PRAISE FOR ROBERT LIVINGSTON AND *THE CONVERSATION*

"Dr. Robert Livingston is a leader in identifying steps to combat bias, and his work is a critical resource for those committed to expanding inclusion and belonging. At Airbnb we have been lucky to partner with him on these important efforts, and know that *The Conversation* will be a tool for anyone seeking to advance equality."

—BRIAN CHESKY, co-founder and CEO, Airbnb

"Social justice is a long game, and it has to start with awareness of the problem. Dr. Livingston's book, just like his live presentations, is one of the most compelling articulations of the problems of racism and discrimination that I have encountered. When a company is prepared to do serious work, the results can be extraordinary. This wonderful book is the place to start. *The Conversation* manages to be both intellectually compelling and substantive while also being infused with warmth and humor, just like Robert. I highly recommend it."

—LAURA W. MURPHY, civil rights activist, consultant, and former director, ACLU Washington Legislative Office

"An extraordinarily timely book . . . Just as companies and organizations in the United States and around the world are focusing anew on the entrenched bias in their culture, *The Conversation* comes along to offer a path forward. Robert Livingston has digested his authoritative understanding of the science into a remarkably approachable volume, one that is animated by his storytelling and voice on the page. *The Conversation* is a major achievement, one that is poised to play a significant role in improving our understanding of bias and addressing systemic racism in the workplace."

—ROBIN J. ELY, Diane Doerge Wilson Professor of Business Administration, Harvard Business School

"After devoting decades of his life working to end systemic racism, Livingston speaks not only with authority but with a refreshing optimism. The thousands of hours he has spent with community leaders across the country have shown that when conversations are candid and respectful, Americans can indeed come together."
—David Gergen, CNN political analyst, adviser
to four U.S. presidents, and Professor of Public
Service, Harvard Kennedy School

"As a product and business innovator, I like to think about how to design globally and execute locally. This is just as necessary when it comes to a company's culture. Candid conversations are among the best ways to dispel myths and false narratives around diversity that hold us back, but we need factual information and a framework. *The Conversation* offers exactly these things. This book should be required reading for leaders and all those who share the goal of a more equitable future."
—William P. Gipson, retired chief diversity
and inclusion officer, Procter & Gamble

"*The Conversation* should be required reading for organizations and individuals that are committed to change. Livingston has made the important and challenging task of truly addressing systemic racism within an organization approachable and achievable. These aren't easy steps, but they are essential for businesses and leaders looking to make a powerful and necessary difference."
—Alex Timm, co-founder and CEO, Root Insurance Company

"This book is a wonderful combination of solid science and gripping storytelling. With clarity and wisdom, Livingston lays out why racism is a problem, why we should care, and what we can do about it. Each chapter sparkles with insights drawn from the sciences, the humanities, and Livingston's own experience.... A rare book that is not just intelligent and entertaining, but also profound and humane."
—Selin Kesebir, Associate Professor of Organisational
Behaviour, London Business School

"A timely and much-needed guide for leaders who value inclusion and want to dismantle systemic racism . . . *The Conversation* is an engaging, practical guide based on scientific research that is as relevant in the workplace as it is in our personal lives. With easy-to-implement actions that move the needle, it should be required reading for anyone in human resources, diversity, and talent functions."

—RITA MITJANS, retired chief diversity and
social responsibility officer, ADP

"Systemic racism is a part of our past, is sadly part of our present, and will be part of our future if we don't educate ourselves on its realities. We all need to seek the truth and be willing to have the uncomfortable conversations necessary to transform ourselves and our organizations. Livingston's thoughtful and instructive book will help us all start these important conversations."

—MIKE KAUFMANN, CEO, Cardinal Health

"Livingston's expertise as a researcher, teacher, and practitioner is on full display in *The Conversation*. This book provides a practical, science-based approach for addressing the seemingly intractable problem of racial inequality in contemporary organizations. . . . A timely and important book."

—MIGUEL M. UNZUETA, Professor and Senior Associate Dean,
UCLA Anderson School of Management

"Dr. Livingston has a unique ability to reach diverse audiences, including those who are new to equity and inclusion work and those who are leaders in the field."

—LETICIA SMITH-EVANS HAYNES, Vice President for
Institutional Diversity, Equity, and Inclusion, Williams College

"Robert Livingston is one of America's most respected social psychologists studying diversity. Robert has a unique ability to strip out the judgmentalism that can warp people's thinking about race and racism; he can treat a difficult topic scientifically, and therefore he can reach a broad audience, educate them about the research, and bring them along when he talks about solutions."

—JONATHAN HAIDT, Thomas Cooley Professor of
Ethical Leadership, NYU Stern School of Business,
and bestselling author of *The Righteous Mind*

"I met Dr. Livingston in 2013 when he made the first of many trips to Asheville to educate our county and city leaders on how racism shows up in organizations. His presentation awakened us to what was possible if we had the courage and commitment to do the work. Fast-forward to today and the progress that Asheville and Buncombe County have made toward reparations and greater racial equity, and you can see Robert's handprint in shaping this change. *The Conversation* is a testament to Dr. Livingston's storytelling skill as he deftly weaves research with vivid examples to make the case for how and why change is possible. This book is a must-read."

—LISA EBY, former human resources and
community engagement director, government
of Buncombe County, North Carolina

THE CONVERSATION

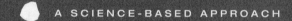 A SCIENCE-BASED APPROACH

THE

CONVERSATION

HOW SEEKING AND SPEAKING

THE TRUTH ABOUT RACISM

CAN RADICALLY TRANSFORM

INDIVIDUALS AND ORGANIZATIONS

ROBERT LIVINGSTON

CURRENCY
NEW YORK

Published in the United States by Currency, an imprint of Random House,
a division of Penguin Random House LLC, New York.

CURRENCY and its colophon are trademarks of Penguin Random House LLC.

LIBRARY OF CONGRESS CATALOGING-IN-PUBLICATION DATA
Names: Livingston, Robert W., author.
Title: The conversation / Robert Livingston.
Description: New York : Currency, [2021] | Includes bibliographical references and index.
Identifiers: LCCN 2020043497 (print) | LCCN 2020043498 (ebook) | ISBN 9780593238561
(hardcover) | ISBN 9780593238578 (ebook)
Subjects: LCSH: Racism. | Discrimination.
Classification: LCC HT1521 .L58 2021 (print) | LCC HT1521 (ebook) | DDC 305.8—dc23
LC record available at https://lccn.loc.gov/2020043497
LC ebook record available at https://lccn.loc.gov/2020043498

Printed in the United States of America on acid-free paper

crownpublishing.com

9 8 7 6 5 4 3 2 1

First Edition

Maps © 2021 David Lindroth, Inc.

TO MATTIE B.
FOR HELPING ME UNDERSTAND
AND APPRECIATE THE VIRTUES OF
COMPASSION, TRUTH, AND JUSTICE

CONTENTS

INTRODUCTION

The lecture hall on the campus of Harvard University was abuzz with the amped-up energy of students arriving for their first day of class. These "students," however, were far from undergraduates. They were a motley crew of corporate leaders, police chiefs, university presidents, military brass, NGO directors, elected officials, social activists, and entrepreneurs.

As they filed into their seats, I couldn't help but notice "Ted," in part due to his towering stature and shiny bald head and in part due to his demeanor. He seemed slightly uneasy and withdrawn. Was his discomfort the result of being surrounded by dozens of strangers from all over the world, or was it related to the topic of the course? I soon discovered that it was the latter. Unlike the other attendees, Ted had no desire whatsoever to attend my six-day executive education course on strategies for building diversity, equity, and inclusion. No way. In fact, he had intended to enroll in a course on authentic leadership that was being offered during the same week. A registration error had landed him in my course instead. A self-described "polite Midwesterner," Ted went along with the mix-up, despite a healthy dose of disappointment and trepidation.

"Oh boy, this is going to be the longest week of my life!" he later admitted thinking as he sat in the lecture hall, preparing himself for what he assumed would be the "Let's beat up on the White guy class."

Ted served as mayor of a small but affluent city located about twenty miles from a Midwestern metropolis. He had grown up on a farm and in many ways fit the country stereotype. He is a strapping man—six-foot-five with a ruddy complexion and a shaved head—the kind of guy who prefers jeans over slacks. Ted began his career as a firefighter in his early twenties and over time rose to become the fire chief before transitioning to his role as the city's chief administrator. He had been surrounded by Whiteness his whole life, both in his hometown and in the nearby city that he ran.

Ted didn't say much that first morning. He sat quietly, intensely absorbing the course material and commentaries from his classmates. It was his first time learning about the dynamics of structural racism and the numerous disparities that it creates. His face expressed a combination of curiosity and skepticism.

When he finally raised his hand, during a discussion on implicit bias, his first comment was "So I guess this means I'm a bigot."

"I'm not sure, Ted," I replied. "But that's not a term that I'd use. We all have *some* type of bias. What differentiates us is what we choose to do about it. We may not be able to control our thoughts, but we have the power to determine our actions."

Throughout that week Ted's assumptions about the world were challenged. The course stretched his comfort zone. After all, he was seeing more racial diversity in one classroom than in his entire hometown. As the days and hours went on, I saw Ted's discomfort dissipate. The fifty-some participants were together almost every waking hour—breakfast, classes, excursions, lunch, dinner, cocktails . . . more cocktails. New friendships were formed.

For many of the students, the course was as much about building relationships with one another and with me as it was about honing skills and expertise. Earlier in my career, I was taken by surprise when people who attended my courses seemed intent on getting to know me personally, asking about my childhood hobbies or my favorite foods. Why would they care? What I've learned over the years, however, is that those hours of small talk dramatically increase the likelihood that people will hear me during the hours of formal presentations. Relationships provide a portal for facts to enter and learning to occur. They create what Bryan Stevenson, founder and executive director of the Equal Justice Initiative and author of *Just Mercy,* refers to as "proximity." People need to get proximate to one another for change to occur.

My hope is that *The Conversation* will bring people together to talk honestly about race, with the goal of creating profound and sustainable social change. What differentiates *The Conversation* from many other books on race is that it is neither a thesis nor a testimonial. My primary aim is not to bolster support for a scholarly hypothesis or assumption. And it is not to give an autobiographical account of my personal experiences with racism. You can find several superb and inspirational examples of these respective genres, including *Stamped from the Beginning* by Ibram Kendi and *Between the World and Me* by Ta-Nehisi Coates, just to name a couple. Instead, *The Conversation* is a tool—a road map and compass for our shared journey toward a more racially just and equitable destination. Its goal is to help us collectively make progress toward solving the perennial problem of racism—particularly as it relates to anti-Black racism in the United States. It's an ambitious endeavor, to say the least, but I am an optimist.

However, it's not blind optimism. Here's a little-known truth: Racial equity is an achievable goal. That's not just my opinion—logic, data, and scientific evidence all speak to the solvability of racism. In addition to being achievable, racial equity is desirable. The overwhelming majority of Americans from all walks of life agree that for the country to reach its full potential, all individuals, regardless of race, must have equal rights, the same economic opportunities, and the same access to quality education: 96 percent of Blacks agree, 93 percent of Hispanics agree, and 93 percent of Whites agree.[1] Moreover, at least 90 percent of respondents from each of the groups believe that establishing greater equity across people of all backgrounds is *critical* for moving the country forward.

If racial equity is both desirable and attainable, then the key questions are: Why hasn't it happened yet, and how can we make it happen now? *The Conversation* aspires to provide answers to these very important questions.

Like other challenges facing individuals (for example, weight loss) and the world (for example, climate change), the problem of racism can be solved, in theory, with the right information, investment, strategy, and implementation. This endeavor has been my life's work for over twenty years. As an academic, I have published research in leading scientific journals on the psychological and organizational implications of racism and sexism. As a practitioner, I have put this knowledge to work serving as a diversity consultant to scores of Fortune 500 companies, police departments, hospitals, universities, federal agencies, and nonprofit organizations. To give but one example of the work I have done: Brian Chesky, CEO of Airbnb, identified me in *Time* magazine as a member of the team assembled to combat discrimination on the company's online platform—designing an antibias training module that was rolled out to millions of users.

Over my years working with this broad range of clients, I have developed and implemented a set of practices that turns difficult conversations about race into productive outcomes. Because my approach is solution oriented—and it works—many have encouraged me to distill it into a book. *The Conversation* is the fruit of that effort.

Here is a peek into my approach: I do not rely too heavily on carrots or sticks. Although external incentives can be useful when used sparingly and strategically, I have learned that they are of limited effectiveness if the goal is to produce *long-term* change. Established research has shown that putting too much emphasis on incentives can undermine intrinsic commitment and motivation.[2] For example, organizational psychologist Frederick Herzberg has argued that negative incentives, or what he refers to as "KITA" (kick in the @$!), can produce *movement* in the workplace—people will often do what you want if you wave around a stick.[3] However, KITA will not lead to a lasting commitment to adopting new behaviors—and will often result in a pendulum swing in the opposite direction. To get people truly motivated, engaged, and devoted to a course of action, they must develop a greater understanding, appreciation, and responsibility for the work that is being undertaken and the reasons behind it.

This isn't just a workplace phenomenon. Anyone with kids knows that time-outs, or treats, only go so far. At some point, you have to sit down and talk to your kids so that they understand *why* they should be behaving in a particular way. Adults are no different. If we could change behavior by simply relying on lawsuits, then many companies would be overflowing with racial diversity. If a swift, hard kick in the @$! could end racism, then we would have eliminated it over 150 years ago with the Civil War. Although many of the formal discriminatory practices in the South were abolished in the wake of the Civil War, the strong motivation to uphold racism did not end with the war. On the contrary, the South, despite being battered and defeated, doubled down on its commitment to racism. New discriminatory structures and policies (such as Jim Crow laws) emerged to replace the old ones. The lesson is simple: If we want to make profound and sustainable racial progress in organizations and society, then we have to reach people on a deeper intellectual, emotional, and moral level.

THE POWER OF CONVERSATION

You might be wondering why I decided to call the book *The Conversation*. It is because conversation is one of the most powerful ways to build knowledge, awareness, and empathy, and ultimately effect change. Conversation is also a primal way for people to form bonds, build trust, and create community. Research has shown that people become connected on a neural level during conversation[4] and that even imagining conversation with others can increase the likelihood of cooperation in difficult social situations.[5] Studies also show that being given the opportunity to have a conversation, in addition to being exposed to new information, can make all of the difference in changing people's behaviors. For example, a classic experiment by Kurt Lewin in 1952 investigated how to persuade volunteers at the Red Cross to serve more nutritionally rich organ meat. The researchers had two conditions in this field experiment. In the first condition, they provided information about the nutritional and societal benefits of serving more organ meat (i.e., kidneys, hearts, throat glands). In the second condition, they not only provided the same information on the benefits of serving organ meat—they also gave the women the opportunity to discuss it. Thus, the only difference between the two conditions was that one condition had the opportunity for conversation and one did not. The outcome of interest was whether the women actually began serving organ meat. In the information-only condition, about 3 percent of the women started serving organ meat. However, in the condition that provided information *and* gave subjects the opportunity to discuss it, more than ten times the number of women (i.e., 32 percent) started serving organ meat.[6] Conversation made a huge difference in changing behaviors.

Our most impactful and consequential learning occurs through our relationships with other people. We are much more likely to talk to, listen to, influence, and be influenced by those who are part of our familial, social, or professional networks. Making progress toward racial equity requires the concerted effort of an entire community. A productive conversation also requires a baseline of real knowledge and factual information.

What I refer to as The Conversation (capital *T,* capital *C*) is a candid sharing of perspectives on race—grounded in facts—that leads to greater awareness, empathy, and action. Occasionally someone will tell me, "Oh, I know all this stuff already." But as demonstrated in the organ meat study, change is not the simple result of information. Furthermore, there is a big difference between information (what is factually true) and presumption (what is assumed to be true)—and between simple information (knowing what is true) and deeper understanding (knowing *why* it is true). One of the primary goals of this book is to provide knowledge in order to facilitate *informed* conversation. Education, conversation, and action—in that order. Let's take a closer look at the critical importance of fact-based knowledge.

THE SYNERGISTIC RELATIONSHIP BETWEEN INFORMATION AND CONVERSATION

What the organ meat study revealed is that the presence of factual information and social dialogue can lead to productive change in behaviors and outcomes. But how can we know what information reflects fact versus opinion? Science is useful for disentangling the two. When scientists conduct an experiment, they often begin with a hunch, presumption, or informed opinion about what the outcome will be. This is called a hypothesis. Here's an example of a hypothesis: *White people, on average, will offer help to another White person more often than to a Black person lying on the sidewalk.* That sounds like a sensible prediction. But is it really true? The only way to know for sure is to test the assumption, or hypothesis. It is also important to provide context. As we will learn in Chapter 2, racial bias is very complicated. Sometimes White people will help other Whites more than Blacks. Sometimes they will help other White people *less* than Black people. And sometimes they will help both groups equally.[7] This complexity reveals why testing is so important.

Scientists and practitioners spend months, and often years, rigorously testing their hypotheses—so that they can move beyond mere presumption to actual knowledge. They are only satisfied when there is hard *evidence* that confirms their assumptions.

However, many people—including some leaders—have little use for data and evidence. They believe what they believe—evidence or not—and to them presumption and knowledge are one and the same. That's not how *The Conversation* treats the concept of knowledge. Throughout the book, we will lean on science as an arbiter of fact when it comes to assumptions about racism.

In the book, I will draw on research and data to answer many of the questions about the nature of racism, where it comes from, why everyone should care about it—and the steps that we can take to eradicate it.

In addition to knowing *whether* something is true, the second challenge is knowing *why* it is true. This reflects the subtle difference between knowledge and understanding. I love to cook, but I'm by no means a chef. I know what to do—for example, add yeast and a pinch of baking soda to bread dough—but I have no idea *why* I'm doing it. What is actually happening at a chemical level? Why do I have to put the dough on a cold surface? Why does it have to sit and rise for a specific amount of time? I am not quite sure. This lack of deep understanding would put me at a huge disadvantage if I were ever a contestant on the Food Network show *Chopped,* where you are handed a mystery basket of unusual and unexpected ingredients (e.g., blood sausage, pineapple, croissants, quail eggs) and given thirty minutes to combine the ingredients into a distinctive and delectable dish (e.g., a blood sausage bread pudding with roasted pineapple glaze). I wouldn't possess sufficient understanding of the basic chemistry and physics (e.g., emulsification, convection) of culinary science to combine and engineer the ingredients in such a masterful way.

Similarly, many managers are "cooks" when it comes to understanding racism—they know the kitchen basics but not necessarily the whys and hows. Other managers do not know their way around a kitchen at all but are willing to learn. By the end of this book, you will be well on your way to becoming a master chef. As on *Chopped,* in many social and organizational situations you will find yourself without a cookbook or manual of step-by-step instructions. But that's okay. After reading *The Conversation* you will be able to draw on a foundation of knowledge and understanding to help guide you. If you have a deeper understanding of what racial bias is, where it comes from, and when it is more or less likely to emerge, then you are in a better position to prevent it, or create interventions and solutions when it does occur.

CREATING A "RADICAL" TRANSFORMATION

When you were reading the book's subtitle, the phrase "radically transform" may have jumped out at you. The word *radical* often gets a bad rap. As I intend it, however, the word doesn't refer to zeal or extremism but rather to *radical*'s true etymology—*radix*—the Latin word for "root" (and the root vegetable "radish"). My hope is that *The Conversation* will produce not a superficial but a "root," foundational commitment to e*radic*ate, or uproot, racism. I have witnessed radical change at the individual level and some at the organizational level, even if society at large has yet to show a "radical" change on racism. Nevertheless, I continue to think that profound societal-level change is possible, and I believe it will happen by leveraging the power of individuals and large organizations. Grassroots efforts, as well as pressure from organizations like FedEx and Nike, in getting the Washington Football Team to drop its racist mascot and moniker are one example of how individuals and organizations can promote antiracism. I will elaborate on other more complex and profound approaches and examples of antiracist strategies in the final chapters of the book.

To be clear, I am not claiming that conversation in general (or The Conversation more specifically) alone is a panacea, or that incentives are not important. Self-interest, economic gain, and short-term gratification can all be effective motivators. Sometimes carrots (or the threat of sticks) are necessary to bring people to the table in the first place. What I have discovered through my work and life experience, however, is that rewards and punishments can induce immediate and temporary movement but rarely generate profound and sustainable change. By contrast, conversation, if done in the right way, can be a powerful tool for bringing people together and developing support for enduring solutions.

Ultimately, people are the regulators and agents of social transformation, which means if enough people want change, then it will happen. But social change requires social *ex*change. In other words, we have to start talking to one another—especially those outside our social circle. Nothing will improve until we begin to have honest and informed conversations about race and decide, as a community, to do something about it. The problem is that many people feel uncomfortable or ill-equipped to talk about race—or they fear that talking about it will only make things worse. Or they dive in too quickly, without a clear structure or objective, and beat a hasty retreat once the dialogue becomes difficult.

The Conversation aims to change all that by increasing confidence, competence, and commitment to engage in racial dialogue. In this book, I have culled theory, data, and research from a range of scientific disciplines, including social psychology, behavioral economics, sociology, organizational behavior, political science, history, and evolutionary and molecular biology to address the fundamental question of how we can better name, understand, discuss, and resolve the problem of racism in society and the workplace. Social science is critical to this effort because it enables us to peer into our minds and into our reality in a way that our subjective perceptions alone do not allow. When we dive into the research findings, it is not to minimize the importance of personal feelings or opinions but rather to test and complement them by providing a more objective perspective on the world. To keep you engaged, I bring personal anecdotes and experiences to the table, integrating the science with vivid stories and metaphors that I hope readers find memorable.

To structure and guide The Conversation, the book follows my PRESS model (*P*roblem Awareness, *R*oot Cause Analysis, *E*mpathy, *S*trategy, *S*acrifice), which can be applied not just to racism but to any personal or societal challenge. The PRESS model is described in detail in my 2020 *Harvard Business Review* article "How to Promote Racial Equity in the Workplace" and in "Forum 1: How to Talk About the Problem," the section that concludes Part 1. It provides a big-picture overview of the necessary steps to achieve stable and enduring racial progress. One secret to doing effective antiracism work is the ability to have open and informed Conversations about the nature of the problem, how to increase concern about the problem, and finally what can be and will be done to resolve it.

The Conversation was written to be accessible to everyone—whether you are a corporate executive in New York, a farmer in Nebraska, a factory worker in Milwaukee, a preacher in rural Utah, an entrepreneur in Atlanta, a police officer in San Diego, a schoolteacher in San Antonio, or a DJ in DC. It is for anyone who is bothered by the current level of racial tension, wants to learn more about its causes, and is invested in becoming part of the solution.

I ask for only one thing as you read the book—patience. Patience with yourself. Patience with others. And above all, patience with the process. After reading the first chapter or two, you may start thinking, "Just tell me what to do to fix it." Please resist the impulse to skip ahead. Einstein once said that if he had only one hour to save the world, he would spend fifty-five minutes thinking deeply about the problem and only five minutes on the solution. A focus on solutions without thoroughly understanding the problem is akin to prescribing medicine without first diagnosing the patient's condition. The palliative approach—soothing the symptoms without treating the underlying disease—is likely to be unproductive, or even counterproductive, in the long run. The same principle applies to social problems.

The book consists of a total of twelve chapters—designed to be read *sequentially*—with each chapter building on the previous one, like a miniseries. Each chapter might take, on average, about two hours to read. So the investment of reading time—to do *The Conversation* right—amounts to twenty-four hours, or one full day. In addition, each part concludes with a "Forum" section, which will help recap the most important topics covered in the part and offer Conversation starters aimed at generating instructive and productive Conversation with others in your family, organization, or community.

Are you willing to invest one day of your life to substantially improve our society? I am confident that it will be worth it.

Before we begin our journey, let's return to Ted, the Midwestern mayor. By the end of the weeklong training, the reticent and skeptical Ted had turned into a fearless and passionate advocate for racial equity. In the years since our first encounter, I've flown to his city many times to conduct trainings and workshops for his workforce—police and fire departments, city managers, heads of parks and recreation, and the like. And these weren't one-hour talks. He cleared his employees' calendars for two full days of antiracism training. You can imagine how thrilled the attendees were about that. Almost as thrilled as Ted was when he first walked into my classroom.

Like Ted, many in the town's workforce have also evolved over time. Now when I go back each year, the "cohort" from the previous year stops by to share sentiments about their continuing journey toward antiracism and offer their support to the new batch of attendees. It's inspiring to witness because it's not just lip service; it's action. And Ted has led the charge. He's faced down resistance and opposition. He's changed policy. He's changed practice. He's changed the culture. He's changed the community. He has changed himself. So much so that Ted now wants to dedicate himself to doing diversity, equity, and inclusion work full time.

My uncle Kenny and his family live in the city near Ted's suburb. Whenever I go to visit my uncle, Ted will make the drive to his house.

Everyone in my uncle's family knows him at this point. He's had dinner with my first cousins and second cousins. He's had dinner with my friends from high school who happen to live in the area. The canine members of the family have even stopped barking at him. Uncle Kenny, a social worker and retired nonprofit foundation executive, is a local racial-justice activist, focusing on at-risk youth in the city. Ted and Uncle Kenny hang out together, even when I'm not in town. Ted inundates us with emails, texts, and links about race-related articles, documentaries, studies, and events. "Nephew, you've created a monster!" Uncle Kenny sometimes jokes. But we recognize his commitment and enthusiasm, as well as the effort, hard work, resources, and political capital—capital undoubtedly enhanced by the fact that he is a White man—that he's spent to promote racial equity.

Ted is not a unicorn. There are millions of people in America just like him. In addition, there are many millions more civic-minded, community-invested, intellectually curious individuals who are already aware of the problem but are not sure what they can do to fix it. If those millions of people could have an honest Conversation about racism, then we could create *real* change. *The Conversation* was inspired by my work over the years with countless individuals and executives like Ted who have grown to embrace the mission of racial equity.

Given the devastating impact of racism in America, we must seize the opportunity to improve our community by committing to education, Conversation, and action. As intractable as it seems, racism is not an insurmountable problem. But we must be willing to put in the work. The most effective interventions produce not just reflexive reactions to rewards or punishments but a deeper engagement with the mind, heart, and soul. Let's get started.

Part I
CONDITION

CHAPTER ONE

Do We All Believe That Racism Exists?

Several winters ago, I was invited by a large corporation to conduct an antibias workshop. I would be working with a department of employees located in Appalachia that was roughly 98 percent male, 99 percent White, and 100 percent rural. As I drove to the venue, watching snow blanket the barren hillsides, I wondered what I had gotten myself into. The organizers had told me I would have my work cut out for me. The "fellas," as I came to think of them, were highly skilled blue-collar employees—welders, plumbers, pipe fitters—who had a history of resisting efforts to promote diversity, equity, and inclusion.

Given the differences in our backgrounds, how was this group going to respond to my efforts? I am a Black man with a white-collar job who lives in a large city. Odds were good that they would assume we were opposites. And yet, lurking beneath the surface, I suspected that we might have some things in common. I was born and raised in Kentucky and am familiar with Appalachian culture. I am a man of faith. I am an outdoor sportsman. And because I rehab houses as a hobby, I know my way around power saws, nail guns, and sledge-hammers.

Despite the possible points of similarity, I still felt a bit anxious. I had led hundreds of Conversations, trainings, and antibias work-shops for organizations all across the United States and the world, with audiences spanning the entire spectrum of awareness and resis-tance. But I suspected that this crowd might be one of the toughest I had ever faced. The research-based approach that works so well for number-crunching executives who relish data and evidence would fall flat here. This audience would respond to facts, but I needed to present them in a different way. And we would have to do some rela-tionship building before any facts were presented. They would never hear me if they could not relate to me.

Fortunately, the workshop was a multiday affair. There would be time to get to know one another before we dove into more controver-sial and potentially divisive topics. On the first day of the training, we spent much of our time engaged in conversations completely unre-lated to race. We talked about the heavy snowfall. We talked about fishing and whether lures are better than live bait. We talked about our favorite sports teams. We talked about whether real chili is made with or without beans. We talked about their company's widely ad-mired benefits plan and how they dreamed of spending their time after retiring. We shared warm food, a generous supply of pastries, and freshly brewed coffee. Mostly, though, we just talked.

After a while, the group had grown more comfortable—and even started calling me "Doc" (I responded with "fellas"). As our conversa-tion segued into a lighthearted chat about whether rich executives and CEOs should work at all or just retire and go fishing, I saw an op-portunity to finally broach the subject of race and power. They knew that the Fortune 500 contained some of the nation's largest and best-known companies, like Walmart, General Motors, Microsoft, McDon-ald's, Amazon, and General Electric, and that these corporations were led by CEOs who typically earned millions of dollars per year.

"Hey, can anyone tell me how many CEOs there are in the For-tune 500?" I asked the group.

After a brief period of silence, one attendee looked around and muttered, "Uh, five hundred?"

"Yep, that's right," I replied. "Trick question. I wanted to see if you were all paying attention." Laughter erupted.

"Okay, so here's a more difficult question. Out of those five hundred CEOs, can anyone tell me how many are Black?"

After a short pause, a few hands went up. That any hands shot up at all was, I suspect, a consequence of the hours we'd spent talking about chili and fishing. I signaled to someone sitting close to me.

"Hmm . . . I'd say around a hundred," he replied. A rumble spread across the room as others pondered the question aloud.

"Nah, I think it's more than that," another man asserted. "I'd say around a hundred and fifty," he stated. The rumbling got louder.

I tried with limited success to maintain a poker face. Perhaps reading my expression, another respondent blurted out, "No way, guys. Y'all are way too high. I'm thinking it's around seventy-five or eighty." I remained silent.

"So what's the answer, Doc?" someone finally asked.

I took a breath, looked around the room, and paused before uttering, "Five."

A groan of disbelief spread through the crowd.

"And that includes both Black men *and* Black women," I added.

The grumbling got louder. "Aw, I don't buy that!" someone exclaimed. The hum of private conversations across the room increased. I heard one man utter "fake news," and a few others chuckled.

"Okay, let's do this," I interjected calmly. "I want everyone to look into this when they get home tonight, and we'll talk about it again tomorrow. Find a list of the Fortune 500 companies on the Internet. Then go to each company's website and click on a link to the page where bios of the company leadership are displayed. Take a look at the photos of the CEOs. If they have so much as a rich golden tan, then I want you to check them off as being Black." The humor lightened the mood a bit. "Let's see how many Black people you come up with."

The next morning the room was somber. Some of the fellas looked sheepish, others annoyed. But it was clear that facts had been absorbed and learning had taken place. Those who had done their homework knew something that they hadn't known twenty-four hours earlier. This new information allowed us to shift the dialogue. Instead of simply speculating about whether the composition of Fortune 500 CEOs did or didn't lack racial diversity, we began to have a conversation about why their guesses deviated so drastically from reality—and ultimately a conversation about why the Fortune 500 lacks racial and gender diversity in the first place. Once again, the hours we had spent getting to know one another had paid off. By this point they felt comfortable enough with me to open up about their feelings.

"When I turn on the TV, I see Obama, Oprah, Jay-Z, Beyoncé, all these rich and famous Black people," one man, whom we will call "Jim," exclaimed. "I live in a trailer. They are doing a helluva lot better than me!" Others nodded their agreement. This was an exciting moment for me, not just because the candor of Jim's comment allowed us to kick-start a real and honest discussion but because the comment also provided an excellent example of a scientific concept that I would eventually introduce to them. The existence in Jim's mind of a few easy-to-recall rich and successful Black exemplars had created the impression that Black people in general are richer and more successful than the reality. This is an example of the *availability heuristic,* a phenomenon discovered by Amos Tversky and Nobel Prize–winning social psychologist Daniel Kahneman, author of the bestselling book *Thinking, Fast and Slow*. It wasn't the only factor that contributed to the fellas' gross overestimation of the number of Black CEOs, but it was a clear starting point.

From the casual banter of the first day, we had now moved fully into The Conversation. We were having a candid exchange of perspectives on race, but grounded in facts. By discussing their thoughts about wealthy Black Americans, we were touching on *racism credence,* or people's beliefs about the existence of anti-Black racism in the United States. What the fellas were telling me, as reflected in Jim's comment and the assent of the others, was that they didn't really see the need for all this diversity training, because Black people were doing just fine. In their opinion, it was the White man who was being stepped on. The notions of White privilege and systemic discrimination against minorities were a joke to them. Where was the privilege in their lives? Looking at me—someone they saw as not just a Black man but a financially secure, cultured, well-educated Harvard professor—they perceived way more privilege than they saw looking at one another. The fact that they even had to sit through this workshop added insult to injury.

The dynamic in my Conversation with the fellas that morning revealed a tension that arises in most of the trainings that I do—namely, how to reconcile a few executives' desire for greater equity and inclusion with perceptions among many employees and middle managers (often referred to as the "frozen middle" when change initiatives handed down from above stagnate at this level) that there is no discrimination within an organization.

As I write these sentences, I can almost feel the tension of some of the readers rising. Some will be disturbed by what they perceive as the fellas' utter ignorance and will be waiting for me to tell them off and set them straight. Other readers will be nodding along with the fellas, thinking, "Exactly! *They* get it!"

I'd like you to sit with those feelings for a moment and recall my plea for patience in the introduction. We will explore the big question of whether racism really exists in the chapters to come. For now, let's continue to focus on racism credence or people's *beliefs* about the existence of racism. Although facts matter, sometimes beliefs matter more. Beliefs, not facts, lead to choices (for example, hiring decisions), which lead to outcomes (for example, economic disparities). Therefore, it is just as important to understand the source of people's *beliefs* about racism as it is to understand the *reality* of racism.

Before condoning or condemning people's beliefs about racism, I would like to invite us to understand where those beliefs come from and bring them into alignment with the reality of inequality. New policies around diversity and inclusion are dramatically more likely to fail if there isn't a critical mass of people within an organization who have an understanding of and appreciation for why the policies are being created and implemented in the first place. The first step in producing profound and sustainable change is raising awareness of the existence of a real problem. Otherwise, the solution will seem like the problem—and resistance will follow.

This is why I chose to begin the book with a chapter on racism credence. It turns out it's not just the fellas who are skeptical about

the existence of anti-Black racism—*many* White people do not believe that Black people are victims of racism and discrimination. Research by Michael Norton at Harvard Business School and Samuel
Sommers at Tufts University shows that a large segment of the White
American population believes that *Whites* now suffer the brunt of discrimination.[1] These researchers asked a large random sample of
White and Black Americans to report the extent to which they believed discrimination against Blacks and Whites existed in the United
States. They also asked the same respondents to estimate the level of
racial discrimination in the past, starting in the 1950s and progressing
decade by decade to the 2000s. Both groups agreed that the level of
racial discrimination against Black people in the 1950s was extremely
high and the level of racial discrimination against White people in the
1950s was extremely low. But that's where the consensus ended. With
each subsequent decade, Whites perceived that the level of discrimination against Blacks in American society decreased while the level of
discrimination against Whites in American society increased. And
the shift isn't subtle:

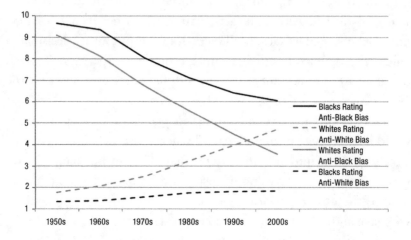

Many Whites believed that by the new millennium they were
more discriminated against in America than were Blacks. In fact, on
a scale from one to ten, with ten being the highest possible rating,
over 10 percent of Whites rated the current level of racial discrimination against Whites at a whopping ten! By contrast, very few Whites

(just 2 percent) rated the current level of racial discrimination against Blacks as a ten. In other words, five times more Whites believed that Whites were *severely* discriminated against than thought that Blacks were severely discriminated against.

Norton and Sommers also found that Whites saw racism as a zero-sum game, meaning that the decrease in perception of discrimination against Blacks and the increase in perception of discrimination against Whites were interrelated. White Americans were convinced that gains for Blacks had to be achieved at the expense of Whites. One group's victory meant the other group's loss.

Black Americans saw the world differently. Although they believed there was less discrimination against Blacks in the twenty-first century than in the 1950s, they still believed that in present-day America there was far more racial discrimination against Blacks than against Whites. They also did not see racism as a zero-sum game. Less discrimination against Blacks did *not* necessarily mean more discrimination against Whites. Blacks believed that a rising tide could lift all boats.

As you can see, we already have a problem: namely, we can't agree on whether there is a problem or whom it afflicts. Moreover, the study's findings were not limited to a specific demographic within each racial group. It's not just rural, working-class White men—like the fellas—who believe that racism against Blacks is a fairy tale and that in reality it is Whites who are getting the short end of the stick. The study's respondents were a nationally representative random sample, meaning that the data likely reflect beliefs across age, gender, social class, educational level, and demographic region. Therefore, the sentiment that Whites have replaced Blacks as the primary victims of discrimination is much more widely shared among Whites as a group.

It is important to pause and reflect on the profound implications of these findings. The very first step to solving *any* problem is being aware that it exists and agreeing on what it is. If someone has a serious illness, such as cancer, but doesn't know it, how can they succeed in treating it? The same applies to social ills. How can we ever resolve racism if we can't first acknowledge its existence?

In case you are still skeptical about Norton and Sommers's findings, know that their study is not a fluke or a relic. More recent data echo their results. For example, a 2016 survey by the Public Religion Research Institute found that 57 percent of all Whites and 66 percent of working-class Whites in the United States consider discrimination against Whites to be as big a problem as discrimination against Blacks and other minorities. And according to a 2019 Pew Research Survey on Race, 52 percent of Whites think that the bigger problem for the country is people seeing racial discrimination where it really does *not* exist whereas only 14 percent of Blacks endorse this belief. In contrast, 84 percent of Black respondents believe the bigger problem for the country is people *not* seeing racial discrimination where it really *does* exist, whereas only 48 percent of Whites endorse this belief.[2]

Although public opinion research conducted since George Floyd's murder in May of 2020 shows an increase in perception of systemic racism among Whites, the spike is not as large as you might assume. For example, a poll in July 2016 showed that 68 percent of Americans said that racial and ethnic discrimination is a big problem in the United States, whereas that number only climbed to 76 percent after the Floyd murder.[3] Looking specifically at the differences between Black and White respondents, there are still large disparities. For example, a YouGov survey administered just a few days after the Floyd murder showed that fewer than half as many Whites (37 percent) as Blacks (78 percent) agreed that "our country hasn't gone far enough in giving black people equal rights."[4] That's a whopping difference of 41 percentage points.

Consistent with Norton and Sommers's data, these surveys did not show that opinions varied much by age, level of education, or geography. However, it would be inaccurate to conclude that all White people deny the existence of racism. There is considerable variability among Whites; it's just not fully explained by age, gender, educational level, or geography. One factor that does differentiate Whites' racism credence is political ideology. Whereas 54 percent of White Democrats agreed that being White helps people get ahead, only 12 percent of White Republicans thought so. And in the same survey, among White respondents, while 72 percent of Democrats believed that Blacks are treated less fairly than Whites in hiring, pay, and promotions, only 21 percent of Republicans endorsed this belief.

How can it be that *beliefs* about racism differ so vastly between Whites and Blacks, and even among Whites? Is it even possible to get these groups on the same page? Getting enough people from various backgrounds to acknowledge that there is a problem and to agree on the problem is the critical first step to a solution. But reaching a common acknowledgment is tricky.

Fortunately, there is a way forward and, here again, scientific research offers hope. The next sections focus on the psychological factors that create disparities in people's beliefs about the prevalence of racism—insights that offer guidance on how we might get people on the same page. For the remainder of the chapter, I will describe two factors that create disparities in racism credence—cognitive heuristics and motivated reasoning.

HOW MENTAL SHORTCUTS AFFECT PEOPLE'S JUDGMENTS: COGNITIVE HEURISTICS

Which kills more Americans each year: floods or asthma?

Think about it for a moment, and jot down your answer. Did you say "floods"? If so, then you're in good company. Most people think that floods kill far more people than asthma. However, asthma kills nearly one hundred times more people than floods do.[5] Why, then, do so many people get this wrong? The primary reason is that most of us have a much easier time calling to mind images of disastrous floods than we do calling to mind an asthma fatality. Media sensationalism, vivid imagery, and emotional impact are all factors that influence our perceptions of how commonly things occur. Because plane crashes are so vivid, many people fear flying more than driving, despite the fact that we are exponentially more likely to die in a car crash than in a plane crash. The availability heuristic, or the tendency to overweight information that is readily available in your mind when making decisions, judgments, or estimates, is now well established by a large body of research.[6]

How does this tendency relate to racism credence, or the belief that racism against people of color really exists? Recall when I invited the fellas to ponder why their estimates of the number of Black CEOs were twenty times higher than the actual figure. Many of them pointed to salient, easy-to-recall examples of rich and famous Black people, like Beyoncé, Oprah, and Jay-Z. Memorable figures like these celebrities have skewed perspectives when it comes to the general economic status of Black Americans. This type of perception skewing is consistent with the availability heuristic.

There is another factor that contributes to lower racism credence: anchors and benchmarks. Ponder this for a moment: Are you old? On the surface, it seems like a simple question. However, the answer can vary tremendously depending on whether you compare your current age with how old you were in the distant past or with how old you will be in the distant future. Many twenty-five-year-olds perceive themselves to be "old" and lament the loss of their youth at the quarter-century mark. Before you laugh, consider that their assessment may be based on comparisons to the "good old days" of high school or college. The point is not whether they are right or wrong but whether they would come to a very different conclusion if they compared being twenty-five with being sixty-five. (Not that sixty-five is old either! It can seem downright youthful compared with being octogenarian—which itself is young in contrast to being centenarian.)

What anchors your thinking on race? Many Whites mentally compare how well they believe Black people are doing now with their views about how badly Black people were doing in the past. The past then becomes an "anchor" for judgments about the present—leading to the conclusion that Blacks are doing much better now than they really are. *Anchoring bias* occurs when people use information—such as a particular quantity or point in time—as a strong foundation or context for making judgments and decisions, often leading to biased conclusions.[7]

Here's an example of how anchoring bias works. Imagine your friend Janet is competing in a marathon and just passed the ten-mile mark. Another friend, Javier, has just shown up at the race and has no idea where Janet is. He asks you whether Janet has run a "long way" so far. It sounds like a pretty straightforward question. However, your answer will depend not only on what you consider to be a "long way" but also on whether the "anchor" for your judgment is the *starting* line or the *finish* line. Being anchored by the starting line, you might conclude that she has already run ten miles—a really long way (I certainly can't run ten miles!). However, being anchored by the finish line would lead to a different conclusion from being anchored at the starting line, because you are more focused on the miles that she has left to go. Now you might conclude that she has *not* run a long way, because she still has over sixteen miles left. The *actual* distance in both scenarios is exactly the same—she has run 10 miles in a 26.2-mile race—but you reach a very different conclusion about whether she has run a "long way" based on whether the anchor is the starting line or the finish line.

Let's apply the marathon example to perceptions of racial progress. Consider research by Richard Eibach and Joyce Ehrlinger that assessed Americans' beliefs about whether we have come a "long way" as a nation. When White participants and people of color (i.e., Black, Asian, and Hispanic participants) were asked how much progress toward racial equality had been made in the United States, Whites believed that far more progress had been made than did people of color.[8] The disparities in perceptions were almost entirely explained by the anchors used by each group. The results suggest that Whites tended to anchor their judgment about how far the nation had come more on an oppressive past (calling forth images of slavery or Jim Crow–era segregation), whereas people of color tended to anchor on a more equitable, ideal future (calling forth images of Dr. Martin Luther King, Jr.'s "I Have a Dream" speech). These disparate anchors resulted in very different conclusions about how far we have come, as shown in the center two bars of the following graph, which depict the "default anchor" (no-prime) responses for Whites and people of color when they weren't given any information and just made the estimate spontaneously. Responses ranged from zero (very little progress) to seven (a great deal of progress).

When the study's organizers gave people information before they

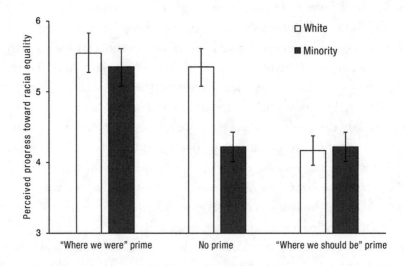

made their judgment, their responses looked very different. As indicated by the two bars on the left, when people of color were given anchoring information about past events and were induced to think about conditions during slavery and Jim Crow, for example, their perceptions of racial progress increased dramatically compared with the default no-prime condition. On the other hand, Whites' perceptions of how far we've come didn't change that much when they were induced to think about the past, because presumably the past was already their default anchor.

Conversely, Whites' perceptions of racial progress decreased dramatically when they were given anchoring information about an ideal future of racial equality and were induced to think about Dr. King's dream. The perceptions of people of color did not change much in this condition, compared with the default, no-prime condition, because presumably this ideal future was the anchor, or frame of reference, that they normally used when thinking about racial progress—comparing the present with the ideal future rather than the brutal past (see two far-right bars).

What do these data and metaphors add up to? They show us that subjective judgments are relative. But that's not necessarily a bad thing. If judgments are relative, then it is possible that people *can* change their perceptions about the prevalence of racism if they are provided with a new frame of reference. Knowledge and objective information can help too. Research has shown that knowing about Black history and past discrimination was associated with higher levels of racism credence, for both Blacks and Whites.[9] In short, it's possible to bring divergent viewpoints into alignment by setting the right frame of reference and making important facts and information available to people when they make judgments.

We are not helpless victims to availability heuristics and anchoring biases. Providing new information or a different perspective can dramatically increase the alignment of people's judgments about racism. This is where The Conversation can help.

Of course, people aren't just computers—cold processors of data. We have emotions, desires, needs, and ambitions, which can create a whole new set of obstacles to perceiving the world in an accurate way. Facts are necessary but not sufficient, as they are of little use to someone who is determined not to see them. This was sagely articulated in a passage by W. E. B. Du Bois, the prominent African American activist, scholar, and co-founder of the NAACP, as he reflected on his life and work:

> My faith in [antiracism's] success was based on the firm belief that race prejudice was based on widespread ignorance. . . . My remedy was truth: carefully gathered scientific proof that neither color nor race determined the limits of a man's capacity. I was not at the time [in 1909] sufficiently Freudian to understand how little human action is based on reason.[10]

Du Bois was right. Because people are not entirely rational or objective, the problem doesn't end with just providing people with factual information. It is important to understand how emotions, needs, and desires impact the interpretation of facts, and ultimately what people accept as truth. Truth isn't just factual; it can be emotional as well, as observed by Harvard philosopher Michael Sandel.[11] Research has shown that our perceptions are affected not only by the information most available or accessible to us but also by our personal wants and needs.

EMOTIONAL TRUTH: WHEN PERCEPTIONS AND JUDGMENTS REFLECT OUR NEEDS AND DESIRES

You can give people accurate information all day long, but it won't do any good if they do not want to see it or hear it. The biggest challenge with the fellas was not persuading them to consider new information; it was increasing their emotional capacity and willingness to digest the information. Once again, they are not alone. There is basic scientific evidence that people literally have a hard time "seeing" things that they don't want to see. Early research by Jerome Bruner, Leo Postman, Elliott McGinnies, and others in the 1940s and 1950s probed the novel but then still-controversial idea that visual perception was not just an objective response to a stimulus in the environment, but that needs, motivations, and emotions can affect what people actually see.

In one study documenting a phenomenon that they called *perceptual defense,* people were presented with words that flashed so rapidly that they were difficult to consciously perceive. The researchers found that people required a longer presentation time before they could visually perceive certain taboo words (e.g., *penis, whore*) compared with more innocuous words (e.g., *broom, apple*) that contained the same number of letters.[12] All of these effects occurred in a fraction of an eyeblink. The difference in the time required to "see" the taboo word versus the innocuous word was less than one hundred milliseconds, or one-tenth of a second. But it was just enough time for the brain's automatic perceptual defenses to, ever so briefly, block the word from entering consciousness. Further evidence of this defensive blocking was obtained from physiological measures, which indicated higher levels of negative arousal when participants were subliminally exposed to taboo words versus innocuous words.

What this study shows is that perception is not simply a function of whether you are *able* to see what's in front of you—it is also affected by whether you *want* to see what is in front of you. When something is aversive, threatening, or discomforting, often you would prefer not to see it. We have built-in automatic defense mechanisms that protect us from seeing things that might upset us. Later research showed that, in addition to blocking subliminal words that it doesn't want to see, the brain is also adept at blocking threatening information and ideas that it doesn't want to hear.[13] This coping mechanism, called *motivated reasoning,* defends us from all manner of psychological threats: threats to our sense of worth and self-esteem, threats to our sense of psychological security and well-being, threats to our sense of power and control, and threats to our cherished views of the world as fair and just.

Consider the famous exchange from the 1992 movie *A Few Good Men,* when Tom Cruise's character, Lieutenant Kaffee, acting as the prosecutor, aggressively questions Jack Nicholson's character, Colonel Jessep, in court about the latter's involvement in a shady military operation. After a fiery exchange between the two officers, the judge indicates to Jessep that he doesn't have to respond to Kaffee's incendiary questions and accusations. Nevertheless, Jessep obliges:

"I'll answer the question. You want answers?" Jessep asks Kaffee.

"I think I'm entitled to them," Kaffee responds.

"You want answers?!" Jessep repeats, this time raising his voice and demanding confirmation from Kaffee that he *really* wants what he's asking for.

Kaffee responds angrily and emphatically that he does indeed want him to answer. "I want the truth!" he shouts.

"You can't handle the truth!" Jessep exclaims, which he uses as his justification for the cover-up and for never having revealed the truth prior to the trial.

It turns out we all have this version of Jack Nicholson living somewhere in our brain—a cognitive defense mechanism that steers us away from inconvenient and unpleasant truths. Ignorance is bliss, as the saying goes.

Imagine a teenager who is socially rejected by popular peers but convinces himself that he never wanted to be friends with those stupid jerks anyway. That's Jack Nicholson at work, alleviating pain. Or imagine an entrepreneur who inherits a fortune but is nonetheless convinced that her wealth is the result of her own genius and diligence. Nicholson once again, enhancing ego. Or imagine a CEO of an oil refinery who has convinced himself that this whole climate change thing is one big hoax. Great work, Jack!

In all these examples, one's desire to think or feel a certain way has produced internalized beliefs about people and the world—emotional truths—that are disconnected from reality. No matter. Increasing accuracy is not Jack's goal. His cognitive job is to insulate our cherished beliefs and worldviews[14] from the truth, a truth that he feels we are too fragile to handle. So he shields our brains from reality, without our even knowing it. In the face of new data that disconfirms our assumptions, we conclude that something is wrong with the new data rather than with our old assumptions. Our brains bend, contort, and somersault in an effort to hold on to inaccurate but comforting emotional truths. When it comes to performing mental gymnastics, most of us are Olympic athletes. The fact that there are so many different idiomatic expressions and ways to describe motivated reasoning in common, everyday language—wishful thinking, having blinders on, burying your head in the sand, turning a blind eye, living in a fool's paradise, or being in denial (not the river)—is indicative of its ubiquity.

What does all of this have to do with racism credence? A lot. It became obvious to me early on that the fellas did not just lack factual information—they were also emotionally invested in their denial of anti-Black racism. One sentiment that surfaced during the discussion with some of the fellas was a deep sense of disappointment and rage over the daily struggles that they endured to make ends meet. Given those, how could they possibly accept the idea that they were born with a big head start in life and still lost the race? That's a bitter pill to swallow, and research confirms that personal failure can lead to a strong denial of White privilege.[15] It's a bitter pill for rich White folks too. The notion that they won the race in part *because* they're White undermines their sense of personal merit and achievement.[16] It may also imply that other people were exploited or oppressed to produce that financial success. These bitter pills may explain why both working-class and upper-class Whites fervently deny the existence of anti-Black racism, as found in the Sommers and Norton study. We like to think that our successes are the result of internal traits, such as our brilliance, and that our failures are the result of something external, such as bad luck—or some other group stealing opportunities. Of course, the opposite logic is applied when judging other people's successes and failures—they succeed because of luck and fail due to ineptitude.[17]

Many people are wedded to the view that the world is just and fair. A large body of scientific evidence on the "belief in a just world" phenomenon[18] reveals that people have a strong motivation to see the world as fair, as a way to mitigate feelings of discomfort, anxiety, guilt, or uncertainty.[19] The downside is that people who endorse just-world beliefs tend to see victims as being responsible for their own misfortunes. And victims often blame themselves.[20] Blaming the victim preserves the false but comforting belief—the emotional truth—that there is a method to the madness in the world. If bad things never happen to good people, then we can rest easier at night. By a similar logic, if bad things happen to Black people (e.g., police brutality), then it must be because they bring it on themselves.

In short, the very existence of racism violates the notion that the world is fair and just, which puts people in a tizzy. People who see the world as fair and just are therefore less likely to see racial discrimination and disparities. For example, research has shown that White people who believe the world is fair are more likely to judge Black and White household wealth as being relatively equal, and this was particularly true for high-income Whites, precisely the people who would tend to experience the most guilt over the racial wealth gap.[21]

Finally, many White people deny the existence of anti-Black racism because they want to see not just the world but also themselves as fair. If White people see racism as bad and themselves as good, this creates a very strong incentive to avoid seeing themselves as "racist."[22] Much of the work on the concept known as "White fragility" argues that Whites' desire to see themselves as good people leads to the defensiveness around recognizing and acknowledging their own biases.[23]

One sure way to get Jack Nicholson to quit his job of constantly deluding you is to show him that you can handle the truth. Research reveals that one of the most effective strategies for getting people to lower their reliance on emotional truth is by increasing their belief that they are competent, worthy, and good—a process known as *self-*

affirmation. Research demonstrates that making White people feel more affirmed increases the likelihood that they will see societal racism.[24]

This is *not* to suggest that White people should be coddled. Mayor Ted, whom we read about in the introduction, was never coddled. But the goal was not to "beat him up" either. The objective was to communicate with him in clear, direct, bold, and unapologetic language, and to also listen to his perspective, as well as to "build him up" by acknowledging his courage to face his fears and his willingness to learn. The message was clear: You are not stupid. You are not evil. You can get better if you try. We will hold you to high expectations. And we expect you to succeed. This formula is similar to the concept of *wise schooling,* proposed by Claude Steele, in which high expectations and challenging lessons are coupled with affirming messages and encouragement.[25] If people are *only* attacked, threatened, or criticized, then they will retreat. However, if they are confronted and corrected while also being given resources, reassurance, and opportunity to grow, then many will rise to the challenge.[26]

As we will see in the next chapter, racism against people of color is very much alive and well. The question, then, is: Why do so many White people not see it? I have provided two answers in this chapter: problems with how we process information and the fact that it's often easier to lie to ourselves than it is to handle the truth.

By raising the findings we discussed in this chapter, it's not my intent to judge, condemn, or belittle—nor is it to condone, excuse, or justify. It's simply an effort to comprehend, and ultimately remedy, the situation. How are you doing so far? It's a step-by-step journey, but it will be worth it in the end. You'll see.

Let's now continue to another important determinant of racism credence: how each of us defines racism in the first place. Before people can decide whether racism exists or not, they first have to reach a conclusion about what it is. It may not surprise you to learn that Americans are not all on the same page.

CHAPTER TWO

What Is "Racism," Anyway?

B elow is a picture of Brenda, a Black girl, standing behind a playground swing, and Sara, a White girl, on the ground near the swing. If I asked you to describe in a few sentences what is happening in this illustration, what would you say? What story would you come up with?

McGLOTHLIN & KILLEN (2006, 2020). ILLUSTRATIONS © 2020 JOAN M. K. TYCKO

We will return to this scenario shortly, but first let's continue the discussion of racism credence we began in the last chapter.

One of the single biggest determinants of racism credence is what people consider to be racism. Is racism necessarily deliberate and malicious, or can it also include actions that are unintentional and inadvertent? Views differ.[1] Similarly, if racism is defined as extreme acts of discrimination or violence perpetrated by a few rotten apples, rather than pervasive institutional policies and practices that differentially advantage some racial groups over others, then people will reach very different conclusions about its prevalence and impact.[2]

Getting on the same page with regard to the question of whether racism exists requires us to first reach a common understanding of what racism really means. Research confirms that both Black and White Americans agree that blatant acts of hatred are clear examples of racism.[3] For example, the vicious hostility that Jackie Robinson endured when he broke the color barrier in Major League Baseball is almost invariably perceived as racism. In addition, nearly everyone denounces individual acts of racial and ethnic violence, such as those perpetrated against the members of the Emanuel African Methodist Episcopal Church in Charleston and the Tree of Life Synagogue in Pittsburgh, who were callously murdered in their houses of worship. Where people disagree, however, is in the extent to which they view more subtle behaviors as racism.[4]

Having a productive Conversation requires a shared understanding of the perspective that each person is bringing to the table. The goal of this chapter is to examine the concept of racism as it exists in America today and to reach a common understanding of how it impacts our lives.

With that in mind, let's return to the picture of Brenda and Sara on the playground on the previous page. What did you think happened there? Perhaps you came up with something like:

> It was a sunny April afternoon, with the scent of cherry blossoms in the air, and the sounds of Sara squealing with delight as she soared higher and higher in the swing—until bad Brenda put an abrupt end to her joy by pushing Sara out of the swing and into the mud. This made Sara sad.

Okay, maybe I included more flowery embellishments than you would have. But research backs up the likelihood that your story would have had something to do with Brenda pushing Sara out of the swing, especially if you didn't know the study was about racism (in this case, the title of the chapter gave it away). Now take a look at the second picture, below. It's a similar scene, except in this image Abby, a Black girl, is on the ground, and Carrie, a White girl, is standing up behind the swing. Do you think someone would tell the same story they would have about the first image?

McGLOTHLIN & KILLEN (2006, 2020). ILLUSTRATIONS © 2020 JOAN M. K. TYCKO

Despite the fact that the two illustrations are virtually identical, except for the race and names of the two girls, study participants tend to describe these scenes very differently. When participants are randomly assigned to view only one of the two scenes, those who see the picture of Carrie, a White girl, standing behind the swing, and Abby, a Black girl, on the ground, they are more likely to describe it something like this:

> It was a sunny April afternoon, with the scent of cherry blossoms in the air, and the sounds of two best friends, Carrie and Abby, squealing with delight as they held hands, skipping gleefully in the park. As they approached the swing set, Abby slipped and fell in the mud. This made Carrie and Abby sad.

These differing descriptions illustrate a phenomenon commonly referred to as implicit or "unconscious" bias.[5] Unlike malicious or deliberate acts of racism, implicit racial bias occurs when race has an impact on perceptions, decisions, and behaviors without conscious awareness, intent, control, or effort. Most people, of all races, have implicit biases that impact how they judge others. Not even children are immune to implicit bias. In fact, the preceding pictures were actually shown to children between the ages of six and nine years old, both boys and girls, with the girls viewing one of the two scenes that we just saw, and the boys seeing a similar scene depicting boys. Not only did children interpret the pictures differently, but they also judged the *children* differently. When asked, "What do you think happened in this picture?" they were more likely to give a negative interpretation of what happened when the standing child was Black. And when asked how "good" or "bad" each *child* was, they were more likely to assign a frowny face (rather than a smiley face) to the Black child than to the White child.[6] These findings are consistent with other lines of research finding implicit bias among children.[7] Children's racial biases can come from a variety of sources, including social interactions, the media, and, of course, their parents.[8]

Adults also interpret situations very differently depending on the race of the actors. One infamous example occurred after Hurricane Katrina. Journalists described similar photos of people wading through the floodwaters carrying essential supplies very differently depending on whether the people depicted were Black or White. The photo was described as an example of "looting" in the aftermath of Hurricane Katrina when it contained a Black person with supplies but was described as an example of "finding" supplies when it contained White people.[9]

Just like the Katrina images, the swing-set illustrations—sans captions—are inherently ambiguous. In the swing-set scenario, it's by no means clear what has happened or what the "right" answer is. It's up to you to fill in the blanks and draw conclusions about what occurred. Research has shown that racism thrives under these conditions of ambiguity, both because racial biases can influence interpretations in fuzzy situations and because ambiguity can provide cover for racist judgments and decisions without them being interpreted as such.

If you answered that Brenda pushed Sara out of the swing, it is not 100 percent obvious that this is a racially biased interpretation. After all, the scenario is vague enough to allow for the possibility that Brenda really did push Sara out of the swing. It's only when we compare Brenda and Sara to Carrie and Abby that racial bias reveals itself. In short, the detection of subtle racism depends on the delta—the change or discrepancy between two similar conditions that differ only by race. The detection of blatant racism, such as the lynching in 1955 of Emmett Till—a fourteen-year-old Black boy who was savagely beaten and murdered by White men for allegedly whistling at a White woman[10]—doesn't require a comparison condition to see that it was an act of racial hatred. On the other hand, the interpretation of Brenda's behavior did require a comparison to see that she was being judged and treated differently. Racism resides in the delta—the change, or difference, in how people from different races are evaluated under very similar circumstances.

Unfortunately, life isn't a randomized, controlled experiment that allows you to check all of your actions and decisions against a comparison or control condition. You get just one situation or the other, which makes it impossible to know what you would have done in the same situation if the person were a different race. But we know from numerous experiments that White people do treat people of color less favorably than other White people, even when they have no idea that they are behaving in this biased manner.

Let's look at another example. Suppose you are on your way to work and someone falls on the sidewalk in front of you. What would you do? If you're a good person, you would help, wouldn't you? Research suggests that the answer depends on whether other people are around to lend a hand. Early investigations of the determinants of helping behavior came in response to the case of Kitty Genovese, who was repeatedly attacked and ultimately killed in New York City in the 1960s despite the presence of several witnesses who neither called the police nor offered to help her. Social psychologists eventually determined that this lack of responsiveness among bystanders could be explained, in part, by diffusion of responsibility. The presence of others gives everyone present an excuse not to help, because "someone else will do it." Ironically, a person in need is less likely to receive assistance when there are lots of people around.[11]

Now, what if the person who needs help is of a different race? How might that further change people's responses? In one study, researchers set up situations in which people encountered a person in need of aid who was either Black or White. The experimenters also varied the context—in some scenarios there was no one else around to help and in other scenarios there were lots of bystanders. What do you think they found? Were Whites more likely to lend a hand to a White person in need, a Black person in need, or both races equally? The answer: It depended on whether the situation was ambiguous enough to give them cover, allowing them to engage in racially biased behavior without it being obvious.

Results indicated that 88 percent of White participants assisted the person in need when no one else was around to help, and this rate of helping did *not* vary as a function of whether the person was White or Black. When they, and they alone, could help, it turns out most people (or, again, 88 percent of them) weren't comfortable leaving others in dire straits, regardless of their race.

By contrast, in scenarios where others were present, the researchers found that the helping patterns were dramatically different. When White participants believed that other people were present— and therefore could take on the responsibility of helping the person in need—75 percent (a 13 percent drop-off) helped a White person in need, but only 37 percent (a 51 percent drop-off) helped a Black person in need. This striking drop-off in the Black condition can be attributed to the fact that the presence of others provided a readily available, race-neutral excuse, both to others *and* to oneself, to keep walking.[12] The ambiguity of the situation allowed White people to refuse help to the Black person without feeling guilty or racist. It is in ambiguous situations, or what some researchers call moments of "plausible deniability,"[13] that bias is most likely to emerge.

Racism can play out in very subtle ways. One of the cornerstones of *aversive racism theory,* a concept originated by social psychologists Sam Gaertner and Jack Dovidio, is that the nature of racism in America has evolved from more blatant acts of exclusion, oppression, and violence, common in the first half of the twentieth century, to more subtle acts of racial discrimination, common in the latter half of the twentieth century and into the twenty-first century. This change is due to the cultural shift toward egalitarian values in the wake of civil rights and other social movements of the 1960s. Although White people in the post–civil rights era began to genuinely embrace egalitarian values—reflecting the belief that all people, regardless of race, should be treated with dignity and have the same access to opportunity— negative feelings toward Black people did not fully disappear. These negative feelings merely went underground. Thus, aversive racism is the paradoxical product of Whites' egalitarian values and anti-Black feelings, which together create an "aversion" or contradiction. To deal with this contradiction of, on the one hand, being someone who genuinely values fairness and equality, while also being someone who harbors negative feelings about people who happen to belong to a different race, Whites push their negative feelings toward Blacks into the subconscious and just focus on their egalitarian values, believing that they are unbiased and they treat everyone the same. This was one of the early theoretical foundations of research on implicit bias.

Aversive racism has also been found in employment and organizational contexts, such as when evaluating job candidates. Dovidio and colleagues found that White evaluators will sometimes give equivalent recommendations for White and Black candidates, but only if both candidates are superstars.[14] In fact, if both candidates are superstars, there might be an ever-so-slight preference for the Black candidate (one could imagine that White evaluators might see Black superstars as a twofer—a great candidate *and* an opportunity to pat oneself on the back for being egalitarian!). If, however, the two candidates have identical résumés that show both of them as being less than perfect, then White evaluators will choose the White mediocre candidate much more often than the Black mediocre candidate. The potentially flawed, less-than-perfect White candidate gets the benefit of the doubt, whereas the potentially flawed, less-than-perfect Black candidate does not.

What is most insidious about aversive racism is that the White evaluators have no idea that they behave relatively equitably in clear-cut situations while being racially biased in ambiguous situations. In White evaluators' minds, their rejection of the Black candidate had absolutely nothing to do with race, because they could point to the candidate's less-than-perfect record. "I didn't hire this candidate because six months is not enough work experience," they will say to themselves or others. "It had *nothing* to do with the fact that they were Black. I don't have a racist bone in my body!" These experiments have been conducted extensively, and we know from decades of research that the same six months of work experience would have been considered plenty sufficient for the White candidate, or a minor deficit that could be fixed with a little bit of training.

Worse still, when White people support one Black person, research indicates that they run the risk of becoming more racially biased against other Black people.[15] London Business School professor Daniel Effron and his colleagues showed that voting for Barack Obama actually increased racism by bolstering White people's "moral credentials," creating greater latitude to discriminate against Blacks who were not Obama.[16] The "moral credential" earned by voting for Obama gave the White voter greater license to behave in a more racist manner toward other Black people without being afraid of being labeled racist.

Organizations can have moral credentials as well.[17] Cheryl Kaiser and colleagues have found that merely having diversity policies can lead Whites to judge an organization as being more procedurally fair and nondiscriminatory compared with organizations that do not have these policies.[18] However, the mere existence of diversity policies can make Whites blind to the racial discrimination that is really occurring, given that we know that companies with and without diversity policies show similarly high levels of racial discrimination.[19] The policies can also lead to harsher and more insensitive reactions to racial minorities who complain about discrimination.[20]

There is a disturbing paradox here—people, and organizations, who claim to value fairness and equality are still treating people of color in ways that are unfair and unequal. This kind of racism is especially difficult to address because any excuse—the presence of others who could help, a flaw in a résumé, a much-touted diversity policy—suffices to leave the delusion of egalitarianism intact. That's a double whammy. It is one challenge to combat blatant racism but quite another to confront racism that many people have no idea they are perpetrating. Most White people believe that they would never treat someone differently because of the color of their skin. This combination of culpability and deniability makes the problem of aversive racism especially challenging.

I suspect that there are two questions coursing through your mind right now: What do I do about all this? And has anything changed in the years since researchers first discovered and documented aversive racism?

In response to the first question, I will reiterate my earlier call for patience as we establish facts before moving toward solutions. However, if you are a White reader, one big thing that you can do right now is acknowledge the almost-certain possibility that you (not "other" White people, but *you*) are discriminating against people of color in this unintentional but insidious way. That's a critical first step. I realize that it's difficult for many White people to digest the possibility that they are an integral part of the problem (after all, their values are the exact opposite). But it is, by far, one of the most important things that you can "do" at this moment.

As to the second question, although most of the foundational work on aversive or modern racism occurred in the three decades following the civil rights movement, its replications, variations, and elaborations continue to the present day. Just like your grandma's chocolate chip cookie recipe or the human-anatomy poster on your doctor's wall (the one in my doctor's office has a copyright from the 1940s), aversive racism hasn't changed much with the passage of time.

Dovidio and colleagues have replicated the job-candidate experiment and found that the results did not vary at all over a period of fifteen years. Other researchers have examined job discrimination over a period almost twice that long (from 1989 to 2017) and found absolutely no change in discrimination against Black candidates over those four decades.[21] Field research indicates that Black candidates continue to get fewer interview requests than otherwise identical White applicants,[22] and laboratory research reveals that asking participants to imagine their "ideal" candidate increased their likelihood of thinking about a White candidate and led them to give more preferential treatment to a White candidate over a Black candidate with matched qualifications.[23]

In addition, psychometric research shows that about 80 percent of White Americans harbor negative implicit biases against Blacks, as measured by the Implicit Association Test (IAT),[24] with a much smaller percentage of Black Americans showing negative implicit bias against Whites.[25] There are many measures of implicit bias, but the IAT is among the most popular and widely studied, with millions of people all over the world having taken it since the test was created in 1996. It measures the strength of association between Black or White people and positive or negative concepts by looking at reaction times to categorize stimuli on a computer. You can take it yourself at implicit.harvard.edu. Although there is some debate and controversy about the meaning of IAT results and what they predict,[26] there is much less controversy about the concept of implicit bias and the impact that it has on judgments and behavior.

So given all of this research, let's return to our original question: How do we define "racism"? Here is my simple definition:

Racism occurs when individuals or institutions show more favorable evaluation or treatment of an individual or group based on race or ethnicity.

That's it. Nothing too complicated or elaborate. However, it's worth taking a closer look at the wording of this definition. First, I intentionally used the phrase "racism *occurs*" rather than "racism *is*" to highlight the idea that racism is more about the consequences of people's behaviors than it is about their particular traits. In other words, racism is more about what people do than who people are. This is consistent with Ibram Kendi's notion of thinking of the racist label as being a "sticker" rather than a "tattoo."[27] A sticker is something that can be applied or peeled off for each action. In contrast, a tattoo is something that is etched on someone always and forever, regardless of what they do. We shouldn't think that racism is fixed and permanent like a tattoo, because few people are racist all of the time and never do anything antiracist. Similarly, there are few, if any, people who are antiracist all of the time and never say or do anything racist.

All of us are guilty of saying or doing something that can be considered racist. And everyone has done or is capable of doing something that is antiracist. Tattooing someone as a racist or antiracist is too simplistic and does not reflect the complexity of people or environments, or the way that the two interact. More and more research points to the idea that implicit bias is not so much an immutable trait of a person, like height, but a malleable feature that is more strongly determined by culture, norms, history, and other social factors.[28] It's not so much hair as it is a hairdo. Research using the IAT has shown that individual people's implicit biases can change with time or context, and that societal-level implicit biases can change as well.[29]

Racism can manifest itself as "evaluation" (what you think) or "treatment" (how you behave). What someone believes about a particular group (e.g., Blacks are athletic, Asians are nerdy, Whites are selfish) is called a *stereotype*. What someone feels about a particular group (e.g., I don't like Blacks) is called *prejudice*. How someone behaves toward a particular group (e.g., I will not hire Hispanic candidates) is called *discrimination*. I highlight these definitions not to split hairs but because they will be very important in later chapters when we discuss systemic causes of racism and the solutions to it.

Let's continue unpacking my definition of racism, specifically the phrase "when individuals or institutions show more favorable evaluation or treatment . . ." The word *individual(s)* refers to one person or a small number of people acting in a personal capacity, whereas *institutions* refers to large organizations within a society or to society itself. This part of the definition captures the fact that racism is not just about individual acts but also about the way in which society is structured and organized. In fact, racism is *mostly* about how society operates, as will become evident in subsequent chapters. For example, extreme manifestations of racism, such as chattel slavery and Jim Crow laws, have more to do with institutional policies and practices than individual decisions and behaviors. Nevertheless, many see racism as something that is primarily perpetrated by individuals rather than something that is perpetrated by systems and cultures. This has profound implications, not just for racism credence but for one's level of support for public policy aimed at ameliorating racism.[30]

Another important nuance in my definition is the phrase "more favorable." That's a *relative* assessment that is focused on differing evaluations and treatments between two groups, regardless of whether the difference is due to too much negativity toward out-groups—the social categories that you do not belong to—or too much positivity toward in-groups, which are the social categories that you do belong to. In other words, racism doesn't have to involve hatred toward the "other." It could be due to excessive positivity or preference for your own group relative to other (out-)groups. In fact, one prominent line of research argues that discrimination is mostly driven by higher in-group favoritism and a "neutral" attitude toward the out-group, rather than by a high level of out-group hatred.[31] It is frequently motivated by an opportunistic desire to promote self-interest or group interest rather than a hateful or sinister desire to harm others because they are different. Nevertheless, the end result is still a disparity between how the two groups are treated or evaluated. Remember, racism resides in the delta.

Finally, note that my definition of racism includes "ethnicity" as well as race, which allows for *intra*racial discrimination to occur. This allows for the possibility of German racism against Jews, Greeks, or Turks, for Japanese racism against Koreans, or even for Black Jamaican American racism against African Americans, or vice versa. It also allows for the possibility of racism among racial minority groups (e.g., Asians vs. Blacks, or vice versa) or from racial minority groups toward Whites, at least at the individual level.

Notice that I did not use words like *malicious, intentional,* and *deliberate* in my definition. Although these attributes sometimes characterize racism, they don't inherently define it. Polite people can, and do, engage in racist behavior. Liberal and progressive people can, and do, engage in racist behavior. Caring and compassionate people can, and do, engage in racist behavior. There are whole books written about how racial biases can contaminate the judgments and actions of people with the best intentions.[32] As we have seen, and the research has established conclusively, differential treatment or evaluation often happens unintentionally. Brenda standing behind the swing gets demonized, the mediocre White candidate gets hired, the Black person who falls in a crowd is avoided, and all of it is done without any awareness that racial bias was being expressed.

Two important elements that are missing from this simple definition of racism involve how "systems" of oppression are formed and the extent to which they influence how racism is expressed. I also did not delve into the complexities of how systemic/institutional racism affects individual racism, and vice versa, via laws and policies, social norms, the media, wage disparities, and other factors. That is a topic that will be explored in detail in the next two chapters. For now, I will offer a metaphor that illuminates the nebulous concept of systemic racism.

SYSTEMIC RACISM: THE SALMON AND THE STREAM

To understand what *systemic* racism is, let's think about individuals as fish and society as the stream that they inhabit and navigate day in and day out. There are forces, or "currents," in the stream that push everything in a certain direction. We can think of racism as one of those currents. Sometimes the current is like white water, very strong and observable, like mass violence against a group. At other times the current is strong but obscured, like an undercurrent that you can't see but that nevertheless pushes you downstream or pulls you under. An example might be widespread but subtle employment discrimination. Sometimes the current gets weaker or stronger, depending on the season or the location of the stream. But it's always there and the basic dynamic is always the same—it moves everything downstream toward the sea.

Racism is not just about movements and actions of the individual fish; it's also about the hydrodynamics of the stream itself (i.e., the current). The current can affect movements of individuals without their knowledge and often against their will. It can also affect outcomes even in the absence of actions. If you do nothing but float in a stream, treading water, then the current will eventually carry you out to sea. If you actively surf or swim with the current, then you will still arrive at the same destination, just much faster. What's important is that the destination is ultimately the same whether you passively float or actively swim with the current. From this systemic perspective, racism has absolutely nothing to do with what's in your heart, your brain, or even your intentions. It's all about how your actions or inactions allow the dynamics that are already in place to move you in a certain direction.

Antiracism requires swimming against and outpacing the current, like a salmon, in order to head upstream toward the pristine headwaters where the whole species can benefit. In the end, what matters is whether individuals are traveling upstream—or downstream—regardless of whether their seaward journey is the result of active swimming or treading water. Therefore, I propose replacing the "racist" versus "not racist" dichotomy with the "complicit" versus "antiracist" dichotomy. Complicit individuals are all of those heading downstream, regardless of whether it's due to action or inaction, whereas antiracists are all of those resisting and overcoming the current to swim upstream to benefit the species and the environment. Of course, being an upstream salmon requires *much* more effort, courage, strength, persistence, and endurance than being a downstream floater or a surfer. And the journey upstream can be exhausting, frustrating, and even dangerous. But the potential benefits for all are too great to stop swimming.

One of the absolute most impactful actions that White people can do is to dedicate a ton of time, thought, and attention to understanding, in concrete ways, exactly how their *own* thoughts, feelings, and behaviors toward people of color are influenced by the current—not their values or intentions. To be sure, many Whites (and some people of color) question the existence of a "current" altogether. They believe that the world is a stagnant pond and the only thing that matters is whether you're willing to swim to where you want to go. Some may even believe that it's a river whose current flows upstream, carrying the salmon to their destination without any struggle at all.

Recall my conversations with the fellas from the last chapter. Many of them felt not only that they were socially disadvantaged but also that their social disadvantage was the result of the river flowing in reverse. Many of the fellas believed that Blacks were the "privileged" ones, pointing to the dozens of Black celebrities, entrepreneurs, and academics who appear to have privilege. Are they right? Is the existence of socioeconomic disadvantage among some Whites evidence that no current exists? On the flip side, are privileged Black people, like Oprah Winfrey or Barack Obama, evidence that racism is nonexistent, or even that "Black privilege" exists?

The answer requires a closer look at the concept of "privilege," which will be examined in the next chapter using a popular Hollywood movie to highlight the important distinction between two types of privilege: individual and institutional.

CHAPTER THREE

How Does Social Disadvantage Differ for Blacks and Whites?

The Oscar-winning movie *Green Book,* directed by Peter Farrelly, is based on the real life of Don Shirley, a talented and successful Black musician in the 1960s, and Tony Vallelonga, his working-class White driver. In the film, Shirley is portrayed as talented, cultured, and financially secure—so much so that he is able to hire Tony to be his driver. While he is a star onstage, playing to sold-out crowds throughout the South, Don is shown suffering the constant indignity of arriving at venues through the service entrance and being refused service at upscale restaurants that cater to Whites. Despite his economic and intellectual "power," Don finds himself relying on Tony for legitimacy, credibility, and protection. Tony, on the other hand, doesn't have a steady job and worries about bills, debt, and providing for his family. However, due to his skin color, Tony has the option of frequenting any establishment that he pleases, regardless of whether he can financially afford to be there. Indeed, he is permitted by society to occupy any space that he chooses to, whether it is a predominantly Black or White venue.

The movie's plotline seems to raise the question of which of these two men possesses more "privilege." But this simple question fails to get to the heart of the matter. A better question is: How does the privilege that each man possesses *differ* from the privilege of the other? In order to answer that question, we need to consider how race shapes the nature of privilege.

As discussed in Chapter 1, many White Americans believe that it is White people, not people of color, who are being systematically discriminated against. This belief is particularly fervid among working-class Whites. For many, talk of "White privilege" creates confusion at best and resentment at worst, as they do not feel privileged in the least. In fact, they feel that they are ignored, marginalized, excluded, and left to endure considerable hardship without any assistance from organizations or society.[1]

Few would challenge the fact that working-class Whites experience hardships. Of course they do. But are the hardships facing working-class Whites, like Tony Vallelonga, equivalent to the racism facing Black people?

Racism is often characterized by two related but distinct foundational forces: *White supremacy* and *anti-Blackness*.[2] White supremacy is the notion that Whiteness and White people are superior and desirable, especially when contrasted with Blackness and Black people. Anti-Blackness is the notion that Blackness and Black people are inferior and undesirable, especially when contrasted with Whiteness and White people. Neither Blackness nor Whiteness is "neutral" in American society, or in the world for that matter. Being White is seen as a positive quality that confers societal status, acceptance, and inclusion. Being Black is seen as a negative quality that produces societal stigma, marginalization, and exclusion.

Because White privilege and Black stigma are both residual effects of enslavement, and European colonialism more broadly, both forces remain prevalent in the United States and throughout the entire world. For example, research on skin-tone bias, or "colorism," shows that in nearly every country in the world "Whiter" is considered better, and lighter skin tone is implicitly and explicitly associated with more positive traits.[3] Indeed, some multinational companies have capitalized on colorism; one estimate predicts that revenues from skin-whitening products will double to $24 billion by 2027. Already skin-bleaching products account for 61 percent of the skin-care market in India, and a staggering 77 percent of women in Nigeria report using them regularly.[4] The positivity associated with White-ness is woven into the fabric, or institutions, of society, as is the nega-tivity associated with Blackness.

Institutional privilege refers to all the advantages of Whiteness that are inherited through these baked-in, foundational forces and their impact on political, economic, legal, and social structures, policies, and practices. Some argue that institutional privilege has nothing to do with individuals' actions. It's something that White people inherit from structures that were put in place long before they, or anyone in their family, were born. Sociologists sometimes refer to this type of privilege as "ascribed" status. Institutional privilege is part of the sys-tem, like a current in a stream, and is impossible to separate from our social world. Consequently, race in the United States functions in many ways like a caste system[5]—a condition inherited at birth from which there is no escape.[6]

But institutional privilege is not the *only* form of privilege or social advantage. There is also *individual privilege,* or advantages that indi-viduals obtain for themselves. This is often referred to by sociologists as "achieved" status. It captures the fact that individuals can, and do, achieve wealth, power, and position through their own merit and labor or through simple luck (for example, winning the lottery).

Consider the diagram below:[7]

INDIVIDUAL PRIVILEGE	INSTITUTIONAL PRIVILEGE	
	Low	High
Low	Poor Blacks	Poor Whites
High	Rich Blacks	Rich Whites

In theory, these two dimensions of privilege are conceptually in-dependent. In practice, however, institutional privilege is tied to indi-vidual privilege—a lack of institutional privilege can constrain or restrict individual privilege. Research shows that being Black will present a hindrance to individual achievement, regardless of merit, whereas being White will enhance the likelihood of individual achievement, all else being equal.[8]

Institutional privilege determines where people "belong." Isabel Wilkerson describes social caste—which keeps people in their place—as being analogous to a plaster cast that keeps bones in place. Both types of "cast(e)s" limit your mobility. If you have institutional privilege, then you are much freer to occupy high-status roles and spaces because there is a "match" between the individual and institutional privilege. If you don't have institutional privilege, it is more difficult to occupy high-status roles and spaces, regardless of your actions as an individual, because you have to deal with social and structural barriers in society in addition to the unique personal challenges in your life. In *Green Book,* Don Shirley's individual privilege did not "match" the institutional privilege of a Black person in America, and his life was burdened as a result.

A more contemporary real-life example is Oprah Winfrey. Despite immense individual privilege—with an estimated net worth of over $3 billion—being Black means that she nonetheless lacks institutional privilege. Because of this privilege "mismatch" (high individual privilege but low institutional privilege), Winfrey has encountered discrimination in elite spaces. In one infamous incident in 2013, Winfrey left a high-end retailer in Switzerland after a salesperson refused to show her a $38,000 handbag that the employee assumed was too expensive for Winfrey, whom the clerk apparently saw as simply a "Black woman," to afford.

More generally, people of color carry the burden of being psychologically and politically excluded from the simple institutional privilege of being a full citizen (i.e., "American"). They are especially barred from the role of American hero—despite the fact that over 40 percent of those serving in the U.S. armed forces are non-White. Early Black intellectuals like W. E. B. Du Bois thought that giving Blacks the opportunity to prove their loyalty and heroism in World War I would translate into increased acceptance and social status back home in the United States. He was mistaken. As Nikole Hannah-Jones puts it: "Black veterans . . . especially those with the audacity to wear their uniform, had since the Civil War been the target of a particular violence." She goes on to state that "many white Americans saw black men in the uniforms of America's armed services not as patriotic but as exhibiting a dangerous pride."[9] In sum,

White people have the privilege of being seen as "real" Americans[10] and of being hailed as national heroes. Black veterans, on the other hand, may be viewed negatively due to the threat their military service presents to the racial caste system.[11]

What all these examples of privilege mismatch illustrate is that the stigma of Blackness can never be completely escaped, even for those who make sacrifices and valuable contributions to the nation. It cannot be escaped even for Black billionaires, despite the nation's deeply ingrained respect for entrepreneurship and capitalism. In fact, research suggests that wealthy and powerful Blacks may face even more racial discrimination than working-class Blacks because they are considered "out of place" by society and do not belong in elite spaces.[12] The book *The Rage of a Privileged Class* by Ellis Cose highlights the unique challenges that wealthy Blacks face because their success defies powerful institutional structures and therefore makes it more difficult for them to operate within a space of privilege.

None of this is news to Black people. Research by Dov Cohen and colleagues revealed that while White people's sense of their own social status or privilege in society was strongly correlated with their income, occupational prestige, and educational attainment, this was not true for Black people. It wasn't that Blacks didn't value achievements. They did, and it increased their *self*-esteem. However, it did not increase their perceptions of their *social* status—or sense of their rank, regard, or standing in *society*. The opposite pattern was true for Whites—income, occupational prestige, and educational attainment enhanced their sense of their social position in society more than it enhanced their self-esteem. The authors argued that Blacks tend to see their (low) status in society as being primarily determined by their skin color, regardless of what they do individually.[13] Relatively speaking, Blacks were less likely than Whites to see a link between their individual privilege and institutional privilege.

Some evidence suggests that other groups also see Blackness as being associated with lower social status. Research that simultaneously examines the impact of race and individual privilege (such as wealth, occupational prestige, or other high-status cues) on implicit evaluations found that high levels of individual privilege enhanced the evaluation of Whites but not of Blacks. Specifically, participants' reaction times to respond to positive words were faster when they were simultaneously primed with White faces paired with high-status cues compared with White faces paired with low-status cues. However, reaction times to positive words following Black faces did not vary as a function of whether the Black faces were paired with high-status or low-status cues.[14] Simply put, high-status paired with Black is still "Black," and therefore doesn't boost evaluations. On the other hand, high-status combined with White yields the most positive outcomes. Other research echoes these findings, showing that when race and socioeconomic status are examined simultaneously, the high-status White group stands apart, being evaluated more positively than all of the other combinations (i.e., low-status White targets, high-status Black targets, and low-status Black targets).[15] In summary, consistent with the notion of a caste system, having money or education or occupational prestige doesn't seem to fully erase the stigma of being Black.

DISENTANGLING THE EFFECTS OF INDIVIDUAL AND INSTITUTIONAL PRIVILEGE

Which form of privilege matters more in the workplace: what you've done as an individual, or where your race places you in the institutional caste system? Let us first consider the well-known résumé study by the economists Marianne Bertrand and Sendhil Mullainathan, conducted in 2004. The authors set out to answer a basic question: Which matters more in the workplace—race or personal accomplishments? To find an answer, they responded to over twelve hundred jobs posted across a variety of sectors in two major American cities, sending out around five thousand résumés. Bertrand and Mullainathan created fictitious résumés to apply for these jobs. The résumés all showed merit in terms of the fictional candidates' accomplishments. The only differences were names. The researchers selected certain names that suggested the race of the candidate (e.g., Lakisha Washington or Emily Walsh). In other words, they varied institutional privilege by making one of the candidates Black and the other White, while keeping individual privilege the same by using the exact same achievements and qualifications for each candidate.

What do you think the researchers discovered? In what percentage of cases do you think a company treated the Black and White applicants equally (e.g., contacted them both)? What percentage of the time would it favor the White applicants (i.e., contacted Whites more frequently than Blacks)? And what percentage of the time would it favor Black applicants (i.e., contacted Blacks more frequently than Whites)? Write down your answers. The percentages you assign to the three possibilities should total one hundred. Remember, in each instance the Black and White candidates are equally qualified.

In their study, Bertrand and Mullainathan found that the likelihood of any applicant being contacted was relatively small, but when applicants were contacted, the most frequent outcome was more favorable treatment toward White applicants. That is, a bit more than 50 percent of the time, the White applicant was called back but not the Black applicant, for example, despite the fact that the applicants were equally qualified. The second-most-frequent outcome was for both candidates to be called back, which occurred around 29 percent of the time. And the least frequent outcome was for the Black candidate to be favored over the White candidate, which occurred around 21 percent of the time. The graph below indicates the probability of each outcome.

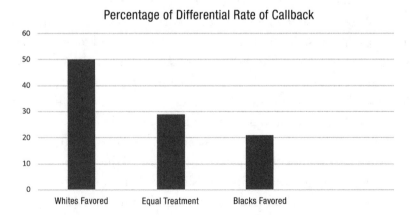

Percentage of Differential Rate of Callback

What these data demonstrate is that institutional privilege, not individual privilege, usually determined which job candidate prevailed. The researchers estimated that the benefit of just being White was the equivalent of an additional eight years of work experience, giving White candidates a considerable head start over equally qualified Black candidates.[16]

Remember the fellas from Chapter 1? The scenario imagined by the fellas to be the most widespread and prevalent outcome—White people being discriminated against in favor of Black people—turns out to be the rarest outcome. The rate of discrimination against Blacks was more than double the incidence of "reverse" discrimination against Whites. And by far the most common outcome of all was special treatment in favor of Whites—much more common than equal treatment.

Let's look at another study that examined how race affects individual outcomes in the United States. In this 2003 study, sociologist Devah Pager looked at how Black and White applicants with or without a criminal record fared in the job market.[17] She created and sent résumés of Black or White applicants to various job postings. In half of the cases, the Black or White applicant had a clean criminal record, and in the other half the applicant was a convicted felon who had been incarcerated for eighteen months.[18] So which job applicant do you think got the most callbacks: the White nonfelon, the Black nonfelon, the White felon, or the Black felon? And who do you think received the second-highest number of callbacks?

You probably guessed correctly that the applicant with the most callbacks was the White nonfelon, who would have both relatively high individual and institutional privilege in this context. And the applicant with the lowest number of callbacks was the Black felon, who most lacked individual and institutional privilege. No big surprises there. The really interesting question is what happened in the situations of privilege mismatch—i.e., the Black nonfelon and the White felon. Is it better to have a clean record and be Black, which one could interpret as high individual privilege and low institutional privilege, or the inverse—to be White but have a felony conviction, which is high institutional privilege but low individual privilege? Who will get more callbacks?

Contrary to many people's expectations, White applicants with felony convictions did not receive fewer callbacks than Black applicants with a clean record. In fact, if anything, the trend was in the opposite direction, with the White felon getting more callbacks than the Black law-abiding citizen.

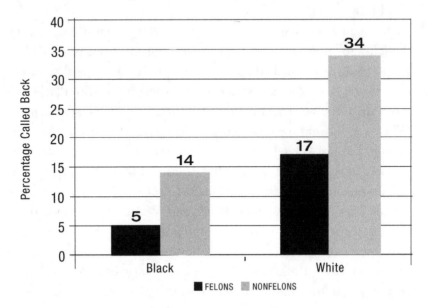

Here, in four bars, is White privilege. Even for people who readily acknowledge the privilege that Whiteness confers, the extent of that privilege indicated by this study can be shocking. In the Bertrand and Mullainathan study, Whiteness was the equivalent of eight years of work experience. In this study, the benefit of Whiteness is even more extreme.

It is profound to think that what you do, your personal merits and demerits captured in such things as a criminal record, can be overshadowed by the caste to which society relegates you based on the color of your skin. Being White provides a staggering amount of unearned privilege, including the luxury of being fallible—whether it's a professional mistake, a social faux pas, or a legal violation—without being condemned for eternity. It is the privilege of not constantly having a cloud of suspicion hanging over you when you haven't done anything wrong. The graph shows that White people are given the benefit of the doubt, the freedom to make mistakes. Black people are not.

Let's leave the data aside for a moment. Can you think of any White convicted felons in the real world who've gone on to live relatively prosperous, happy, stigma-free lives? I can think of several. First, there is Frank Abagnale, the convicted fraudster who, after serving time in prison, was offered a consulting gig by the FBI, a Hollywood script (*Catch Me if You Can*, starring Leonardo DiCaprio), and a book deal (*Scam Me if You Can*). There are thousands of skilled Black, Hispanic, Asian, and Arab criminals as well, but to my knowledge none has landed a federal consulting contract or a lucrative movie or publishing contract. Other examples include Jared Kushner's father, Charles Kushner—a convicted felon who spent over a year in prison. This has not kept him from a profitable career in real estate development, nor has it destroyed his social standing—he still hosts elegant parties, fundraisers, and receptions for big-name politicians.

The image of the celebrated White criminal goes back centuries, as does that of the condemned Black "criminal" (in quotation marks because there was often no crime).[19] For example, Jesse James was a brutal murderer and compulsive thief, but his image is often exalted and glorified in American lore, in part because he was a Confederate sympathizer. I could go on, but I think the point is clear. As the Pager study suggests, criminality is not as damning for White people as it is for Black people. A criminal conviction provides a convenient and socially acceptable excuse, consistent with aversive racism theory, to throw a Black person in the trash can. Heck, technically speaking, you don't even need to be convicted to get tossed in the rubbish bin if you're Black—just ask O.J.

In my work, when I observe a breakthrough with an individual like Ted or a group like the fellas, the lightbulb goes off when they realize, perhaps for the first time in their lives, that race really does matter. And that it's the Black person who gets the short end of the stick. This moment of revelation can be a jarring awakening. It can also be emotionally painful to learn that people of color are treated so harshly. Most people know someone who has made a mistake and come out okay in the end. Have you yourself ever made a mistake or done things that you would undo if you could relive the past? We all have. But the sad truth is that the graces of forgiveness and redemption that can follow human error and imperfection are privileges that are differentially afforded to people based on their race.

This was an earth-shattering moment for Ted when he first became fully aware. At the same time, it is a shock to many people of color that a White person could live their entire life and *not* know that race strongly impacts life outcomes. There are many reasons for this lack of awareness, as discussed in Chapter 1, including motivated reasoning, or seeing the world through rose-colored glasses, as well as deliberate ignorance, or intentionally shielding oneself from the truth.[20] Deliberate ignorance is not an option for people of color. Their survival and prosperity depend on understanding the dynamics of race.

Many people of color intuitively understand the insights of the studies we've just discussed, purely from experience, and adjust their lives accordingly in order to cope and prosper. For example, I once spoke to the CEO of a Fortune 500 corporation who talked about a female employee who used her middle name (let's say "Ann") rather than her first name (let's say "Shanice") because it was less ethnically identifiable. She had been passed over many times as Shanice but found it easier to get her foot in the door as Ann. A colleague of mine at Harvard has talked about the different responses she gets if she describes herself using her first initial and last name, let's say "N. Bradford," rather than her full name, "Nekesha Bradford." People have used many terms, such as "covering"[21] or "Whitening the résumé,"[22] to describe the practice of deemphasizing one's race to avoid job-market discrimination.

Data collected by Sonia Kang and colleagues found 31 percent of Black professionals and 40 percent of Asian professionals whom they queried admitted to Whitening their résumés, either by changing their name or by omitting club memberships or extracurricular experiences that might reveal their racial identities. One possibility is that although people of color *believe* that they need to Whiten their résumé to increase the likelihood of a callback, in reality there is no benefit of a Whitened résumé. In fact, one could make the case that an un-Whitened résumé would increase callback rates, particularly for companies seeking diversity.

To address these possibilities, Kang and colleagues conducted a field experiment to investigate whether the practice of Whitening résumés actually led to higher (or lower) callback rates, and whether this varied based on the organization's commitment to diversity. In this study, they sent Whitened or un-Whitened résumés of Black or Asian applicants to 1,600 different real-world job postings across a variety of industries and geographical areas in the United States. Half, or 800, of the job postings contained language expressing a strong desire to seek diverse applicants, and the other half of the job postings did not contain such language. The résumés were Whitened by changing the names to appear less ethnic and/or by omitting extracurricular experiences or memberships that revealed ethnicity.

Whitening the résumés of Black and Asian applicants increased their callback rate by up to 150 percent. For example, the callback rate for un-Whitened résumés was 10 percent for Black applicants and 11.5 percent for Asian applicants. However, this rate jumped to nearly 26 percent for Black applicants and 21 percent for Asian applicants who Whitened both their name (for example, "Susan Lee" rather than "Xian Li") and their extracurricular experience (for example, omitting membership in an ethnic sorority or fraternity, or using a more generic label).

What's particularly unsettling is that the preference for Whitened résumés held true even for companies that explicitly stated a desire to seek diversity. The level of discrimination at these prodiversity companies was the same as the discrimination levels of companies without prodiversity statements. These data suggest that if you are not White, you will increase your chances of getting a callback if you Whiten your résumé—even when applying to a position at a company that claims to value diversity.[23]

I want to be abundantly clear on one point: The results of the studies cited in this chapter do not suggest that working-class White people don't experience hardships. As seen in the graph on page 44, Whites with a felony receive half the callbacks of Whites without a felony. Thus, the data do not support the idea that Whites are completely impervious to any social disadvantage. What these studies do underscore is how important it is to avoid conflating hardship and racism. They are not the same thing. Remember, racism resides in the delta. And in the graph we see a clear shift in the way that Blacks are being treated relative to Whites who are otherwise identical. And the treatment is usually less favorable.

I am also not making the case that one type of disadvantage is better or worse—they are simply different. The fellas saw me as being privileged because they were focused on individual privilege—they saw a Harvard professor talking to them from a position of authority. I saw the fellas as being privileged because I was focused on institutional privilege—I saw a roomful of White men who represented the gatekeepers of access, not just to their department but to almost every major organization and institution in the United States. What is particularly noteworthy is that we both failed to see the big picture. I initially failed to understand how they could possibly consider themselves, as individuals, to be less advantaged than a Black person. And they initially failed to see how being Black presents a permanent and indelible challenge in America.

Hardship can be caused by many different factors, such as poverty, disability, and social stigma. One interesting question is whether Black and White people believe to the same extent that their race can be a direct cause of hardship. According to a 2019 Pew Survey, most Whites believe that their race is neutral—slightly more than 50 percent believe that being White neither helps nor hurts them. Despite low levels of racism credence, many Whites, including working-class Whites, believe that being White in the United States does confer some institutional-level social advantages, with 45 percent of Whites acknowledging that being White helps them to get ahead.

What's fascinating is what happens when the question is flipped to focus on *disadvantages* or hardship rather than advantages or benefits. While a majority of Black respondents (52 percent) reported that being Black *hurt* their ability to get ahead, only 5 percent of White respondents reported that being White *hurt* their ability to get ahead. Similarly, in the E Pluribus Unum survey administered in the fall of 2019 to six hundred White, six hundred Black, and six hundred Hispanic adults living in the American South, only 5 percent of White respondents reported that their race made it *harder* for them to get ahead in life, whereas 49 percent of Blacks and 25 percent of Hispanics believed that their race made it harder for them to get ahead in life.

This subtle distinction between believing that one's race confers an unearned benefit in life versus believing that one's race creates an onerous hardship is worth highlighting. While many Whites believe that the color of their skin grants them no special privilege, almost no White person believes that the color of their skin is a burdensome cross to bear (a mere 1 percent in the 2019 Pew Survey reported that being White hurt them "a lot").[24]

After one of my sessions, I had a conversation with a White executive named "Sean" who was absolutely infuriated by the concept of White privilege. "First of all, I am not White," he exclaimed. "I'm Irish!" Although he was born in the United States, he believed that someone with an Irish last name like "O'Malley," for example, would never be accepted by high society, and therefore he was not privileged. "I would never be accepted into the Boston Brahmins or invited to tea at Buckingham Palace," he declared. So where was all of this "White privilege" that I was talking about? he wanted to know.[25]

There are two issues here. The first is that he was focused primarily on benefits rather than burdens, which the aforementioned survey data indicate are very different. Not having the benefit of attending tea with the queen is not the same as having the burden of harassment or violence by the police. In some cities, Black motorists are ticketed at a rate that is eighteen times higher than the rate of ticketing for White motorists.[26] In addition, a widely cited 2017 study that analyzed data from police body camera footage found that Black motorists are treated with less respect than White motorists, even when taking into account the severity of the infraction, the location of the stop, and the race of the officer.[27] Finally, a 2019 study shows that the risk of being killed by a police officer is far higher for Black, Native

American, and Hispanic males than it is for White males, especially in the twenty-to-thirty-five-year-old age group. In fact, police use of force is among the leading causes of death for young men of color.[28] (The next chapter will be dedicated to outlining the dynamics that create these disparities and outcomes such as the tragic deaths of George Floyd, Eric Garner, Ahmaud Arbery, Sandra Bland, and other Black people.)

Second, and more important, Sean defined benefits very narrowly. If the definition of "White privilege" is being able to have tea with the queen, then he is right. That is very much an individual privilege, not an institutional privilege. There are some Black and biracial individuals—think Meghan Markle and her mother, Doria Ragland— who get to enjoy that privilege, despite the fact that the vast majority of White people, and Black people, do not. The same goes, more or less, for the Boston Brahmins, those wealthy, multigenerational Boston families who did, and to an extent still do, set the city's social calendar. Most White (and Black, Asian, Hispanic, or Native American) Bostonians are not invited.

This attempt to invalidate the notion of institutional privilege by conjuring up isolated and extreme contexts in which it does not exist is what I call *compartmentalization*. Being a woman might be an advantage in a child custody hearing, all else being equal, because of cultural stereotypes of women as nurturing and selfless. It doesn't mean that males don't have *institutional* privilege. Being a gay man might be an advantage if you're pursuing a career in the fashion industry. This doesn't mean that being gay is a societal advantage. Defining institutional privilege as having *any* privilege at any time reflects a gross misunderstanding of what "institutional" means. Far from being defined by isolated examples, institutional privilege is, by definition, what happens in general, across myriad contexts in society.

One might argue that being disabled confers an advantage when driving around a parking lot. But believing that people with disabilities have more privilege than able-bodied individuals in general because they get access to closer parking spaces is an example of compartmentalization. Living one's entire life being wheelchair bound, for example, would create far more obstacles than advantages—even for getting out of the car once you've parked in that closer space. Again, the real question concerns what happens most of the time. Would a White person voluntarily choose to live their entire life, permanently and irreversibly, as a Black person in American society? Not a chance. In fact, it would take huge sums of money—tens of millions of dollars—before some White people would even consider it.[29]

If we put all these data together, the conclusion is that many Whites do endure hardship and socioeconomic disadvantage—whether they realize it or not. Often they do not realize it. During a recent conversation with Mayor Ted, he digressed to tell me about a meeting that he had with some of the first responders in his city a couple of weeks prior. He discussed with them how a lot of the city's zoning laws, which were created long before he took office, were designed to exclude not just people of color but working-class White people.

Here's how Ted, both excited and amused, described the meeting to me: "You know, most of the people who work for [my city] can't afford to live in [my city], and I asked them, 'Why do you think it is that you can't afford to live here . . . that you gotta live in the next town over and commute to work every day? Why do you think that is?' I told them that it didn't just happen by chance. A bunch of well-to-do White guys sat around and talked about the [property] lots having to be a certain size, and you gotta have brick on all four sides of the house and not just the front. 'Why do you think they did that? It was to make sure only a certain type of buyer could afford to live here. And guess what? You ain't that buyer!' Oh my gosh, Dr. Livingston, you should have seen their faces. Their mouths literally dropped open!"

I was amused—and surprised—as well. And then I became a little curious.

"[Ted,] do you think you would have come to this same conclusion years ago, or is that something that you think resulted from learning about racial inequality?" I asked. Would he have thought about the larger socioeconomic problems that affect both working-class Whites and Blacks?

"Absolutely not," he responded emphatically, shaking his head.

"There is *no* way I would have been thinking this way before I took your class."

This was a powerful moment for me because it illustrated how greater awareness of one type of privilege can awaken consciousness of other types, building solidarity among all people who face *any* type social disadvantage.

There is a long history of privileged White people exploiting less privileged White people while convincing them that their hardships are because of Blacks, Hispanics, and people living in faraway lands. Lots of books have covered this subject in great depth, so I won't go into detail here.[30]

Lyndon B. Johnson once said, "If you can convince the lowest White man he's better than the best colored man, he won't notice you're picking his pocket. Hell, give him somebody to look down on, and he'll empty his pockets for you."

Ted and many of his colleagues have begun to notice that their pockets are being emptied, and that their complicity and investment in a racist system has facilitated the robbery.

I hope this chapter will help you to have an honest Conversation about at least three points. The first is that many White people are socioeconomically disadvantaged. The second is that there is a racial caste system, which makes the nature of the social disadvantages facing Whites and Blacks quite distinct. Third, the angst of working-class Whites is misdirected. There are historical reasons for this. It's ironic that some working-class Whites are White nationalists, because an all-White country would put them at the *very* bottom. Low-road capitalism, as *Evicted* author Matthew Desmond calls it, is here to stay, and if immigrants and Blacks are no longer around to be exploited by the ruling classes, then it will be working-class Whites. It's happened before and has been chronicled in history books (e.g., *White Trash* by Nancy Isenberg), classic fiction (e.g., Upton Sinclair's *The Jungle*), and, of course, Hollywood cinema (e.g., *Gangs of New York,* directed by Martin Scorsese).

Although there are some clear parallels between classism and racism, as well as complex intersectional effects when you combine the two,[31] it would be a mistake to assume that working-class Whites and people of color face the *same* challenges. They don't. Although the only *full* privilege in the United States is held by high-status Whites, who have *both* individual and institutional privilege, race, not class, is still the strongest predictor of life outcomes in a racial caste system. But why does the color of one's skin so strongly determine institutional privilege and life outcomes? In the next chapter we will begin to examine and demystify the concept of the "system," how it was created, how it is maintained, and how it creates enduring challenges for those whom it was not built to serve.

CHAPTER FOUR

What Are the Structural Origins of Racism?

E very society in the history of humankind has contained "haves" and "have-nots." That's not news. What often comes as a surprise is the magnitude of the twenty-first-century divide between these two groups,[1] as well as how much this economic inequality is tied to race.[2] Indulge me with a quick quiz.

The United States has a population of approximately 330 million people. How many ordinary Americans' assets would have to be combined to match the joint wealth of the country's three richest people—Bill Gates, Jeff Bezos, and Warren Buffett? In other words, if you started with the least wealthy person in the country, what percent of the entire U.S. population would you have to assemble before their combined wealth added up to the combined net worth of just these three White men?

    A. 1% (or 3.3 million people)
    B. 2% (or 6.6 million people)
    C. 5% (or 16.5 million people)
    D. 10% (or 33 million people)
    E. 25% (or 82.5 million people)
    F. 50% (the entire bottom half of the U.S. population, or 165 million people)

G. More than the bottom half of the U.S. population
(> 165 million people)

I will reveal the answer a bit later in the chapter, but for now let's continue our discussion of the extent to which prosperity is determined by institutional factors rather than individual factors. In this chapter we will dive deeper into the mysterious origins of institutional forces, or the "system." Recall the metaphor of the salmon and the stream introduced in Chapter 2. If racism is the current in the stream, then what is the source of this current?

Imagine a very tall mountain, one that is wide at its base and narrow at its peak. The mountain's triangular shape has a steep slope, and because it's tall, whenever it rains or snow melts, the water traveling down the mountain gains speed and momentum. The dynamic movement of this water creates the "current" that we've been discussing throughout this book. The important thing to note is that once the mountain structure is in place, no one has to *do* anything to generate the current; it is created by the sheer force of gravity.

Social hierarchies are often shaped like mountains, with a wide base and narrow summit. This symbolically indicates that there are far more people at the bottom than at the top. Indeed, all large-scale human societies, without exception, have been organized into some form of *group*-based social hierarchy, with some groups (for example, wealthy White males) having disproportionately more power and privilege than other groups (for example, the poor, non-Whites, women, etc.).[3] Social hierarchies are also quite stable, often lasting centuries or millennia. Like mountains, they don't crumble from one day to the next; erosion is very, very slow.

Social hierarchies are inherently paradoxical, because the number of people who are disadvantaged by the structure far exceeds the number of people who benefit from it. If the masses are getting the raw deal, and they greatly outnumber the elites, then why wouldn't they simply oust them and get rid of the hierarchy altogether?

Centuries of thinkers, from Plato to Machiavelli to Marx, have contemplated this question. More recently, Jim Sidanius at Harvard University and Felicia Pratto at the University of Connecticut developed a comprehensive theory and large body of empirical research to speak directly to the question of how group-based social hierarchies are established and maintained. Their *social dominance theory* identifies two primary mechanisms that help to maintain social hierarchies. The first mechanism is *legitimizing myths,* which are widely held but often fictitious beliefs that explain why people occupy different positions of power within the social hierarchy. The defining characteristic is not whether the beliefs are actually true or false but rather that most people *accept* them as valid explanations for social hierarchical positions. Meritocracy—the idea that people determine their own outcomes in life through talent and hard work—is an example of a legitimizing myth. When people stop believing in the myths, the second mechanism, *institutional terror,* actively maintains the social hierarchy through the use of force—intimidation, violence, or oppressive legal policies or practices.[4] Let's look at the first mechanism.

THE MYTHS THAT BIND

Legitimizing myths provide digestible explanations for why some people are at the bottom of the mountain and others are at the top. Despite the fact that they aren't necessarily true, they are believed by many people across all levels of the social hierarchy. I realize this may be a fuzzy idea in the abstract, so let's illustrate it using some concrete examples, starting with the Middle Ages and working our way to the present.

Imagine that the year is 1412. A young serf named Johan is toiling in the fields in the blazing midday sun. He is exhausted. His hands are calloused. His feet are sore. As he wipes the sweat from his brow, he looks around and begins to wonder why serf families work their fingers to the bone fourteen hours a day for just a few stale bushels of barley. Meanwhile the king, who never lifts a finger, enjoys banquets of roasted pheasant and wild boar. Johan shares these thoughts with his father, who is toiling alongside him.

His father sighs and responds: "My dear Johan, it is not our right to question the will of God. God chose the king to lead us, and He chose us to follow. Our job is to serve His Majesty without hesitation or rancor. By being faithful servants of His Majesty, we are serving the will of God and will be rewarded in the kingdom of heaven."

With these words, Johan's father expresses the legitimizing myth known as the *divine right of kings*. This myth, widely accepted in medieval Europe, legitimized the power of monarchs by proclaiming that their authority to rule was granted by God and that any disobedience or act of treason against the Crown constituted a heinous sin. The result of this myth was that millions of serfs went on toiling while the nobility and royalty went on reaping the rewards of the serfs' efforts for many centuries.

Essentially, legitimizing myths increase the likelihood that people at the bottom of the social hierarchy will accept situations that are not fair,[5] and they increase the likelihood that people at the top of the hierarchy will feel entitled to their privilege. These myths are narratives that provide stability to the social hierarchy.

Well, we've come a long way since the Middle Ages, you might be thinking. People back then probably didn't know any better. Surely these legitimizing myths do not exist in twenty-first-century modern society. Alas, they do. From a socioeconomic standpoint, we have the equivalent of kings and queens in contemporary American society: Bill Gates, Warren Buffett, Jeff Bezos, and other titans of corporate America. Remember the quiz question posed at the beginning of the chapter? These three men have more wealth than the combined bank accounts and assets of how many ordinary Americans? The answer is G—the combined wealth of the poorest 165 million people in the United States *still* falls tens of billions of dollars short of the combined wealth of just three White men.[6] To give you some idea of the purchase power of tens of billions of dollars, you could buy a brand-new Tesla for every single person living in the country of Iceland—and still have millions of dollars left over. And that's just what you could buy with the *difference* between the combined wealth of half of the country and these three men.

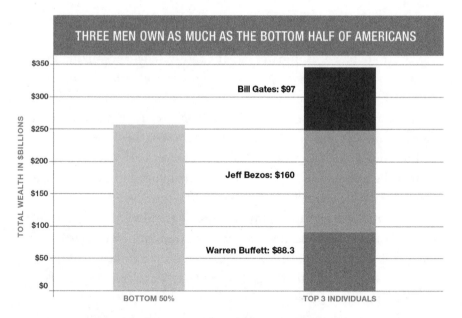

Sources: Institute for Policy Studies, Forbes. Bottom 50% data from 2016. Top 3 from 2018.

To put it in even greater perspective, the combined wealth of *all* of the Black people in the United States—including Oprah, Michael Jordan, Jay-Z, Beyoncé, Barack Obama, LeBron James, Will Smith, and Robert Smith—would not add up to the wealth of even *one* of these White men.

In light of this reality, is the distribution of wealth in America today really all that different from that of the Middle Ages? How do most of us feel about the lopsided distribution of wealth? Do we feel righteous anger and resentment toward Buffett, Bezos, and Gates or feel wondrous awe and admiration toward them? Unlike the notion of the *divine right of kings* endorsed by the serfs, our myths today support the idea that you too can become "king," or Bill Gates. All you need is sufficient talent and hard work. It is the framework of the American dream. If you're a serf in this age, it's only because of your ignorance or indolence. Work harder. Go to school. Be persistent. And you too can become a billionaire. This is the essence of the *myth of meritocracy*—the belief that economic disparities are determined *only* by differences in talent and/or effort.

In many ways, the meritocratic assumption that "you too can be a billionaire" mirrors the logic of lottery slogans such as "You can't win if you don't play." They imply that the power is in your hands. If you work hard, then you can become a billionaire. If you play, then you can win. But is this really how the world works? You may be thinking that people *do* build successful businesses, like Bill Gates or Jeff Bezos. And people *do* win the Mega Millions. Both statements are factually correct. The question is whether these facts hold any meaning or relevance for *you*. The data suggest that they don't. Your individual odds of winning the Mega Millions jackpot are still one in approximately three hundred million—or essentially zero. Yet even with these abysmal odds, a person of color might still have a better chance of winning the Mega Millions than of becoming Bill Gates. Why? Because the lottery is completely random, meaning that everyone has the same odds. However, scientific research suggests that everyone does not have the same odds of becoming CEO or landing venture capital funding, even if their qualifications are identical.[7]

Becoming Bill Gates, Warren Buffett, or Jeff Bezos depends on a whole host of factors, including accumulated financial capital, social capital, human capital, and the right gender, race, religion, sexuality, and even physical height.[8] For example, Bill Gates came from generations of wealth, and his mother was friends with John Opel, then CEO of IBM, who helped Bill Gates to launch Microsoft. Jeff Bezos received hundreds of thousands of dollars from his family, in addition to venture capital, to start Amazon. On the other hand, talented Black people, like Stephanie Lampkin, founder and CEO of Blendoor, found it nearly impossible to land venture capital despite possessing engineering and business degrees from Stanford and MIT.[9]

Let me be perfectly clear: I am not making the claim that merit is bogus. It's not. There are individuals who are talented and hardworking, and they are rewarded for it. Bill Gates, for example, is both brilliant and diligent. He's also wise and provident.[10] But there are plenty of smart, hardworking people with multiple jobs who struggle to make ends meet. The point is that meritocracy, as a *large-scale* explanation for the distribution of outcomes at the broader societal level, is largely unfounded. In this chapter we are discussing systems, not outliers. Looking at one individual or isolated situations will tell you very little about the *system*. The aggregated outcomes of the Mega Millions lottery, or of casinos, are highly predictable because they follow reliable mathematical laws. Similarly, outcomes in society, broadly speaking, are the result of systems and structures that follow certain "social laws," producing very predictable outcomes. Such is the nature of the current—reliably pushing everything in the stream in a certain direction. Sure, there are anomalies and exceptions, but they don't negate the fact that the water is swiftly moving in one direction, dragging everything along with it.

The notion that meritocracy is a myth is tough for many people to swallow, because it goes against everything that we (including myself) have been taught and want to have faith in. We want to believe that we can succeed if we just work hard enough. And sometimes it does work out. But often it doesn't. The myth of meritocracy is swallowed hook, line, and sinker, not just by a handful of wealthy people at the top, for whom motivated reasoning would support such a belief, but by people at all levels of the social hierarchy.[11]

It is important to question our internalized myths and assumptions because the social implications of blindly accepting them are profound. We have a system that isn't fair but is widely accepted and seen as fair. This contributes to the maintenance of group-based social hierarchy because people are less likely to question or challenge the status quo. Research confirms that the belief in meritocracy or economic mobility creates tolerance for income inequality, because we then believe that people's financial status is the product of their own effort.[12] The blind acceptance of legitimizing myths reduces the likelihood that people will challenge the status quo. In brief, myths keep people in line by providing a false sense of opportunity for success, like winning the lottery. However, unlike the lottery, it's not by chance or bad luck that many people don't win—it's by design.

This notion that many of our most cherished beliefs may not be entirely true is depressing news, and some of you may now be thinking, "I thought you said this was going to be an optimistic book!" It will be. I promise. But we have to investigate the truth before we get to reconciliation. If you are having a hard time coping with all of this but you're still reading, I applaud you for not giving up. Keep going! I invite you to indulge your skepticism—write down any objections or counterarguments that come to mind, and keep them handy as we forge ahead.

Legitimizing myths are not the only mechanism of social hierarchy maintenance. Institutional terror also plays a role in maintaining the status quo. For some readers, this next section may be particularly challenging. Take a deep breath and approach it with an open mind, again exercising the freedom to take exception with anything that you read. These intellectual and emotional reactions to the text are an important part of the Conversation.

THE SINISTER FACE OF INSTITUTIONAL TERROR

Although legitimizing myths are widespread, clearly not everyone buys them.[13] So what happens when people stop believing legitimizing myths and other hierarchy-enhancing ideologies? In the 1960s, when large portions of the population became socially conscious and began to directly challenge the social hierarchy, there was a corresponding manifestation of *institutional terror* that forced those who threatened the stability of the social hierarchy into submission. We saw these institutional forces rear their ugly head again in 2020, after people became overwhelmed by systemic injustice in the wake of George Floyd's murder and chose to make their discontent known.

Institutional terror is the result of blatant, and often brutal, efforts to create, maintain, or enhance the social hierarchy. It can take many forms, including the passage of laws and policies to restrict liberties (e.g., voter suppression, mass incarceration), acts of intimidation, social or economic oppression, or state-sponsored violence.

The enslavement of Africans by White Americans and Europeans is the clearest example of the intentional creation of a group-based social hierarchy, with each group's position in the hierarchical structure being determined by skin color and continent of ancestry. The institution of chattel slavery was created for the sole purpose of economic exploitation, and the benefits were asymmetrical. That is, Blacks were used for the benefit of Whites. Whites were not used for the benefit of Blacks. This asymmetry is important because it relates to the asymmetry of racist beliefs and ideologies—meaning that anti-Black and anti-White racism are not the same thing, as discussed in Chapter 3. This unidirectional exploitation was supported not only by legitimizing myths around the biological inferiority of Africans and superiority of Europeans but also through institutional terror, which took the form of oppressive policies restricting legal rights, land ownership, and even one's full humanity (e.g., the infamous three-fifths compromise),[14] as well as physical intimidation, sanctioned violence, rape, and murder. Slavery was a caste system in which every social, political, economic, and legal right was predetermined at birth—making it the exact opposite of meritocracy.

The centuries-old "mountain" of racial hierarchy that was created by slavery did not collapse even after slavery itself was abolished in the United States. Laws and policies such as Jim Crow were intentionally enacted to maintain status differences between Blacks and Whites.[15] The intentional effort to oppress Blacks did not end with the civil rights era and the overturning of Jim Crow legislation. As the activism of the 1960s and the civil rights movement worked to attenuate the racial hierarchy, it was met with counterefforts to preserve and enhance the hierarchy, for example, through criminal justice legislation.

The history of the shift from slavery to mass incarceration is masterfully chronicled in the book *The New Jim Crow* by Michelle Alexander and brilliantly showcased in the 2016 Academy Award–nominated documentary *13th,* directed by Ava DuVernay. The title is based on the Thirteenth Amendment to the U.S. Constitution, which states: "Neither slavery nor involuntary servitude, *except as a punishment for crime whereof the party shall have been duly convicted,* shall exist within the United States, or any place subject to their jurisdiction" (italics added).

Although slavery was abolished de jure, the italicized clause provided a loophole that allowed some version of it to be re-created de facto through policies that disproportionately targeted, prosecuted, and imprisoned Black people. Not only were Blacks robbed of their freedom as the result of disproportionately high rates of arrest, conviction, and incarceration—typically without a formal jury trial—but their imprisonment often generated economic profit, for example, through cheap prison labor or private prison revenue. To the extent that such practices fortify and perpetuate traditional racial hierarchy—by forcibly warehousing and exploiting Black people—they represent clear instances of institutional terror.

Was there an intentional effort to maintain the racial hierarchy in the United States? In many ways, it doesn't matter if the process was intentional or accidental, because the disparate outcomes are the same. However, there is evidence to suggest that drafters of discriminatory policies knew exactly what they were doing, well into the late twentieth century. As discussed in the documentary *13th,* Nixon's policy chief John Ehrlichman stated the following during an interview with journalist Dan Baum when discussing their administration's stance and strategy around incarceration and drug policy:

> The Nixon campaign in 1968, and the Nixon White House after that, had two enemies: the antiwar left and black people. You understand what I'm saying? We knew we couldn't make it illegal to be either against the war or black, but by getting the public to associate the hippies with marijuana and blacks with heroin, and then criminalizing both heavily, we could disrupt those communities. We could arrest their leaders, raid their homes, break up their meetings, and vilify them night after night on the evening news. Did we know we were lying about the drugs? Of course we did.

And policies continued to unfairly target and prosecute Blacks. The Anti–Drug Abuse Act of 1986 set a five-year *mandatory* federal prison sentence for possession of five grams of crack cocaine, whereas possession of powder cocaine was deemed a misdemeanor that could potentially, not mandatorily, be punishable by up to a maximum of one year in prison. For trafficking, you would have to be caught with half a kilo of powder cocaine to receive the same criminal sentence you would get for carrying only five grams of crack cocaine.[16]

The law disproportionately punished Blacks relative to Whites because of the differential prevalence of rock versus powder cocaine in Black and White communities. Creating even deeper disparities, these policies were then enforced much more zealously in Black communities than in White communities. For example, although Blacks constituted less than 40 percent of the crack cocaine users in 2003, they represented over 80 percent of the crack cocaine convictions. And whereas Whites constituted over 45 percent of the crack cocaine users,[17] they represented only 7.8 percent of the crack cocaine convictions.[18]

By creating different penalties for drugs that were relatively more prevalent in Black than White communities, by enacting different levels of vigilance and enforcement by the police in Black and White communities, by treating Black and White offenders differently (e.g., arrest versus warning), and by giving them differential access to legal rights (e.g., plea bargain versus jury trial), the authorities caused the prison population to soar from 300,000 inmates in 1972 to well over 2 million inmates in recent years. To put this in perspective, the general U.S. population increased by roughly 50 percent during this time period while the U.S. *prison* population increased by over 600 percent.

DuVernay's documentary also chronicles other damning statements by White House officials on the intent of their administration's policies. Lee Atwater, a strategist for Ronald Reagan, was caught on tape describing the "southern strategy," which aimed to increase support for the Republican Party among Whites by capitalizing on racial appeals:

> Y'all, don't quote me on this. You start out in 1954 by saying "nigger, nigger, nigger." By 1968 you can't say "nigger." That hurts you. It backfires. So you say stuff like "forced busing," "states' rights," and all that stuff. You get so abstract. Now you're talking about cutting taxes. And all of these things you're talking about are totally economic things. And the by-product of them is Blacks get hurt worse than Whites.

The Ehrlichman and Atwater quotes reveal an intentional effort, at the highest levels of power, to preserve a racial hierarchy by creating policies that would negatively impact Black Americans. These examples also reveal the covert and insidious nature of such efforts. In Chapter 2 I highlighted the role of "ambiguity" when discussing aversive racism theory—the idea is that White people will racially discriminate only in situations where the actions can be attributed to something other than race. Atwater's statement reveals a strategy to create "abstract" policies that were designed to hurt Blacks more than Whites. The more abstract the policy, the more plausible it is to deny that race had anything to do with it (e.g., we are just being "tough on crime"; it has nothing to do with race).

Government policies have a reverberating impact not just on the criminal justice system but also on more mundane activities that affect all citizens—such as purchasing a home. In his book *The Color of Law: A Forgotten History of How Our Government Segregated America,* Richard Rothstein makes a compelling case that Black Americans were intentionally excluded from the housing market in the United States, not just by prejudiced private citizens but by the U.S. government itself. This was accomplished through practices such as "redlining" and lending practices that made it difficult for Blacks, even Black war veterans, to get mortgages. Even Black people who had cash to buy homes could not legally purchase them in certain neighborhoods due to "racial covenants" that prohibited the sale of homes to non-Whites. These restrictive legal clauses were not simply stipulations that private citizens decided to put in home purchase contracts—they were often required by the U.S. government for developers to secure funding for real estate projects.

Some readers might be thinking, "All of this happened a really long time ago. Why are we discussing it now?" Research suggests that policies and practices constructed decades or centuries ago still have an impact on the racial attitudes and outcomes of Americans today. For example, a 2019 study reveals that the current level of implicit racial bias at the county or state level is positively related to the number of slaves living in those counties or states in 1860. Moreover, the relationship between a region's level of slavery and the same region's level of implicit racial bias now—more than 150 years later—is accounted for by long-standing economic inequalities in those regions. Statistical analysis reveals that the relationship between Whites' present-day implicit bias and the number of slaves in 1860 was statistically explained by the current proportion of poor people in the county who are Black.[19] In other words, the magnitude of slavery in 1860 was related to the preponderance of Black poverty in 2019, presumably due to lingering social structures that restrict Black socioeconomic mobility in those geographical locations. This persistent socioeconomic gap between Blacks and Whites in those regions was related to Whites' current implicit racial attitudes toward Blacks in those regions.

Laws and practices of the past affect not only present-day racial attitudes but financial outcomes as well. Take housing, for example, where policies of prior decades have an impact on the wealth of Black Americans today. Given that home ownership is a big source of wealth for most Americans, the ability to purchase a home is tied to the ability to create wealth. A home purchased by someone's great-grandfather in Levittown, New York, for $7,000 in the late 1940s would be worth about $500,000 today. Buying that home was an opportunity afforded to White World War II veterans in the late 1940s but denied to Black World War II veterans, in spite of their equally honorable service to their country.[20] In addition to enjoying the intangible benefits of owning a home, such as stability, community, sense of security, and pride of ownership, White veterans and their families were also able to economically benefit from home ownership across generations. This wealth could be passed down to future generations and used for college education, new business opportunities, and future home down payments and ownership—further compounding wealth over time and contributing to the present-day racial wealth gap. The GI Bill of 1944 is another example of government policy that provided life-changing benefits disproportionately to White World War II veterans but largely excluded Black veterans. Other examples of government policies designed to aid and assist Whites but not Blacks are detailed in the book *When Affirmative Action Was White,* by Ira Katznelson.

THE IMPETUS BEHIND THE INJUSTICE

At one recent presentation I made for a Fortune 500 company, a soft-spoken, middle-aged White woman remarked that the notion of systemic oppression by design is hard to accept because it's difficult to believe that human beings could be so devious.

"Why would anyone *do* something like that?" she asked earnestly.

There are at least two assumptions embedded in the woman's statement and subsequent question. The first is that devious intent is rare or nonexistent. Contrary to popular belief, not everyone *wants* social justice. There are people who prefer oppression and social inequality—as long as their group is doing the oppressing. Indeed, there is much to be gained by oppression, both financially and socially. If it can be morally justified by making the other group seem inferior or deviant, oppression can be converted into a reward without the guilt.

The notion that some people prefer group-based social *in*equality in society can be measured by a widely utilized individual difference scale called *social dominance orientation* (SDO) developed by the originators of social dominance theory.[21] People who are high in SDO are more likely to agree with the following statements:

> An ideal society requires some groups to be on top and others to be on the bottom.
> Some groups of people must be kept in their place.
> We should not push for group equality.
> Some groups of people are simply inferior to other groups.

In contrast, people high in SDO tend to *dis*agree with statements such as the following:

> No one group should dominate in society.
> No matter how much effort it takes, we ought to strive to ensure that all groups have the same chance in life.

Although SDO is not specifically about race, research has shown that it strongly predicts racism, in particular racism toward groups that are seen as being low in status.[22] There are many individuals who actively strive to make societies more *un*equal, which includes creatively designing and implementing policies to keep Blacks "in their place." For these individuals, supporting discriminatory legislation is very much a *deliberate* process that closely aligns with their personal preference, values, and ideology.

But racist systems can remain in place even when many Whites do not consciously want to see Black communities subjugated. Racism is perpetuated to the extent that people are willing to turn a blind eye to racist systems. These systems created hundreds of years ago—and still with us today—continue to perpetuate racial inequality without requiring that those who benefit from the systems be aware that the systems even exist. This is an example of the "complicity" described in Chapter 2. Some tread water in the stream and allow the current to move them—often without knowing it. Fish may not notice that they are immersed in water, let alone the dynamics of the stream they live in, because they have become habituated to swimming in a current that has always been there.

A case in point is the tragic death of George Floyd in Minneapolis. His murder and its aftermath was an emotional time for Black people, as well as for many White people, in America. I had numerous colleagues and acquaintances calling me after the event to express how utterly disgusted they were by the video, some of them in tears, demanding that the officers involved be charged and locked away. That would be justice in their minds. But does the solution lie in putting away a few bad apples, or is the problem much deeper? A more difficult question concerns the extent to which ordinary people, like my colleagues and acquaintances, may be complicit in upholding a system that permits Black people to be harmed so that they can feel safe and protected.

Here's another way to think about it from a purely metaphorical perspective.[23] People often buy certain breeds of dogs, such as Rottweilers or pit bulls, *because* they have loyal but aggressive tendencies that can be leveraged to provide deterrence and defense with very little risk to the owners. The pit bull owner would feel genuinely terrible if the dog attacked the mailman or hopped the fence and mauled a child. But the reality is that the owner bears a certain level of responsibility for the attack for condoning, or encouraging, canine aggression in the first place. Have our police forces become the pit bulls of White citizens—who feel absolutely devastated when an innocent person is harmed, but at the same time value and appreciate the pit bull's willingness and ability to bite because it helps them feel safer, especially since they run very little risk of being bitten themselves?

Of course, there are also those who relish the power to sic the pit bull on others. One such case in 2020 was that of Amy Cooper, a White woman who threatened to falsely report (and subsequently did falsely report) to the police that Christian Cooper, a Black man who was out birding, was threatening her life in Central Park.[24] In reality, he simply asked her to put her cocker spaniel on a leash, as required by the park's rules. So the police can be used as not just a security blanket but a weapon of institutional terror—to put Black people "in their place."

Another question is whether police officers of any race, and White people in general, feel emboldened to show aggression because of a system that, historically, has not held them accountable. The answer seems to be, at least partially, affirmative. How else could you explain the audacious decision to kneel on the neck of another human being, who is pleading for air, for nearly ten minutes in broad daylight—all with his hands casually placed in his pockets—ignoring the desperate pleas of various witnesses who are all actively videotaping the incident? That's as bold as robbing a busy bank in broad daylight without a mask, biding your time as you push the loot down the street in a wheelbarrow. You'd only really do that if you were criminally insane—or your family owned the bank.

We see the same audacity shown not just by police officers but ordinary White men—the actions of the McMichaels, the father and son, who chased and gunned down jogger Ahmaud Arbery on a residential street in broad daylight, or of George Zimmerman, who in 2012 murdered a Black teenager, Trayvon Martin, as he was returning to his father's fiancée's gated community after a trip to a convenience store.

The point is that the problem is much larger than a few bad apples. Putting Derek Chauvin and the other officers present at the Floyd killing in jail will treat the symptoms but not the disease. When White people feel secure enough and concerned enough to renounce a pit bull–like system that protects and privileges them (while maiming people of color), then we will have made tremendous progress.

Until then, it's important to realize that the ugly images from the George Floyd video were merely a reflection of deeper structures that lie beneath the surface. Most people do not realize how their actions (e.g., voting behavior, assumption that the Black person must have done something) or inactions (e.g., silence, indifference) create and uphold a system that licenses White people to harm Black people with a high level of impunity.

EGO INVESTMENT IN RACIAL HIERARCHY

Finally, racist outcomes can result from envy and insecurity rather than malice, hatred, apathy, or ignorance. The role of ego threat and psychological insecurity in fueling racism and other forms of prejudice have been well documented in the social sciences.

As a movie buff, I can't resist including an example from a film that illustrates this idea of envy/threat as a source of racism. In the classic 1988 movie *Mississippi Burning,* there is a scene in which a White man remembers the envy experienced by his father when a Black farmer nearby started to prosper:

You know, when I was a little boy, there was an old Negro farmer that lived down the road from us, name of Monroe. And he was . . . well, I guess he was just a little luckier than my daddy was. He bought himself a mule. That was a big deal around that town. My daddy hated that mule, 'cause his friends were always kidding him that they saw Monroe out plowing with his new mule, and Monroe was going to rent another field now he had a mule. One morning, that mule showed up dead. They poisoned the water. After that, there wasn't any mention about that mule around my daddy. It just never came up. One time, we were driving down that road, and we passed Monroe's place and we saw it was empty. He just packed up and left, I guess, he must of went up north or something. I looked over at my daddy's face. I knew he done it. He saw that I knew. He was ashamed. I guess he was ashamed. He looked at me and said, "If you ain't better than a nigger, son, who are you better than?"

Although the *Mississippi Burning* example is fictitious, there are many real-world examples that corroborate the basic idea that mere Black achievement can produce feelings of insecurity, threat, and envy, which can lead to sabotage, or even murder, by Whites who feel threatened by that achievement. The 1921 Greenwood Massacre in Tulsa, Oklahoma, is but one historical example among many. Greenwood was a prosperous Black community known as "Black Wall Street" until several blocks of it were leveled by an angry White mob, destroying over $30 million dollars of property and killing hundreds of Black citizens, many of them women and elderly.

It's not just that dominant groups have more power than subordinate groups. It's also that people come to believe, consciously or subconsciously, that dominant groups *should* have more power than subordinate groups. To many people, the world makes more sense that way, and they will vehemently, and sometimes violently, resist any disruption to the current hierarchical structure. Any deviation from traditional status arrangements, such as a White man reporting to a Black boss, may arouse curiosity, tension, or outrage—and a general sense of threat. In the next chapter we will delve deeper into the role of psychological threat as an underlying reason that many White people are so deeply invested in preserving racial hierarchy.

CHAPTER FIVE

How Does "Threat" Perpetuate Racial Inequality?

Take a look at the six statements below. On a scale from one to seven, with one indicating strong disagreement and seven indicating strong agreement, how much do you disagree or agree with each of them? Write your answers down in the space next to each statement:

1. Our country will be great if we honor the ways of our forefathers, do what the authorities tell us to do, and get rid of the "rotten apples" who are ruining everything. _____

2. Some of the best people in our country are those who are challenging our government, criticizing religion, and ignoring the "normal" way things are supposed to be done. _____

3. The "old-fashioned ways" and the "old-fashioned values" still show the best way to live. _____

4. Everyone should have their own lifestyle, religious beliefs, and sexual preferences, even if it makes them different from everyone else. _____

5. The only way our country can get through the crisis ahead is to get back to our traditional values, put some tough leaders in power, and silence the troublemakers spreading bad ideas. _____

6. There is no "one right way" to live life; everybody has to create their own way. _____

Add up your responses to the odd-numbered questions (1, 3, and 5): _____.
Next, add up your responses to the even-numbered questions (2, 4, and 6): _____.

We will return to these totals later in the chapter. In the meantime, let's pick up where we left off regarding our discussion of caste, hierarchy, and threat as pillars of Black oppression. In the current chapter, we will undertake a more nuanced exploration of the concept of threat by making a distinction between *structural threat,* which is a disruption to the racial hierarchy or status quo, and *psychological threat,* which compromises an individual's sense of competence, certainty, status, or self-worth. Both types of threats can occur simultaneously. The Black farmer in the film *Mississippi Burning,* mentioned in the previous chapter, posed both types of threat to the White farmer. First, he was a threat to the existing social structure, because a Black farmer who is more successful than a White farmer is at odds with the racial hierarchy. Second, he was a psychological threat to the White farmer, whose self-esteem suffered because a Black man had outperformed him. If we are going to talk honestly about racism, we need to discuss the manifestations of these two types of threats in organizations and society in general, in addition to the formidable challenges that they pose for people of color who are simply trying to make a living.

STRUCTURAL THREAT: THE DRIVE TO KEEP RACIAL HIERARCHIES INTACT

As we established in the previous chapter, social hierarchies don't just represent the way that things are; they also symbolically represent people's assumptions about the way that things "should" be. When outcomes deviate from traditional hierarchical structures, it destabilizes the status quo and creates a structural threat. These structural threats can assume various forms, including changes to representation and/or rank. For example, research has shown that giving White people information projecting that they will no longer represent the majority in America three decades from now is sufficient to increase both implicit and explicit racism. In one study, participants were randomly assigned to read a newspaper article that reported either the current racial demographics in the United States (with Whites as the majority group) or the projected U.S. racial demographic in the year 2042 (with Whites no longer as the majority group). The authors found that Whites exposed to the article describing racial demographics in 2042 later expressed more negative implicit and explicit racial attitudes, not just toward Blacks but toward Hispanics and Asians as well. In addition, they expressed a stronger preference to interact with and be surrounded by Whites, compared with White participants who read about current U.S. racial demographics.[1]

Structural threat can be activated not just by shifts in numerical representation, and in which groups constitute the majority or minority, but also by individual behaviors that challenge who is supposedly superior or inferior. In other words, one high-achieving Black person can also represent a threat to the racial caste system. Being successful if you're Black, as in the case of the farmer in *Mississippi Burning,* represents a direct threat to the established social order.

Black success isn't what White America signed up for when enslaved Africans were brought to America. Blacks were never meant to be prosperous, or powerful, or even educated, and measures were put in place during and after slavery to ensure that they did not rise above their prescribed station. Even though America's slave-owning Whites are long dead, versions of the structures they established still linger, affecting people's attitudes, beliefs, and expectations or prescriptions for who should be in power. As a result, Blacks who are "too" successful—meaning more successful than White people think that Black people should be—are seen as a threat.

The notion that achievement can be perceived as a negative thing may seem puzzling to many people. The Black farmer's success depicted in *Mississippi Burning* seems particularly innocuous, given that he is not on a soapbox bragging about his farming genius, nor is he leveraging his success to gain political power. He's just trying to make a decent living. Blacks who display any measure of confidence, competence, or ambition may be seen as "uppity," potentially rendering them a structural threat, thereby provoking hostile responses from Whites. Journalist Trymaine Lee has written about the true-life story of Elmore "Buddy" Bolling, a successful Black farmer and businessman in Alabama who was shot seven times by a group of White men in 1947 because he was apparently "too successful to be a Negro."[2] There is also the case of Anthony Crawford, whom civil rights activist and attorney Bryan Stevenson describes as a man who in 1916 "was lynched in South Carolina for being successful enough to refuse a low price for his cotton."[3] You may be thinking, "But those examples are from the Deep South in the first half of the twentieth century." Is Black achievement a threat in the twenty-first-century workplace?

Unfortunately, the idea of Black excellence or power is still something the country struggles with in this day and age. Consider the prominent example of the election of Barack Obama. Entire books have been written on the subject, analyzing whether, how, and to what degree race played a role in resistance to his presidential legitimacy and authority.[4] But it's not just Obama and the highest office in the land. Black leaders in general are seen as a threat, in large part because they contradict people's profile of the ideal or typical leader as a White male.[5] It's not just images and ideals that Black leaders violate; they also threaten established patterns of actual leader representation, dominated by White males. This tendency can be seen acutely in the C-suite. Although White men are roughly 30 percent of the overall U.S. population today, they represent over 90 percent of U.S. Fortune 500 CEO positions. As discussed in the last chapter, what is descriptive becomes prescriptive, so the overrepresentation of White males also reinforces the notion that only White males "should" occupy leadership roles.

A plethora of empirical evidence supports the idea that White people have a hard time accepting Black leadership. One recent study reveals that White male managers identify less strongly with their organization following the appointment of a minority CEO, and they subsequently provide less help to colleagues in the organization, particularly ethnic minority colleagues.[6] A different study analyzed interviews with White male CEOs and found that racial bias and envy increased their tendency to overly blame minority CEOs in other companies for any low performance in those respective firms, rather than making situational attributions. Furthermore, this bad-mouthing of minority CEOs by White CEOs led journalists, particularly White male journalists, to write negative articles blaming the minority CEOs personally, rather than taking into account situational factors.[7] Because White male leaders are far less likely than minority leaders to be disciplined or fired when they make performance-based mistakes on the job,[8] it is unlikely that the negative evaluation of minority CEOs is due to genuine concerns about competence.

Even when Black leaders are perceived as supremely competent, it simply produces a different set of problems. Recall the Black farmer again. Competence itself makes Black men threatening. A 2019 study from the finance sector bolsters this idea. Asset-allocation managers, who were predominantly White, responded differently to venture capital funds led by a competent or incompetent Black or White fund manager. In one experiment, the asset-allocation managers discriminated against the *competent* Black fund manager who had a track record of high performance compared with the White fund manager with a similarly competent track record. Even more interesting, further analysis showed that after reviewing the highly competent, Black male–led proposal, asset allocation managers rated their own social status as being lower. These findings echo the sentiment of the White farmer in *Mississippi Burning:* If White managers are not better than a Black person—especially in a domain, like finance, that White males have traditionally dominated—then who are they better than?[9] Consistent with this idea, after reviewing the low-competence, Black male–led proposal, asset allocation managers rated their own status as being higher.[10] A real-world example of the vulnerability of high-performing Black professionals can be found in the case of Tidjane Thiam, the former CEO of Credit Suisse, who endured race-based harassment—and was ultimately forced to resign—despite demonstrating a very high level of competence.[11]

Black people are well aware of the negative consequences that their high performance can produce. Empirical research suggests that Black employees and students often downplay their achievements out of fear that they could produce negative repercussions for them. In one study, social psychologists Julie Phelan and Laurie Rudman provided feedback to Black participants indicating that they had excelled on a portion of the LSAT that ostensibly measures leadership aptitude and ability. They also measured participants' actual performance on the test. Black students who scored highest on the test were the most likely to express fear of negative backlash.[12] Moreover, they found that fear of negative backlash explained their reluctance to publicize their outstanding score on the test when given the choice.[13]

Again, it may seem strange to many readers that someone would be punished for being competent.[14] But Blacks in America live in a complex and maddening catch-22 where you're damned if you do, damned if you don't. Blacks who behave consistently with negative stereotypes (e.g., incompetently) are often preferred, both because they justify racism and because they do not represent a threat to existing hierarchical structures. At the same time, Blacks who challenge negative stereotypes by succeeding are applauded and admired, on some level, while also being resented and castigated for upending the status quo. This is particularly true if their high competence is coupled with high confidence, rather than the meekness and modesty displayed by high performers in the aforementioned study.

Let's explore examples of the need to neutralize Black competence with docility. One would think that sports might be a domain in which Blacks might be permitted to be competent *and* confident, on account of pervasive stereotypes about superior Black athleticism. But a closer look at both anecdotal and scientific evidence tells a very different story. For decades we have witnessed the backlash suffered by competent and confident Black athletes such as Serena Williams and Tiger Woods. At first blush, one might discount these two examples because they excel in "country club" sports that are traditionally and currently dominated by Whites.

What about sports with higher Black representations, like basketball and football, with Blacks representing roughly 75 percent and 67 percent of all the players, respectively? Ta-Nehisi Coates compared the treatment LeBron James received in the media in 2010 when he confidently and unapologetically exercised his freedom to leave the Cleveland Cavaliers to join the Miami Heat to that of a "runaway slave."[15] Mr. James was widely condemned as being too "uppity." We find similar dynamics in the NFL. Terrell Owens, considered by many to be the greatest wide receiver to ever play the game, had a delayed induction into the Hall of Fame, not based on his record—that spoke for itself—but because of his perceived arrogance.[16] Colin Kaepernick faced ostracism and alienation when he had the temerity to protest racial injustice by kneeling during the national anthem, which was perceived by many as an act of arrogance as well as a lack of patriotic gratitude. For years, journalists and sports commentators have made the case that backlash against Black athletes is essentially an expression of White disdain for Black arrogance, and in football, this contempt has traditionally been instituted in policies such as the "celebration penalty" against players who performed after touchdowns.[17]

Scientific data supports the commentators' conclusions in the case of celebration penalties.[18] After both analyzing NFL archival evidence and conducting in-person studies, researchers found that Black football players were more likely than White football players (remember Tim Tebow and "Tebowing"?) to be punished for celebrating after touchdowns. In the laboratory, non-Black participants who read about Black or White football players who celebrated after touchdowns were more likely to negatively evaluate, and confer a lower salary on, Black players compared with White players. However, White players and Black players were treated equally when they did not celebrate their touchdowns.[19] Further analysis demonstrates that both Black and White players who celebrate after touchdowns were rated as being more arrogant than players of either race who did not celebrate after touchdowns. However, the more arrogance was associated with Black players, the less money these players were given. By contrast, White players' monetary bonus was not reduced due to arrogance. Stated differently, White players were entitled to arrogance, whereas Black players were punished for displaying arrogance. These divergent reactions to Black and White players' arrogance, and even their roles—White and Black quarterbacks, for example, are perceived and described differently[20]—reflect deeper hierarchical assumptions and prescriptions about the "place" of Black

and White people, and which behaviors are deemed acceptable or un-
acceptable.

Although Black confidence and arrogance are punished, Black
humility and deference are rewarded. Indeed, research confirms that
Blacks benefit from *disarming mechanisms,* or features, traits, or behaviors that make them appear more meek, affable, or docile and less
assertive, confident, or authoritative.[21] Some examples of disarming
mechanisms include smiling behavior,[22] speaking softly or using non-
ethnic English,[23] not having a tall physical stature,[24] being more as-
similated into White culture and less identified with Black culture,[25]
or even whistling classical music to signal erudition and sophistication.[26] Because disarming mechanisms can make Blacks appear less
threatening to Whites, they sometimes facilitate Blacks' access to leadership roles.[27]

My own research reveals that Black CEOs tend to be more baby-
faced than White CEOs, because the more cherubic facial structure
makes them appear less threatening.[28] And the more baby-faced Black
CEOs were, the larger their company revenues and personal salary
tended to be, compared with Black CEOs who were relatively less
baby-faced. The opposite effect emerged for White male CEOs. Being
more mature-faced, with a strong jaw and angular features, was more
predictive of success among the White male CEOs, because White
male leaders do not need to be disarmed—they need to be "armed."
Because hierarchical prescriptions entitle them to lead, White males
benefit the most from facial features that display the gravitas, matu-
rity, competence, and authority that people associate with leaders.

Similarly, White male leaders are allowed to behave in a dominant, forceful, or assertive manner, whereas Black male leaders are
punished for showing the exact same behaviors. In one study, participants read about a meeting between a leader—a senior vice president
of a Fortune 500 company—and a subordinate employee who was
failing to meet performance expectations. The leader behaved in either a dominant and assertive manner, demanding that the employee
improve their performance, or in a more docile and communal manner, kindly encouraging the employee to improve their performance.
The researchers varied the race and gender of the leader, so that par-

ticipants read about either a Black man, a Black woman, a White man, or a White woman senior vice president who behaved in a dominant or docile fashion.

The results showed that the Black male leader and the White female leader were rated significantly more negatively when they showed dominance rather than docility. On the other hand, the evaluation of the White male leader did not depend on what type of behavior he adopted. White male leaders could show dominance without suffering any penalty for it. Interestingly, Black women also were not penalized for showing dominance.[29] However, follow-up research suggests several caveats. First, Black women can show dominance only when they exhibit what is referred to as *administrative agency*—assertiveness to get the job done, rather than *ambitious agency*—assertiveness to get ahead or gain personal power.[30] Second, Black women can show dominance only when their performance is nearly perfect. If they make mistakes, they are penalized *more* than either White women or Black men, presumably because they don't fit the ideal "leader" profile, being neither male nor White.[31] Finally, Black women are given more latitude because they are seen as less feminine than White women and less threatening than Black men, which frees them to behave in a more dominant manner.[32]

If we summarize the origins of racism (and sexism) in a single word, it is *power*. It is both the desire to maintain power and the fear of losing power. The name of the game is preservation of the existing social hierarchy, in large part because it is an arrangement that feels comfortable, secure, and familiar to many White people. On the flip side, feeling uncomfortable or insecure can lead to higher levels of racial bias. In the next section, we will examine why this happens.

PSYCHOLOGICAL THREAT: HOW FEELINGS OF INSECURITY, UNCERTAINTY, AND INSIGNIFICANCE FUEL RACISM

All organisms have a basic drive to survive, which compels them to steer clear of danger. However, there is a difference between actual danger and simply being fearful of danger. Fear can emerge even when environments are perfectly safe. The conscious or unconscious sense of fear or anxiety, in the absence of any real danger, is what I refer to as psychological threat (in contrast to realistic threat). Psychological threat manifests itself in numerous ways, including fear of uncertainty, fear of chaos, fear of inadequacy, and even existential fear of one's own mortality. And they all can lead to heightened levels of racism.

Remember the questions that you answered at the beginning of the chapter? Look back at your totals. If your odd-numbered total (for questions 1, 3, and 5) was above fifteen and your even-numbered total (questions 2, 4, and 6) was below nine, then you might be high on a personality trait that social scientists call *right-wing authoritarianism* (RWA).[33] RWA taps into people's desire for order, reverence for strong "legitimate" authority, affinity for traditional values, and belief that there is a right and a wrong way to live, with the "right" way being the old-fashioned way. They subscribe to these beliefs to combat feelings of fear, uncertainty, or lack of control.

When confronted by fear and chaos, some people tend to get behind a "strong" leader who promises to crush evil, return to traditional values, and restore order. Decades of research have shown that authoritarians—people who score high on RWA—are more likely to support leaders who emphasize security and structure, as well as impose the rule of law. Some of these leaders are demagogues, who thrive on fear and are most likely to emerge under conditions that produce fear, such as economic and/or cultural uncertainty. Their tyrannical social contract boils down to *Make me all-powerful and I will keep you safe and bring society back to its former glory*. The problem with this arrangement is that it leaves little room for diversity or dissent, as any departure from the very straight and narrow path is not tolerated.

Authoritarianism was first investigated as an explanation for the rise of fascism and anti-Semitism in Europe in the 1930s, and one of the original authoritarianism scales was a measure of fascist ideology.[34] Because fascism promises order and stability, it is acceptable, even appealing, to authoritarians due to their need for psychological security. Studies have shown that people who score high on the authoritarianism scale are much more likely to believe that the world is a dangerous place, compared with those who have a low score.[35] High scorers on the authoritarianism scale are quicker than low scorers to identify threatening words such as *snake* or *cancer* on a computer screen, but they are not quicker to identify nonthreatening words such as *tree* or *telescope*.[36]

At this point, you may be asking yourself what any of this has to do with racism, particularly because none of the RWA questions mentions Blacks, Whites, Hispanics, or even the word *race* itself. It might surprise you that over five decades of research in the social sciences have found RWA to be one of the most reliable predictors of racism. This robust relationship between RWA and racism is due to a couple of factors. First, authoritarians believe in the sanctity of "legitimate" authority and have a strong affinity for what they perceive as "normal" or mainstream; people outside of the mainstream are viewed with suspicion or contempt. Because White people are seen as normal in the United States and other Western countries, based on their numerical majority and cultural dominance, ethnic minorities are viewed by authoritarians as not just different but deviant—*especially* if they do not assimilate to mainstream norms. Authoritarians do not celebrate difference. As a result, RWA is strongly associated not only with racism but also with sexism, heterosexism, xenophobia, and other forms of bias.[37] Second, authoritarians tend to be self-righteous, moralistic, and judgmental. A strong component of the ideology is the notion that there is only one "right" way to live, which is decided by traditional authority. Authoritarians endorse ostracism, punishment, and aggression (rather than inclusion or compassion) toward anyone who deviates from this narrow, righteous path.

Another big question that you may be asking yourself: What the heck do I do if I scored high on RWA? Am I forever doomed to be a racist? As I mentioned in Chapter 2, I see the world in terms of complicit and antiracist behaviors, and being an authoritarian doesn't mean that you can't become more antiracist. You absolutely can. The purpose of the questionnaire was not to knock anyone but rather to inform and empower. Raising one's awareness about their psychological orientation toward the world and how it can inadvertently impact their social and political judgments and behaviors is an important first step. But it's not by any means the last step. I have witnessed some of the biggest authoritarians turn into some of the biggest champions of racial justice. Once they become cognizant of how their fears and insecurities about the world produce a set of behaviors that create racial injustice, they stop feeling fearful and start becoming courageously committed to upholding their values around compassion and social justice.

If you scored high on the scale, and you're bothered by it, sit with that discomfort, but don't let it define you. Know that what *really* matters is what you do. And if you scored low on the scale, this does not automatically qualify you as someone who is antiracist. Most low scorers are also complicit, albeit in different ways from high scorers.

You may also be wondering where authoritarianism comes from. Researchers hypothesize that rigid, harsh parenting styles lead children to internalize the idea that there is a clear "right" and "wrong" way to do things. Interestingly, people's RWA scores are highly correlated with their parents' scores, and adults who remember their parents as being angry tend to have higher RWA scores.[38] Such strict upbringing may teach children from an early age to both resent and revere authority, which leads to anger, anxiety, and insecurity on the one hand, while also producing a certain level of acceptance of, comfort with, and respect for rigid authority figures.

Although authoritarianism is correlated with political conservatism, and many studies have also found a correlation between political conservatism and racism,[39] it would be a mistake to draw the simple conclusion that conservatives are racist and liberals are not. For one thing, there is wide variation in racial attitudes among conservatives, just as there is wide variation in racial attitudes among liberals. Some individuals have more racial bias than others no matter their political affiliation.[40] The differences in levels of racial bias between liberals and conservatives is not always as marked as people might assume. Liberals, and even progressives, can sometimes demonstrate equal, or higher, evidence of racism than conservatives. Classic research on aversive racism, discussed in Chapter 2, found that compared with conservatives, liberals were quicker to hang up on a

Black-sounding person asking for help. However, among people who stayed on the phone, liberals were more likely to help.[41] Other research has found that Democratic political candidates use different words when addressing White audiences compared with audiences of color. Specifically, liberal politicians were more likely to "dumb down" their speech when talking to audiences of racial minorities compared with Whites. However, Republican politicians tended to use the same caliber of speech with both White and non-White audiences.[42] This finding also held true for nonpoliticians. Liberals used simpler language than did conservatives when interacting with a Black compared with a White partner.

As someone who has worked in both highly liberal and highly conservative work spaces, I can confirm that racism occurs in each of them. And I've observed some of the most egregious transgressions from die-hard White progressives. Moreover, social scientific research reveals that activities such as voting for Obama, volunteering for the Peace Corps, or dating/marrying interracially can all but convince liberals that they are immune to racism, which ironically licenses them to be even more bold in their racial transgressions.

Even in the crucible of enlightenment and progressive liberalism—academia—racism can be found. Researchers sent out identical meeting requests to over 6,500 professors from dozens of disciplines across hundreds of colleges and universities. The meeting requests ostensibly came from interested students, asking to discuss research opportunities and possible doctoral work. The researchers varied the names of the interested students to sound White or non-White and female or male. They found that professors were significantly more responsive to requests coming from White male students than requests from women or people of color.[43]

One reason that both liberals and conservatives discriminate is that they are both exposed to the same cultural stereotypes. Moreover, both liberals and conservatives can suffer damage to their identity or their self-esteem—which can then lead to higher levels of racism. For instance, a White woman who experiences sexism from White men may respond by exhibiting racist attitudes toward ethnic minorities.[44] Evidence suggests that when our feelings of worth are diminished, we find solace in diminishing someone else's.[45] But when we feel good about ourselves, racism is less likely to emerge. The same researchers showed that when White women's resilience and values were affirmed prior to their experiencing sexism, they did not show more racism.

Similarly, in a study conducted by Steve Fein and Steven Spencer, White participants seized on the opportunity to denigrate an ethnic out-group member after they thought they failed a test, but not when they thought they passed the test or when their self-worth was affirmed prior to being told that they failed the test.[46] Another study by Lisa Sinclair and Ziva Kunda found that when Whites' sense of competence was threatened by being given negative feedback by a Black professor, they dismissed the professor as "Black" and activated negative racial stereotypes related to incompetence to discredit both the professor and the feedback.[47] A student who received negative feedback might think: "Yeah, that Black professor didn't like my paper on Hemingway because she wouldn't know good writing if it bit her on the nose. Plus, I bet she doesn't know anything about Hemingway. She's probably only read Toni Morrison and Alice Walker. I'm sure that they gave her a PhD to avoid a discrimination lawsuit." On the other hand, positive feedback by a Black professor activated positive stereotypes and the tendency to think of this person as a "professor" rather than as "Black." A student who received positive feedback might think: "Cool, my Black professor loved my paper on Hemingway. She's one of the world's top experts on twentieth-century American literature and has done some pretty amazing research. I feel honored to have someone of that stature think so highly of my paper!" These wild pendulum swings in evaluations of Black professionals reveal just how complicated racism can be. They also demonstrate that racism often has more to do with psychological issues of the person doing the judging than with any fault of the person being judged. This is an important point for both managers and ordinary people to keep in mind before they jump to conclusions about the validity of their evaluations of others.

Taken together, these studies show that a sense of failure can trigger the expression of racism. And there are always going to be people who experience failure. This gets us back to the White farmer in *Mississippi Burning,* and to the fellas. People who feel vulnerable or "less than" are poised to fall into all sorts of racism traps.

Fortunately, there are ways to break the cycle. One is to make people aware of this phenomenon. It may not consciously occur to people that their feelings about their own shortcomings are directly tied to their political leanings and racial evaluations of other people. Another path to intervention when threat is involved is to make people feel more secure about themselves through a process called *self-affirmation.* I will elaborate on these and many other strategies in later chapters. What is critically important for now is to understand—to *really* understand—that the heart of racism is power and the soul of racism is fear, with the heart striving to protect the soul. This fear is not mortal fear, what one might experience when facing a lion or shark, but psychological fear grounded in feelings of inadequacy, uncertainty, failure, and insignificance. Power has a palliative effect on fear. It does nothing to cure the underlying insecurities caused by fear, but it sure does make people feel better about themselves by providing the illusion of invulnerability.

A ton of research over the past forty years has taught us that the root causes of racism are historical contingencies, institutional structures, and social policies. These social factors or hierarchical structures work together with the dominant group's psychological needs, desires, and motives. But difficult as this is, the real picture is even trickier, because these systemic structures and psychological threats are not the only factors that breed racism. Evidence has accumulated over the last several decades to reveal that human intergroup bias is wired into our DNA, figuratively speaking, and to get the complete picture of racism we have to dig deeper into our basic psychology and evolution.

CHAPTER SIX

What Are the Psychological and Evolutionary Origins of All Intergroup Biases?

As a child, I was always intrigued by the story "The Sneetches" by Dr. Seuss. It is a tale of two groups of whimsical-looking creatures that resemble a cross between an ostrich and the Grinch. Though these creatures are quite similar in appearance, and equally homely, they live in a divided society demarcated by their only physical difference—their bellies. Some of them have green stars emblazoned on their tummies and others do not. The Star-Belly Sneetches are the more privileged of the two groups, and they tend to stroll around "with their snoots in the air. They sniff and they snort 'We will have nothing to do with the Plain-Belly sort!'"[1]

The misfortune of the Plain-Belly Sneetches soon changes, or so it seems, with the arrival of a slick hustler named Sylvester McMonkey McBean. For the right price, he promises to turn their frowns upside down with a magic machine that puts a bright green star on their bellies. Allured by the prospect of social acceptance, the Plain-Belly Sneetches pony up large sums of cash and go into McBean's machine one by one with their bellies bare and emerge with newly minted stars.

They hurry over to share the news of their star-studded transformation with the "original" Star-Belly Sneetches. Finally one big happy family! Right? Well, no, not quite. Appalled by the thought of being confused with these nouveau Star-Bellies, the original Star-Belly Sneetches return to Sylvester McMonkey McBean—cash in hand—to have their stars removed! Of course, the original Plain-Belly Sneetches have their newly minted stars removed too. In response, the original Star-Belly Sneetches have their stars put back on. And so begins an endless cycle of assimilation and differentiation. The result? Sylvester McMonkey McBean becomes rich and the Sneetches all end up broke and befuddled.

It turns out that we humans are not so different from the Sneetches. Like them, we divide ourselves into "us" and "them" based on all sorts of random and insignificant traits.[2] Although specific markers of difference (e.g., skin color) are arbitrary, the mechanisms that determine which types of groups we join are very predictable. According to *optimal distinctiveness theory,* developed by Marilynn Brewer in the early 1990s, humans are drawn to social groups that simultaneously fulfill two conflicting needs—a need for *assimilation,* or the desire for social connection, affiliation, inclusion, and belonging, and a need for *differentiation,* or the desire to be unique, special, and distinctive.[3]

The attempt to optimize or balance these two competing needs leads to some intriguing yet foreseeable outcomes. The first is that human social groups tend to follow the Goldilocks rule—not too big, not too small, but just right. A group that includes everyone is too inclusive and doesn't satisfy the need for differentiation, and a group with too few members is not inclusive enough and thus doesn't satisfy the need for assimilation. The way to satisfy both at the same time is by joining optimally distinct, or medium-sized, groups of similar others.

But what does similar mean and what is a "medium-sized" group? The answer is that it depends on context, which largely determines both perceptions of similarity and group size. In the context of a business school, for example, the marketing department is a medium-sized group that considers itself relatively distinct from the accounting department. In the context of the university, the entire business school is now a medium-sized group contrasted with the law school or the medical school, bringing a dimension of similarity and unity to the marketing and accounting departments. And in an intercollegiate context, the entire university is a medium-sized group. People's identities will shift with each context, leading them to identify with the marketing department, for example, within the business school, with the business school within the larger university, and with the university during an intercollegiate football or basketball game.

Our perceptions of larger social groups are driven by context as well. For example, people from Northern Ireland might be viewed as being very similar to one another within a broad global context because they share a common ancestry, nationality, culture, language, and physical appearance. However, the national context *within* Northern Ireland could produce lots of potential differentiators. Being Protestant or Catholic, for instance, might become a source of social identity, and a source of conflict, even though the differences between these two denominations of Christianity are minuscule in the larger context of world religions. Similarly, if the context is only the United States, then we might focus on all sorts of differences within the country (Northern versus Southern, East Coast versus West Coast, urban versus rural, Democrat versus Republican, White versus Black). But if the context becomes global, whether due to the Olympics or due to a war, then we all tend to rally around a common "American" identity and those *intra*national divisions matter much less. This optimal distinctiveness phenomenon can also partially explain why some social movements begin to fragment as they grow large enough for "medium-sized" factions to gain critical mass. As a gender movement gets larger, it could become factionalized by racial, socioeconomic, or other factors. As a racial movement becomes larger, it could become factionalized by differences in ethnic, religious, or ideological (e.g., militant versus nonviolent) factors. In short, as groups become increasingly larger, dimensions of "difference" within the group become increasingly evident—and inevitable.

The second implication of optimal distinctiveness theory is that there will always be an "other." People will probably never see all of humanity as one big happy family, because the category "humans" is too big and too inclusive. It clearly satisfies the need for assimilation but does not satisfy the need for differentiation. We might start identifying as "human beings" in the wake of an alien invasion or a robot uprising. But without extraterrestrials or rogue machines to unite us, we will likely have to grapple with some form of social fragmentation and "othering." Research has shown that this tendency to label the "other" and to show favorable treatment toward "us" compared with "them" has been found in children as young as six[4] and may have a genetic basis.[5]

The phenomenon of in-group favoritism is so powerful that it even surfaces in bizarre ways. In one zany example, a team of researchers asked a male student to exercise and sleep in the same T-shirt for seven days. Needless to say, the T-shirt reeked by the end of the week. The researchers stored it in a Ziploc bag to preserve the pungent body odor. They then recruited dozens of hapless students to participate in an experiment in which their job was to sniff the smelly T-shirt and to rate their level of disgust. Half of the students were told that the shirt belonged to a student from their own university, while the other half were told that it belonged to a student from a rival university.

Even though all of the students sniffed the exact same T-shirt, students were less disgusted by the foul odor when they thought that it came from an in-group member (a student from the same university) rather than an out-group member (a student from a different university). This belief affected not just their level of visceral disgust but their behavior as well. After handling the rancid T-shirt, participants had the opportunity to clean their hands. Students who thought the T-shirt came from someone from their university used fewer pumps of hand sanitizer and took more time to get to the hand sanitizer, compared with students who thought the T-shirt came from someone from a different university—those participants made a beeline to the sanitizing station.[6]

While there will always be an "other," who constitutes this "other" is malleable and depends on the social context. In one context, the "other" can be students from a different university. Within the university, it could be students from one major versus another major, or one fraternity or sorority versus another fraternity or sorority. The context rules. Savvy leaders can unite or divide groups by simply manipulating the social context or frame of reference. For example, working-class Whites and working-class Blacks might see each other as enemies in a (deliberately) racialized context but see each other as allies (against the hegemonic establishment) in a context where socioeconomic status is salient. Remember the Lyndon B. Johnson quote from Chapter 3 about making "the lowest" Whites feel superior to "the best" Blacks so that you can rob them blind? Or Ted's story from that chapter about working-class White first responders not being able to afford to live in the city where they work, where the building codes have been designed on purpose to price out people like them?

This contextual malleability of social identity highlights the fact that we are *not* wired to be racist. Or homophobic. Or xenophobic. What *is* wired is tribalism—the propensity to form a distinction between "us" and "them." Who ends up "us" and who ends up "them" is completely fluid—often determined by factors such as history, environment, and social structures rather than genes or evolutionary pressure. Tribalism is so deeply ingrained that the groups don't even have to be real or relevant. In one famous example, individuals were asked to estimate the number of dots on a page and then were randomly assigned to groups labeled "dot overestimators" or "dot underestimators." Importantly, the people in the study didn't know they were *randomly* assigned to one group or the other; they assumed it was based on how they viewed the dots. The dot overestimators started favoring their own group, allocating more resources to other people who were overestimators than they did to the underestimators. The same pattern of discrimination occurred for the underestimators, who gave more to their group compared with the out-group.[7] Even though these groups were completely arbitrary and fabricated, they became real to the people involved, resulting in discrimination against the "other." This experiment shows that people have a strong propensity to latch on to and defend their "tribe," even if the basis for tribal affiliation is utterly meaningless. The big question is why.

WHY CAN'T WE ALL JUST GET ALONG?

From an evolutionary perspective, there are good reasons why we, and other social animals, are wired to join tight-knit, relatively exclusive social groups and to favor the in-group over out-groups. In early humans, this tendency enhanced the likelihood of survival. Across the animal kingdom, there are numerous parallels. Wild canids such as wolves or African wild dogs, for instance, are like most social animals: They live in packs because it provides a survival advantage over solitary existence. A lone wolf might survive, but it's harder than being in a pack, where the presence of other wolves provides greater protection from larger predators and leads to greater hunting success. The hunting success rate of African wild dogs, for example, far exceeds that of solitary predators, such as leopards.

But more isn't necessarily more when it comes to pack size. The effectiveness of the pack grows with the size of the pack—but only up to a certain point, after which a larger pack becomes more of a liability than a benefit. For example, a pack of four canines has an advantage over a pack of three canines, which has an advantage over a pack of two. But once the pack reaches a certain size, those advantages begin to level off and quickly wane. A pack of fifty wolves would be unruly, and a pack of five hundred wolves would be way too large to function effectively. Thus, the advantages of wolf packs are optimized by a size that is not too big, not too small, but just right—the Goldilocks principle once again.

Early human groups were not that different from wolf packs. Humans evolved to live in tight-knit hunter-gatherer tribes that were large enough to provide protection but small enough to manage. This resulted in bands that numbered a few dozen people who were socially connected and often genetically related, much like a wolf pack or a lion pride. Our astonishing intelligence, propensity for cultural learning, and ability to accumulate knowledge across generations allowed us to master the art and science of plant and animal reproduction, radically changing how we lived. The advent of farming set the stage for human civilization and the rise of large, densely populated cities and, eventually, nation-states. People went from living in dispersed hunter-gatherer tribes of a few dozen familiar people to living in large, bustling cities of millions of strangers, almost overnight by an evolutionary timescale.

Human culture has changed much more rapidly and profoundly than our genetic code. Many of our biological propensities developed during the early stages of human evolution. We have lived in civilizations for only six thousand years or so, and in globally interconnected societies for just a few centuries—a mere eyeblink in the long span of human existence. Consequently, we live in a cosmopolitan, interdependent world that is a far cry from the relatively parochial hunter-gatherer world that we evolved to inhabit. Wild canine culture hasn't changed much in the last million years, but human culture has changed dramatically in that time period. This means that some human tendencies that were adaptive and functional during the Paleolithic era have become maladaptive and dysfunctional in today's society.

Nevertheless, research suggests that our primal tendencies continue to shape our modern-day decisions and behaviors. For example, physical height and strength continue to play a huge role in our selection of leaders and in how we allocate resources,[8] even though leadership responsibilities no longer involve hunting or hand-to-hand combat. Consider this: While barely 15 percent of men in the general population are over six feet tall, almost 60 percent of male leaders are over six feet tall.[9] Although physical size and strength may have mattered a lot in the caveman days, leadership tasks in the modern world have no direct relationship with physical height or strength.

Evolutionary success requires adaptation to the environment. When environments change, the organism must change too, or it might end up in big trouble. Just because an impulse or tendency was useful 250,000 years ago doesn't mean that it is useful today. This is a point missed by people who selectively use evolutionary arguments to justify current inequalities. Who cares if men brought home the bacon a million years ago? What works *now*? Are women good leaders in today's world? If so, why aren't they better represented? It's important to tailor behavior to the "here and now" as opposed to the "used to be."[10] As every good business leader knows, if you don't adapt, you will perish.

Intergroup bias has a basis in our evolutionary history, but this doesn't mean that it's useful or beneficial today. And racism does not have an evolutionary basis at all; it's an arbitrary, socially determined classification.[11] In fact, your Stone Age enemy would have been more likely to have a skin tone similar to yours than different from yours. People with widely divergent skin tones or phenotypic features would have likely lived in a different climatic region thousands of miles away—they weren't in the next valley over the hill. History and socialization are responsible for our current social stratification based on skin color. Indeed, in ancient civilizations such as Egypt and Rome, differences in skin tone were pervasive but were not the basis for social interactions or economic stratification.[12] Slaves came in every hue. So did rulers. There was a veritable rainbow of skin color among Egyptian pharaohs, from olive to ebony, and Rome had a number of Black emperors of African ancestry, including Septimius Severus and Caracalla.[13] Differences in skin color in antiquity would have been as meaningful as differences in hair color or eye color today.

In addition to processes related to social group formation, our biases also are a result of our tendency to simplify and streamline the perception of a highly complex world. Our brains are wired to save energy, and research shows that when people use categories and stereotypes when perceiving other people, it frees up their brains to focus on other cognitive tasks.[14] But this comes at a cost. Although "boxes" help us to preserve cognitive resources, they also reduce accuracy because they induce us to attend to and process information very selectively. If you have a normal-functioning human brain, then you will have biases in the way that you process the world. The key is to be mindful of the impact of these biases on the conclusions that we draw.

SIMPLICITY: HOW OUR BRAINS ARE WIRED TO TAKE SHORTCUTS

I remember strolling one day with a colleague down State Street, a pedestrian thoroughfare in downtown Madison that is lined with restaurants, bars, shops, and people. We had walked the entire mile or so from the State Capitol to the University of Wisconsin, and after reaching campus, my colleague, who was visiting from another city, said: "It's a shame there are so many homeless Black people asking for money. The city should do something to help them." At the time, I was a professor at the University of Wisconsin and was much more familiar with the street than my out-of-town White visitor. In reality, we had passed over a dozen people asking for money and only two or three of them were Black. All of the others were White. So why did my colleague think that she saw "so many" Black people asking for money?

The answer is that, despite the fact that there were many more White people asking for money on State Street, my colleague didn't notice their race. She didn't notice them because our brains focus on what is distinctive. We've all seen posters or photographs that show one item that is different in a sea of similarity: for example, one green apple among forty-nine red apples. What is the first thing you notice when you look at the poster? The green apple, of course. Effortlessly, your eye goes right to it. Our brains work the same way when it comes to people. When my colleague looked around on our stroll, White people were the equivalent of the red apples in the photograph. On a street with mostly White people, they just blended into the background. However, she did notice the Black people asking for money—the green apples. Similarly, on a street where most people are strolling, people approaching others for money stood out. Put these two together, and it gives the impression of a lot of Black people asking for money, despite the fact that the vast majority of people asking for money were White. This is an example of an *illusory correlation*—an erroneous assumption about the relationship between two things based on the extent to which they are distinctive or stand out.

The *illusory correlation* phenomenon was first discovered by Loren and Jean Chapman[15] and was an early inspiration for Daniel Kahneman and Amos Tversky's work on heuristics and confirmation bias. The theory of illusory correlations was later developed by David Hamilton[16] and his colleagues, who showed that if two things stand out because they are different from everything else around them, people will assume that the two things are more strongly correlated than they really are. For example, when distinctive people perform distinctive behaviors, we are much more likely to erroneously assume that there is a correlation between the people and the behaviors. Being Black and asking for money on the street are both distinctive in Madison. People notice the "Black" race of the person and the "asking for money" and believe that the two traits are more highly correlated than they actually are. The result: People's brains will trick them into believing that they saw more Black panhandlers than they actually did. In contrast, they don't notice "White" because it is not distinctive, and they therefore don't reach the conclusion that they had seen a lot of White panhandlers. This distinctiveness mechanism explains the formation of stereotypes.

To see more clearly how illusory correlations explain the formation of stereotypes, let's delve into a classic study conducted by David Hamilton and his colleagues in the 1970s.[17] They presented people with two fictitious groups so that they could allow brand-new stereotypes to emerge where none had existed before. One group was the numerical majority and was simply referred to as group A. The other group was the numerical minority, and it was referred to as group B. Group A had twice as many members as group B, such that about 67 percent of the total population belonged to group A and about 33 percent of the total population belonged to group B. The researchers gave participants a list of mildly positive and mildly negative behaviors performed by members of both group A and group B. Importantly, both groups engaged in positive and negative behaviors in exactly the same proportion. In both groups, about 70 percent of individuals' behaviors were positive (e.g., visited a sick friend in the hospital, conversed easily with people) and about 30 percent of their behaviors were negative (e.g., always talked about himself and his problems, showed up late for work).[18]

Even though the percentage of good and bad actors in each group was exactly the same, the researchers discovered that the *impressions* that outside participants formed of the two groups, after reading about their members, were *not* the same. Participants were much more likely to associate negative behaviors with group B. How is this possible, given that the percentage of negative behaviors was exactly the same across the two groups? Because group B was a numerical minority, they were distinctive, like the green apple on the poster. Negative behaviors for each group were also distinctive, as they were less common, so they were noticed more than positive behaviors. Because people noticed "group B" and "bad behavior" more than their counterparts, they formed the (erroneous) impression that negative behaviors were more characteristic of group B than of group A. Again, we know that there is not a shred of truth to this belief, because the ratio of positive to negative acts was *identical* for both groups. But it *seemed* true to people because they formed an illusory correlation based on what was distinctive in their environment. This is the same process by which my colleague would form an illusory correlation between "Black" and "panhandler."

Illusory correlations explain not only how stereotypes form but also why they persist. Stereotypes persist partly because people are more likely to notice events that are consistent with their preexisting associations, due to confirmation bias.[19] For example, people are better at remembering behaviors that are consistent with stereotypes than behaviors that are inconsistent with stereotypes.[20] As a result, they tend to overestimate stereotype-confirming instances. To test this idea, Hamilton and colleagues asked people to read several sentences that described salespeople, doctors, or accountants using traits that were stereotypically associated with these groups (e.g., talkative, wealthy, or perfectionistic, respectively) or not. What they found was that people reported seeing the trait "talkative" more often than other traits like "timid" when it was used to describe a salesperson. Conversely, they reported seeing "timid" more often than other traits when talking about an accountant. Similarly, people like my colleague may think that they are seeing "poverty" more often than is reality when it is associated with a Black person compared with a White person, because a Black person asking for money is consistent with people's stereotypes of Black people being poor. In contrast, a person asking for money is not consistent with people's stereotypes about White people and is therefore less likely to be remembered.

I have heard multiple White people self-righteously claim that their disdain for group X is due to a bad experience with that group. For example, people's anti-Muslim bias is because of 9/11. People have anti-Black bias because they were picked on by Black kids when they were little. They have anti-Hispanic bias because of a negative encounter with a Hispanic person, and so on. The assumption is that if members of a group didn't behave in such a way, then there would be no prejudice against them. The theory of illusory correlation challenges this assumption by showing that even if there isn't a difference in the frequency of negative behaviors committed by Whites and people of color, White people will *still* view people of color more negatively just because they noticed their race and/or they already hold negative stereotypes about them.

Here is a different way to think about it: Is there any act committed by a U.S.-born White man, no matter how heinous, that could get Americans to get behind a ban of White men from the country? By far, most of the deadliest attacks (e.g., mass shootings) against people on U.S. soil have been perpetrated by White men. Has this produced changes in screening policy affecting White men or led to laws targeting White men? Are there White kids attending all-White schools, say, in Wyoming or New Hampshire, who get bullied and beaten up by other White kids? If so, has it led parents to consider moving out of their all-White neighborhoods or states because the bullying endured by their kids leads them to fear or resent all White people?

What the research on illusory correlations shows us is that White people who commit negative behaviors are almost never encoded as "White." The negative behaviors are noticed, but the Whiteness of the individual committing the behaviors doesn't register. That is why White people can have unracialized personal identities and the privilege of simply being an individual person.[21] The result is that negative actions perpetrated by White people are attributed to characteristics of the individual (e.g., "lone wolf") and/or their presumed state of mental health. It is also why White criminals, even the most egregious ones, do not affect the image of White people in general the way Muslim or Black criminals, for example, are used to justify discrimination against those groups in general. When negative behaviors are committed by people of color, both the behavior *and* the person's race or ethnicity are encoded and become part of the memory, automatically producing the tendency to overestimate how often negative acts are committed by people of color. This is, in large part, a result of the way that our brains process distinctive information. But being aware of this, being able to name it, and exercising due caution before drawing conclusions is one way to counteract the effect.

An alternative possibility is that beliefs about racial groups in the real world really are accurate, and that people are treating others differently based on real differences rather than racial biases. If we are going to have an honest Conversation, then we need to expose all the elephants in the room. Is there truth to the idea that real differences exist between the races? Is it possible that all of the disparities that we have discussed are due not to systemic or psychological biases but rather to something innate to people of color? This and other questions that challenge the existence of racism will be examined in the next chapter.

CHAPTER SEVEN

Is Inequality Due to Racism or Race?

Here is another quiz. Take a look at the three images below of a polar bear on the left, an arctic fox in the middle, and a grizzly bear on the right. Which two animals do you think are more genetically similar to each other? Jot down your answer—we will come back to the question later in the chapter.

In the preceding chapter, we covered various systemic factors leading to disparities in the lives and experiences of Black and White people. However, there is an elephant in the room that needs to be acknowledged before we can have an honest Conversation about racism—that elephant is the common presumption that there are biological differences among races.[1] Often, White people will quickly reject notions of innate racial difference because it isn't consistent with their egalitarian values—nor is it polite or socially acceptable.

However, deep down, many White people wonder if there are bio-logically based competence differences between Whites and people of color, particularly Blacks. These suppositions are the result of deeply ingrained historical and cultural narratives, as well as influential books like *The Bell Curve,* published in 1994, which attempted to make a case for racial differences in intelligence.[2]

For those who attribute racial disparities to something inherently different about Black people rather than something inherent to the system, a shift in mindset about race itself is needed to combat racism. One person who believes that notions of Black inferiority remain prevalent among White people today is Derek Black. Derek's father, Don Black, founded the White nationalist website Stormfront, and his godfather is David Duke, the former grand wizard of the Ku Klux Klan. Derek told me that he attributes much of his own renun-ciation of White nationalism to learning that racial differences are not real.[3] "There are two pillars of White nationalism," he said. "The first is the belief that American society is anti-White, and the second is that there are biological differences among races. Even though both of these things are false, I think most White people, not just White nationalists, believe one or the other or both of them, to some extent."

If we have any hope of changing many people's mindset about race, we must gather the facts. It turns out there is considerable em-pirical and anecdotal evidence supporting the idea that beliefs about inherent racial differences (i.e., *essentialism*) and the belief that Blacks are base, animalistic, and inferior (i.e., *dehumanization*) are more prevalent than people may assume.[4] For example, research by Philip Goff and colleagues found that implicit associations between Black people and apes exist in the general population, and that these asso-ciations occur regardless of a person's level of implicit racial bias. That is, both those high and low in implicit racial bias associated Black people with apes to an equivalent degree.[5] The most disturbing finding is that the association between Black people and apes pre-dicted a higher tendency to justify police violence against Blacks.

The impact of this dehumanization of Black Americans is seen clearly in social movements for racial justice, where slogans and calls to action are rooted in pleas for the recognition of full humanity. In the 1960s the rallying cry was "I am a man." The mere need to make such an obvious statement implies that Black men were somehow seen not as men but rather as something else. In recent years, the mantra "Black Lives Matter" is a counterpoint to the dehumanizing assumption that Black lives do *not* matter. It's important to emphasize that "matter" is not asking a lot. I once read a sign during a rally that read "Matter Is the Minimum" and went on to proclaim that Black lives are "worthy," "loved," and "valuable."

Beliefs about the full and equal humanity of Black people affect not only the nature of police interactions but the quality of medical treatment as well. Even physicians fall prey to the assumption that Black bodies are biologically different from White bodies in ways that transcend skin color. Multiple studies reveal that doctors are more likely to underestimate the pain experienced by Black patients compared with White patients and are less likely to prescribe the recommended or appropriate pain treatment for Black patients, even when they report the same level of pain as Whites.[6]

In Linda Villarosa's 2019 *New York Times* piece as part of the newspaper's "1619 Project," she wrote about the historical evidence of White doctors believing that Black people would be unaffected by pain that would be unbearable to a White person. She recounts a particularly gruesome example of a doctor in the late eighteenth century who claimed that Black people had assisted him during the amputation of their own limbs.[7] These beliefs about Blacks as being simultaneously (mentally) subhuman and (physically) superhuman[8] conveniently served as justifications for the harsh exploitation and treatment of enslaved Africans. If Blacks don't feel the same pain as Whites, then brutally whipping them isn't so bad (never mind the logical question of why someone would bother to whip someone if they truly believed the person would be unfazed by it). Another common myth, perpetuated by the physician Samuel Cartwright in the mid-nineteenth century, was that Black people had lower lung capacity than White people (never mind that many of the best marathoners in the world are African). Dr. Cartwright also believed, quite conveniently, that this lung deficiency could be corrected by strenuous manual labor. These purported differences thus not only justified hard forced labor but even framed it as a benefit to slaves.

Antiquated notions persist among some White medical professionals today. For example, a 2016 study by Kelly Hoffman, Sophie Trawalter, and colleagues found that about 8 percent of White first-year medical students believe that Whites have a more efficient respiratory system than Blacks. That number drops to 2 percent by the third year of medical school, once students gain more knowledge and experience. Similarly, 21 percent of White first-year medical students believe that Blacks have stronger immune systems than Whites, and 29 percent believe that Black people's blood coagulates more quickly than Whites'. Again, the percentage of medical students who hold these false beliefs falls dramatically by the third year of medical school—to 3 percent for each of these two beliefs.

These false beliefs did not appear to be malicious or intentional, as the researchers found that neither implicit nor explicit racial biases predicted differential pain assessment or treatment.[9] In other words, people low in racial prejudice were not less likely than people high in racial prejudice to believe that there are biological differences between Black and White bodies. Nevertheless, these false beliefs are still harmful because they predicted the medical professional's ability to accurately diagnose and treat Black patients. Those who were more likely to believe, for example, that Blacks had thicker blood, stronger immune systems, or lower respiratory capacity than Whites were more likely to underestimate the pain of Black patients and were less likely to prescribe the appropriate treatment.

In addition to antiquated beliefs about Black bodies, other racist notions that existed during slavery persist today, even among Whites who reject racism. These beliefs affect not just everyday interactions but policy decisions as well.[10] As taboo and uncomfortable as the topic may be, the question of biological differences merits our further attention. Unlike the days of Samuel Cartwright, when musings about inherent racial differences were based on nothing more than pseudoscience (e.g., phrenology) and the motivated desire to justify oppression, we now have more scientifically sound answers to the question of racial differences. The mapping of the entire human genome—a Herculean effort considered to be one of the most ambitious feats of modern science—was completed in 2003. This means that we can rigorously address the validity of the belief that race accounts for human differences. What does the scientific evidence reveal?

Based on genomic data, the majority of human geneticists and molecular biologists in the world would accept each of these claims as true: (1) Every single human being alive today can trace their lineage back to the *same* great[x]-grandmother, a woman who lived about 150,000 years ago.[11] (2) All of the 7.8 billion human "cousins" alive today have a 99.9 percent overlap in their DNA. That's a much higher genetic overlap than one can find in most other species[12] and is due to the relative youth of *Homo sapiens*.[13] For example, the average genetic difference between two randomly selected chimpanzees is twice as large as the average genetic difference between two humans randomly selected from the entire world's population,[14] despite the fact that chimpanzees tend to *look* more similar to one another than humans do. (3) The 0.1 percent genetic variability that exists among the billions of "cousins" is not easily or adequately explained by traditional racial categories (e.g., Blacks, Whites, Asians, Native Americans). Indeed, the range of genetic differences among individuals of the same "race" are far greater than the average differences between any two racial groups.[15]

This is a difficult concept for many people to wrap their heads around. The range of human phenotypic diversity reveals conspicuous differences in skin color, hair texture, eye shape, and body shape, and it's therefore easy for people to assume that we must be very different on the inside (i.e., genetically). They may hear that race is a social construct but might not fully understand what that means.

Home kits for genetic testing have become extremely popular in recent years. Some readers have surely spit in a vial, sent it off to Ancestry.com or 23andMe, and, in response, received a report stating the percentage of their DNA linked to forty-five different "populations." What these tests trace is *ancestry*. These DNA tests are not necessarily able to discern your "race," or even your skin tone.

The distinction between tribal ancestry (or "ethnicity," to use the term loosely) on the one hand and race on the other is an important one. *Within* each race there exist many different tribes or ethnicities—Yoruba, Fulani, Celtic, Basque, Filipino, Korean, Navajo, Wampanoag—each having a unique genetic profile. Furthermore, the genetic profiles of these tribes can be more distinct from other tribes within the same "race" than they are from tribes of a different "race." For example, data show that the genetic differences between a randomly chosen person who is Celtic and one who is Basque—both European ("White") ethnicities—can be *greater* than the genetic differences between the Celtic person and a randomly chosen person of Yoruba (African or "Black") or Filipino (Asian) ancestry.[16]

Let's explore this idea in greater depth using a more mundane analogy. I'd like for you to imagine two White families living in Iowa—the Smith family, with a mother, a father, and eighteen biological children, and the Wilson family, with a mother, a father, and eighteen biological children. If you randomly chose two people from the Smith family, they would almost always be more genetically similar to each other than to a randomly chosen member of the Wilson family. Why? Because the Smith children really do share a close genetic kinship due to their common biological ancestry. The same goes for the Wilsons. Therefore, the chance of a Smith being genetically more similar to a Wilson than to another Smith is very slim, less than 1 percent, or one out of one hundred.[17]

Now let's assume that you did this same experiment, but instead of using nuclear families composed of parents and their offspring, you made up artificial groups using forty White people randomly selected from all across the state of Iowa and randomly assigned to two different groups—twenty people to group A and twenty people to group B. Now the likelihood of one person from group A being more genetically similar to another person from group A than to a person from group B is pure chance—about 50 percent, or one out of two. Why is it a coin toss in this case? Because the genetic similarities and differences between the groups are not systematically determined by shared family ancestry. The genetic differences between group A and group B are random.

So, what about race? Imagine the same premise as before, except now the people who are selected are not from biological families or random groups but from different races (e.g., Whites and Blacks). Do you think race operates more like families (the Smiths and Wilsons) or random groups (group A and group B)? In other words, what do you think is the likelihood that a randomly selected White person and a randomly selected Black person will be more genetically similar to each other than two randomly selected White people?

Several studies have investigated this question in different ways. Research by Michael Bamshad and colleagues examined the degree of genetic similarity between people of different "races," determined by traditional continent-based categories—Africans, Europeans, Asians, Native Americans—by assessing how many of 377 "genes" (more precisely, short tandem repeat alleles) they shared.[18] Each racial group contained people from different ancestral tribes or ethnicities (e.g., French, Sardinian, Russian, etc. for "Whites" or Mandenka, Yoruba, Bantu, etc. for "Blacks"). They looked at the number of overlapping genes between two randomly selected individuals from the same "racial" group and between randomly selected individuals from different "racial" groups (e.g., one White person and one Black person).

It would seem intuitive that people of the same race are more genetically similar than people of differing races. If race is a biological reality, then a White person and a Black person should almost never be more genetically similar to each other than two White people—just as a Smith and a Wilson should almost never be more similar to each other than two Smiths. But that's not what the study found. Far from being a remote possibility—say, 1 percent, or one in one hundred—the likelihood was much closer to one in two. Specifically, a White person and a Black person were more genetically similar than two White people about 36 percent of the time, or slightly more than one out of three. Although higher within-race similarity was more common, higher between-race similarity occurred quite frequently.

Have a look at the photos of the three scientists on the next page: James Watson, a White man, on the left; Seong-Jin Kim, a Korean man, in the middle; and Craig Venter, a White man, on the right. Which two men do you think are most genetically similar?

Based on a full analysis of the actual DNA of all three men, which computed the number of alleles that they shared, the two most genetically similar men were James Watson and Seong-Jin Kim.[19] In fact, the number of shared alleles between these two men was more than 20 percent higher than the number of shared alleles between James Watson and Craig Venter.[20] The genetic similarity between Kim and Venter was also greater than the genetic similarity between Watson and Venter. So much for judging a book by its cover.

You may be wondering whether this finding depends on which "races" are being compared. For example, are Whites and Native Americans relatively more similar to each other than Whites and Blacks? Nope. The likelihood of a White person and a non-White person being more genetically similar to each other than two White people are to each other is approximately one in three, regardless of whether Whites are being compared with Asians, Blacks, or Native Americans.[21] Indeed, we are *all* "cousins."

What's even more astounding about the results of the Bamshad study is that they used "Old World" ancestral populations of Blacks, Whites, Native Americans, and Asians, providing a more extreme test of racial differences. If the study had compared Black Americans to White Americans, rather than Black Africans to White Europeans, then the results would have been even closer to chance, because of the admixture (i.e., miscegenation) of Blacks and Whites in the United States. That is, almost all Black Americans have some European ancestry (in fact, the average Black American is roughly 25 percent White) and many White Americans have some African ancestry (in some Southern states, up to 12 percent of the White population has significant African ancestry).[22]

To be clear, I am not implying that European Whites or African Blacks are "pure." All human tribes have some degree of admixture with other human groups. Some human tribes even have traces of admixture with other hominid populations (e.g., Neanderthals).[23] No one is pure anything. It's helpful to think about this concept of "purity" using a color analogy. The notion of pure green or pure orange is problematic because they both have other colors "baked in" (e.g., yellow). Similarly, "pure" Spaniards have Moorish ancestry (and Iberian, Phoenician, Celtic, and other groups) baked in. And "pure" Moors have sub-Saharan African ancestry (there is a reason Colin Kaepernick, who is Black-White biracial, was thought to be Moroccan by some of my North African friends). A large proportion of "pure" Britons have Syrian and Turkish ancestry (these settlers introduced early British tribes to farming).[24] Of course, Britons also had contact with Romans, who themselves were not racially or ethnically homogeneous. As previously mentioned, there were even Black Roman emperors, such as Septimius Severus, who fortified Hadrian's Wall in England. Archaeological evidence abounds of members of other African peoples living in England during antiquity, many of them people of high status and wealth (e.g., the Ivory Bangle Lady). This means that a White American whose ancestry is 100 percent English may also have Syrian, Italian, or African ancestry mixed in—just as "pure" green is infused with yellow. There is no racial purity in the human world. To discover our "primary colors," we would have to go back to the African ancestors that we all share.

It's somewhat amusing that many see Prince Harry and Meghan Markle as being an interracial couple, because Harry, like Meghan, is himself biracial to some degree. For over half a century the royal family, including the queen herself, has acknowledged its African ancestry, which comes from at least one ancestor—Queen Charlotte (Queen Victoria's grandmother), whose Blackness is apparent in both her ancestral bloodline and her physical appearance.[25]

Science reveals that we humans are basically distant "cousins" who do not always resemble one another, despite our common DNA—just as orange and green don't really resemble each other, despite the underlying yellow in both. So why do we look different, and how are these phenotypic differences related to judgments about competence and capacity? We'll explore these questions next.

THE IMPACT OF PHYSICAL APPEARANCE

Let's return to the quiz from the beginning of the chapter. Which two animals did you think are more genetically similar? I've posed this question to highly educated audiences, and there is always a substantial minority (i.e., 10 to 25 percent) who believe that the polar bear and the arctic fox are more closely related than the polar bear and the grizzly bear. And this is not because they thought it was a trick question. Because the polar bear and the arctic fox are both white and from the same geographic region, they reason that the two are somehow united on a deeper genetic or molecular level. Those who arrive at this answer have unconsciously created an artificial biological category of "arctic creatures," which may include not only polar bears and arctic foxes but arctic hares and snowy owls as well—anything "white" and "arctic." If you haven't realized it by now, it's scientifically untenable that a bear could be genetically more similar to an owl or a fox of the same color than to a bear of a different color.

What about the three scientists? Did you assume that the two White scientists were more genetically similar to each other than to the Korean scientist? Lumping people together based on skin color (e.g., "White people") is akin to constructing the category "arctic creatures," because it focuses on *one* superficial trait (i.e., skin/fur/feather color) and disregards all of the other differences among members of the category, as well as the commonalities with members of other categories. This is what it means to "construct" a race. One might as well pick eye color as a defining characteristic of "race" and make attributions about personality traits and intellectual abilities based on eye color alone. In fact, this is exactly what Jane Elliott did in her famous blue eyes/brown eyes experiment to demonstrate to White school-age children what it would feel like to be categorized and treated differently on the basis of an arbitrary physical characteristic, such as their eye color.[26]

So if we humans aren't so different on the inside, why do we look so different on the outside? Science has revealed that skin color is not a dichotomy but rather a "cline" or continuous spectrum that gradually changes across the human geographical range.[27] A Black-White dichotomy might make sense if you just compared Sudanese and Swedes, for example. But if you made a picture book of all the people whom you would encounter on a hike from South Sudan to Sweden, you would see a full spectrum of black, brown, tan, olive, beige, and white, with varying cocoa, bronze, golden, peach, and ruddy undertones, due to infinite combinations of the skin pigments eumelanin (black, brown) and pheomelanin (yellowish, reddish).

Skin tones differ by geographic location because our skin must perform two functions simultaneously. First, our skin performs a photoprotective function, shielding us from harmful UV radiation that can cause both folate damage—which impedes fertility—and skin cancer. This is where darker skin has an advantage. At the same time, our skin must absorb and synthesize UVB photons into vitamin D,[28] which helps our bodies absorb minerals and nutrients critical for heathy bones, teeth, and muscles. This is where lighter skin has an advantage. To optimize the balance between these competing needs, the skin tone of a given human population tends to correspond to the intensity of sunlight in its indigenous geographic region. Pale white skin in Uganda is suboptimal because it does not provide sufficient protection against the equatorial sun. On the other hand, dark brown skin in Scotland is suboptimal because it deflects the faint rays of sunshine that occasionally emerge, resulting in vitamin D deficiency. People living in between the two extremes—say, Greeks, Turks, Iraqis, Egyptians, and Bangladeshis—represent various intermediate shades of beige, olive, tan, and brown, because UV exposure in those regions is more intense than in northern Europe but less intense than in equatorial Africa.

To test the connection between skin color and geography, anthropologists Nina Jablonski and George Chaplin measured ground-level UV radiation all around the world using satellite data. They also measured the skin color of native populations in each of those regions using a light meter to measure skin reflectance. Their results revealed a very strong correlation between skin color and UV intensity, with lighter skin in the areas with lower UV radiation and darker skin in the areas with higher UV radiation.[29]

The diagram below, taken from an anthropological study, is a crude approximation of the many shades of skin color (crude because there is a wide spectrum of skin tones, not just seven) and how they are distributed across the planet.[30] If you circumnavigated the earth at the equator, making stops to greet all of the people that you encountered, every single population across the world—whether in Asia, Africa, Oceania, or South America—would have brown skin due to the intensity and consistency of sunlight at that latitude.

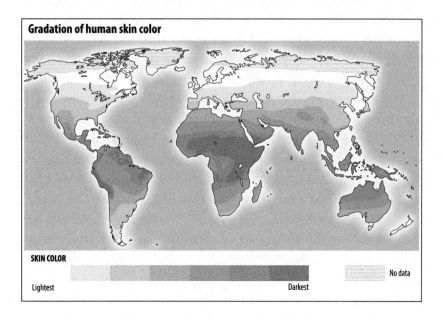

Gradation of human skin color

SKIN COLOR

Lightest   Darkest   No data

Although there is strong evidence for this environmental account of skin color, the full story is even more complicated, as revealed by recent studies. Science knows relatively little about the genetic architecture and determinants of skin color, especially among African populations.[31] Although it's evident that skin color is not determined by just one gene, it's not clear how many genes are implicated or how they interact with one another.[32] The result is that it is very difficult to accurately predict an individual's skin color from their DNA.

I experienced this firsthand when I received my own report from 23andMe. Although it got nearly all of my traits correct—for example, a 92 percent likelihood of no balding, a 99 percent likelihood of not having red hair, a 74 percent likelihood of detached earlobes, a 91 percent likelihood of dark brown eyes, even an 88 percent likelihood of no photic sneeze reflex (i.e., when bright sunlight makes you sneeze)—the two things that it got wrong were my skin color and my hair texture. The report only gave me a 7 percent chance of having the texture of "Black" hair (i.e., "very tight curls" or "small curls") but a 58 percent chance of having the texture of "White" hair (i.e., "straight hair" or "semistraight hair"), with the remaining 35 percent corresponding to my chance of having the texture of "Olive," or Mediterranean hair (i.e., "wavy" or "big curls"). More important, it estimated my likelihood of having dark brown skin at only 3 percent, which was lower than the estimated likelihood of having "fair" skin (or "beige," "olive," or "light brown" skin).

It was surprising that the test was able to discern my tribal ancestries (mostly from West Africa) but not my skin color. Armed with just this ancestral information, most anyone's guess about my likely skin color and hair texture would have been more accurate than the genetic report's estimate. Ironically, reaching this conclusion based solely on my DNA proved more challenging. My 23andMe experience was further evidence that the link between skin color (or hair texture) and any underlying DNA structure is extraordinarily complex. This complexity was beautifully captured by the cover of the April 2018 issue of *National Geographic,* which featured a photograph of dizygotic (fraternal) twins, one who appears White and the other who appears Black. Despite the striking difference in their physical appearances, they share a 100 percent overlap in biological ancestry, given that they have the same mother and father.

Some of the most prominent Black people in U.S. history (e.g., Angela Davis, Rosa Parks) have lighter skin than some southern Europeans, adding more intricacy to the notion that African ancestry means dark skin whereas European ancestry means light skin. Even within "Old World" ancestral populations of Africa, there is astounding variation in skin color.[33] For example, the San people of South

Africa have relatively light skin, whereas the Surma people in Ethiopia have very dark skin.

Despite all the complexity revealed by science, people have tried to turn race into something simple and biologically deterministic. The fact that race has been "essentialized" by our society makes it harder for people to grasp the notion that skin color does *not* reflect a deeper underlying "essence" and one's ability to learn, govern, socialize, or prosper. In addition to robust evidence that race is not biological, there is compelling evidence that achievement gaps, across a variety of domains, are environmentally determined. There is a big difference between disability and disadvantage. For example, left-handed people are just as able as right-handed people. However, if you put them in a world designed for right-handed people, they will be at a competitive disadvantage and will likely underperform relative to right-handed people. What research has shown again and again is that schools and workplace environments can be structurally—and culturally—inhospitable to members of socially disadvantaged groups, which can lead to decrements in performance.

For instance, cross-cultural research has shown that groups that are stigmatized and academically disadvantaged in one country or context may flourish academically when they move to a different environment where their social identity is not stigmatized. One concrete example is the Burakumin, a highly stigmatized, low-caste group in Japan that performs far below the mainstream Japanese population in Japan but excels in the United States, where there is no knowledge or expectation of social differences between Burakumin and other Japanese students.[34] Much social psychological research has shown that cultural expectations and self-fulfilling prophecies can affect outcomes.[35] Providing further empirical evidence that environmental messages can undermine performance, a vast body of research originated by social psychologist Claude Steele has shown that women and people of color can fall victim to *stereotype threat*. Stereotype threat occurs when mere knowledge about negative cultural stereotypes regarding a group's competence in a particular domain, such as math for women or academics in general for Blacks, creates a fear of confirming the stereotype—which leads to anxiety and underperformance.[36]

Positive stereotypes can also boost performance. In one clever study, researchers asked Asian American women to indicate either their race or their gender (or neither, in the control condition), before taking a difficult math test. Because cultural stereotypes about Asians reflect high mathematical aptitude, whereas stereotypes of women reflect low mathematical aptitude, they expected that activation of those respective social categories would correspond to better or worse performance outcomes, respectively. That is precisely what they found—Asian women who thought of themselves as "Asian" performed better than the control group, whereas Asian women who thought of themselves as "women" performed worse than the control group.[37]

Context and the environment are very powerful outcome determinants, in general, and can affect performance for reasons unrelated to race. Research examining the effect of birth order, for example, has shown that children who are born first consistently show higher levels of academic achievement and professional success than children with a later birth order. For example, in families of four or five children, the firstborn child was more likely to become a National Merit Finalist (an honor that is determined primarily by performance on an aptitude test very similar to the SAT) than the second-, third-, fourth-, or fifth-born child.[38] In families with five children, firstborns, on average, become National Merit Finalists more often than all the later-born children combined.[39] This example is particularly salient because if we cited those same differences based on five different races rather than five different birth orders, then people might be very quick to jump to the conclusion that the high performer (in this case, the first-born) is "biologically" superior to the other four. But given that the children are products of the same biological stock, a much more plausible explanation for the differences in performance has to do with differences in parents' rearing and expectations of their first child compared with their younger children.

If nonbiological but environmentally relevant factors such as birth order can have a substantial impact on performance and life outcomes, then how could it be that nonbiological, environmentally relevant factors as pervasive as systemic racism would *not* have a big impact on performance and life outcomes? Nevertheless, there is a long-standing misperception that gaps are due to some combination of biological or cultural deficits. In other words, people of color create deficient cultures due to their biological deficiencies. This is consistent with the notion that people of color are barbaric and incapable of civilization, while White people are the creators and purveyors of civilization. This idea is inherently flawed because "race" must biologically exist before biological racial *differences* affecting people's capacity for "civilization" can exist—and we have just established that race is biologically not a tenable idea. The argument further breaks down when we take a closer, more objective look at the relationship between civilization and skin color over human history.

THE MYTH OF BLACK BARBARISM

Philosopher David Hume once wrote:

> There never was a civilized nation of any other complexion than white, nor even any individual eminent either in action or speculation. . . . (*Of National Characters,* 1753)

The notion that White people were the original, primary, or exclusive creators of civilization is a fallacy. The fact of the matter, based on centuries of history—much of it written by White people—is that Hume got it completely wrong. That is, one could make the exact opposite case—that ancient civilizations came in every complexion *except* White. Here is another look (see the following page) at the diagram that I showed you of skin tones across the world. I placed stars on the map to indicate the locations of the principal civilizations mentioned by books on "ancient" or "Western" civilization.

As mentioned previously, skin color is a biological cline—it is difficult to determine where white ends and brown begins. However, if we define "White" as pale-skinned, blond-haired, blue-eyed northern Europeans, then few, if any, early civilizations were White.

The producers of early civilization were the tan- and brown-

complexioned peoples of Iraq (Mesopotamia), Iran (Persia), and India
(Indus Valley), the bronze-complexioned peoples of Mexico (Aztec),
Guatemala (Maya), and Peru (Inca), the beige- and olive-complexioned
Mediterranean peoples of Greece, Turkey, Malta, and southern Italy,
and the mahogany- and ebony-complexioned peoples of Egypt, Zimbabwe (Great Zimbabwe), Mali, Senegal (Awkar), and Sudan (Kush).
Furthermore, many of the civilizations of Asia, Africa, and the
Americas predate the civilizations of (southern) Europe. The Romans were deeply influenced by the Greeks, who were influenced by
nearby Asian and African civilizations. The historical evidence for
this argument is thoughtfully and rigorously expounded in the 1987
book *Black Athena: The Afroasiatic Roots of Classical Civilization* by
Martin Bernal.

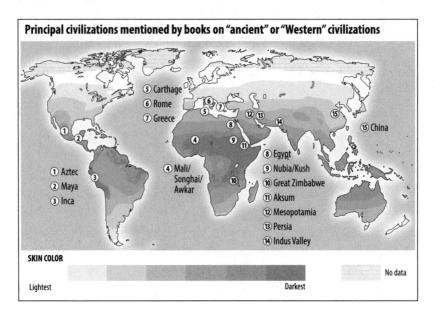

A recurring theme throughout my book has been the difference
between factual and emotional truth. There is a deep and emotionally
charged investment in the belief of European superiority and African
inferiority. So history will be construed to cater to those needs—or
ignored entirely. Indeed, most Americans have never heard of the
Mali Empire, or Great Zimbabwe, or ancient Kush in Sudan and
southern Egypt. They have no idea that this Nubian civilization of

black-skinned Africans built pyramids and a mighty empire that conquered and ruled Egypt for centuries. In fact, due to Hollywood portrayals, many of them may not know that Egyptians themselves were dark brown–skinned people whose empires were located hundreds of miles south of the Mediterranean Sea (e.g., Valley of the Kings). In short, history shows that it was people of color who civilized White people, not the other way around. Indeed, it was Germanic tribes who constituted the original "barbarians." Research by Patricia Balaresque, Mark Jobling, and others found that early tribes of the British Isles and northern Europe were still hunter-gatherers before people from Syria and Turkey introduced them to farming— the cornerstone of civilization.

Although Hume's notion of Whites as the original and exclusive creators of civilization is completely inaccurate, the point of setting the record straight is not to suggest that White people have made no contributions. Western Europe has made undeniable artistic and technological advances in the last six hundred years, as has every other group on the planet at some point in the last six thousand years—a relatively brief period of time for a species that has existed for a million years. My hope is that your primary takeaway from this chapter is that race is an illusion—we share vastly more similarities than differences.[40] And the physical differences that do exist are in no way related to our character, competence, or human worth. But it's not an easy illusion to shake, as some scientists have noted:

> Moving from race-as-biology to race-as-socially constructed is as profound as learning that the earth is round, when [we] always knew it was flat. It requires a paradigm shift. While this paradigm shift will not be sufficient to eliminate racism in our time, it is surely a necessary step in the right direction.[41]

The first step toward making the change is recognizing that tribes and individuals of all complexions from every corner of the globe have contributed to the knowledge, advances, and achievements made by humankind. The next step, and perhaps a more difficult one, is asking why many people wouldn't *already* recognize this fact. Based on everything that we have covered in the book until now, why might some White people continue to harbor the belief that people of color are not as capable as Whites? To answer *that* question is to begin to get to the heart of the Condition of racism.

How to Talk About the Problem

This final section of Part 1, which I call a "Forum," is designed to help people share and integrate their individual reading experiences through the dialogue and social exchange that *The Conversation* is meant to create. The Forum for Part 1 provides a springboard for interactive discussion with others in your network, community, or organization, including specific prompts or conversation starters. Two additional Forum sections will conclude Parts 2 and 3, respectively. Some of you are likely reading this book as part of a social group, book club, community event, or specific initiative at your workplace. The Forums will help guide your group discussion about the book. For those of you who came to the book on your own, I hope the Forums will inspire you to find ways to raise the book's key questions in your own mind, as well as with others in less formal social settings.

Before I invite you to begin your dialogue, I want to return to the PRESS model, which I briefly mentioned in the book's introduction. *The Conversation* is organized around five stages of my PRESS model—a simple, straightforward framework I first wrote about in my article "How to Promote Racial Equity in the Workplace," published in 2020 in *Harvard Business Review*.[1] It outlines the sequential steps necessary to make impactful progress toward racial equity.

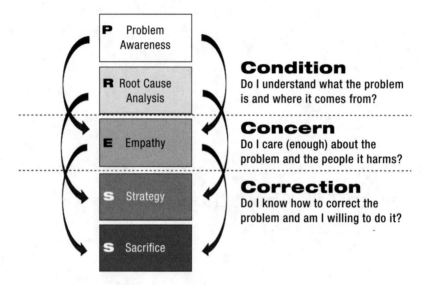

The model applies not only to racism but to almost any personal or social problem (e.g., weight loss, addiction, climate change, etc.). The very first step in solving any problem is becoming aware that a problem even exists. If someone doesn't believe that climate change is real, then they are unlikely to be concerned about the problem (hence the arrow from *P* to *E*). In Chapter 1 we explored the issue of racism credence, or whether people believe that anti-Black racism really exists. Acknowledging the problem is necessary but not sufficient. It's also important to understand what's causing the problem. Assuming that climate change is real, is it the result of fossil fuel emissions or is it part of the natural geological cycle of the earth? The answer will give clues to an effective strategy for solving it (hence the arrow from *R* to *S*). If it's caused by carbon emissions, then there are many things we can do to reduce the problem. Similarly, determining whether racism is caused by a few bad apples or an entire structure will guide the most promising steps toward its eradication.

Of course, information is useful only to the extent that there is motivation to do something about the problem. People are unlikely to take steps toward solving a problem if they don't believe that it concerns them. But assuming there is knowledge of the Condition as well as sufficient Concern, the next question becomes: What do I do to fix it? This is the stage that most individuals and leaders want to jump to *first,* rather than last—which would be a mistake. It is akin to a doctor prescribing medicine for symptoms (e.g., headache) without performing an examination to better understand the patient's underlying condition and whether the patient will comply with the prescribed regimen. If the headache is being caused by severe dehydration, for example, and the patient is given ibuprofen to get rid of the headache without any plan for rehydration, then the headache will recur—not to mention the likelihood of more serious medical problems. In many ways, Strategy is the "easiest" of the five stages.

Once you understand the Condition, have sufficient Concern, and know what to do to fix it, are you actually willing to get it done? The answer will depend, in part, on how much sacrifice you think it will take and how much sacrifice you're willing to make. That will be determined, to some extent, by how much you care (hence the arrow from E to the second S). Let's take a concrete example that most people can relate to—dieting. There is no shortage of diets for losing weight, and gyms are ubiquitous—you can even turn a public park or the walls and floors of your home into a makeshift gym. The real question is whether you are willing to incur the cost, inconvenience, trade-offs, and "sacrifice" to commit to the diet or exercise plan. I put *sacrifice* in quotation marks because these commitments often involve less sacrifice than one might suspect. When I moved from Chicago to England nine years ago, I lost a lot of excess weight. I didn't have a car and the city I lived in was quite hilly. Moreover, the portion sizes are much smaller in the UK. However, when I moved back to the United States about six years ago, I put on roughly a pound a week for several months. It was so gradual, and I was so focused on other things, that I barely noticed the twenty-five-pound weight gain—until a colleague who hadn't seen me in a while pointed out that I had "grown" substantially since the last time she saw me.

At that point, not only did I become fully aware of the problem, but I was also able to quickly diagnose the cause (too many desserts and not enough exercise), and my level of concern (quite high, due to health and other concerns). The strategy wasn't mysterious. There are many effective diets and several gyms within a half mile of my house. However, it all came down to whether I was willing to make the "sacrifice." I hate running like a hamster on a treadmill and I love chocolate—sometimes even the decadent, two-thousand-calorie-slice-of-double-chocolate-brownie-fudge-cheesecake variety. My assumption was that losing weight required incurring the pain of exercise and giving up the pleasure of chocolate. But a meeting with a wellness counselor revealed otherwise. Even though I despise gyms, I love nature (hence the copious wildlife examples throughout the book). Why not buy a bike and explore the beautiful trails that surround the river where I lived? This simple idea transformed exercise from drudgery to pleasure. I actually began looking forward to my daily bike rides. What about the chocolate? After a little research, we discovered that Hershey's kisses have fewer than twenty calories each. That meant that I could get a little chocolate fix ten times a day and still not top two hundred calories!

The point here is that making any profound and sustainable change involves starting with the problem—not the solution—and ending with a thoughtful and meticulous consideration of what one is *willing* to do, given what the "cost" may be. Many individuals and organizations desire greater racial equity but may not be willing to invest the effort, energy, time, and commitment necessary to make it happen. In their book *Immunity to Change,* Robert Kegan and Lisa Lahey discuss useful techniques for identifying and overcoming barriers to successful transformation.

THE CONVERSATION

The "deep structure" of this book follows the logic and sequence of the PRESS model, so it's important that you understand it. The first stage (Problem Awareness) was addressed in Chapters 1 and 2. The second stage of the model (Root Cause Analysis) was covered in Chapters 3 through 7. If I have done my job, you should now be convinced that there is a problem and have a solid understanding of where it comes from. The next section of the book (Chapters 8–10) will investigate *Concern,* and the last section of the book (Chapters 11–12) will focus on *Correction*.

As I mentioned in the introduction, *The Conversation* is a book that is written for everyone who wants to learn and grow, regardless of their current level of knowledge. This means that readers may represent a broad diversity of awareness and experience. It's important to recognize and accept that it will be hard for all. It will be difficult for White readers, for example, because the experience will create defensiveness and challenge assumptions about the world as they are *seeking* the truth about racism. It will be challenging for people of color due to the vulnerability that they assume when *speaking* the truth about racism, in addition to sheer fatigue and frustration from having discussions about the same problems over and over.

To be clear, it is *not* the case that all White people will *seek* and all Black people will *speak*. Across racial categories there will be a broad mix of seeking and speaking. The process will require investment and effort, and people will have to decide for themselves whether it's worth the work. I believe it is. Think of it this way: If your muscles never ached after pushing through those last ten minutes of spin class or that last set of bench presses, that might be a sign that your workout routine is ineffective, especially if the goal is to transform your body. The same is true for the transformation of your mind and community. My colleague Hugh O'Doherty describes the "learning zone" as the sweet spot nestled between the "comfort zone" and the "danger zone." This learning zone is where The Conversation needs to take place. Therefore, you should expect from the outset to experience, and have to work through, a certain amount of discomfort and unpleasant emotions—tension, anger, guilt, frustration, confusion, and awkwardness—when working toward personal and social transformation. It may not be pleasant, but it is often a necessary part of growth. No pain, no gain.

It's also important to consider how best to approach The Conversation. For everyone involved, the process will require a certain level of patience—patience that many people of color in your organization or community may, very understandably, not have. As a teacher and trainer, it's my job to have patience and to meet people where they are. Therefore, the suggestions for how to have The Conversation are based on my experiences and what I have seen work very effectively for me. While there is no magic formula for a smooth ride, I will propose four rules for increasing the likelihood of a productive Conversation—one that promotes mutual learning and advances positive social change.

RULE #1: GATHER THE FACTS . . . *AND* MAKE SPACE FOR THE FEELINGS

It is often easier to begin with a discussion of facts because they are easier to verify and tend to be somewhat more value neutral. Imagine that someone said to you, "Capital punishment is wrong." That's their opinion. You could disagree, and a philosophical debate or heated argument might ensue. However, it's impossible to confirm or refute the truth of their statement. On the other hand, if someone said, "Capital punishment does not lower the crime rate," then you could begin to support or refute the veracity of the statement by examining the pool of scientific evidence around whether capital punishment is a crime deterrent or not. One major goal of this book is to put hard facts at your fingertips so that you are better equipped to offer (or rebut) arguments in a way that is grounded in fact, not simply opinion. As you may recall, "the fellas" (from Chapter 1) had all sorts of opinions about the representation of Black CEOs in America (e.g., one hundred out of five hundred were Black, according to one respondent), but there was no denying the facts. However, a focus on the facts doesn't mean that emotions are not important too.

During one of my workshops in Mayor Ted's Midwestern city, I presented facts about discrimination to a group of police officers a dozen different ways, using charts, graphs, studies, stories—you name it. The officers were nodding along, but I could see that they weren't completely convinced. It wasn't until one of the Black police officers in the room broke down emotionally and began talking about the hardships and discrimination he faced as a Black man on the city's police force that they really began to listen. He spoke about one incident in which a citizen called the police on *him* as he was walking the beat on foot patrol. For that audience, seeing one of their colleagues voice his pain gave the facts a whole new level of significance. After that, they were ready to receive my data. In fact, one of the White officers on the force, whom I perceived to be one of the most resistant people in the room prior to this emotional moment, became one of the most voracious consumers of the facts. He's now an ally.

As mentioned in the introduction, researchers found that Red Cross volunteers started serving more organ meat as a function of being given information about its nutritional benefits, as well as being given the opportunity to discuss it. In the information-only condition, about 3 percent of the women started serving organ meat, whereas 32 percent of the women started serving organ meat when they were provided information *and* given the opportunity to discuss it.

More generally, research has shown that people are more likely to tune in when there is the opportunity to form a personal connection. For example, a photograph of a single needy child will generate many more charitable donations than a pamphlet with hard data about millions of starving children, as paradoxical as it seems.[2] Mother Teresa once said, "If I look at the mass, I will never act. If I look at the one, I will." At the other end of the moral spectrum, Stalin once said, "A single death is a tragedy; a million deaths is a statistic." What all of this means is that many people need to be able to emotionally connect to another person for the data to even matter. Black Lives Matter has been around for years. Police brutality has been around for decades. The data are out there and readily available. However, the Black Lives Matter movement did not hit home for many White people until they witnessed the protracted murder of George Floyd unfold in front of their eyes in an intensely personal and visceral way.

The idea here is that conversations should not *exclusively* focus on facts—or feelings—but on a combination of both. My general rule of thumb is 70 percent facts and 30 percent feelings, but that varies depending on the context. Following the death of George Floyd, my sessions were 30 percent facts and 70 percent feelings, because people just wanted to process their emotions. Many couldn't even digest data at that moment. What is important to realize is that both are needed to support a constructive Conversation.

Facts allow us to distinguish between impressions that are valid and those that are not—which gives us more reliable information on the nature of the problem and what can be done to fix it. I often try to push opinions or value judgments (e.g., "Capital punishment is wrong") toward testable statements (e.g., "Capital punishment does not reduce crime" or "The criminal justice system can make wrongful convictions") by simply asking the question "Why?" after people make value judgments, and listening to the response. Once discussions and disagreements enter the realm of statements that can be tested, then relying on the science, data, and observable facts as arbiters of factual truth can push the Conversation forward, which is what I did when the fellas' emotions made them skeptical about the low representation of Black Fortune 500 CEOs.

RULE #2: MAKE PEOPLE FEEL AFFIRMED WHEN POSSIBLE

Feeling threatened or insecure can disrupt, even derail difficult conversations, particularly in their early stages. Science reveals that people are more open to inconvenient but factual truths when they feel personally affirmed, psychologically safe, and socially connected. When people feel wounded or threatened, they are more likely to disengage or lash out—which curtails real communication. There is an old saying, "An enemy is someone whose story you do not know." People's vulnerabilities stem from a prior history of wounds and difficult experiences. Take the time to build a relationship with the person you're having a Conversation with.

In their book *Difficult Conversations: How to Discuss What Matters Most,* Douglas Stone, Bruce Patton, and Sheila Heen posit that when individuals feel threatened, it often involves one of three core personal identities: "Am I competent?," "Am I a good person?," and "Am I worthy of love?"[3] Research has also shown that these identity triggers affect individuals from different social groups differently during interracial interactions. For example, White people are more likely to be triggered by information that suggests that they might be racist (i.e., "Am I a good person?"), whereas Black people are more likely to be triggered by information that indicates that they are not being respected (i.e., "Am I competent?").[4]

Being triggered has an effect not only on how we process information but also on how we interact with others. When we are angry or upset, we have a higher tendency to attribute malicious intent to others, and we have a lower ability to connect with and empathize with them. We are also less likely to receive what they are saying, no matter how valid the message might be. When we are heated up, what we hear becomes filtered and distorted, or we get so riled up we don't process anything at all.

With identity as a trigger, we can see how conversations on race can derail. White people who have built an identity around being a "good person" cannot imagine how they might be racist or contributing to a racist system. This sets up a big trigger for people of color—namely, White people getting defensive, or even passive-aggressive, when talking about race. Robin DiAngelo's book *White Fragility* goes into great detail about the many ways in which White people do this. One is by denying that racism has anything to do with them. If you still believe this, then go back and reread Chapters 1–7.

Another trigger is the belief that Black people are making up things and playing the race card. A third one is when White people position themselves as the victim in addition to, or instead of, Black people (remember the Irish American man from Chapter 3 who talked about not being able to get into the Boston Brahmins). DiAngelo talks in depth about White women's tears and how they can derail The Conversation. You are allowed to be emotional; just be mindful of its impact on others. If you believe it will be disruptive, consider stepping out for a moment.

White people have triggers too, such as when people of color assume that White people don't care or are not trying. Realistically, many White people don't care about systemic racism (as we will discuss in the next chapter), but I never make that assumption. Many do care. And there are some who don't care in the beginning but end up embracing the cause over time. So I give White people the benefit of the doubt until they prove that they are not invested in making the effort. Perhaps that's being too generous, but it's part of that hope and optimism that I spoke about in the introduction.

I also try to make them feel affirmed for even joining The Conversation. One benefit of White privilege is that you have the choice of opting out of conversations about race. Therefore, if a White person has made the decision that they want to talk about it and do something about it, then I acknowledge that investment while demanding they put in the work required to do it right.

RULE #3: FOCUS ON THE PROBLEM, NOT THE PERSON

Multiple studies have shown that people working together are more effective at solving complex problems than individuals working alone.[5] The downside is that having more than one person in the room also creates the possibility of conflict. Fortunately, not all conflict is created equal. Task-based conflict (as when a colleague says, "I think we would be more effective if we did it this way instead of that way") can enhance group performance and outcomes, even if people experience some tension and discomfort during the process. In contrast, person-based conflict (as when a colleague says, "I think you're an idiot for suggesting that we do it that way") is toxic and counterproductive.[6] Any conflict resulting from task-oriented problem solving will yield more fruitful outcomes than conflict characterized by personal attacks.

It's helpful to keep in mind that the "real" problem resides not in individual people but rather in the broader system or culture. Remember, it's more about the current than the fish swimming in it. This is not to excuse individual ignorance but rather to provide yet another reason why it makes more sense to focus on the problem rather than on the person.

RULE #4: SHOW CURIOSITY, NOT ANIMOSITY

When people are speaking in good faith (rather than disingenuously or with intent to offend), it makes more sense to listen with curiosity than to react defensively. This requires switching into "inquiry" mode versus "advocacy" mode.

Research outlines an important distinction between "inquiry," which involves seeking new information, pondering possibilities, asking questions, and listening to others, and "advocacy," which focuses on asserting arguments, making persuasive appeals, and trying to convince others. In initial Conversations, it is beneficial to start off in "inquiry" mode and to avoid the temptation of jumping too quickly into "advocacy" mode.

Consider the following two statements:

Everyone is different.
Everyone is similar.

Which is true? Clearly, they are both true to some degree. Thus, the real goal of someone who is seeking the truth is to talk about when, how, why, and how much each statement is true, rather than adopting a strong political or advocacy position that one is true and the other is false. Bear in mind that they do *not* have to be true to the same degree. Indeed, if we look at the totality of evidence, one statement might ring truer than the other. However, the goal is not "winning" but rather fostering a deeper understanding of the multifaceted nature of an issue in order to be better informed about solutions. If you immediately assume a strong stance and defend it, then you will miss out on a wealth of information. Adopting an inquiry mode also increases the likelihood that the other party will in turn listen to *you,* which may ultimately make your advocacy more effective. This is because listening to other people increases the likelihood that they will be more receptive to your ideas and suggestions.

One tactic for engaging curiosity and inquiry is to view oneself as a dispassionate juror during conversation, rather than a prosecutor or defender, who often operates in advocacy mode (in fact, the Latin word for *attorney* is *advocatus*). For attorneys in advocacy mode, the truth may be of secondary importance—the primary goal is gathering evidence to defend a position. Success is determined by whether that position aligns with a favorable verdict. To be sure, not all verdicts or outcomes reflect the truth, and when they don't, we call that injustice. In contrast, the job of the juror is to try to discern "what *really* happened" so that they can arrive at the truth—and therefore justice. *The Conversation* endeavors to embark on a journey toward truth and calls on you to be a juror.

I want to make it crystal clear that these rules are not mandates. They are merely a set of principles that have worked for *me* in most situations when leading Conversations with audiences composed of people from all different backgrounds and levels of awareness. In the section that follows, I provide a list of possible discussion topics that range in nature from informational (e.g., "What do you think about the data?") to testimonial (e.g., "How does this relate to you personally?") to ideological (e.g., "How does this affect your view of the world more broadly?").

As you build your Forum around the themes of Part 1, feel free to pick and choose any of the questions below, modify their wording to fit your needs or perspectives, or add completely new and different questions. These questions are meant to be Conversation starters, not Conversation fortresses.

CONVERSATION STARTERS

General Questions to Begin *The Conversation*

What do you think?

1. Ask yourself: What are three concepts, theories, studies, or statements that resonated with you from reading the chapters in this section?

   Was there anything in particular that you underlined, high-lighted, or wrote down that you'd like to share?

   What made this information so intriguing, powerful, or note-worthy to you?

2. What were some ideas that did *not* resonate with you—things that you took exception with? Which aspects of these ideas, studies, or findings did you find inaccurate, objectionable, or offensive?

3. Which concepts do you think your family/friends would have a hard time buying?

How do you feel?

1. How did you feel before you began reading the book?

    How do you feel now, after finishing Part 1? What did you learn that you did not know before? How has this information affected the way you feel?

    How do you feel about your role in The Conversation? Do you feel empowered by the information, or are you sad or nervous?

2. Did this reading highlight a personal trigger that you did not know you had? Can you name it? Was it connected to your identity? Was it connected to your values or morality? Was it connected to your sense of competence or self-worth? If so, what have you learned about the trigger?

3. Do you think the identity of the messenger impacts how you receive information about race?

How Much Awareness Is There Really?

1. In your network, community, or organization, have you seen a leader express genuine shock or disdain after a person of color raises an issue around race?

    What do you think contributes to these reactions?

    How have you responded in these situations? What barriers exist within you to speak out effectively?

2. How do you reconcile the two conflicting findings on White people's perceptions of racism reported in the data? On the one hand, data from Norton and Sommers and the surveys presented in Chapter 1 reveal that Whites tend to see the same amount of racism directed against them as against Blacks—if not more.

On the other hand, survey data from Chapter 3 revealed that only 1 percent of Whites believe that being White would hurt them "a lot" (and only 5 percent reported that it would hurt them at all).

So do White people believe that being White hurts them in the workplace, society, etc., or do they feel that it helps them? Or is it some complex combination? Do you think most White people would choose to be Black? If not, what does this say about their level of awareness?

3. Do you think there is motivated reasoning involved in how White people view racism, meaning that Whites can see themselves as being perpetrators, innocent bystanders, or even victims, depending on the context and/or what is convenient or advantageous?

4. Do you believe there is racism in your workplace? How do you know? What data, metrics, or evidence can be collected to convince others of this situation?

5. How do you think we can increase racism credence, or people's belief about the pervasiveness of racism? Or do you believe that people, like the fellas, for example, already know deep down? How are beliefs changing today around this concept? What factors are at play?

MORE FOOD FOR THOUGHT: CONVERSATION IN CONTEXT

Long Time Ago

Imagine that Ned Smith, a White man, knew my great-great-great-grandfather, Wallace Livingston, a free Black man who owned a general store in the mid-1800s. Wallace worked hard and, over the years, saved a lot of money, the equivalent of $10 million today. There were no reliable banks in his town, so he kept the money in his mattress. Ned got wind of the money and stole every penny of it while Wallace and his family were out one day. Wallace was financially ruined, and the family fell into poverty while Ned prospered. It was so much money that Ned shared it not only with his family but with the entire White community of one hundred people in the town where he resided, including the Preston family. Everyone knew about the theft, but none of the authorities did anything.

Fast-forward to the year 2021. I meet Brandon Smith, a descendant of Ned Smith. I present him with several pieces of evidence from the 1800s showing that his ancestor stole a fortune from my ancestor. His response is that it happened a long time ago and had nothing to do with him. He felt that he didn't do anything and was neither guilty nor responsible for the actions of his great-great-great-grandfather. I also run into Emily Preston, a descendant of the Preston family, who tells me that her great-great-great-grandfather never personally stole any money from anybody, so she definitely had no responsibility. They both insist that everything that they have is based on their own talent and hard work. They politely express their sympathy and wish me a good day.

First, sticking literally to the story, how would you characterize the reaction of Brandon? What about Emily? Are either of their responses appropriate, in your opinion? Do you think their responses would be different if it were Brandon's father who committed the misdeed, rather than his great-great-great-grandfather?

What do you think about their claims of meritocracy and being self-made?

Generalizing this scenario to the real world, many, if not most, White people argue that they had absolutely nothing to do with slavery. Many will further argue that their ancestors never even owned slaves. For example, Senate Majority Leader Mitch McConnell said, "I don't think that reparations for something that happened 150 years ago, for whom none of us currently living are responsible, is a good idea."[7]

How important is the distinction between being a perpetrator and creator of a corrupt and immoral scheme versus being an enabler, or just a beneficiary, of a corrupt and immoral scheme? Does it matter legally? Does it matter morally? Does it matter consequentially? Is it possible for any White person to be *completely* self-made?

How does this story further relate and generalize to other racial and ethnic groups, such as Native Americans in the United States?

Taking a Knee

A White male leader confided in me that he once felt opposed to NFL players kneeling during the national anthem. To him, the anthem was a tribute to our veterans, and it was wrong not to honor them. Now he sees it differently. Many of our veterans, past and present, are people of color who have also fought for America—ever since this country's very first war (e.g., Crispus Attucks). "Why wouldn't Colin Kaepernick take a peaceful stance in a spot that would bring attention to a problem?" this leader now asked. "What better stage could be picked to send a message? He's been trying to tell us something, but we weren't listening to him." I asked when this change of heart occurred, and he responded that it occurred after the murder of George Floyd.

The murder of George Floyd has had a profound impact on both the racism credence and the antiracism of Whites and other non-Blacks. Why do you think this is the case? Do you think that it's something that will have an enduring effect for decades to come, or is it like the images of the 1960s, such as the photograph of the lynched fourteen-year-old Emmett Till, or the televised images of Bloody Sunday in Selma—which had an immediate impact on people's attitudes and behaviors at the time but not decades later? What does White people's (negative) response to Black protest signal about their commitment to Black dignity and equality?

My Ancestors Made It. Why Can't Yours?

Some White people reason that every group who sailed across the Atlantic and arrived in the United States has faced hardships. For example, some may argue, rightfully so, that their ancestors arrived at

Ellis Island with nothing but the shirt on their back. They further argue that these White ancestors faced discrimination too but were able to make a life for themselves and their family through hard work and determination—with no "handouts" or "special favors." They wonder, then, why can't Black people do the same?

Have a Conversation about this issue, referring back to Chapter 3 if you need to. I realize that it is a fraught topic, and one that may be difficult to kick-start, so I offer some suggestions below for how you might go about framing the discussion.

1. **Skills and Preparation.** How is immigration fundamentally different from slavery? Do immigrant groups (Black and White alike) arrive with a certain set of skills and/or credentials that will assist them in building lives in their new country?

2. **Drive and Ambition.** When people come to the United States in search of a better life, how are their attitudes and mindsets likely to be different from those of people who were taken from a better life and forced into slavery? More important, how is the system likely to treat these two broad categories—native underclasses and newly arrived aspirational groups—differently?

3. **Race as Capital.** Do certain immigrant groups have an automatic advantage over other immigrant groups, even given the same level of preparation and aspiration? Does physical appearance facilitate assimilation for some groups more than others? Do certain laws based on physical appearance (e.g., segregation, miscegenation) also make life easier for some groups than others? Do you believe a caste system exists in America?

4. **Stereotypes as Capital?** If certain groups are rumored to be good at something, does that provide members of these groups with a leg up or create a positive self-fulfilling prophecy or stereotype boost, as discussed in Chapter 7? Specifically, if people from a certain group are seen as being good cooks, will that help them in the restaurant industry? Good woodworkers in

the building industry? Good bankers in the financial industry? Good athletes in the sports industry?

5. **Community Support.** Do some groups have a built-in network that aids success due to a strong and tight-knit community? Historically speaking, were African Americans permitted to show strong solidarity and support to one another? Or was loyalty to the Black community perceived as a threat to Whites—given that Blacks far outnumbered White people on Southern plantations? Were there deliberate measures put in place to "divide and conquer" and incentivize Black people to betray one another? Are there divisions within the Black community today that are the consequences of these colonial structures and practices?

6. How do all, or some subset, of the five factors above answer the opening question ("My ancestors made it. Why can't yours?")? Are there additional factors that can be brought to bear on this question? Do you think this question has profound implications for public opinion, public policy, and the continuation of structural racism in this country? Why or why not?

Do White People Need to Believe in Black Inferiority?

In the documentary *I Am Not Your Negro,* James Baldwin states in an interview (I'm replacing Baldwin's original use of the *N*-word with "n*****" to make The Conversation more comfortable for all involved): "What White people have to do is try to find out in their own hearts why it was necessary for them to have a [n*****] in the first place because I'm not a [n*****], I'm a man. If I'm not the [n*****] here, and you invented him, you the White people invented him, then you have to find out why. And the future of the country depends on that. Whether or not [America] is able to ask that question."

What do you think Baldwin meant? Based on what you read in Chapters 4 and 5, how might data support or refute his statement?

Baldwin posed this question over fifty years ago. Do you think that it is a question that is still relevant, and should be asked, today?

Shattering the Concept of Black Inferiority?

Related to the previous question, is the concept and presumption of Black inferiority made of glass or titanium? Is it something that can be shattered with a few hard blows or something that is extremely durable?

In 2020 Nicholas Johnson became the first Black valedictorian of Princeton in its nearly three-century history. Being the first Black valedictorian at Princeton is an unquestionable achievement.

Does this fact change White people's perceptions of Blacks as a group? What about all of the other examples of Black achievement over the past centuries? How many can you name? What would need to happen for White people to believe that Black people are as capable as Whites?

Or do White people not *want* to believe it? Do White people *need* to believe that Black people are inferior, as Baldwin suggested, because the idea of the successful Black farmer or Black Wall Street is much more threatening that the caricature of the "*N*-word"?

Beyond Anti-Blackness

How is anti-Black racism similar to or different from other forms of racism against other groups? What about sexism, ableism, and heterosexism? How is it similar? How is it different? Does anti-Blackness exist *within* communities of color? In other words, does "colorism," or negativity against darker-skinned group members, exist among Hispanics, Asians, and Native Americans? Does it exist among Black Americans too? Where do you think these prejudices come from?

The Lion and the Lamb

Research has found that police officers use less respectful language when dealing with Blacks compared with Whites, even when the severity of the offense is the same.[8] Is it possible that, as my colleague Naisha Bradley put it, police officers start off like a lion when they interact with Blacks, but start off like a lamb when they interact with Whites? In other words, do officers lead with an aggressive stance when dealing with Blacks and soften up if they notice that the situation is nonthreatening, whereas they lead with gentle stance with Whites and become tougher if they perceive that the situation is threatening?

First of all, do you believe that this is true? What concrete examples can you offer (e.g., Tamir Rice, armed White protesters at state capitols). If so, why might it be the case? Most important, what are the implications and consequences that you think this differential initial treatment of citizens, based only on race, has for escalation, incidents of brutality, trust between communities, etc.?

Part II

CONCERN

CHAPTER EIGHT

How Much Do White People Care About Racism?

I magine you and a colleague were chosen to participate in a free money giveaway. There are thousands of people at your organization, so chances are that you don't know the other person and will probably never meet them in the future. You have been chosen to be the sole decision maker for how money will be distributed between yourself and the other person. Once you make a decision, you will be given an envelope of money and the other person—who is in another room on a different floor—will be given an envelope of money, without knowing that you had anything to do with the decision. You have three options: A, B, or C.

	A	B	C
You Receive	$500	$500	$550
Other Receives	$100	$500	$300

If you choose option A, then you will receive an envelope with $500 and the other person will receive an envelope with $100. If you choose option B, then you will receive $500 and the other person will also receive $500. Finally, if you choose option C, you will receive

$550 and the other person will receive $300. The total sums are different in each option. The differences in sums between yourself and the other person are different in each option. You can't combine or mix and match offers—you have to choose either A, B, or C. Which option would you choose?

I will return to this example later in the chapter. (Have you detected a pattern by now?) In the meantime, let's begin our discussion of *Concern*. How much do White people care about racism, even when they acknowledge and understand it? The recent interest in Black Lives Matter and the various steps that organizations have taken to increase racial equity and inclusion—from Quaker Oats' plans to retire the Aunt Jemima brand and Mars's plan to end Uncle Ben's, to NFL commissioner Roger Goodell's reversal of the ban on national anthem protests and NASCAR's decision to ban the Confederate flag—suggest that people from all walks of life are beginning to take seriously the pervasiveness of systemic racism and the harm that it inflicts on people of color. But is this a movement or merely a moment?

Skeptics may assume it's the latter, arguing that we have seen this movie before. In the 1960s, for example, we witnessed a period of social unrest that led to increased White awareness around racism—followed by feelings of sympathy, empathy, or fear—and ultimately changes to some laws, policies, and practices. However, this temporary solidarity eventually reverted back to apathy and business as usual. Some scholars have argued that these conciliatory actions—throughout U.S. history—follow a very predictable pattern and are the result of appeasement efforts rather than an earnest interest in effecting real social change.

Research by Rosalind Chow and colleagues has shown that ordinary White people, especially those who tacitly support a racial hierarchy of White supremacy, experience substantial levels of discomfort when Blacks feel angry at Whites. They respond by increasing their support for diversity and equity-based initiatives, but they do so only until the racial hierarchy stabilizes and returns to the status quo. Therefore, the researchers argue that these initiatives are designed by prohierarchy Whites to appease people of color, rather than to dismantle the racial hierarchy.[1] The goal is to restore peace while preserving power, and appeasement can achieve a certain "peace on the plantation" that attains both objectives simultaneously. Judging from multiple objective measures, power differences have been maintained across the decades. Indeed, many racial disparities across a wide range of indices, such as wealth, health, education, and incarceration, just to name a few, are greater now than they were in the 1970s.

In addition to appeasement, other studies reveal evidence of apathy, or no response at all, when encountering racism. Unlike sympathy, which involves feelings of sorrow or pity toward the target of discrimination, or empathy, which entails experiencing the same emotions as the target of discrimination (e.g., righteous anger), apathy involves no emotional or behavioral response. A study published in the journal *Science* revealed apathy in the presence of blatant examples of anti-Black racism. The findings revealed that non-Black participants *believed* that they would be very upset and would respond negatively to a White person exhibiting overt racist behavior against a Black person. However, when these individuals were placed in an actual situation where they observed racist behavior firsthand, they were emotionally unaffected and behaviorally unresponsive.

In this experiment, Kerry Kawakami and colleagues brought non-Black participants into the laboratory to participate in a study with two fellow "students," one Black and one White (both actors). Participants were randomly assigned to one of three conditions in the study: no comment, mildly racist comment, and extremely racist comment. In all three conditions, the Black actor got up to briefly exit the room and on the way out gently brushed against the White actor's knee. In the no-comment condition, the White actor didn't say anything. In the mildly-racist-comment condition, once the Black actor was out of the room, the White actor said: "Typical. I hate it when Black people do that." In the extremely-racist-comment condition, once the Black actor was out of the room, the White actor said: "Clumsy n*****." Shortly afterward, participants had the opportunity to rate how they were feeling (e.g., upset), as well as to choose the Black or White actor to be their partner in a subsequent task.

In addition to these three scenarios in which participants were actually in the room as the incident unfolded ("experiencers"), other participants were randomly assigned to merely read about one of these three conditions and to indicate how they *would* feel if they were present and which person they *would* pick as their partner if they were in the room ("forecasters").

The data revealed that "forecasters" who read about a White person making a mildly racist or extremely racist comment reported that they would be much more upset than did "forecasters" where the White person made no comment at all about the Black person (see the graph on the following page). Similarly, the "forecasters" in the two scenarios in which a racist comment was made reported a lower intention to choose the White person as their interaction partner for a subsequent experiment—on average 17 percent of the time—compared with those in the no-comment condition, who reported the intention to choose the White person 68 percent of the time.[2]

However, those who were actually in the room when the incident happened—the "experiencers"—showed a very different pattern of emotions and behavior than people who merely read about the incident. "Experiencers" who witnessed the racist comments in person felt no more upset than those who were in the condition where no comment at all was made. These findings hold true regardless of whether emotions are measured via self-report (as in the current study) or using physiological measures of emotional arousal (e.g., cortisol level, skin conductance, heart rate).[3]

As shown in the graph, those in the no-comment condition chose the White actor to be their interaction partner in a subsequent experiment about 53 percent of the time, whereas those in the racist-comment conditions chose the White actor about 63 percent of the time, on average. So if anything, racist behavior led to a slightly increased likelihood of actually choosing the White actor over the Black actor as an interaction partner. In a nutshell, witnessing racism against Black people wasn't really all that upsetting to non-Blacks—and because they were not upset, they had no qualms about choosing the White actor as the interaction partner.

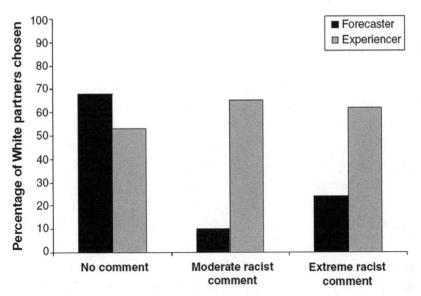

These findings have enormous implications for organizations, as people of color often have to deal not only with hostility from those who oppose diversity but also with indifference, or even complicity, from those who truly *believe* that they support diversity and racial justice. I have witnessed apathy in various forms (e.g., indifference, denial, dismissal of racism) at every job I've ever held. However, most similar to the Kawakami scenario was a situation that I encountered when I was still a student in graduate school. A White male student in the program ostensibly had no reservations about expressing overtly racist sentiments about Black people, and often used the *N*-word when doing so. Like the Black actor in the experiment, I was never in the room when it happened. There were a couple of White students who were disgusted by it and decided to cut ties with the individual (the one who informed me of the situation now has a Black spouse). But, similar to the experiment, this racist individual was not socially ostracized by the majority of the White students in the program. When it came time to pick an interaction partner, whether it was a roommate or a date, he was often chosen. In fact, he probably dated more women from the program than any other student—ultimately marrying one of them. This all took place in a liberal context of highly educated people earning doctorates in a field that is heavily focused on social justice.

These studies, and my anecdote, show examples of apathetic responses to blatant discrimination where some White people who honestly feel that they support racial equity also condone racism by doing nothing when they see it, or providing a half-hearted slap on the wrist. The likelihood of apathy only increases the more subtle the discrimination becomes. Everyday microaggressions—racial slights that are subtle and often inadvertent[4]—are often not even acknowledged as racism. And this White indifference can turn to White scorn when people of color complain about the real discrimination that they face within organizations.[5] The stories of Black people being ignored or trivialized when they bring up examples of microaggressions at work are too countless to list. They are often told: "Oh, you're being too sensitive." "I don't think she meant it that way." "There must be some misunderstanding. . . . I know Johnny isn't racist." "I wasn't there, so I don't know." "Just try to ignore it and get your work done." These dismissive responses often end up enabling racism. Other types of microaggressions (e.g., a higher tendency to interrupt people of color who are speaking, ignoring input from people of color, or displaying cold or hostile nonverbal behaviors) manifest racism directly—so much so that some scholars and practitioners have begun using the term *racial harassment,* in place of *microaggression,* to convey the seriousness of their impact.

Some of this indifference can be attributed to White people not being willing or able to recognize discrimination or intentionally deciding to remain blind to it. But in the aforementioned study, the experiencers saw it and heard it themselves. There is little room for misinterpretation. Most of them simply didn't care. This chapter will more closely examine why many White people experience little concern about racism, exploring three distinct but interrelated factors: tribalism, self-interest, and moral values.

TRIBALISM AND GROUP DYNAMICS

Research suggests that many White people not only tolerate but appreciate racism from other Whites because it signals loyalty to the in-group. For example, Italian researchers have found that White school-age children prefer White children who play exclusively with other White children to White children who are seen playing with a Black child.[6] They have found similar results with Italian adults, who *overtly* reject racist behavior from other Whites but *tacitly* approve of such behavior because the perpetrators are seen as loyal in-group members.[7]

Of course, these results are not confined to Italy. In the United States, White people with implicit racial biases express greater affinity toward White people who do not feel comfortable around Black people than toward White people who do feel comfortable around Black people.[8] Even explicitly egalitarian White people who happen to hold implicit racial biases show a preference for Whites who feel uncomfortable around Black people. Moreover, we have both anecdotal and empirical evidence, from the United States and multiple Western countries, of broad (not fringe) White support of White political candidates who explicitly express pro-White and overtly racist and anti-immigrant sentiments.[9] Again, the underlying rationale seems to be that White people who express racism are signaling loyalty, or White solidarity,[10] which elevates their status among other Whites, on average.

In addition to increasing the standing of the White person who is expressing racism, these incidents can also decrease the status of the Black person who suffers the racism. In other words, when White people observe a Black person being discriminated against, they tend to think less of the Black person who is the target of the discrimination—not the White perpetrator of the discrimination. Thus, racism becomes a perverse type of status signal, sending the message that if people are discriminating against you, then it must mean that you are not worth much. This paradoxical idea might help to explain why participants in the Kawakami study were more likely to select the White actor and shun the Black actor as an interaction partner after he was called the N-word by the White actor, despite believing that they would have been less likely to choose the White actor.

There is scientific data to support the idea that racism further stigmatizes the victim in the eyes of bystanders. One study showed that overhearing a Black person being referred to as the N-word by a

White person further lowered perceptions of the competence of the *Black* person.[11] In another study, participants read the transcript from a courtroom trial in which a Black or White attorney represented a White defendant. Similar to the Kawakami study, there were three conditions: one in which a White actor, posing as a participant, said nothing; one in which he referred to the Black lawyer as a "shyster"; and one in which he referred to the Black lawyer as a "n*****." Similar to the previous study, overhearing the Black lawyer being referred to as a racial slur led to more negative evaluations of the Black lawyer. Moreover, the participants gave harsher verdicts to the White defendant represented by the Black lawyer who was called a racial slur.[12] These results even extend to nonverbal behavior, with one study showing that when Whites exhibited negative nonverbal behavior toward Blacks, this "contaminated" other White observers' evaluations, leading Whites to judge the Black receiver of the negative nonverbal vibes more negatively than they did the Black person who received positive nonverbal vibes. The researchers did not find the same results when a White person received negative nonverbal behavior from another White person—the negativity vibes affected only the judgments of Blacks.[13]

These results all point to the fact that racism is a double whammy for Black people—serving as both insult and injury. Not only do Black targets of racism suffer the psychological damage and emotional abuse of the insult, but their social and professional image may also be diminished in the eyes of White observers of the incident. There are a number of social and political implications of these findings. The first is that Black lives are continuing to be damaged while White people remain indifferent or complicit. The second implication is that if White people tend to be emotionally unmoved by what happens to Black people,[14] then White people may need to be involved before other Whites will take notice. This was arguably the case during the civil rights movement, when White involvement catalyzed national support for the Black cause. In one horrific incident, known as the Freedom Summer murders, a Black activist, James Chaney, and two White activists, Andrew Goodman and Michael Schwerner, were abducted and killed in June 1964 after meeting with members of the Black community to promote voting rights in Mississippi. Rita Schwerner, the widow of Michael Schwerner, was quoted in the history documentary *Eyes on the Prize* as saying, "It's tragic that White Northerners have to be caught up into the machinery of injustice and indifference in the South before the American people register concern. I personally suspect that if Mr. Chaney [the Black man] had been alone at the time of the disappearance, that this case, like so many others that have come before, would have gone completely unnoticed."

Fast-forward five decades to the Black Lives Matter movement and the brutal violence perpetrated on Eric Garner, Freddie Gray, Sandra Bland, Tamir Rice, Breonna Taylor, Trayvon Martin, Ahmaud Arbery, Philando Castile, and so many others—if the same harm had been inflicted on White men and women, would the system have been reformed decades ago? White people may become concerned when there are particularly vivid and visceral incidents, such as the murders of Emmett Till and George Floyd, but the default response for many Whites, when harm is done to Black people, is low concern. Similarly, if the victims of the 1980s crack epidemic had been White and suburban rather than Black and urban, then it would have been treated as a public health issue rather than a criminal justice issue—like the opioid epidemic of the 2010s.[15] If the staggering death toll caused by COVID-19 disproportionately afflicted young, slender, wealthy, White people, rather than elderly, obese, poor, Black and Brown people—those considered less "valuable" by society—then the pandemic would have been taken much more seriously by citizens and politicians alike.

All of these examples point to the fact that tribalism strongly determines concern—so much so that White people often prioritize their comfort over Black harm. Several sources chronicle the importance of White women's tears, both in terms of how the distress of White women can take priority over real harm that is occurring to Black people and also with regard to how the distress of White women can be weaponized against Black people.[16] The whole world witnessed this weaponization of White distress in the 2020 case of Amy Cooper—the Central Park dog walker discussed in Chapter 4.

Disregard for Black harm relative to White comfort can assume multiple forms. Another example comes from a Black colleague of mine at Harvard. When he was in his midtwenties he interned in the UK for a member of the House of Lords. Lord Avebury, a White civil rights advocate in England, was a presiding member of the Parliamentary Human Rights Committee in the 1990s. He invited my colleague, Rob, to come to his home to start working on a project. Being excited about the work, Rob arrived early and sat on the front porch quietly waiting for Lord Avebury to get home. When some of the neighbors saw him there, they decided to call the police. The police arrived and began to aggressively question him. Despite calmly explaining that he worked for Lord Avebury, he ended up being thrown to the ground by the officers as they went through his backpack (finding only papers and briefs). While he was pinned facedown on the ground, Lord Avebury arrived—appearing baffled and bothered by the incident—and asked the officers why they had Rob on the ground. He explained to the officers that Rob was working for him, at which point they began apologizing profusely to Lord Avebury.

What's noteworthy about the incident is that the officers never uttered one word to Rob after Lord Avebury arrived. During their obsequious interchange with Lord Avebury, Rob was left on the ground like a sack of potatoes. No one apologized. No one attempted to give any context or explanation. No one offered to help him up. Once he was no longer the target of physical aggression, he essentially became invisible. The officers were very concerned about how Lord Avebury felt but showed no regard whatsoever for Rob. After they were finished with the apology and explanation to Lord Avebury, they got in their car and left.

The main point here is that decisions, behaviors, and public policy are profoundly affected by whether the beneficiaries seem familiar, endearing, or relatable. Perhaps this explains why White people's responses to Bosnian or Syrian refugees are often quite different from their responses to Sudanese or Rwandan refugees. People have a higher tendency to care for and empathize with those whom they perceive as being similar to themselves. For these reasons and others, psychologist Paul Bloom, author of *Against Empathy,* believes that we would be much kinder and fairer people if we did *not* allow empathy to influence whether we help others. In the book, he states that the capacity to feel "what you think others are feeling—whatever one chooses to call this—is different from being compassionate, from being kind, and most of all, from being good." This interesting and provocative argument contends that empathy is not a necessary ingredient for the promotion of social justice. Rather, people's actions and decisions should be based on what Bloom calls *rational compassion*.

In describing what he means by this term in the book, he states, "We are smart enough to intellectually grasp that the lives of those in faraway lands (people who aren't related to us, don't know us, don't wish us well) matter just as much as the lives of our children. . . . We can appreciate that favoring one's own ethnic group or race, however natural and intuitive it feels, can be unfair and immoral. And we can act to enforce impartiality—for instance, by creating policies that establish certain principles of impartial justice."[17] Empirical research also makes a distinction between empathy and desire to help (similar to rational compassion) and has shown that the latter more strongly predicts people's actual behaviors and prosocial actions.[18]

In short, our social identification and emotional connection with racial groups can affect the extent to which we experience empathy or apathy. As suggested by Bloom, one escape hatch is to focus on one's conscious and deliberate commitment to help others, rather than the extent to which one can emotionally relate to others. But part of this commitment will depend on how much people care about other people in general, versus being concerned only about themselves. In addition to social group dynamics, concern can also be affected by people's prosocial orientation toward others relative to their investment in their own individual self-interest.

SELF-INTEREST, SHARING, AND COOPERATION PREFERENCES

Apart from tribalism, and the dehumanization that often accompanies it, another reason that many White people are not more concerned about racism has to do with simple self-interest. Let's return to the example from the beginning of the chapter. Which option did you choose: $500/$100, $500/$500, or $550/$300?

Research has shown that these choices reflect "social value orientations," or sharing tendencies with others. These tendencies typically fall into one of three categories: prosocial, individualist, or competitor.[19] Prosocials are those who are concerned about community and equality. They seek to increase joint outcomes for the entire collective, and they like to distribute those outcomes in a relatively equal way.[20] In this case, the option of $500/$500 provides a total of $1,000 to the "community," broadly construed, as well as equal amounts to each person.

On the other hand, there are two different "proself" sharing tendencies where the primary goal is to advance one's own self-interest. Individualists are those who seek to maximize personal outcomes, *regardless* of other people's outcomes. They would take the $550/$300 option. This increases personal gain because one ends up with $50 more than with any other option. What's important to understand is that this choice is indifferent to what the other person gets—they could receive $300, $100, $0, or even $600. It doesn't really matter. The primary focus is on maximizing gains for oneself, and little attention is paid to the sum allocated to the other person.

The second type of "proself" tendency is where people seek to maximize their personal gain *relative* to other people. In contrast to the individualist, who is indifferent to what other people get, the competitor is very focused on what others receive because their primary aim is to maximize the *difference* between their outcomes and everyone else's. They would pick the $500/$100 option, because the difference between what they get and what the other person gets is $400—the highest disparity of all the options. Their objective is "beating" the other person, even if it means less money in their own pocket (in this case, $50, because they could have gone with the $550/$300 individualist option). To the competitor, life is a zero-sum game with clear winners and losers. The big-picture implication is that competitors tend to have a strong commitment to inequality and are even willing to incur a cost to establish and maintain dominance over others. To give a simple summary, prosocials are strongly invested in equality, competitors are strongly invested in *in*equality, and individualists can go either way depending on what's in it for them.

These different sharing tendencies are important to understand because they shed light on people's preferences for how resources should be allocated, as well as their broader social philosophies and orientation to the world. Suppose you were extremely wealthy, with a beautiful mansion overlooking the sea. Most of the other citizens in your community live in dilapidated shacks with no running water or electricity. One day you discover a magic lamp and a genie appears, granting you the power to change your community. At your wish, the coastline could be magically extended and everyone in the community would have a beautiful mansion by the sea, allowing them to enjoy the good life too. Would you command the genie to transform the neighborhood in this way? Prosocials certainly would. For them, it would be a win-win situation, because they would be "expanding the pie," growing the entire community's wealth, as well as distributing it more evenly among everyone.

For individualists, it would depend on what they would stand to gain or lose. If having more people on the coast increased the tax base of the city, providing better schools for their children and raising property values, then they would be all for it. However, if the influx of people created more traffic and noise without countervailing benefits, then they would likely be against commanding the inclusive coastline expansion.

Competitors are likely to oppose the expansion no matter what. After all, what is the point of having a mansion on the coast if it isn't a trophy and object of envy? You need "have-nots" in order to be one of the "haves." One interesting observation is that competitors are more interpersonally invested than individualists because they actually pay attention to other people's outcomes (even if only to outperform them), whereas individualists tend to ignore other people's outcomes altogether. This distinction between dominance and indifference is overshadowed by the shared tendency of both individualists and competitors to elevate their own personal interest over the greater good, which makes them "proself" rather than prosocial. Research has found that most of the differences in political, economic, and social preferences are explained by the prosocial-versus-proself distinction, and not by the individualist-versus-competitor distinction.

The neighborhood example that I just provided is not that far from reality. Decades of research have linked these different sharing tendencies to political conservatism (e.g., tolerance for economic inequality), racial prejudice, right-wing authoritarianism, and social dominance orientation (discussed in Chapters 4 and 5), with prosocial individuals scoring lower on all of the aforementioned variables than proself individuals (i.e., individualists and competitors combined).[21] For example, one study found that prosocial individuals tended to score higher than proself individuals on questions such as whether "all races, religions, and nations of the world have the same value" and "schools should teach more about the culture and religion of other countries."[22]

These sharing tendencies are also related to people's perceptions of morality. For example, if someone reneges on a promise or fails to reciprocate kindness or generosity, prosocial individuals are more likely than proself individuals to get angry and view it as a violation of justice or morality.[23] On the other hand, proself individuals are more likely to associate cooperation and generosity with weakness or stupidity and lack of cooperation with strength or intelligence.[24] These divergent reactions are partly explained by the level of trust in others.[25] That is, prosocials are more likely to approach a situation with the default assumption that people are trustworthy, fair, and cooperative, whereas proself individuals are more likely to believe that the world is a dangerous game where you either eat or get eaten.[26] Proself individuals expect opportunism and self-serving behavior from others, so they are relatively unfazed when they encounter it. Prosocial individuals, on the other hand, expect integrity and cooperation from others, so they become infuriated when they run into people who are unscrupulous and opportunistic.

All of this has tremendous implications for how prosocial and proself people view "fairness" and morality more broadly. Proself

individuals are much less likely than prosocials to be morally outraged when businesspeople or politicians lie, cheat, steal, or stab
their best friend in the back to get ahead. They either shrug it off as
being the way life is or applaud it as shrewd self-promotion. They
can watch businesspeople break promises or witness world leaders
violate treaties and shirk obligations, and they either react with indifference or give the selfish actor a cigar and a pat on the back. On
the other hand, prosocials are more likely to be repulsed by what
they would view as "dishonorable" and immoral behavior. To take
a fictitious and facetious example, prosocials might be less likely
than proselfs to cheer for the Lannisters than the Starks when
watching *Game of Thrones*. But (spoiler alert to those who are woe-
fully behind in the series) consistent with the final outcome of the
series, real life also shows that those with honor are neither weak
nor stupid and sometimes win the marathon, even if they lag behind in the sprint.[27]

There are two million-dollar questions here. The first is: What
percentage of the population falls into these three categories? When I
present the opening options to audiences, not surprisingly, about 90
percent of them claim that they would choose B, or $500/$500, with
nearly all of the rest choosing C, or $550/$300. I have only had a small
handful of people choose A, $500/$100, in public. But what do you
think is the actual proportion of people who choose competitor, prosocial, and individualist options in private, when there are real points
or money on the line? Do you think it corresponds to the 1 percent/90
percent/9 percent distribution? Bear in mind the Kawakami study—
what people say they would do, hypothetically, is often very different
from what they really do, in actuality.

One meta-analysis of multiple samples shows that about 46 percent of the population are prosocials—accounting for the largest percentage of the three—whereas 38 percent are individualists, and
about 12 percent are competitors (with 4 percent uncategorizable).[28]
Another large sample put those numbers at 52 percent, 37 percent,
and 11 percent, respectively.[29] The exact numbers are difficult to pin
down and will depend on numerous sampling, geographic, and cultural factors. However, it's safe to assume that about half the popula-

tion is prosocial and the other half is proself. What's striking about the 11 percent estimate of competitors in the latter study is that this is exactly the same as the percentage of White respondents in the 2019 E Pluribus Unum survey who reported that equity, or the "fair opportunity for everyone to attain their full potential regardless of demographic, social, economic or geographic status," was *not* important to moving the country forward (87 percent thought that it was important, and 2 percent offered no response).

A *really* important difference between individualists and competitors is that the former will engage in prosocial behavior if convinced that they themselves can benefit from it in the long run, whereas it's extremely difficult to get competitors to engage in prosocial behavior no matter what.[30] The bright side is that it's possible, at least in theory, to get close to 90 percent of the population to get on board with a prosocial agenda, with the right logic and incentives. A supermajority of that magnitude could really change the world, in a democratic system. But competitive individuals disproportionately wind up in positions of power because they are more attracted to power, and more willing to do whatever it takes to attain and maintain powerful positions.[31] People who are more competitive and dominant are often perceived as being more competent, regardless of their actual competence,[32] and often end up being empowered by prosocials and individualists.[33]

The second million-dollar question is: What do seaside villas, monetary allocations, and sagas with fire-breathing dragons have to do with concern about racism? At the root of all of these examples is the foundational consideration of power and self-interest. As I mentioned in Chapter 5, if we had to summarize the origins of racism in one word, it would be *power*—not hatred, not color, not crime, not segregation. Slavery was not perpetrated as a personal vendetta against African people. It was done to seize resources and power, both in the individualistic sense (more money is better) and in the competitive sense (my group having more privilege relative to other groups is better). But even during slavery there were prosocial White people (e.g., abolitionists) who believed that the system should be more equal and either begrudgingly conformed to the status quo or actively resisted it, going against the current like a school of salmon.

These sharing tendencies are empirically related to social, political, and economic tendencies because they capture how people approach the world in relation to others. Do you care about the outcome of the person in the other room? Do you care about the outcomes of those living outside your neighborhood? Any solution to racism will involve sharing of resources and hence power, and some people simply don't want to share. What they want is "peace on the plantation," where subordinate groups accept their position without resistance or resentment. Power is more important to them than equity. In the next section, we will take a closer look at what is important to people—as reflected by their values. All of this information will be critical to understanding both the perpetuation of the problem of racism and people's diverse perspectives during The Conversation.

THE SCIENCE OF HUMAN VALUES

Values reflect what is truly important to us in life. Social psychologist Shalom Schwartz has spent decades studying what is important to people across dozens of countries and how these values are linked to their judgments, decisions, and behaviors. This research reveals a number of fascinating findings. One is that we humans have a finite number of core, universal values that tend to be clustered in a predictable way. Across cultures and individuals, human values can be summarized by ten categories that compete with one another in a systematic manner.[34] There are values related to determining one's own path in life (e.g., self-direction) that are the opposite of values that express the importance of going along with established norms (e.g., conformity, tradition). And related to our discussion of sharing tendencies, there are values associated with enhancing your own outcomes (e.g., power, achievement) that are the opposite of values that are about helping and supporting other people in your community (i.e., benevolence) or the world more broadly (i.e., universalism).

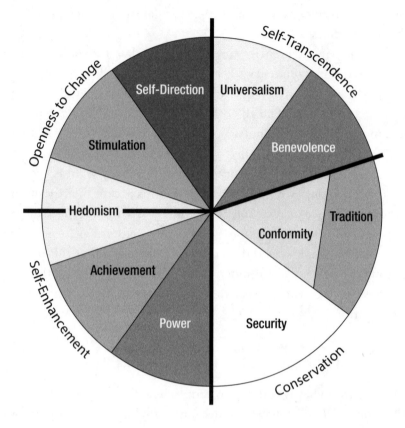

What the researchers have found is that, all over the world, these ten values can be statistically clustered into a circular pattern where adjacent values positively correlate with each other while values that are located across the wheel from each other are negatively correlated. For example, people who value universalism, or social justice, also tend to value benevolence and helping out others in their community. People who value universalism, however, tend not to place a high premium on money and power. You might ask, What if someone values both money and social justice? The way the values are measured takes into account your *relative* prioritization of values, or which ones are more important than the others.[35] There are tremendous differences in what is important to different people, and research has shown that these values explain not only how we see the world but our actions as well.[36]

What values do you think are important to an executive who raises the price of a life-saving drug, like Daraprim, 5,000 percent in one month—meaning that a patient would wake up one day to learn that a pill that cost $40 the previous month now costs $2,040? What about a White Baptist preacher who conspires to murder three young people in their early twenties whose only crime is helping Black people exercise their legal right to vote? Finally, what do you think are the values of someone who refuses to wear a face covering in public during an outbreak of a highly contagious disease? And what do you think is important to an NFL player who is willing to risk his professional career to stand up for the dignity of all people?

It's possible that Martin Shkreli (aka Pharma Bro), the notorious pharmaceutical executive who increased the price of Daraprim by 5,000 percent, values both money and helping patients in need. But clearly he values money much more. Colin Kaepernick, the former NFL player who knelt during the national anthem to protest racial injustice, probably valued money and achievement, but he obviously valued social justice much more. Understanding a person's values is important because their values can determine their behaviors. Values are generally stable but can sometimes shift. Would Kaepernick have taken a knee if he had a spouse and three children? No one can say for certain. If the situation called for a trade-off between what was best for his immediate family (i.e., benevolence) and what was best for the world (i.e., universalism), then he might have chosen family. Or perhaps, like Nelson Mandela, he would have chosen what was better for the world over what was better for his family.

People often see power as being "dirty" or corrupt. However, it's important to distinguish between the value of power as an end and power as a means to obtaining another valued goal or outcome. One cannot deny that Mandela, Gandhi, and Dr. Martin Luther King, Jr., all had tremendous power. But they used their power to bring about universalism. Stated differently, theirs was more of an uplifting "power to" than an oppressive "power over." One could argue that there is some element of "power to" embedded in all of the values—the power to define one's own path in life (self-direction), the power to party and have a good time (hedonism), the power to protect oneself (security), and the power to promote social justice in the world (universalism). This is distinct from the value of power in the Schwartz model, which is an end unto itself, manifested as "power over" people, resources, decisions, and outcomes.

This chapter reveals that not everyone cares about people. Some are more concerned with power and resources. And even those who do care about other people are not always responsive to racism when they see it, because of tribalism. The challenge then becomes, How do we get everyone to show greater concern for racism and become invested in its eradication? Three broad approaches are "carrots" (incentives/rewards), "sticks" (disincentives/punishments), and "better angels" (moral appeals). Each approach will have a different degree of effectiveness for different people or contexts. For example, carrots might be the most effective approach when dealing with individualists, because they are more likely to respond when something is in it for them, even if that something is the chance to feel good or look good. In a corporate setting, these are the people most likely to resonate with the "business case" for diversity or to engage in "window dressing" and adopt diversity initiatives to promote the company's image.

Sticks might be the most effective (or *only*) way to get competitors to be more inclusive. It is difficult to persuade them to cooperate—they won't be egalitarian or inclusive unless they are strongly compelled to do so. For them, it truly is a "game of thrones" where "might is right." Further complicating the matter is that this 11 to 12 percent is not randomly distributed. They tend to disproportionately occupy positions of power, so they have a disproportionate impact on culture.

Prosocials truly care about other people and their community. For them to be more antiracist, you need to appeal to their better angels by educating, inspiring, and empowering them to invest in racial justice. Too many carrots might offend them and too many sticks might break their spirit.

To be clear, competitors are not necessarily antisocial, individualists are not mercenary, and prosocials don't all promote social justice. It's much more complicated than that. I am using these social value orientation categories as a loose interpretative lens for understanding differences in people's approach to others, rather than a literal assessment or diagnosis of who people are. The key idea here is that increasing concern and compliance does not take a one-size-fits-all approach. Effectively addressing racism requires a deeper understanding of people's motives and values and therefore what they will respond to: carrots, sticks, or better angels. As mentioned in the introduction, KITA (kick in the "pants") will only get you so far when it comes to motivating people and therefore creating profound and sustainable change.

My own perspective is fairly aligned with that of Michelle Alexander, author of the bestselling book *The New Jim Crow*. She writes:

> I no longer believe we can "win" justice simply by filing lawsuits, flexing our political muscles or boosting voter turnout. Yes, we absolutely must do that work, but none of it—not even working for some form of political revolution—will ever be enough *on its own*. Without a moral or spiritual awakening, we will remain forever trapped in political games fueled by fear, greed and the hunger for power [italics added].[37]

The question then becomes: How do we create that moral awakening? Why *should* White people care about racism?

CHAPTER NINE

The Moral Cost of Condoning Racism

Which of the two scenarios below would you judge as being more "fair"? In the scenario on the left, each individual receives an equal number of crates to stand on, but not everyone can see the soccer game. In the scenario on the right, each person receives a different number of crates, but everyone can enjoy the game. We will return to these scenarios, and an alternative version of them, in a few pages.

ILLUSTRATION © 2020 JOAN M. K. TYCKO

As we learned in Chapter 8, not all White people are bothered by the existence of racism—due to tribalism, differing propensities toward self-interest, or the relative importance of self-transcendent values. In addition, many White people may be apathetic because they do not believe that racism really exists (Chapter 1)—or they believe that even if it does, they have no personal role in creating or perpetuating it (Chapters 2–4). Regardless of the reasons underlying this indifference, the next two chapters make the case that *everyone* should be concerned about racism, for moral or practical reasons, respectively. Chapter 9 focuses on the moral case by exploring philosophical and scientific notions of what it means to be a good human being and examining how racism violates basic standards of moral decency.

Morality has been a topic of philosophical inquiry for millennia. More recently, it has become the subject of scientific investigation. In this chapter, I'll use our current scientific understanding of morality to examine why apathy toward racism is problematic. One of the most prominent, scientifically validated theories of morality today is the "five foundations" model developed by social psychologists Jon Haidt and Jesse Graham. The model proposes five basic foundations of morality: two that define morality for almost everyone (fairness, harm) and three that serve as moral domains for certain individuals or cultures (loyalty, authority, purity).[1] The first foundation of morality—fairness/justice—dictates that people should judge and treat others fairly. But what exactly does it mean to be fair?

Suppose you and three other people go out to dinner and each of you orders different items from the menu. The total bill comes to $200. What is the "fair" way to split the tab among the four of you? If you were to ask a roomful of people, you would likely get a variety of responses. Some might believe that splitting the bill four ways, with each person paying $50, is the fairest (and easiest) way to do it. Others might not see an even split as fair because each person ordered different dishes—the person who ordered the filet mignon should pay $70, while the person who ordered the less-expensive Cobb salad should only owe $30. Finally, others might contend that fairness depends on who is attending the dinner. A professor dining with three graduate students or a parent dining with three children might pay the entire $200, with the other three contributing $0. Similarly, it might be okay for someone to pay $0 if it was her birthday, even if she ordered the filet mignon, while the other three split the $200. What all of these conceptions of fairness have in common is that they seek to establish a balance between the outcome (i.e., payment) and some input—the number of people present, the cost of each person's meal, the relative financial means of each individual, or some consideration of merit.

These various conceptions of fairness can be roughly classified into two categories—equality and equity. Equality means that everyone gets the same thing—or in this case, everyone pays the same amount. Equity means that the outputs vary based on some input variable—such as the price of the dish you ordered or what you can afford to pay. Our progressive tax system in the United States, and in most countries of the world, is designed on the principle of equity. The percentage of tax that you pay varies as a function of your income, the assumption being that wealthy people can afford to pay more while still living very comfortably, compared with people who barely make enough money to scrape by.[2]

Thus, equity entails treating people differently, but in a way that makes sense. There is a logic behind why the person who ordered the steak would pay more than the person who ordered the salad. It makes sense that the multimillionaire would pay a higher tax rate than the person whose income is at the poverty line. Some people do not buy this argument, however. Indeed, many wealthy people are wholeheartedly in favor of a flat tax. There is no objectively right or wrong perspective on what is fair, and judgments of fairness will subjectively depend on a wide array of factors, including self-interest, social values, and ideological beliefs, as well as attitudes toward the recipients of resources. This will become clearer as we move through the chapter.

For now, let's return to the illustrations of the soccer spectators that opened the chapter. Which scenario did you select as being more fair? If you chose the scenario on the right—and most people do—then you made an equity-based judgment of fairness rather than an equality-based judgment of fairness. In other words, you subscribe to the notion that "fairness" can require treating people differently—as each individual in that scene receives a different number of crates. This concept may challenge some individuals and organizations who embrace the notion that fairness requires treating everyone exactly the same. But if you think about it, we rarely treat people the same when we are striving to be fair. For example, if you have more than one child, it is likely that you treat them differently due to their different ages, personalities, needs, and challenges. But your treatment is nevertheless equitable because the toddler may need to be spoon-fed whereas the eight-year-old may not. Similarly, a child with a confident and independent personality may require less guidance and attention than a child who is more diffident and dependent. In our families, we know that fairness doesn't always call for equal treatment.

What about organizations? Should they treat all of their applicants and employees the same? Should a business school admissions committee treat an applicant with a 3.9 GPA who grew up in an affluent, supportive family with access to tutors the same as an applicant with a 3.9 GPA from the same high school who grew up in poverty, working after school and on weekends, and shouldering the responsibility of caring for five younger siblings at home? A 3.9 GPA despite tremendous hardship shows resilience. Wouldn't that be an important quality for a business school student, and future leader, to possess?

While many of us share the intuition that the student from the socially disadvantaged background should be given a chance over the student with the supportive background—not due to pity and sympathy but due to sheer logic and reason—some critics might argue that equitable treatment results in lower standards and therefore will have the effect of reducing the overall quality of the institution. Flip back to the illustrations that opened the chapter. If we think of height as being analogous to competence or intelligence, then one could claim that the little guy on the right is less "qualified" than the other two people. Why should the organization allocate extra crates to prop up the "short" person who simply isn't able to see over the fence?

Now let's look at a different way of conceptualizing the scenario with a second pair of illustrations:

ILLUSTRATION © 2020 JOAN M. K. TYCKO

Here, everyone is the same "height." But this time the ground under their feet differs in elevation, and the fence in front of them differs in height. We can think of the elevation of the ground as analogous to privilege and the height of the fence as analogous to discrimination. In this case, providing extra crates does not prop up a "shorter" person—it merely corrects for external barriers and hardships that have nothing to do with the height of the person, or their inherent potential. In these circumstances, are we morally obligated to treat each person *differently* in order to provide *equal* access when there is an unlevel playing field?

Different treatment is not the same as "special" treatment. The latter is based on pure favoritism or cronyism, not need, merit, obstacles, or other criteria of commensuration. The scenarios presented in this chapter make us recognize that different treatment is not the same as special treatment. Indeed, sometimes fairness requires different treatment, particularly when there are different needs or obstacles. In an environment devoid of external barriers—where the ground is level and the fence is equal height (or absent altogether)—fairness could boil down to everyone being treated equally. In the absence of a level playing field, however, one could argue that the failure to treat people differently is the real violation of fairness—not the failure to treat everyone the same. Equal treatment in the face of unlevel playing fields and disparate barrier heights merely perpetuates systems of injustice that are already in place.

FAIRNESS VERSUS ENTITLEMENT

Imagine a mom, Betty, who has identical twelve-year-old twins, Frances and Zelda. Betty bakes a batch of butter cookies every Sunday, and she gives Frances four cookies and Zelda zero cookies every day of the week. Although both kids love butter cookies, Betty gives them all to Frances, her favorite child. When other parents catch wind of the situation, they are outraged. In response to social pressure, Betty decides to change her policy and starts giving Zelda one cookie a day and reduces Frances's allocation to three. Betty is surprised to learn that, as a result of her new allocation, instead of having one child who's unhappy about the cookie situation, she now has two disgruntled kids. Zelda is angry because she still doesn't believe the situation is fair, and Frances is furious because, despite the fact that she is getting three times more cookies than Zelda, it is still fewer cookies than she is used to receiving. Therefore, Frances now feels *deprived*.

Although Frances's reaction might make sense from a purely emotional perspective—she *feels* that she has been treated unfairly—from a more objective standpoint her umbrage stems from what I would consider to be a sense of entitlement rather than principled fairness. Because she has grown accustomed to receiving four cookies—regardless of whether it was ever fair or not—Frances now feels cheated. It doesn't even occur to her that she's been receiving an unearned cookie bonus all these years, thanks to Betty's favoritism. For Frances, bounty is the "normal" state of affairs. This example illustrates that *perceptions* of fairness can be based entirely on habit or history and the expectations they create about future outcomes. Objective considerations of social justice fall out of the picture completely.

This story gets to the heart of how many White people see merit and fairness in the workplace. Some leaders voice concern that diversity initiatives will be perceived as unfair because they result in "discrimination" against White men. However, as the story illustrates, there is a big difference between fairness/justice and entitlement/satisfaction. Whether something *feels* fair and whether it *is* fair are not one and the same. Growing accustomed to an imbalanced status quo can bias perceptions of fairness. Allow me to clarify what I mean.

Until the midtwentieth century, White men held 100 percent of the top executive positions in corporate America and in the executive branch of the U.S. government, despite the fact that they were less than 40 percent of the population. Is that fair? Today that representation ranges from 80 to 90 percent of all top leadership positions, despite the fact that White men compose about 30 percent of the population. There are at least two ways to interpret the situation. One is that the situation is unfair to White men because in the past they held 100 percent of Fortune 500 CEO positions, for example, but now they hold "only" 90 percent of those positions. Therefore, they have been "cheated" or deprived of goodies, much the same way that Frances felt unfairly deprived of a cookie when Betty changed her policy due to mounting pressure from the other parents. Who's at fault? You could make the case that it's Betty for having established such an egregiously unfair cookie policy in the first place. You could make the case that it's Frances, because, at twelve, she's old enough to know that the situation is unfair, regardless of her mom's policy, and she should have taken the initiative to give her sister what she was due. Instead, she chose goodies over goodness.

Regardless of who is to blame, the outcome is that Zelda is being treated unfairly. And as a result of the unfair treatment, she is enduring harm and suffering. The "cookies" are a metaphor for many different "goodies" that are unequally distributed in society. I previously mentioned the gross overrepresentation of White males in leadership positions (e.g., 80 to 100 percent), as one example. There are huge disparities in everything from wealth to health, as discussed in Part 1. Judgments of fairness have to be examined in a larger social context, taking into account both the processes and the outcomes.[3] Justice in the face of systemic inequality will appear unjust to those who benefited from the previous system. This is because they are comparing the way things used to be with how they are, rather than comparing the way things *should* have been with how they are. As civil rights leader Laura Murphy once explained to me, "Part of the problem [in America] is a belief system that made it okay to treat Black people as less than human. And that has been ingrained in our culture. So now when you include Black people, it's as if you're doing *them* a favor. And people run out of favors." If the default assumption is that Zelda shouldn't have any cookies—or should just be satisfied with the crumbs that Frances leaves behind—then you begin to understand how one whole cookie becomes seen as a favor that Zelda is "lucky" to receive.

In addition to entitlement, judgments of fairness and who deserves what may depend on the identity of the recipient, as well as how much cost or effort is required. In the opening picture, someone might be more inclined to give two crates to their own child but not to a stranger's child—or to someone from their own racial group but not someone from a different racial group. Some White people who oppose affirmative action in college admissions are actually in favor of legacy policies[4]—giving preferential admission to children and grandchildren of alumni—despite the fact that it's much easier to make a principled case for the person who faces institutional hardship than for the person who is fortunate enough to be born into a well-connected family.

Effort is an important factor to consider as well. Some people would be in favor of giving two crates to the child if they are already built and lying on the ground. But they might not be willing to grab an ax, chop some wood, and spend the time required to build two crates for the child to stand on. That would require a sacrifice that they would be unwilling to make—unless, perhaps, it was their own child.

In summary, while everyone agrees that fairness is critical to being a moral and decent person, people's perceptions of what is fair can vary depending on a number of factors, including motivated reasoning, or what they *want* fairness to be.[5] It's important for individuals to establish objective, justifiable, and consistent standards for what is fair.

MORALITY REQUIRES DOING NO HARM . . . AND RACISM HURTS PEOPLE

The second component of the "five foundations" model of morality is harm. Almost everyone agrees that good people do not inflict harm on others. In fact, they should do just the opposite—treating others with care and compassion, keeping them safe from harm, and lending a helping hand whenever possible. Racism is a textbook example of harm because it hurts people of color in every sense imaginable—psychologically, physically, financially, and professionally. The suicide rate for Black children between the ages of four and twelve is two times higher than that for White children of the same age group, and much of the disparity can be explained by the soul-crushing experience of racism, stigmatization, and lack of belonging.[6] The general rates of suicide are the highest in the Native American community and are also high among immigrant communities. In fact, one study found that suicide rates among immigrant populations are linked to the prevalence of ethnic slurs and hate speech against their group[7]—demonstrating once again how the soul-crushing experience of racism severely harms people. Racism even affects infants—Black babies are less likely to be adopted,[8] and are more likely to end up in foster care. Among adults, racism leads to impaired physical and mental health, even when controlling for other variables.[9] Notably, Harvard professor David Williams has published numerous studies documenting the link between racism and deleterious health outcomes.[10]

In addition to health, racism harms educational and economic outcomes. As mentioned in Chapter 7, over twenty-five years of research on *stereotype threat* demonstrates that racist stereotypes have a negative impact on the education and performance of Black students.[11] Stereotype threat can also have detrimental effects in the workplace, leading people of color to disidentify with high-ranking jobs, as they absorb the cultural message that people of color lack the ability to succeed in these roles.[12] We saw in Chapter 4 how racism is linked to access to housing and economic wealth through home-ownership. Racism can also perpetuate intergenerational economic harm. Even when Blacks and Whites are raised in families with similar economic means, Black boys will earn less than White boys.[13]

All of these disparities can be traced to slavery—an institution that flagrantly violated both of the core components of morality. It wasn't fair by any measure—equality or equity—and it brought tremendous harm and trauma to millions of Black people and their descendants. Most people in America acknowledge the harm of slavery but fail to see how it impacts our world today or how White people who are currently living are accountable for the damage caused by racism. Understanding the causal link between the past and the present is critical to increasing Whites' concern about racism. The next section explores how seemingly distal events occurring in the past can profoundly shape reality.

DISTAL IMPACT: HOW THE PAST IS LINKED TO THE PRESENT

Genuine concern about racism is attenuated by what I call distal impact. Because enslavement happened centuries ago, many people don't see how it still affects social structures today. Furthermore, because it isn't the White people alive today who enslaved Black people, many fail to see how they still play a role in upholding systemic racism. So there are two assumptions here that require examination:

1. Events in the past do not impact the present.
2. People without direct involvement in slavery have no role in creating or perpetuating systemic racism.

A comment by Kentucky senator Mitch McConnell captures both sentiments. As previously mentioned, in discussing reparations to the descendants of slaves, he stated that restitution for "something that happened 150 years ago, for whom none of us currently living are responsible" would not be a good idea. Note that he is not denying that harm occurred—rather the premise is that the harm occurred so long ago that it's no longer relevant. This belief directly contradicts what we know. I presented evidence in previous chapters (e.g., Chapter 4) that social, political, economic, cultural, and structural elements of the past linger into the present, including the results of a study showing that implicit racial bias in a state or county today is predicted by the number of slaves in that state or county in the 1800s.[14] Further evidence comes from the medical fields of psychiatry and epigenetics. The defining feature of posttraumatic stress disorder (PTSD), for example, is a traumatic experience that continues to affect functioning and well-being years or decades after the event. Of course, people do not always acknowledge the impact of past traumatic events on current psychological conditions and instead attribute them to emotional fragility or weak character. Otherwise, there would be more sympathy, support, and resources available for military veterans, sexual assault survivors, medical providers, and other individuals who have endured trauma and/or work in professions that involve high exposure to crisis or mortal danger.

Although racism is not an example of PTSD (for a multitude of reasons, one being that the traumatic events are continually recurring, so there is never a "post" period), it epitomizes how past events continue to produce harmful attitudes and outcomes in the present. The social, economic, political, and health disparities created by historical structures are still with us today. If we had to assign a disorder to the condition of being Black in America, it might be OTSD—ongoing traumatic stress disorder. Black people in corporate America rarely inhabit a situation where their race doesn't have the potential to create a stressor or negative impact. Nevertheless, in the case of both PTSD and racial trauma, people often blame the victim for their plight rather than external circumstances.

The second assumption in Mitch McConnell's argument is that White people alive today had nothing to do with the enslavement of Blacks in centuries past. I agree that Whites today bear zero responsibility for *creating* the institution of slavery. However, it does not logically follow that White people today have zero culpability or complicity in creating other racist structures (e.g., mass incarceration) or in perpetuating the racial caste system created by slavery. For starters, there are still many Whites today who endeavor to preserve racial hierarchy. Even White people who do not actively promote racial hierarchy are often complicit in its continuation. The institution of slavery created a system of privilege from which all Whites benefit relative to Blacks, all else being equal. And without active attempts to dismantle that system—because of self-interest or any of the other motives discussed in Chapter 8—Whites continue to be the beneficiaries of a morally unjust and abusive system. Do you remember the discussion question in the Forum following Chapter 7 that described a scenario in which a White ancestor stole a Black ancestor's money and passed it down to future generations of White people? The White benefactors may not be the thieves, but they are the beneficiaries of the theft.

The concept is similar to that of blood money or dirty money. Even if you didn't pull the trigger, you're still complicit if you accept money from someone who did. In fact, our government has a policy of seizing dirty money and assets, even from innocent family members who have received "gifts" from those who obtained the money through illicit means. For instance, a drug dealer who buys his mother a house will see the home seized and his mother removed from it—if it can be proven that her home was bought with funds that he earned from drug trafficking. So the question is why blood money and assets from slavery should be treated any differently. This point should be considered in any discussion about the moral rationale for reparations.

INTENT VERSUS IMPACT

Most people realize that it is possible to cause injury without any intent to harm. In the legal realm, this distinction is reflected by a charge of manslaughter versus homicide. What is especially ironic is that one can also inflict harm when there is genuine intent to help. Indulge me while I recount a personal story to illustrate this point.

As a child, I loved spending summers at my Aunt Sarah's house in Cleveland, Ohio. She and her husband, along with my three older cousins, would be waiting for me when my plane landed (in the 1970s nonpassengers could wait at the gate). I was a fearless young traveler who took my first solo flight to Cleveland at age five, despite the initial trepidation of my parents. Some of the best memories of those summers in Ohio were our trips to various amusement parks—Cedar Point, Geauga Lake, but especially SeaWorld. I was enamored with Shamu, the performing killer whale, and upon my arrival would start counting the days to our next trip there.

"Hey, Rob, your commercial is on TV!" Aunt Sarah would exclaim, letting me know that Shamu was about to appear. I'd come racing into the den from wherever I was in the house to hear the sounds of the delightful jingle that I still remember after all these years: *"I like rubbery dolphins, and blubbery whales . . ."* I couldn't contain my excitement.

"Ooh, when can we go?! How about tomorrow?" I pleaded on one such occasion.

"I have to work tomorrow, but we can go this Saturday," she said with a smile, which produced cheers of joy. Saturday couldn't come fast enough.

The whole family spent the entire day at SeaWorld, Aunt Sarah patiently letting me dictate our journey through the park, despite the displeasure of my older cousins, who preferred more "big kid" activities and rides, including the adjacent amusement park Geauga Lake. I remember spending lots of time at a tide pool exhibit where you could pick up starfish and touch sea urchins. But then, the big event— Shamu! I was in awe as Shamu performed tricks and splashed the crowd (we always got there early enough to get splash seats up front). We would see the show at least twice during each visit to the park and visit SeaWorld at least twice during each of my visits to Cleveland. Sometimes it would just be the two of us—Aunt Sarah and me. For many years, one of my most treasured possessions was a plush orca that she bought for me during one of the visits.

Fast-forward forty years and my fascination with orcas, and wildlife in general, hasn't waned a bit. In fact, during a recent trip to visit Aunt Sarah's granddaughter Michaela, who is an engineer in Seattle, we went on a whale-watching tour to observe wild orcas in Puget Sound. One thing that has changed, however, is my consciousness around the plight of orcas and how my childhood affinity for them ironically contributed to their exploitation and suffering. Nowhere is this exploitation more poignantly chronicled than in the documentary *Blackfish*—from the woeful wails of the wild adult orcas as they watch their calves being taken from them to the crestfallen (their dorsal fins slump over in captivity) orcas reduced to the indignity and torment of life in concrete vats. The film highlights the range of psychological traumas endured by the orcas as a result of cramped living quarters, lack of stimulation, and social deprivation.

The orcas do not take all this suffering lying down. They exhibit active resistance in ways ranging from behavioral noncompliance to, in extreme cases, what seems to be targeted assassination, including the well-publicized death of a SeaWorld Orlando trainer in 2010. In one tense and powerful scene in *Blackfish,* we witness what I understood to be an "activist protest" on the part of the orca (watch the documentary and decide for yourself whether my memory and anthropomorphic interpretation seem accurate to you). During one of the training sessions, the orca, which has spent years in captivity, seems to reach the end of its patience and decides to communicate its pent-up frustration to the trainer in a clear and unambiguous way. The orca firmly but gently grabs the trainer by the foot (were it not gentle, the bite would crush and sever the trainer's foot) and drags him underneath the water. The orca seems to instinctively know how long a human can hold his breath before drowning (orcas routinely drown seals before eating them, which takes a lot more time than drowning a human). Before the critical drowning point is reached, the orca returns to the surface the surely terrified trainer, who is now desperately gasping for air, his foot still in the orca's mouth. Despite the gravity of the situation, the trainer somehow manages to keep his cool. He begins gently caressing and talking to the orca in an effort to placate the animal.

The orca seemingly allows the trainer to catch his breath while the other trainers helplessly watch from the safety of the pool deck. After the trainer's breathing stabilizes, the orca dives once again. It's a harrowing scene to watch, as the two remain submerged for what seems like an eternity. Eventually the orca resurfaces with the trainer, who again begins gasping for air. Remarkably, he still retains his composure. Finally the orca releases its grip on the trainer's foot and the trainer slowly backs away before making a desperate dash for the edge of the pool. He recovers with only minor foot injuries.

In my reading of this incident, the orca was making a strong effort to communicate its frustration and outrage against its captivity. Any orca could devour a human in mere seconds if it wanted to, and catching the trainer trying to swim away would not have been a challenge. But it didn't do either one of those things, suggesting that it wanted to send a message rather than do real harm.

I tell this story to illustrate my own complicity, and the difference between intent and impact. In my case, ignorance was responsible for the disconnect between the two. As a child at SeaWorld, I would never have wanted to hurt Shamu, and yet I was inflicting tremendous harm on Shamu because I didn't understand how the SeaWorld "system" worked. As a five- to twelve-year-old, I hadn't thought that deeply about how the whales got to SeaWorld or what life was like for them out of the spotlight.

In the case of the trainers, the inconsistency between their good intentions and the negative impact on the whales was likely due to motivated reasoning and necessity. If SeaWorld disappeared, so too would their jobs. Many of the trainers in the documentary express tremendous guilt for their role in exploiting the orcas. However, their dependency on the organization for their livelihood makes it easier for them to psychologically accept, on some level, SeaWorld's claim that the orcas are doing fine. Motivated reasoning at its best.

At the end of the day, it is irrelevant whether or not I (or the trainers) adored Shamu, or orcas in general. The real question is whether we were engaging in behaviors that are harmful to orcas, and if so, why. Is it due to ignorance and a lack of awareness? Is it due to awareness coupled with low concern? Or is it due to a competing commitment, such as pleasure, convenience, or remuneration, that we prioritize over the well-being of the orca? If you really want to save the orca, then dismantle the system that torments, abuses, and confines these magnificent creatures—even if it means that you will have to find a less entertaining or fulfilling line of work or spend a summer without a visit to SeaWorld.

In the same way, it is irrelevant whether White people like Black people or not. As I will discuss in the final section of the book, implicit biases are not the most consequential consideration. The real question is whether you are taking actions that actively or passively support a system that oppresses Black people. In many respects, some White liberal progressives are like the orca trainers—staunch champions of the oppressed who are nevertheless complicit in their oppression because the system benefits them. Like the orca trainers, people often must wrestle with competing commitments—or two highly desirable but directly opposing goals that they are trying to fulfill simultaneously.

WRESTLING WITH COMPETING
MORAL FOUNDATIONS

In addition to fairness and harm, there are three additional components of the "five foundations" model of morality: loyalty, authority, and purity. These foundations can sometimes compete with, and deactivate, the first two. What would you do if you learned that someone from your hockey team harmed an innocent person? Would you report it to the police or stay silent to protect your teammate? This situation represents a conflict between the moral foundations of harm and loyalty. Or what if your boss ordered you to fire someone for unjust reasons? Would you refuse or obey? This would be a conflict between fairness and authority. Classic research demonstrates that subjects are willing to administer harmful shocks to others if a legitimate authority figure orders them to do so.[15] This represents a conflict between harm and authority. Or what if you were a juror on a murder trial for a defendant who didn't believe in showering or personal hygiene? Would your judgment of guilt or innocence be affected by the disgust evoked by the defendant's presence? This example pits fairness against purity.

These conflicts and inconsistencies between different moral foundations are really important to ponder. So let's consider a few more socially relevant examples. Honor killings—when individuals are deliberately murdered for doing something that undermines a family's social standing—are the epitome of a moral-foundations conflict. The complexity of social considerations necessary to adequately analyze the concept of honor killings extends far beyond the scope of this chapter. I highly recommend the forty-minute documentary *A Girl in the River: The Price of Forgiveness* for anyone interested in more background on the topic. The point that I want to make here is that the act of honor killing—by definition—requires doing harm to another person in the name of purity (e.g., the murder victim is seen as having committed a "dirty" or sinful act), authority (e.g., the murder victim is seen as having disobeyed a parent), or loyalty (i.e., the murderer is perceived as protecting the "honor" of the in-group/family).

Researchers have found that the relative importance of these five moral foundations—fairness, harm, loyalty, authority, and purity— varies not only among individuals but also between different political ideologies. In general, conservatives tend to endorse all five foundations to a relatively equal degree, whereas liberals tend to value the first two more than conservatives, and the last three less than conservatives.[16]

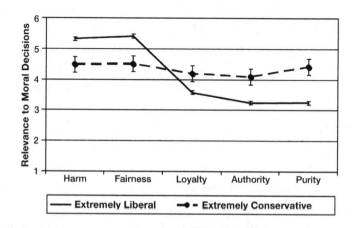

These data reflect responses averaged across many individuals and tell us about general tendencies. However, each unique individual can deviate from these general patterns in the relative importance they put on each of the five foundations. These individual patterns have consequences for moral behavior. For example, one study found that individuals who endorse fairness over loyalty are more likely to engage in whistleblowing when wrongdoing occurs.[17] Finally, subjective perceptions of purity, dirtiness, or sinfulness can affect judgments of who should be treated with care and compassion, with stigmatized groups being morally excluded.[18]

The institution of slavery clearly violated the first two of the basic foundations of morality. There was nothing *fair* about it, and it inflicted tremendous *harm* to the mind, body, and soul. The extent to which slavery violated the other three foundations of morality is less clear, which may explain, in part, why it was able to endure for so many centuries. In many respects, one could argue that it supports the foundations of authority and in-group loyalty. One could make a similar case for many current-day examples of racism. Specifically, what happens during and after police shootings can be interpreted as a conflict of moral foundations. Does an officer denounce a partner who has done something wrong or cover it up to show loyalty to the force? Do rookie officers do what they feel is right or follow the lead or orders of more senior officers or commanders—a question central to some of the defendants in the George Floyd murder case?

When asking the questions of whether you care about racism and why, it is important to also examine *what else* you care about, and why. Sure, you care about fairness—but do you care about loyalty more? Why is loyalty important? Does in-group loyalty serve the function of protecting those whom you deeply love, or is it merely an effective way for dominant individuals to consolidate power? Is authority about paying respect to wiser elders, or is it a way to keep a rigid social hierarchy intact? Do purity standards help to protect the body from disease and toxins, or are they used to stigmatize and ostracize groups who are different?

Navigating the moral landscape is tricky. Many people look inward for guidance. Others look to established religion for a spiritual compass. In many ways, the various religious compasses all point in the same direction—themes of compassion, peace, love, interconnectedness, and harmony with others and the universe. Christianity—the religion that I am most familiar with—prioritizes some moral foundations over others. It is clear from my reading of the Bible which of the moral foundations Jesus valued most. He did not want to be a king (authority), he did not take sides (loyalty), and he embraced even those society considered "unclean," such as lepers, beggars, and harlots (purity). He was all about justice (fairness) and compassion (not harming others)—so much so that he even showed humanity and forgiveness toward those who betrayed, tortured, and murdered him.

Given this truth, how could a self-professed Christian, like the Baptist minister in Mississippi who murdered three innocent people in 1964, feel licensed to harm other human beings for not subscribing to his own hierarchical concept of authority? They were simply exercising their legal right to vote. The "might is right" philosophy is something that the ancient Romans, not Jesus, would have subscribed to. Therefore, it seems more than a little ironic that the people who are the most fervently committed to authority, loyalty, and purity also tend to be the most fervently religious. And that is a trend that exists not just in the United States but worldwide. My objective here is not to judge but to foster a greater understanding of the complex nature of morality, and get people more in tune with their moral compass.

Again, the intention is not to point fingers—nor is it to provide excuses. It is to increase knowledge and awareness so that we can decide, as a community, what is really important to us and how our actions advance or inhibit that moral agenda. Racism violates basic principles of decency, whether we define them secularly or religiously. Although it is both unfair and harmful, racism persists, in part, because people allow self-interest, tribalism, and other factors to conveniently distort their conception of fairness (and perhaps harm). It also persists because enough people prioritize some values (e.g., power) and moral foundations (e.g., loyalty) over other values (e.g., universalism) and moral foundations (e.g., compassion/no harm). When people are given the choice between doing the right thing and doing what is politically, economically, or socially beneficial, many choose the latter. In that sense, the world has not changed in the four hundred years since the first enslaved Africans were brought to the American East Coast. If twenty-first-century White Americans and Europeans were faced with the choices of seventeenth-century White Americans and Europeans, would they do anything differently? Have we progressed morally in the last four hundred years?

We will turn to the question of how people can shift their moral strategies in the book's final chapter, but education is one powerful tool. Education is what happened when I watched *Blackfish* and became informed about the evil system that created Shamu. Inspiration can also come from religious or nonreligious sources. Many White people have pointed to spirituality as a catalyst for their antiracist actions. For example, Jay Neal, a White pastor who became a Republican state legislator in the Georgia House of Representatives, would have seemed like an unlikely candidate for criminal justice reform, given its lack of popularity among his constituents. Friends and supporters even admonished him to stay away from the issue, for fear that it could harm his reelection efforts among conservative White Georgians. He refused to back down. Neal stated:

> I could have just went [sic] with the flow and been elected over and over again, and not accomplished anything, and I wouldn't have felt like I was successful. But if I do what I felt like God placed me there to do, and I helped change the culture of Georgia, and somebody somewhere down the road spends a lot of money and convinces voters that I've been soft on crime and I've had the shorter political career than I otherwise would have—then I'm okay with that.[19]

Similar sentiments were echoed by Mayor Ted, whom readers met in the introduction, when I asked him why he was so deeply invested in racial justice. He shook his head and replied, "As a man of faith, I can't just stand by and do nothing." Inspiration can come from nonreligious sources as well, including philosophy, literature, or cherished leaders (e.g., Nelson Mandela). And inspiration can lead to antiracist action. At the end of the day, it's the action that matters. As stated by the late congressman John Lewis: "When you see something that is not right, not fair, not just, you have to speak up. You have to say something; you have to do something."

Doing something isn't just the right thing to do; it's the smart thing to do. In the next chapter, I will move past the moral case to the more practical case that ending racism makes organizations and society better—for everyone.

CHAPTER TEN

The Practical Importance of Redressing Racism

I magine you are a carpenter and you have the choice between two different toolboxes. The first box contains eight brand-new titanium hammers. They are the best quality that money can buy, but each hammer is exactly the same. The second box has eight different tools—a hammer, a screwdriver, a wrench, a saw, and four other tools—but all of the tools are worn and used, and they are made of standard-grade steel rather than high-end titanium. Which toolbox would you choose?

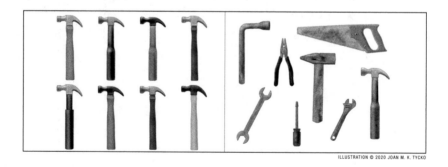

ILLUSTRATION © 2020 JOAN M. K. TYCKO

Your answer probably depends on what you plan to do with the tools. If your only job is pounding nails, then you would likely choose the titanium hammers. However, if your task is more complicated—like building a shed—then you would be better served by a diverse set of tools. Having just hammers will only get you so far, no matter how top-notch they are.

This analogy illustrates what Scott Page, author of *The Difference: How the Power of Diversity Creates Better Groups, Firms, Schools, and Societies,* calls "superadditivity."[1] With diverse components, the whole of a set is greater than the sum of its parts, as if 2 + 2 were equal to 5, 15, or even 50. In other words, a hammer, saw, screwdriver, and wrench working together offer exponentially more possibilities in terms of output than four hammers working together, regardless of their superior quality. The more complex the problem at hand, the greater the superadditive advantage of diverse tools over homogeneous tools. Page's argument is that diversity trumps individual ability.[2] Let's explore this idea further with some real-world examples.

One organizational implication of this superadditivity principle is that diverse groups solving complex problems will very frequently outperform groups of exceptional individuals who lack diversity in their approach to the problem. This point is highlighted in the book *The Medici Effect,* by Frans Johansson.[3] The title was inspired by the explosion of knowledge and creativity that characterized Florence in the fifteenth and sixteenth centuries, when the Medici family became patrons and sponsors of thinkers from a wide range of disciplines—astronomers, painters, philosophers, physicists, sculptors, engineers, architects, and writers. This concentration of diverse interests and expertise in one place led to a cross-fertilization of knowledge that gave rise to the period of renewed intellectual and cultural discovery that we call the Renaissance.

Johansson argues that an explosion of innovation and creativity is more likely to occur at what he calls the "intersection." At the intersection, diverse pools of knowledge or cultural perspectives meet and mingle. One vivid example cited by Johansson is the design of the Old Mutual building in Harare, Zimbabwe. The seemingly insurmountable challenge was erecting a multistory building—without air-conditioning—where people on the upper floors wouldn't feel like Cornish hens in a Crock-Pot. The solution was found at the intersection of two seemingly disconnected disciplines: architecture and entomology—the study of insects. It turns out that termites know a thing or two about building "skyscrapers," constructing mounds that can rise to heights of over twenty feet—an astonishing feat for ant-sized insects. They build these structures not only as shelter but also as farms where they grow the fungus that they eat. Fungus farming requires a constant temperature of around eighty-five degrees Fahrenheit inside the mound, even when the temperature outside soars above one hundred degrees. How do the termites manage to keep the mounds cool under the searing African sun? They do it by cleverly engineering systems that use wet mud to cool air that is strategically channeled through wind tunnels.

By incorporating termite technology—the only building in the world to do so—the designers were able to create a structure that can maintain a constant internal temperature of around seventy-five degrees for most of the year, using less than 10 percent of the electricity consumed by other buildings of similar size.[4]

What are the organizational implications of this example, and many others? Homogeneity may be fine if you're pounding nails, building standard old widgets, or doing a job that is routine and doesn't involve high levels of creativity or problem solving. In fact, you may want people to think, work, and perform exactly the same way. For example, Marriott has meticulously created a sixty-plus-step guide to cleaning hotel rooms[5]—the idea being that all of the house-keepers should do it exactly the same way. This standardized approach streamlines efficiency and increases consistency and quality control compared with each individual adopting their own unique method. But if your job is to create new technology or to discover a cure for cancer, then you will benefit from people with diverse ideas, perspectives, methodologies, and approaches. In these situations, a question that every manager should be asking is: What perspectives are missing? Whose voice needs to be in the room?

Maybe some of you are thinking that too much diversity could be a negative—that diversity, if not properly managed, might create a veritable Tower of Babel, with people on so many different wavelengths that they fail to communicate effectively, creating conflict and discomfort. Research has shown that conflict is not detrimental to team performance and can actually be beneficial, as long as it is task conflict rather than relationship conflict. The former focuses on how to approach or solve a problem, whereas the latter involves hostility toward others in the group.[6] Similarly, research has shown that a little discomfort doesn't hurt either. In a 2019 study, ethnic diversity increased discomfort while also enhancing team performance.[7] It's also worth bearing in mind that the extra effort and challenge associated with diversity are front-loaded. In the long run, the advantages of diversity far outweigh the disadvantages, as people learn how to coordinate and cooperate.[8]

Let's return to our example of the toolbox. If you have eight hammers, all you need to learn is one skill—how to use a hammer. Easy. On the other hand, if you have eight different tools, it's going to be more daunting (and possibly frustrating) at first, because you have to master eight different skill sets. Over time, though, you'll be in a better position to perform a much larger variety of tasks (e.g., building a shed). However, a diverse set of tools is of limited utility if one is not willing to invest the time to discover and appreciate the unique potential and capability of each tool.

Extending this metaphor to organizations, it's not sufficient to just have diverse people on a team—it's also important to recognize and utilize the unique capabilities that they bring to the table. This is a prerequisite for teams being able to achieve "superadditivity," or what is also referred to as "collective intelligence"—when the performance capability of a group of people exceeds the average or maximum performance capability of any individual in the group.[9] Imagine that a group has five members with varying levels of ability on a particular skill: Person 1 has a skill level of 80, person 2's is 90, person 3's is 100, person 4's is 110, and person 5 has a skill level of 120. The average skill of the group is 100, and the maximum skill is 120 (i.e., person 5).

In theory, the group should only be able to solve a problem with a difficulty level of 120, because that is the maximum level of skill in the group. However, what the collective-intelligence research shows is that the five people working together can collectively generate a level of skill that allows them to solve a problem with a difficulty level of 130, 150, or possibly even 200. The reason that collective intelligence far exceeds individual intelligence is that persons 1, 2, 3, 4, and 5 all have unique and nonoverlapping knowledge and information— sort of like architects and entomologists. Any given architect and any given entomologist may each know a thousand things, but together they know two thousand things (or more likely seventeen hundred things, for example, if there is a 30 percent overlap in their knowledge). When you aggregate all of this information, you expand the overall pool as well as create lots of new combinations, permutations, and possibilities. The trick to making it work, however, is that people have to be willing to communicate and share their unique information with the group. What are the conditions that maximize information sharing and collective intelligence?

Carnegie Mellon professor Anita Woolley and her colleagues have found three conditions under which collective intelligence is more likely to emerge. First, it is more likely to emerge in groups where the members show high levels of emotional intelligence, social sensitivity, and perspective taking—a finding that echoes other research.[10] So paying attention to other people in the group is important. Second, collective intelligence is more likely to emerge in groups where members take turns speaking, rather than when one person or a subset of people dominate the conversation while the others sit silently. For example, if architects are discussing how to construct a building without air-conditioning, and the junior architect, who is interested in insects, never gets to speak because the senior architects have hijacked the discussion, then the unique information about termite mounds is lost to the design team. This shows that diversity cannot thrive without inclusion and equity—people need to have a sense of belonging and an equal voice before they will speak up.

Finally, the researchers found evidence that demographic diversity (gender, in their study) contributes to collective intelligence; teams with a higher proportion of women had higher collective intelligence than teams with fewer women. This result was explained, in part, by higher levels of emotional intelligence and social sensitivity among women in the sample. Similarly, other research has found that racial diversity can enhance the performance or decision making of groups.[11] For example, one study revealed that simply having a person of color on a team of three people increases the likelihood that the two White people will express dissenting opinions, which brings unique information to the discussion and produces better-quality decisions. In contrast, a racially homogeneous group of three White people is less likely to express dissenting opinions or bring unique information to the table.[12] Similarly, researchers have found that racially diverse juries consider a wider range of information, provide more facts, and make fewer errors than racially homogeneous juries.[13]

Although research on collective intelligence supports Scott Page's claim that diversity trumps ability—as well as Frans Johansson's claim that the intersection of different buckets of knowledge stimulates innovation and high performance—it also shows that positive outcomes are contingent on having the right social dynamics in place. Hiring candidates diverse in race, gender, or any other demographic category will not automatically release pennies from heaven. Whether people feel accepted, appreciated, and validated is critical to whether diversity becomes a liability or an asset. In an article appearing in the November/December 2020 issue of *Harvard Business Review,* Harvard business professor Robin Ely and president of Morehouse College David Thomas are explicit in their argument that an "add-diversity-and-stir" approach is insufficient. Rather, understanding how diversity is perceived, received, and managed is critical in determining whether it becomes an asset and benefit to the organization.[14]

To get diversity to work, organizations need to create an environment in which people from diverse backgrounds experience a sense of equity and belonging. Research suggests that this is more likely to happen in organizations that do not see the "business case" as their primary reason for caring about diversity. They should care because it's the right thing to do—and caring for the "right" reasons will make people more likely to feel included and committed to the organization.[15] This, in turn, will make it more likely that organizations will reap tangible benefits from diversity. In other words, the business case for diversity and the moral case for diversity are intertwined—the former requires the latter in order to work. A strictly diversity-for-profit approach runs the risk of alienating and offending the very people whom the company wants to attract.

Researchers at London Business School investigated whether this is the case by randomly assigning participants from underrepresented backgrounds (e.g., LGBTQ+, women in STEM) to read one of two versions of a corporate statement in favor of greater diversity. For half of the participants, the company emphasized the business case, with statements such as "We strongly believe in promoting diversity because it simply makes good business sense." The other half of the participants read statements that emphasized the moral case, with statements such as "We strongly believe in promoting diversity because it's simply the right thing to do." Participants then answered a series of questions about how much they would feel that they belonged at the organization, based on the statement that they had read. Those who read about the business case anticipated that they would feel a weaker sense of belonging and a stronger sense of rejection at the company, compared with those who read about the moral case.[16]

However, as discussed in Chapters 8 and 9, not everyone will resonate with the "right thing to do" motive. Are there any other (rational) reasons for organizations to care about diversity? In a classic paper, Robin Ely and David Thomas outline three reasons for valuing diversity and how these three different approaches serve as milestones for diversity progress.[17] In the first approach, which they label *discrimination-and-fairness,* diversity is a numbers game that can keep companies from getting sued. The idea is that the lack of diversity in the 1950s and 1960s in the United States reflected a deliberate effort to exclude women and people of color, which constituted discrimination and a lack of fairness. Now that such discrimination is both legally and socially problematic, companies must pay attention to the demographic composition of their workforce to avoid fiscal liability and public shaming. The goal of what I refer to as "Diversity 1.0" is to simply get people of color in the door and onto the roster. Failure to do so could result in lawsuits, as well as reputational damage that could hurt the company financially.

With what I am calling Diversity 2.0, or *access-and-legitimacy,* the assumption is that having people of color in an organization can provide a portal to new markets. A Vietnamese executive, for example, can provide useful information to the company about how to market its products to the Vietnamese community. Moreover, having a visible Vietnamese executive can help the company establish legitimacy with the Vietnamese community, increasing the likelihood that its members will support the business. One potential drawback of this approach is that people of color often end up feeling that their job is to play the role of spokesperson and cultural ambassador, rather than doing the technical work (e.g., electrical engineering) that they were hired to undertake. For example, imagine an American soldier of Iraqi origin who wants to be a helicopter mechanic. Because she speaks Arabic and has phenotypic Arab features, she is asked to serve as a cultural liaison between other American troops and Iraqi villagers. In many ways, her role becomes playing an Iraqi, rather than contributing her expertise as a helicopter mechanic. Or she ends up doing double duty—serving as both diplomat and mechanic—which can be psychologically and professionally burdensome. In short, the access-and-legitimacy approach can make people of color feel pigeonholed—and thwart their professional advancement—even if their presence and cultural knowledge benefit the organization.

Interestingly, some organizations and communities also leverage racial diversity to gain legitimacy within the White community. Once I worked with a mayor who did not strike me as personally passionate about diversity, but he nevertheless invested a lot of energy and resources into seeking it. When I inquired about his motive for spending so much time and effort on diversity initiatives, his response was simply "growth." He continued by saying, "We've got to become better at diversity so we can grow our population. These gray-haired White people in our community are not going to be around that much longer, and White millennial and Gen Z families with children don't want to move into a community that doesn't have any racial diversity." In essence, his focus on racial diversity was a strategy for shoring up the town's tax base—and attracting young *White* people. Corporations have made similar claims—that having a more diverse workforce makes their company more attractive to young White job seekers. They also realize that the need for greater access and legitimacy will only grow in the years to come as the proportion of people of color in the population grows.

The holy grail—Diversity 3.0, if you will—is the *integration-and-learning* model, which reflects the idea that diversity is a valuable asset unto itself, and that diverse teams can generate higher levels of creativity and effectiveness—for all the reasons discussed throughout this chapter. But remember, it's not simply an add-diversity-and-stir approach. As demonstrated by multiple lines of research, the company will have to be committed to equity and inclusion for diversity to pay dividends.

Finally, diversity can be a benefit not just to organizations but to communities more broadly. Scholars across multiple fields have demonstrated that there are social benefits of racial diversity, despite the fact that people often assume that diversity reduces social cohesion. When I interviewed Robert Putnam, author of the influential 2000 sociological work *Bowling Alone: The Collapse and Revival of American Community,* he expressed to me his disappointment that his work is often cited out of context. Although diversity can undermine the sense of community in the short term, he emphasized that, in the long run, diversity improves the sense of community—and his work clearly demonstrates this. Other research confirms the idea that diversity benefits communities in the long run.

A 2019 study published in the *Proceedings of the National Academy of Sciences* provides cross-national, longitudinal evidence—looking at a twenty-year time span across one hundred countries—that although diversity initially reduces trust and quality of life, over time diversity becomes a benefit rather than a detriment.[18] Another study found that people living in more racially diverse neighborhoods were more prosocial and willing to help others than were those living in less diverse neighborhoods. This effect was explained by the fact that people living in diverse neighborhoods were more likely to identify with all of humanity.[19] What's also striking is that the study contains experimental evidence demonstrating that people who were asked to merely imagine living in a racially diverse neighborhood were also more willing to help other people in need, and that this causal link was explained by the fact that imagining life in a more diverse neighborhood led them to have a broader human identity.

Apropos of a broader human identity, it's important to realize that racism can have a negative effect on all of humanity. We'll explore why in the next section.

THE COLLECTIVE IMPACT CASE

In addition to the business case, strong reasons for ending racism can be made on the basis of both self-interest and collective interest. Systems of racial oppression don't just harm Black people; they harm other people of color, and many White people as well. People who are prone to racism, such as right-wing authoritarians, tend to be hostile toward any group that is perceived as deviating from the conventional establishment—including immigrants, LGBTQ+ individuals, and nontraditional women. This means that people who are prejudiced against one social group are very likely to be prejudiced against multiple social groups.[20] In a classic investigation of the "prejudice as general attitude" idea, people were asked to rate their feelings toward a variety of different social groups, some real (e.g., Blacks, Jews) and some fictitious (e.g., Danerians, Wallonians).[21] Results showed that people who reported disliking Jewish people, for example, also tended to dislike Black people and other social groups. What's fascinating is that this antipathy extended to groups that weren't even real, such as the Danerians and Wallonians. Simply put, they didn't like *anyone* who was different, regardless of whether they knew anything about them or not. More recent research has refined this idea by showing that generalized prejudice is not just about "us" versus "them" but tends to be aimed specifically at groups that are socially stigmatized.[22]

We see tragic examples of this phenomenon in the real world. For example, the Poway shooter who viciously murdered worshippers at a synagogue north of San Diego in April 2019 posted a lengthy online diatribe denouncing not just Jews but also Muslims, immigrants, and various racial and ethnic groups. Providing further support for the notion of generalized hatred, he confessed to being inspired by the Christchurch mosque shooter in New Zealand, who murdered fifty-one

Muslims. Prior to that rampage, the shooter posted a seventy-plus-page manifesto vilifying numerous non-White and non-Christian groups.

The sad irony here is that Jews and Muslims in the United States, and abroad, are often viewed as being two sides of very different coins. So the fact that a man who perpetrated the mass murder of Muslims could serve as the inspiration for a man who wantonly murdered Jews speaks to the incredibly indiscriminate and generalized nature of prejudice. The moral of the story is this: When you condone hatred against one group, you simultaneously enable or increase the likelihood of hatred against other groups, including, quite possibly, your own. Hypothetically speaking, a Jewish person living in the United States who might have initially felt that the attack on Muslims half a world away in New Zealand had nothing to do with them—or actually made them safer because hatred against Muslims would signal indifference or affinity toward Jews—would have been terribly mistaken. Working to ensure compassionate and socially just practices can be a benefit to *everyone,* regardless of whether you are a member of the (initially) targeted group. This sentiment is powerfully captured in the words of Martin Niemöller, a Lutheran pastor who spent many years imprisoned in concentration camps in Nazi Germany:

> *First, they came for the Socialists, and I did not speak out—*
> *Because I was not a Socialist.*
>
> *Then they came for the Trade Unionists, and I did not speak out—*
> *Because I was not a Trade Unionist.*
>
> *Then they came for the Jews, and I did not speak out—*
> *Because I was not a Jew.*
>
> *Then they came for me—and there was no one left to speak for me.*

History shows that the establishment even came for many of the early White American immigrants. There is a reason you're much more likely to come across surnames such as Hancock, Franklin,

Middleton, Witherspoon, and Walton than Romano, Lewandowski, Sarkisian, Schwartz, and O'Reilly if you peruse the list of the fifty-six signers of the Declaration of Independence. Among other reasons, it is because the vast majority of the Italian, Polish, Armenian, German, and Irish immigrants to the United States arrived over a century later—after the country was already established. And they were not universally welcomed, nor were they universally considered "White." Entire books have been written on the capricious conceptualization of Whiteness through American history, including *The History of White People* by Nell Irvin Painter, *How the Irish Became White* by Noel Ignatiev, and *How Jews Became White Folks and What That Says About Race in America* by Karen Brodkin.

Religion was just as important as ethnicity in early America. For example, anti-Catholic bias was profound and pervasive. The movie *Gangs of New York,* directed by Martin Scorsese, touches on the ethnic and religious conflict of nineteenth-century America. It references the Native American Party (the "Know Nothings"), which wasn't a party of Native American Indians, as one might guess, but rather a party of native-born White Protestant Americans who were against recent immigrants—mainly the newly arrived Irish and German Catholics. Whenever there is a hierarchy, *anyone* who is not at the top of it can become the target of discrimination. And in the past, many White groups were indeed targets, and some still are (e.g., Jews, the poor, LGBTQ+, etc.).

Given this history, it's shocking that many Whites today see themselves as being more "American" than Native Americans (who have the oldest and strongest ties to the land), Blacks (who have been here since the beginning and built the economy), Hispanics (who were the original owners and inhabitants of the entire southwestern portion of our nation), or Asians (who have been in America for centuries and built the transportation infrastructure of our nation). In a nutshell, the presence and contributions of people of color to the United States are as real and valid as those of Whites. Recognizing this basic fact will not only fortify historical accuracy; it will also strengthen our national unity. The indisputable fact is that we are all Americans, despite our diversity.

Therefore, it is important to be concerned about systems of racism, oppression, and persecution, because they could affect anyone who is not able to check *100 percent* of the boxes that define the elite hegemony within a given society. A very small minority of individuals (perhaps 1 percent within most societies) check *all* the boxes. Even groups that enjoy some measure of individual or institutional privilege can quickly become targets of discrimination if a context or situation changes.

The marked surge in anti-Asian racism due to persistent political attempts to racialize the COVID-19 pandemic shows that Asian Americans, often seen as the "model minority," are not immune to the sting of racism.[23] According to a 2020 Pew survey, a majority (58 percent) of Asians in America believe that it became more common for people to express racist views toward Asians after the coronavirus outbreak than it had been before.[24] But a closer look at history reveals a detailed record of anti-Asian sentiment in the United States: from anti-Chinese practices of the nineteenth and twentieth centuries to the forced relocation and detention of roughly 120,000 Japanese (but not Germans) living in the United States during World War II—most of whom were American citizens. Even today, Asian Americans are at least as likely as Blacks or Hispanics to report being the target of verbal harassment, if not more so. According to a 2019 Pew survey, 61 percent of Asians said that they had been subject to racist slurs or jokes, whereas 52 percent of Blacks, 46 percent of Hispanics, and 37 percent of Whites said the same. Even when it comes to intelligence, a higher percentage of Asians (36 percent) than Whites (26 percent) reported that people acted like they thought they were *not* smart because of their race.[25]

Arab Americans witnessed a similar increase in racism against their group in the wake of September 11, 2001, when their "honorary White" card was essentially revoked.[26] In one heartbreaking example, a former student confessed to changing their last name from their father's name, which sounded Arabic, to their mother's maiden name to avoid constant hassles at the airport. By contrast, consider that White people do not have to undergo an identity transformation when a heinous act (e.g., the 2017 Las Vegas shooting massacre) is perpetrated by another White person.

Nevertheless, oppression against people of color can even have negative consequences for working-class Whites. Sociologist Matthew Desmond argues that "low-road capitalism," or the most base form of economic exploitation, first created by slavery and the plantation economy, was one of the major sources of working-class White poverty, historically speaking. The existence of slave labor lowered wages—and therefore economic security—for most Whites in the South. Because abject poverty was better than the horrors of slavery, poor Whites accepted the deal rather than fighting the system. Desmond writes:

> Labor power had little chance when the bosses could choose between buying people, renting them, contracting indentured servants, taking on apprentices or hiring children and prisoners. . . . Witnessing the horrors of slavery drilled into poor white workers that things could be worse. So they generally accepted their lot, and American freedom became broadly defined as the opposite of bondage . . . a malnourished and mean kind of freedom that kept you out of chains but did not provide bread or shelter.[27]

Thus, racism, slavery, and the low-road capitalism that it supported also created a perverse conception of freedom and miserable standard of life for most Whites in the South. And it's not just the past. In the book *Dying of Whiteness,* Jonathan Metzl makes a similar point—namely that present-day poor and working-class Whites would be better off if they did not fall victim to the allure of racism and instead focused on the systemic oppression that faces all non-elites.[28] It's a general theme that, in various forms, crops up time and time again. In the book *Strangers in Their Own Land,* Arlie Hochschild discusses the negative impact of rapacious capitalism on White communities in southern Louisiana—particularly pollution and hazardous waste.

Long-standing research has documented the prevalence of "environmental racism," or the observation that toxic industries, substances, and contamination are disproportionately likely to occur near people of color. A notorious example is the water crisis in Flint, Michigan—

a city that is predominantly Black, with over 40 percent of the population living below the poverty line—where the city's water became undrinkable due to excessively high levels of lead. Such hazardous contamination is likely to occur in low-income areas more broadly, making poor Whites more susceptible than rich Whites to exposure to toxic materials.[29] This is depicted in the 2019 film *Dark Waters,* starring Mark Ruffalo, which highlights the true-life poisoning of a rural White community in West Virginia by the DuPont corporation. Another example is the 2000 biographical film *Erin Brockovich,* starring Julia Roberts, which deals with Brockovich's efforts to seek justice for those afflicted by the contamination of groundwater by Pacific Gas & Electric in California. The main idea here is that racism leads to inequality, which leads to suffering, for many people of many backgrounds—including Whites.

What's unfortunate, however, is that the temptation to avoid stigma and shame causes poor and working-class Whites to direct their frustration about their economic plight toward Blacks rather than the elite Whites who are the source of the oppression. Although the derogation of one stigmatized group by another stigmatized group is an effective way to remove oneself from the very bottom of the barrel, it serves merely as an emotional salve that temporarily assuages feelings of threat and shame. It does nothing to address the actual problem and, if anything, enables and exacerbates it by ignoring its real source.

When the social justice tide comes in, all boats rise. For example, Nikole Hannah-Jones, in her Pulitzer Prize–winning *New York Times* piece, makes the case that poor Whites in the South also benefited from post-Reconstruction legislation following the Civil War. She writes:

> Public education effectively did not exist in the South before Reconstruction. The white elite sent their children to private schools, while poor white children went without an education. But newly freed black people, who had been prohibited from learning to read and write during slavery, were desperate for an education. So black legislators successfully pushed for a universal, state-funded system

of schools—not just for their own children but for white children, too.[30]

Rights for some groups can lay the foundation for rights for many groups. In their book *The Inner Level: How More Equal Societies Reduce Stress, Restore Sanity and Improve Everyone's Well-Being,* Richard Wilkinson and Kate Pickett present compelling data showing that greater equality reduces all manner of personal and social ills, including bullying, gambling, cheating, hostility, homicide, imprisonment, child abuse, mortality, obesity, depression, drug abuse, and psychosis— while increasing trust, cultural participation, social mobility, educational attainment, environmental sustainability, and solidarity.[31]

Each of these elements, in turn, has potential ripple effects on other issues. For example, greater solidarity can also bolster national security. The motto of my home state of Kentucky is "United We Stand, Divided We Fall." We want to stand. Lincoln invoked this sentiment to condemn slavery when he quoted the scripture:

And Jesus knew their thoughts and said unto them, every king-dom divided against itself is brought to desolation; and every city or house divided against itself shall not stand.

Diversity does not mean divided. Indeed, history suggests just the opposite. As previously discussed, diversity is not new to the United States. It is also not new to the world. Many ancient civilizations (e.g., Rome, Egypt, Persia) were multiethnic and multicultural. This occurred, in part, because they were located near the intersection of three different continents—Africa, Asia, and Europe. Indeed, the name *Mediterranean* comes from the fact that it is a sea located between different large land masses. Based on what you just read about the Medici effect, do you think it is a coincidence that so many civilizations emerged in that geographic vicinity? Or might it be possible that the rich intercontinental diversity was a factor that contributed to the cultural and technological advancement of the region? There is considerable empirical evidence, obtained from samples all around the world, that living abroad and having extended contact with and exposure to other cultures is linked to increased creativity and cognitive complexity.[32]

The main point here is that multiculturalism is neither new nor negative. It has existed in the world for a long time—and it seems to be a good thing. Furthermore, racial, ethnic, religious, and cultural diversity have existed in America since the nation's inception. We have always been diverse; we will always be diverse. The only question we must ask ourselves as a nation is whether we want that diversity to be an asset or a liability. Our country's growing racial divisions are not just a social justice issue. Racism harms us all in various ways. Our challenge is to explore the most effective way to end it.

How do we begin the work toward improving racial attitudes and creating greater social justice for everyone? Part 3 of the book provides some answers.

Addressing Concern and Commitment

CONVERSATION TOPICS

General Questions to Begin *The Conversation:*

What do you think?

1. Ask yourself: What are three concepts, theories, studies, or state-ments from the chapters in this section that resonated with you?

   Was there anything in particular that you underlined, high-lighted, or wrote down that you'd like to share?

   What made this information so intriguing, powerful, or note-worthy to you?

2. What were some ideas that did *not* resonate with you—things that you took exception with? Which aspects of these ideas, studies, or findings did you find inaccurate, objectionable, or offensive?

3. Which concepts do you think your family/friends would have a hard time buying?

How do you feel?

1. How did you feel before you began reading Part 2?

   How do you feel now, after finishing Part 2? What did you learn that you did not know before? How has this information affected the way you feel?

   How do you feel about your role in this process? Do you feel empowered by the information, or are you sad or nervous?

2. Did Part 2 highlight a personal trigger that you did not know you had?

   Can you name it? Was it connected to your identity? Status? Sense of worth?

   If so, what have you learned about the trigger?

How Much Do People Really Care?

1. What made you decide to read this book? How much are you genuinely concerned about the problem of racism? Based on the content of Part 2, what might be some of the factors that contributed to your decision to invest time in reading it?

   What relative importance do you assign to the five moral foundations? Which is most important to you? Which is least important? Which are in the middle? What about the values in the Schwartz model? How does this relative importance of values affect your decisions and behaviors around diversity, equity, and inclusion (DEI)?

2. In your network, community, or organization, have you seen leaders express concern about racism?

   Do you think the reasons are intrinsic or extrinsic? In other words, *why* do you think the leaders care? Is it Diversity 1.0, 2.0, 3.0, or some combination?

Finally, do you believe that empathy is necessary for antiracism? Or, like Paul Bloom's book *Against Empathy,* do you think empathy creates more racism because people mostly empathize with similar others?

MORE FOOD FOR THOUGHT: CONVERSATION IN CONTEXT

A Reexamination of Fairness: Does White Entitlement = White Rage?

Many books show that Whites, particularly working-class Whites, feel alienated from society. In a 2017 Harvard Business School symposium, sociologist Arlie Hochschild, author of the book *Strangers in Their Own Land,* talked about the "deep narrative" that many working-class Whites have. It goes something like this:

> There is a line leading up a hill. And on top of the hill is the American Dream. And people are waiting patiently in line for their turn. Then all of a sudden, people start to cut the line. Someone on the top of the hill is signaling to them to come up to the front. Upon closer inspection, it's Obama. He's signaling to the people of color to break line.

After describing this deep narrative that some working-class Whites have, I asked Dr. Hochschild whether it is possible that there is an even deeper "subnarrative." Could it be that there is the assumption among the White people standing in line that they should be served *first*—before any Black person—because they are White? Any Black person ahead of them, regardless of how long they have been standing in line, needs to get to the back of the line. If there are any American dreams left over after *all* of the White people have been served, then we'll see about Black people and other ethnic minorities.

What are your opinions about this deep narrative and the "subnarrative"? Do you think either, none, or both of them are valid? How do they relate to the distinction between entitlement and fairness that we discussed in Chapter 9? How do they relate to the butter cookie analogy? Who should get cookies first? And how many? Do some Whites feel that Blacks should be happy with one butter cookie—even though Whites have three—because Blacks are lucky to have any cookies at all?

How does it relate to the zero-sum-game perception that we discussed in Chapter 1 (i.e., Whites believe that less racism against Blacks necessarily means more racism against Whites)? Explore the idea that antiracism is racist because it, by definition, undermines White supremacy . . . which in some way impacts White people.

This chapter was largely about everyone benefiting from a more equitable distribution of "cookies." How can this be done without some being deprived and others *feeling* deprived?

What Is the Path to Peace?

In Chapter 8 I highlighted that not everyone cares about social justice. However, almost everyone wants peace and social harmony, even if they have different approaches to achieving it. Talk about each of the statements below:

"If you want peace, work for justice."
"If you want peace, beat 'troublemakers' into submission."

Which do you think represents the ideal approach to peace? Do you believe that there are ideological or political differences in which approach people see as more viable? How might we reconcile these vastly different perspectives on how to achieve peace?

Managing the Comfort Trade-off

Michael Norton and colleagues have an interesting study showing that on planes with first-class cabins, there is more air rage. They found that it is caused by coach passengers having to walk through first class without being able to stay there. On planes that board from the rear, no increase in air rage occurred. I fly a lot—sometimes in first class—so this presents a dilemma for me. I want to be comfortable on my flight, but I also want everyone to feel happy and dignified.

Is it the case that the existence of racism presents a dilemma for White people? On the one hand, it makes them the beneficiaries of all sorts of good things—preferential treatment, like first class. On the other hand, it creates suffering. How do you think most White people deal with this dilemma, if at all?

In Chapter 8, I presented data showing that White people were quite apathetic to racism—even egregious instances. What do you make of these findings? Do you believe they reflect reality?

Where do you think this tacit apathy comes from? Do you believe that it is the result of pure indifference, or is it due to a trade-off between social justice and other values or moral foundations, such as loyalty, power, or self-interest? Feel free to incorporate the research on values and moral foundations, as well as your own opinions and personal experiences.

Sympathy for In-group Transgressors?

Following up on the previous question, is there greater cultural sympathy for immoral actions that stem from White people?

We can see it in the media and movies. One example is Hannibal Lecter. Despite his depravity, he is not dehumanized because he is portrayed as clever and cultured, even a bit funny. He also shows loyalty to certain characters (e.g., Clarice/Jodie Foster). It's the image of the sympathetic psychopath.

Another example is Joaquin Phoenix's character in *Joker*. Despite his murderous depravity, he is portrayed in a way that tries to make the viewer feel sorry for him, not his countless victims, some of whom are people of color.

First, do you agree with this interpretation? Are there any portrayals of lovable psychopaths who are people of color?

Do we see this sort of sympathetic portrayal of real-life people as well? There were many media posts about the Vegas shooter that, instead of demonizing him, sought to understand what went wrong.

Did he lose his job? Was he depressed and didn't seek help? It was seen as a mental health crisis rather than an act of evil, because he fit the image of the hardworking, blue-collar White guy—the archetype that this nation celebrates. How much do these images and portrayals impact our concern for White people versus people of color, if at all? What are other examples or ways in which Hollywood or media images create different perceptions and levels of concern?

Life Goals at the Individual and Societal Levels

Based on research from a number of sources, including research by Susan Fiske, Daniel Gilbert, and Shalom Schwartz, there seems to be considerable overlap and consensus that human beings are looking for just a handful of basic things.

> Prosperity—having sufficient or surplus resources
> Belonging—being accepted and socially integrated into family
>   and the community
> Happiness—experiencing joy and freedom
> Fulfillment—finding meaning and purpose
> Control—limiting danger and chaos

How important are each of these to you, relatively speaking? How might a Black person experience achieving these life goals compared to a White person in our society? Do you see any synergies or conflicts among these five different life goals among individuals? What about among different racial groups? Does Black prosperity mean White unhappiness? Can we find a way to make these life goals more synergistic at the group/societal level and not just the individual level?

Part III
CORRECTION

CHAPTER ELEVEN

What Everyone Can Do to Promote Racial Equity

We have now arrived at the book's most important question: What can I do to fight racism?

Believe it or not, many of you have already been engaged in this effort for the last ten chapters. As we learned from the PRESS model, antiracism requires a reckoning with *Condition* and *Concern* before arriving at *Correction*. Before taking action to address racism, you must first be aware that it exists and understand its origins and complexity. Learning about the nature and history of systemic racism can effectively reduce racial bias.[1] Moreover, having interactive conversations increases not only social connectivity and trust but also the very depth and accuracy of one's understanding.[2] Therefore, by simply seeking and speaking the truth about racism, you've already been *doing* something.

As we learned in Chapter 1, some people have no awareness of systemic racism and may even believe that the true victims of racism are White people.[3] In other cases, people have an awareness of the existence of racism, but only in certain contexts. There are many people of all races who wholeheartedly believe that systemic racism exists but that they themselves are not culpable or complicit in upholding it. Others believe racism exists but that it happens only among individuals and not systematically.[4] Finally, many organizational leaders may acknowledge racism in the world but deny its presence in their organizations—assuming the absence of overtly discriminatory policies or the mere presence of diversity initiatives renders them immune to racial discrimination.[5] After reading Part 1, you have a better understanding of why such assumptions are untenable and why racism is so prevalent.

The second step, which we undertook in Part 2, was to investigate and establish the level of *Concern* about the problem. This requires some serious moral introspection and soul searching. *Why* is this work important to you? Is antiracism an integral part of your being? Or is it an effort to avoid social ostracism or civil litigation? Now that you have a fuller understanding of the scientific and historical facts regarding racism, do you feel a greater level of responsibility for addressing it? Asking these questions is more important than the response; there are no right or wrong answers. The goal is to better understand where you, and others, stand on the issue. Knowing whether people adopt antiracism for intrinsic or extrinsic reasons is important because it has profound implications for their behaviors.[6] The answers are meant to serve not as the basis for condemnation but rather as a practical gauge for understanding how much effort one is willing to invest in this work, and under what conditions. Doing this work requires trade-offs, so having awareness of where it sits in your pecking order of priorities is critical.

Now that we have pondered and assessed Condition and Concern, the next step is *Correction*—or what we can do to fix it. Correction can be broken down into three distinct but interrelated approaches to addressing the problem of racism: individual, cultural, and institutional. Individual strategies are geared toward modifying personal attitudes, behaviors, and habits. Interventions at the cultural level emphasize the role of social norms and expectations for what constitutes appropriate or inappropriate behavior. Institutional approaches focus on changing formal policies, practices, or laws within communities and organizations as they relate to racism.

Chapter 11 will focus on the actions individuals can take—personally, culturally, or institutionally. Chapter 12—the book's final chapter—will examine what leaders can do to reduce racism among employees, within an organization's culture, or as it manifests in their institutional structures and policies. If any readers, eager for "solutions," skipped Parts 1 and 2 and jumped straight to Part 3, I strongly urge you to return to Chapter 1. The approaches we will discuss in these final chapters will make less sense to someone who is not familiar with the science of the previous chapters. People truly committed to doing the work are willing to make a substantial investment of resources—including time—rather than taking shortcuts. *Correction* must build on *Condition* and *Concern*—otherwise the results will be suboptimal and short-lived.

Let me give you an example of how simple strategies that ignore Condition and Concern can go awry. Nancy Reagan's "Just Say No" campaign against drug use among minors in the 1980s is a prime example of a "strategy" in isolation that reflects a deep lack of awareness of the nature of the problem, its root cause or, in my opinion, empathy or concern for the people afflicted by the problem. In this instance, the Reagan administration offered a simplistic solution rather than a thoughtful, informed strategy that included resources for schools, jobs, and mental health services—interventions that would have gotten closer to the root causes of youth drug use. At the same time, Nancy Reagan was not completely wrong. On some level, you do have to say no. But that's not *all* you have to do.

Or consider dieting, as another example. I've talked about losing weight in simple terms—eating less and moving more. If you do both of those things, you will lose weight, in most cases. But will you keep it off? To produce sustainable change, we would have to ask deeper questions: What are the psychological, biological, economic, or social issues underlying the eating or exercise habits of the person? Is the person enduring stress, depression, or abuse? Is food being used as a source of comfort or security? Is there access to anything more than postindustrial processed foods with a high glycemic index? Is there time in the day for someone working three jobs to make ends meet, while taking care of children, to steal away for an hour to go to the gym? If the goal is profound and sustainable change, then you *must* perform a deeper analysis of Condition and Concern before jumping to the Correction stage. Otherwise, you risk encountering the same problem again and again. However, with a more holistic approach there is hope for a sustainable solution.

A WORD ABOUT OPTIMISM

Before we begin exploring the concrete steps that individuals can take to combat racism at both the psychological and structural levels, I want to take a moment to emphasize the importance of one more factor: optimism. *Racism is a solvable problem.* One cannot look to the past for definitive evidence about the future. The fact that racism hasn't been solved doesn't mean it's not solvable.

When approaching the work of antiracism, it's important to have a "yes, we can" attitude. Research shows that idealistic thinking motivates social engagement and action.[7] Barack Obama must have been at least a little idealistic to have the "audacity of hope" that served as the animating theme of his race barrier–breaking presidential election.[8] If you think a situation is hopeless, why would you ever invest the time and energy? And if you don't invest the time and energy, then you've rendered the change hopeless by not even trying. It's the quintessential self-fulfilling prophecy. Assumptions can have a profound effect on actual outcomes. For example, your assumptions or expectations about contact with another racial group can affect how those interactions turn out. One study showed that people with positive expectations about contact with an out-group ended up positively evaluating the other group when the actual contact was positive. However, participants who had negative expectations about contact with an out-group ended up negatively evaluating the group, regardless of whether the actual contact was positive or negative.[9]

Stanford social psychologist Carol Dweck has extolled the virtues of positive thinking and having a growth mindset (i.e., people or situations can change) as opposed to a fixed mindset (i.e., things are what they are and people don't change) as a prerequisite for success across multiple facets of life,[10] including race relations.[11] The idea here is not to promote naïveté or Pollyanna-ism. It is not foolish to think that there are many, many decent people in the world. It is not absurd to believe that people really can change. These are facts, not fantasies. You have taken the first step by gathering the facts, exploring your emotions, and learning how you can engage meaningfully with others in The Conversation. Your job now is to translate that knowledge into action, while keeping in mind that the goal is not to boil the ocean. It's to boil the water in your pot or kettle—the bigger the better—and put it in the ocean. With a sufficient number of pot boilers, a pond will boil, as will a lake, and potentially an ocean.

In a story called "The Star Thrower" by Loren Eiseley, later adapted by Scott Plous, a man is walking along a vast stretch of beach, collecting stranded starfish and returning them to the sea one by one. Another person comes along and questions the man's actions, pointing out the many miles of beach and the millions of starfish that litter the sand. The skeptic tells the man that his work couldn't possibly make a difference, given the countless number of starfish that need rescuing. Undaunted, the starfish collector continues his endeavor, pausing to state, "It makes a difference to this one," as he gently places the starfish into the ocean.[12] Are you ready to become a starfish collector? Working together we can undoubtedly clear the beach.

THOUGHTS VERSUS ACTIONS

In addition to the benefits of an optimistic mindset, I want to emphasize one other important theme as we begin to explore the actions individuals can take to address racism: the distinction between prejudice and discrimination, first introduced in Chapter 2. Prejudice is an attitude—a set of internal beliefs, feelings, and preferences. Discrimination refers to actual behaviors, decisions, and outcomes. The distinction is important because behaviors are often easier to regulate than attitudes. Let's take a hypothetical example. Imagine that *The New England Journal of Medicine* has published a set of groundbreaking, "incontrovertible" studies demonstrating that brussels sprouts are a miracle vegetable and that eating three servings per day will reduce your risk of cancer and other chronic illnesses to zero. Great news! There is just one problem—you despise the taste of brussels sprouts.

How can you reap the nutritional benefits of brussels sprouts in light of your gustatory aversion to them? By simply eating them. To be sure, you cannot control whether you *like* brussels sprouts. No amount of will or determination will make your taste buds respond to brussels sprouts the way they do to chocolate pecan pie. That's okay. You <u>can</u> control whether you *eat* brussels sprouts. All you need to do to reap the nutritional benefits of brussels sprouts is pop them into your mouth, chew, and swallow. The experience may be unpleasant at first, but over time you may "acquire" a taste for brussels sprouts through a process of mere exposure and gustatory reconditioning.[13] It's the brain's "fake it until you make it" mechanism. Similarly, if you jump into a swimming pool with chilly water, it will feel uncomfortable at first. But after a few minutes, once your body becomes habituated to the temperature, you may think, "This is actually nice."

Now let's apply this thinking to interactions among people. Imagine you are a taxi driver in New York City who has negative attitudes toward Muslims. You see a couple who appears to be Muslim standing in the rain attempting to hail a cab. Although you don't have as much control over your visceral feelings toward Muslims, especially at the implicit level, you *do* have control over whether you decide to stop the cab to pick them up or keep driving. You also have control over whether you behave in a professional and respectful manner toward them once they enter the cab. And you have control over whether you engage in pleasant conversation and wish them a pleasant day after you drop them off. These minimal courtesies are enough to avoid creating undue hardship for the passengers, who might have otherwise spent several minutes in the chilling rain waiting for a cab.

This scenario is an example of values overriding attitudes. Your personal beliefs about what is right or wrong can render your feelings irrelevant. The Muslim passengers didn't need you to become their best friend forever; they just needed to get from point A to point B. Such a scenario would be an example of prejudice without discrimination. The beauty of the situation is that you've given yourself an opportunity to interact with Muslim passengers—perhaps listening in as they discuss challenges at work, or squabbles with the in-laws, or their children's violin recitals—because you didn't allow your attitudes to prevent you from picking them up. Over time, research suggests, allowing yourself these interactions may change your negative feelings toward Muslims via a process of repetitive exposure and reconditioning. In the meantime, you can feel empowered knowing that your actions are much more important than your attitudes.

This approach of the behavior overriding the attitude is a quick fix. A bigger goal explored in this chapter is how to get rid of the negative attitudes altogether. We will begin this journey by examining the profound impact of intergroup contact and social interaction on both attitudes and behaviors.

THE POWER OF INTERGROUP CONTACT

If controlling your behavior to eliminate discrimination during brief interactions is a good first step, decades of research have shown that seeking out repetitive contact with or substantive exposure to outgroup members is an effective second step. The *contact hypothesis,* first articulated by Gordon Allport in the 1950s, maintained that both discrimination *and* prejudice could be substantially reduced by increasing social contact between members of different social or ethnic groups.[14] However, unlike brussels sprouts and chilly water, mere contact—by itself—won't do the trick. Certain conditions must be met in order for the intergroup contact to have a positive effect—rather than a negative effect—on racial attitudes. The first necessary condition is *equal status.* Consider the frequent interpersonal contact between Blacks and Whites that took place on plantations in the antebellum South. In those settings, there was an obvious absence of equal status—all the Black people were placed in subordinate positions to the White people, due to slavery. This dynamic served to reinforce the status quo, despite the frequency of the contact between groups. Some of these imbalances persist today. If there is an integrated school where all the White people are rich and all the Black people are poor, then contact will likely worsen rather than improve racial attitudes.

The second condition is *friendship potential.* Even if the groups are of equal status, relations between the groups must be characterized by respect and cooperation rather than rancor and competition. The third condition is *institutional sanction*. This means that the intergroup contact must be viewed positively, by formal and informal institutions and authority figures, rather than as something that is legally or socially inappropriate. The fourth condition is *common goals*. This means the groups want to attain the same superordinate goals and rely on each other to achieve these outcomes.[15]

Many real-world situations can satisfy all four of the necessary preconditions. One example is a racially integrated sports team. On the court or field, the players are of relatively equal status (with any status differences being attributable to skill, not race). They have a high level of camaraderie and cooperation, if not outright friendship. The social relationship has the blessing and approval of coaches, fans, and society in general. And the members of the team are all working toward the same goal—a tournament win, for example—and they have to rely on one another to achieve it. Thus, one could reason that Whites who are part of a racially integrated sports team will have more positive racial attitudes than Whites who are part of a racially homogeneous sports team.

Research by Kendrick Brown and colleagues in 2003 tested this hypothesis by examining the racial attitudes and policy preferences of 375 White student athletes across twenty-four colleges and universities in the United States who participated in individual or team sports. They examined the percentage of Black people on the White athletes' main high school athletic team (ranging from 0 to 99 percent) as a possible predictor of both attitudes and policy preferences. (Earlier research from the 1980s had shown that cross-racial contact can improve Whites' racial attitudes toward Blacks, but not necessarily their support for government policies designed to increase equal opportunity for Blacks.)[16]

Brown and his colleagues' findings revealed that White student athletes who had a higher percentage of Black teammates tended to have more positive emotions and attitudes toward Black people. Importantly, they also found that a higher percentage of Black teammates was also associated with greater support for government policies to improve the social and economic position of Blacks. Interestingly, these positive effects were true only for White athletes who played *team* sports (e.g., basketball, baseball). For those who played individual sports (e.g., tennis, wrestling), having more Black people on the team was actually associated with more negative racial attitudes and lower support for government policies designed to help Blacks.[17] The authors reasoned that direct competition with Black teammates (for seed position in tennis, for example) in individual sports may have undermined the positive effects of interracial contact. Moreover, the level of interdependence between team members is not as high for individual sports compared with team sports, thereby compromising the second and fourth preconditions necessary for obtaining the positive effects of intergroup contact.

You might be wondering whether contact with Black people lowers Whites' prejudice level or whether White people who are already lower in prejudice tend to have more contact with Blacks. In fact, both scenarios are true to some degree—with the causal arrow pointing in each direction. However, research by Thomas Pettigrew shows that the effect of contact on prejudice reduction is stronger than the effect of low prejudice on increased contact.[18]

Additional evidence bolsters the notion that contact leads to more positive attitudes. Do you recall the playground illustration from Chapter 2, depicting a Black girl standing and a White girl on the ground near a swing set? It turns out that children attending racially homogeneous schools are far more likely to describe that scene in a racially stereotypical way than children who attend racially diverse schools.[19] Because children don't get to choose the students at their school, and often parents don't get to choose which public school their children attend, it's likely that the difference in racial bias between the groups of kids is explained, in part, by different levels of interracial contact.

The notion that contact can lead to more positive attitudes is also buttressed by anecdotal evidence. You might be able to point to some examples in your own life. One former student of mine described how his grandmother's negative attitudes toward LGBTQ+ people changed 180 degrees after he revealed to her that he is gay. The change did not happen overnight, but their close relationship was a catalyst for what eventually became not only a reduction in his grand-mother's anti-LGBTQ+ attitudes but her eventual strong allyship with the LGBTQ+ community. In a similar vein, one might question whether Dick Cheney, the ultraconservative former vice president of the United States, would have been so enthusiastically in favor of marriage equality if his daughter Mary Cheney were not a lesbian. Indeed, some researchers argue that the precipitous decrease in anti-LGBTQ+ prejudice in society over the past few decades, on both an implicit and explicit level,[20] is due to the fact that the LGBTQ+ community touches so many people and cuts across so many different social, ethnic, gender, and class categories. As a friend once told me, "Everybody has a gay cousin." And with changing social norms, more people are open about their sexuality than was the case thirty years ago.

Anecdotal evidence suggests that close racial contact can have a similar effect. The 2019 movie *The Best of Enemies,* starring Taraji P. Henson and Sam Rockwell, is about the real-life circumstances surrounding the unlikely friendship between former Klansman C. P. Ellis and Black racial justice activist Ann Atwater in Durham, North Carolina, in the 1970s. In this situation, many of the preconditions for social contact were met, including—believe it or not—a common goal. Both Ann Atwater and C. P. Ellis needed to focus attention on a Black elementary school in need of repair. Atwater wanted it fixed because her daughter attended school there. C. P. Ellis wanted it fixed so that the Black kids would not have to attend the White school that his kids attended. Notwithstanding the different motives, they had to work together in the context of a charette—a collaborative racial forum—to solve the problem. In addition to a superordinate goal and cooperation, the charette assigned everyone equal status (and an equal vote), as well as opportunities for casual conversation and relationship formation (lunches together with assigned seating so they could not choose whom they wanted to sit next to). The process of extended social contact led to a gradual but profound change in C. P. Ellis. Recent examples of the transformation of ex–White nationalists, such as Derek Black, contain similar narratives of intergroup contact leading to attitude shifts.[21]

Does contact always work to reduce prejudice toward everyone in the outgroup? Unfortunately, no. Increased positivity toward an individual does not always extend to the racial group as a whole. Even in the team sports example, White athletes and coaches might develop very positive attitudes toward their Black teammates but not toward Black people as a group. For example, a study of over two thousand NBA players and 163 coaches across a forty-five-year span revealed that coaches, who were predominately White, gave more playing time to players of their own race, regardless of the players' actual performance.[22] However, this racial bias in favor of White players lessened over time as the coaches spent more time interacting with their Black players. Although White coaches began to show less racial bias against specific Black players the longer they worked together, they did not show reduced bias against Black people in general.

Many scholars have explored the complicated reasons behind these seemingly contradictory tendencies.[23] One hypothesis is that White people see their Black friends as unique "exceptions" and put them in a different category than other Black people.[24] This results in increased positivity toward those "special" Black individuals, with little or no change to the negative impression of Black people as a whole.

Researchers have also found that intergroup contact benefits Whites more than Blacks. In fact, some research has found that greater contact with White people can lead to higher levels of internalized racism among Blacks, due to a greater awareness of the negativity and contempt that White people and society hold toward Blacks.[25] There is also evidence that White and Black people walk away from interracial interactions with different perceptions, with Whites having more positive impressions than Blacks. White people who see themselves as allies tend to communicate messages of social support (e.g., sympathy) rather than social change (e.g., solidarity) with people of color, despite the fact that messages of social change are viewed as more comforting and supportive by people of color.[26] Similarly, researchers have shown that many misunderstandings and negative feelings resulting from interracial interactions stem from the different goals and motivations that Whites and people of color have. A study out of Princeton University showed that White people enter interracial interactions wanting to be liked and seen as moral by people of color, whereas Blacks and Hispanics enter interracial interactions wanting to be respected and seen as competent by White people.[27]

Interracial interactions are especially taxing and depleting for people of color when White people adopt a color-blind approach ("I don't see people's color") versus a more multicultural approach ("I value and celebrate diversity").[28] Beverly Daniel Tatum's book *Why Are All the Black Kids Sitting Together in the Cafeteria?* discusses many of the challenges facing Black people during interracial interactions.[29] Being mindful of these challenges is especially important due to the asymmetrical necessity of intergroup contact for Black people compared with White people.

It's nearly impossible for a Black person to exist in the United States without having any contact with White people, especially Blacks who work in professional settings. However, it is very possible to be a successful White person in the United States and have no interaction with Black people. This is true even for White athletes—as 44 percent of the White athletes in the study by Kendrick Brown and colleagues reported zero Black people on their high school sports teams. This means that Black people do not have a choice about interracial interaction, whereas White people do. Power asymmetries are at play during those interactions—even when there is "equal status"— because White people write the rules on every aspect of the interaction: the appropriate way to speak, how emotion should be expressed, and even whether the interracial interaction occurs in the first place.

Much has been written about how people of color often "code-switch," essentially having to become bilingual or bicultural to effectively interact or communicate with White people. The pressure many people of color feel to code-switch complicates the idea of authenticity, and constrains when they are able to act as their "true selves."[30] Authenticity is not a luxury afforded to people of color, despite research showing that being authentic bolsters your subjective sense of power, as well as other people's perceptions of your power and leadership.[31] These are in addition to the microaggressions[32] and drain of energy and cognitive resources[33] that can characterize inter-racial contact for people of color. Thus, people of color are automatically at a disadvantage during interracial interactions, and it is important for antiracist Whites to be aware of this reality.

Being mindful of these challenges is something that White people can do to increase the likelihood of more positive intergroup contact, in addition to striving to satisfy the four aforementioned preconditions. In short, contact can be a powerful tool in the fight against racism. But it's not as simple as add-and-stir. White people who have not had much contact with out-groups understandably may approach the situation with considerable trepidation. What can they do to increase the likelihood of a smoother interaction? I could provide a laundry list, but instead I can boil my advice down to a single maxim that readers can adapt to the unique circumstances of their lives: Be mindful of societal-level power differences (e.g., systemic racism) without perpetuating them yourself. If you believe that the experiences of a Black person and of a White person in America are the same, then you are demonstrating a lack of awareness and a level of insensitivity that might offend. You should also avoid creating inappropriate power dynamics in your interpersonal interactions. For example, men often interrupt women. White people often interrupt (or ignore) Black people. Sometimes these power-relevant transgressions are flagrant (e.g., touching Black people's hair without permission), and sometimes they are unconscious or nonverbal (e.g., not making eye contact).[34] In a nutshell, be respectful—bearing in mind that being respectful is not always the same as being polite. The former requires more thought, knowledge, cultural awareness, and intentionality.

Leaders should devote considerable effort and attention to creating the right conditions for optimal intergroup contact—understanding that if they want *diversity* to work, then they also have to attend to *equity* and *inclusion*. Recall the research discussed in the last chapter showing that conditions for more equitable participation increase collective intelligence. Situations that involve shared hardship and commiseration can also magnify the benefits of contact. In one experiment, researchers brought strangers into the laboratory and asked them to undertake a grueling challenge, such as submerging their hand in a bucket of ice water or eating a hot chili pepper. They found that the shared hardship, challenge, and pain promoted group formation and strengthened trust, bonding, and cooperation among the group members.[35] Staging retreats where people from diverse backgrounds are given really difficult challenges to overcome while relying on one another (e.g., rock climbing) can go a long way toward bolstering solidarity and improving intergroup attitudes.

DISRUPTING SOCIAL CATEGORIZATION

Taking people out of their day-to-day environments to go on a retreat not only provides the opportunity for intergroup contact, but also can reduce people's reliance on social categories altogether. As we learned in Chapter 6, this basic human tendency to place people into social categories is a big factor in the production of racial bias. But is categorization by race inevitable? A fascinating experiment by Robert Kurzban and colleagues challenged the long-held assumption that racial categorization is inevitable by arguing that what is really important is coalitional affiliation—whether someone is friend or foe.[36] They argue that race has become a cue—albeit not an entirely valid one—of coalitional affiliation. For example, if White U.S. politicians assumed that Russians are friends—despite decades of deep enmity and recent intelligence reports of Russia paying Taliban soldiers to kill American soldiers—simply because they are White, then race would be an erroneous affiliation cue. Similarly, if the same politicians believed that Black Americans—who have fought and died for the country in every war, beginning with the Revolutionary War—are enemies simply because they are not White, that would be yet another example of race leading to erroneous assumptions about affiliation.

What Kurzban and colleagues set out to do was to pit actual coalitional affiliation against race to ascertain which one people relied on more heavily when perceiving and categorizing others. In their experiment, the researchers had participants listen to statements from four speakers wearing gray T-shirts who were clearly friends with one another (but enemies with another group who were wearing gold T-shirts). They also listened to statements from four speakers, each wearing a gold shirt, who were clearly friends with one another but enemies with those in the group wearing the gray T-shirts. Each team was racially integrated, two Blacks and two Whites on the gray team and two Blacks and two Whites on the gold team. After the participants listened to all the statements, the experimenters gave them a memory test to see whether they were more likely to confuse the four Black (or White) people with one another *or* whether they were more likely to confuse the four members of the gray team (or gold team) with one another. The results were clear—people paid a lot more attention to coalition-based cues than to race-based cues, getting members of the gray team mixed up with one another in a recall test more than they got the Black people mixed up with one another. Thus, the encoding of groups by actual coalition, not race, occurred at a deep, perceptual level.[37]

Stated differently, their results suggest that people are wired to detect coalitional affiliations. Using a set of evolutionary arguments similar to those presented in Chapter 7, Kurzban and his colleagues reasoned that prehistoric humans would not have evolved the tendency to detect race. Because hunter-gatherers didn't have planes or dune buggies, they would not have been able to span the globe. And the people whom they encountered within the forty-mile radius of their existence all looked relatively similar. However, much like other primates, they would have needed to develop cognitive mechanisms to discern who was friend or foe. Those would have been the most important cues—not race. Despite participants' lifelong habit of using race as a predictor of social affiliation, the authors were able to weaken this tendency—on a deep cognitive level—in less than four minutes. Such studies provide promising evidence that race can be unlearned as a basis for perceiving people, if people are provided with an alternative way to see the world.

Researchers have identified two general approaches to disrupting social category tendencies: decategorization and recategorization. The former occurs when people see others as *individuals* rather than as members of a social category.[38] For example, being seen as Robert Livingston rather than as a Black man is an example of decategorization. Recategorization occurs when individuals who were once members of rival categories become reassigned to the same category, creating a *common in-group*.[39] For example, White students at Ohio State who see Black students as the out-group "Black people" on a regular campus day might see Black students as the in-group "Buckeyes" during the Ohio State–Michigan football game, temporarily creating a common in-group of Black and White students from Ohio State. Researchers have found that both decategorization and recategorization at least partially explain the positive benefits of interracial contact. In other words, contact improves intergroup attitudes because it increases people's perceptions of others as individuals and not just a category.[40] Contact can also increase the realization of overlapping similarities and commonalities,[41] resulting in a common in-group, which reduces prejudice.[42]

Building on the college example of recategorization, another set of studies found that when Black and White faces were grouped separately based on race, White people showed more accurate recognition of White faces than Black faces. However, when the exact same Black and White faces were recategorized and grouped based on university affiliation rather than race, White participants showed better recognition of faces from their own university compared with another university, regardless of the race of the faces.[43] Once again, this led researchers to conclude that the well-documented tendency for people to think that individuals from other races "all look alike" is not based on differences in perceptual expertise—that people are more familiar with faces of their own race. Rather, simply categorizing someone as "other," regardless of what they look like, makes it more difficult to recognize their face.

Another example of recategorization is a scenario in which White participants played a simulated dodgeball game where their teammates were Black and their opponents were White. In the simulated game, their Black teammates saved the game and were good sports, whereas the all-White team cheated and were bad sports. Following this simulation, the White participants showed a dramatic reduction in their levels of implicit anti-Black bias on the Implicit Association Test (IAT, described in Chapter 2).[44] You might notice similarities between this situation and the conditions of intergroup contact on sports teams discussed earlier in the Kendrick Brown et al. study.

An interesting example of a sort of hybrid between decategorization and recategorization is a technique developed by UK social psychologist Richard Crisp. Getting people to categorize others using multiple different categories—rather than trying (perhaps futilely) to avoid categories altogether—steers the mind away from simple us-versus-them thinking. When you encounter a coworker from a different race, try to develop the habit of seeing them as four *additional* categories besides their race. Yes, John is Black—but what other categories can you assign to him? John is an engineer. John is a father. John is a New Yorker. John is deaf. The trick is to let go of the delusion that you do not see race, and instead simply add four other characteristics you are able to come up with, to dilute the impact of race. Undergoing this process of multiple recategorization eventually leads to decategorization (i.e., seeing the person as an individual), which leads to lower bias and less dehumanization of out-groups.[45] What is particularly powerful about this technique is that it works regardless of which groups you choose or whether you yourself belong to any of the groups.[46]

You can make this technique a mental habit by establishing what are called implementation intentions. These are goals that we create in our minds that follow an "If X, . . . then Y" pattern (e.g., "If I see a Black face, I will think 'safe'").[47] You can tell yourself every morning, "If I see a Black person, then I will think of four other categories that person belongs to." It seems very simple, but these if/then statements have been scientifically shown to decrease racial bias across numerous different studies.[48]

For example, research by Saaid Mendoza and his colleagues has shown that implementation intentions can improve performance on a video game simulation that mimics police scenarios. Participants must quickly decide whether to press a "shoot" or "don't shoot" key in response to Black and White male targets that appear carrying guns or harmless objects like a wallet or cellphone.[49] Although participants should simply focus on the threat of the objects being carried, the race of the targets tends to interfere with their shooting decisions. Shooter bias occurs when the participant is more likely to erroneously "shoot" an unarmed Black versus unarmed White person, or mistakenly "not shoot" an armed White versus armed Black person. Studies have shown that mentally rehearsing an implementation intention designed to disrupt social categorization helped them perform better overall, thereby reducing the expression of racially biased shooting errors compared with a control condition in which people did not mentally rehearse the instructions.[50]

CREATING OPPOSITE IMAGES

As the police training example above suggests, social categories can come with a lot of baggage. Another technique that researchers have used to reduce racism based on stereotypes is *vivid counterstereotypicality*. This is just a fancy term for flipping the script on stereotypes (e.g., Black people being seen as heroes rather than villains).

In one of the most rigorous investigations of implicit bias reduction strategies to date, Calvin Lai and colleagues compared the effectiveness of seventeen different interventions for reducing implicit bias.[51] Among the interventions that worked (most of them did not), the most effective of all was a technique designed to create vivid counterstereotypicality. In the experiment, researchers asked participants to read a story in which the participant was the main character. In the story, the participant is walking down a street late one night after drinking at a bar. A White man in his forties attacks the participant and throws the participant into the trunk of his car and drives away. After a while, he pulls over the car, opens the trunk, and begins beating the participant once again. A young Black man notices the assault in progress and rushes in to intervene, rescuing the participant and saving the day. When participants were instructed to keep the story in mind while they completed the Implicit Association Test, this resulted in dramatically reduced levels of anti-Black implicit bias. Researchers have found that this intervention works for three reasons. First, it uses characters and events that strongly challenge stereotypes (i.e., Black hero and White villain). Second, it is emotionally evocative. Third, it is self-relevant. This means that the participants imagined *themselves* in the scenario rather than someone else.

Other studies have employed counterstereotypicality in less vivid and self-relevant ways but have nevertheless obtained significant reductions in implicit bias. In one such study, Nilanjana Dasgupta and Anthony Greenwald created three experimental conditions: pro-Black, pro-White, and control.[52] In the pro-Black condition, participants were exposed to photos of ten admired Black people (e.g., Dr. Martin Luther King, Jr., Will Smith, Colin Powell) and ten disliked White people (e.g., Al Capone, Charles Manson, Jeffrey Dahmer) with a correct or incorrect description of who they were or what they had done (e.g., "leader of the Black civil rights movement in the 1960s" or "former vice president of the United States" for Dr. King). The job of the participants was to identify which statement was correct. In the pro-White condition, they were exposed to ten admired White people (e.g., John F. Kennedy, Tom Hanks) and ten disliked Black people (e.g., O. J. Simpson, Marion Barry) with the appropriate descriptions. In the control condition, they were exposed to pictures of ten flowers (e.g., sunflower) and ten insects (e.g., beetle) with a correct or incorrect name of the flower or insect.

After being exposed to the photos in their condition twice, participants completed the Implicit Association Test. Results showed that participants randomly assigned to the pro-Black condition had significantly lower levels of implicit racial bias than those in the pro-White or control condition. Remarkably, the positive effect of this counterstereotypical exposure appeared even when participants retook the IAT twenty-four hours later. Interestingly, the pro-White condition had no effect. The level of racial bias in the pro-White condition was exactly the same as that of the control condition. Being exposed to negative images of Black people and positive White people did not increase racial bias, presumably because the default association—created by society—is that Black is negative and White is good.

Another high-tech form of creating opposite images is through a process called virtual embodiment, using VR technology. In one study, White participants were brought into the laboratory and embodied in a Black or White virtual body using virtual reality. Not only did the simulation, which lasted for about thirty minutes, reduce implicit racial bias for those White people embodied as a Black person, but the effect also endured for much longer than other interventions—participants who were retested seven days later still showed a reduction in implicit bias.[53]

These studies suggest a couple of everyday strategies that individuals can take to change their attitudes. First, be mindful of the images that surround you. Are there any Black people? Are they stereotypical images or heroic images? Make a list of the five Black people whom you admire most, and put pictures of them in your home or office. Or buy a book featuring the person and put it on your coffee table, so that both you and your guests will see it daily. Watch movies or read biographies with positive and heroic descriptions of Black people, and be sure that your children's books and cartoons contain similarly positive depictions. The data also suggest that practicing vivid empathy and imagining what it is like to live as a Black person can reduce bias.[54] Pick a day and challenge yourself to think deeply about the experiences of each person you encounter, whether a coworker or a clerk at a gas station. Put yourself in their shoes and imagine what it would be like to experience life from their perspective. Do you catch yourself making unfair assumptions about their level of education or interests? Challenge yourself to "flip the script" on your stereotypes. Simple empathetic mental exercises like this one can go a long way toward making us not only less biased but also more humane in general toward one another.

COMMITMENT TO REDRESSING HYPOCRISY

Pointing out the discrepancy between what people practice and what they preach can create dissonance, leading people to take steps to bridge the gap between their words and deeds.[55] This technique is known as a *hypocrisy induction,* and it's been proven effective in reducing biased behavior. Here's how it works: First someone publicly declares support for racial equality. Next they consciously recall times when their behavior was not consistent with those publicly declared values. Finally they take advantage of the opportunity to reduce the discrepancy between their principled position and their inconsistent actions.

When people hold intrinsic nonprejudiced values, research has shown that it is possible to change their attitudes and behaviors by inducing hypocrisy. In Chapter 2 we learned how aversive racists have genuine egalitarian values but behave in racist ways. This discrepancy between values and behaviors is especially likely in ambiguous situations, where they can justify their behavior with thinking that goes something like: "I didn't help the person in need because someone else was around to lend a hand, not because the person in need was Black." The hallmark of aversive racism is that many White people are not aware of their true level of bias against people of color because they push it into the subconscious and deny it. However, if such people can be cognizant of when they are behaving in a prejudiced way, then they will change their behaviors, due to their egalitarian values.

In one study led by a group of Canadian social psychologists, aversive racists (in this case, people with implicit anti-Asian biases but racially egalitarian values) were given the opportunity to write an essay on why they believed it was important to treat Asian students fairly. Those in the hypocrisy condition (but not the control condition) were then asked to recall and write about two situations in which they did not treat or react to an Asian student fairly. Participants were told that the study had concluded. Later, in a presumably unrelated task, the researcher asked everyone to submit an anonymous ballot on how the university should allocate certain budget cuts among ten different student groups. Among them was the Asian Students' Association. The researchers found that students with egalitarian values but high anti-Asian bias made significantly fewer cuts to the Asian Students' Association when they were in the hypocrisy condition compared with those in the control condition.[56]

Keep in mind a few caveats. First, this hypocrisy induction works only among people who have intrinsic, not extrinsic, reasons for wanting to be antiracist. Second, it works only when people are able to recall times when they have behaved in a racist manner. If they are unwilling or unable to see how their behavior violates their values, then the process will not work. Finally, people have to be given a chance or opportunity to do better.

We have now surveyed the most effective, scientifically validated techniques for reducing implicit bias and discriminatory behavior (e.g., intergroup contact, decategorization, recategorization, implementation intentions, vivid counterstereotypicality, hypocrisy induction). However, these are not the only strategies that individuals can employ to reduce racial bias. In the next section, I will explore other approaches for combating racism on both a psychological and a structural level.

THREAT AND SELF-AFFIRMATION

In Chapter 5 we examined how a deep-rooted cause of racism is fear and insecurity, which leads people to form a rigid definition of how the world should be and express intolerance toward those who deviate from these standards. This tendency is reflected in classic research on authoritarianism as well as more recent studies. A 2018 study showed that feeling ashamed, demeaned, humiliated, or otherwise devalued led people to seek clear-cut meaning and a sense of certainty in the world, which in turn led them to embrace more extremist ideologies.[57] Specifically, this research shows that the values of power and security are related—people often crave power because it functions as a security blanket. In other words, feeling scared increases the need and desire for power. The implication of all of this research is that prejudice, dominance, intolerance, and ideological rigidity can be the result of people not feeling good about themselves or secure in their current situation. If people felt more affirmed, safe, secure, valuable, worthy, respected, and competent—in a deep and genuine way, not just a mantra or story that they tell themselves—then levels of prejudice would decrease.

In Chapter 5, I mentioned a study by Steve Fein and Steven Spencer that investigated the extent to which prejudice stems from the desire to maintain feelings of self-worth. They hypothesized that expressing prejudice can restore one's sense of diminished self-esteem. In one experiment, they demonstrated that making study participants feel less self-assured and more threatened (by giving them negative feedback on a test) made them become more prejudiced. Participants were given a difficult exam and were told either that they did very well (scoring in the ninety-third percentile) or not so well (scoring in the forty-seventh percentile). This feedback was bogus, so the results described had, in truth, nothing to do with the participants' actual ability.

After providing the feedback to participants, the researchers then measured the participants' level of self-esteem and found, not surprisingly, that those who were told that they scored in the forty-seventh percentile had significantly lower self-esteem than those who were told that they scored in the ninety-third percentile. Participants were then asked to evaluate the personality of a Jewish or Christian student, which was signaled by religious iconography on jewelry that they were wearing. Those participants who received negative feedback were more likely to negatively evaluate a Jewish student than a Christian student. And this opportunity to negatively evaluate a Jewish student increased their self-esteem.[58]

Similarly, White women in one experimental condition were led to feel threatened by reading an article about the prevalence and economic and social consequences of sexism against women. White women in the control condition read an article about left-handedness and the brain—with no mention of sexism or other social ills. The women who read about sexism subsequently showed more racism against Blacks and Hispanics, and this was due to higher levels of threat that they experienced from reading the article.[59]

Fortunately, in both of these studies the propensity to show bias against ethnic and racial out-groups was decreased when the subjects were affirmed—either by writing about values that were important to them or by reading about a recent accomplishment of women, respectively.

A more secure and happy person is a more tolerant person. The mere state of being angry, for reasons that have nothing to do with race, is sufficient to trigger higher levels of racial prejudice.[60] The chronic state of being positive and chill is associated with higher levels of *non*prejudice. In an interesting investigation of the psychology of truly nonprejudiced White people (i.e., the roughly 7 percent of the population who show no evidence of racial bias on implicit or explicit measures) one of the biggest factors that differentiated them from the other 93 percent was their emotional susceptibility to positive versus negative stimuli in the environment. Participants were shown neutral stimuli (i.e., different Chinese characters) paired with photos of either positive/pleasant stimuli (e.g., cute puppies, smiling faces) or negative/threatening stimuli (e.g., vomit on a sidewalk, a pointed gun) in a classical conditioning-style procedure. The researchers then measured how much those participants later reported liking or disliking each Chinese character as a function of which type of photos the character had been paired with previously.

The truly nonprejudiced people were much less prone to forming negative associations than were ordinary people and were also more prone to forming positive associations. And this difference in their general susceptibility to positive versus negative affective conditioning correlated with their level of racial bias.[61] So where do these nonprejudiced unicorns come from, and how did they become so resilient to the formation of negative associations? There are at least two possible answers: socialization and genetics. And there is indirect evidence of both.

Although the 93 percent of ordinary people were both liberal and conservative, to a relatively equal degree, the 7 percent of truly non-biased people were almost exclusively liberal. Prior research has often characterized conservatives as prejudiced. These data refute that characterization. What it shows is that everyone has racial biases— liberals and conservatives alike. However, among the very small handful of White people who do not have racial biases, there is an overwhelmingly high likelihood that they will be liberal. Research by John Jost and colleagues has argued that, like authoritarianism, conservative ideology is in many ways grounded in perceptions of threat.[62] Remember, authoritarians tend to see the world as a dangerous place and have a low tolerance for disorder. Also recall that the biggest determinant of authoritarianism is a strict, rigid parenting style that instills fear in children. To the extent that political ideology is socially transmitted, like authoritarianism, this could be a factor in producing differences in emotional susceptibility and racial prejudice. Teaching your children that the world is a cruel and chaotic place, for example, may be linked to higher levels of racism in adulthood.

You may be wondering if their more positive emotional orientation to the world renders nonprejudiced people more vulnerable to harm and danger. That does not seem to be the case. A follow-up survey on the likelihood of being mugged, assaulted, scammed, or otherwise victimized showed no difference in the likelihood of victimization between nonprejudiced and ordinary people. It's also not the case that they are clueless. They see threats, just not behind every rock. And negative people or experiences do not linger for them the way that they do for ordinary people.

There may be genetic factors related to vigilance to threat as well. Researchers have found that genes associated with the processing of threat-relevant information are implicated in the prevalence of racial biases. For example, the serotonin transporter polymorphism 5-HTTLPR in the gene SLC6A4 influences the regulation of serotonergic neurotransmission. This polymorphism has been identified as a genetic mechanism associated with threat-relevant racial bias.[63] Simply stated, there are genetic markers that regulate people's responsiveness and reactivity to environmental threat. And individual differences in this genetic marker can also be related to differences in certain forms of racial bias.

What all of this research suggests is that you can reduce prejudice simply by feeling good, calm, and secure. Before engaging in an interracial interaction, write down three things that you like about yourself or that you do well, and remind yourself of why you are a person who is worthy of love. This practice of self-affirmation will not only reduce racial bias but also increase your general well-being. Also, ponder the ways love and kindness in general are important. Although it sounds a bit new age and touchy-feely, it actually works. Several lines of research have shown that loving-kindness meditation, for example, can substantially reduce racial bias.[64]

CONFRONTING PREJUDICE

To do the work of antiracism well requires having the right head, heart, and stomach. You have to understand what's going on, you have to care, and you have to have the courage to do something. However, many people do not speak up or act when they witness racism occurring, as was the case in the Kawakami study discussed in

Chapter 8. The research on the impact of confronting racism has revealed a number of interesting findings. First, when people speak up against racism, it often leads the person confronted to feel guilt and to engage in subsequent efforts to do better. However, this impact is much stronger when the person who confronts a White offender is White rather than Black.[65] A Black person confronting a White person about racism is often not taken seriously and can even be seen as a "complainer."[66]

In an intriguing set of experiments, Cheryl Kaiser and Carol Miller assessed responses to a Black person who attributed his poor score on a test of "future career success" to the quality of his answers (self-blame) or to racial discrimination by one of the eight White people evaluating the test. They also manipulated the likelihood that the White person evaluating the test actually did discriminate against the Black person. Of the eight people judging the test, participants were told that none, four, or all eight of them had a history of discriminating against Black people. This manipulation was designed to vary the actual likelihood of discrimination as being low, medium, or very high. They found that the Black person was judged as being a "complainer" (i.e., hypersensitive, irritating, emotional, argumentative, and a troublemaker) when he attributed the low score to discrimination by one of the eight White judges rather than to his own answers. What is particularly stunning about the study is that the Black person was seen as being as much of a complainer regardless of whether he was in the low-, medium-, or high-probability condition. In other words, the Black person was treated as negatively in the condition where all of the judges had a history of racism as he was in the condition where none of the judges had a history of racism.[67]

This finding is troubling because it suggests that White people's negative reaction to Black people who raise grievances about discrimination has nothing to do with whether the complaint is valid or not. Rather, they just don't want to hear about it—either because they are apathetic (as shown in the Kawakami study in Chapter 8, when White people witnessed a Black person being called the N-word) or because it makes them feel awkward. Indeed, White people do feel more *awkward* when confronted by a Black person compared with a

White person, even though they feel less *guilty* when confronted by a Black person compared with a White person.[68]

This creates a frustrating situation for Black people, who have to bear not only the heavy cost of discrimination but also the additional burden of being punished for speaking up about it. And when no Black people speak up, White people may assume that all is well in the organization—erroneously concluding that racial discrimination does not exist. A further consequence of this trend is that when Black people engage in all-out, unfettered, in-your-face confrontation and activism, White people are often confused (and scared) and left wondering where all this "anger" is coming from. This study provides an answer—subtle appeals fall on deaf ears.

However, White people *will* listen to other White people—which creates an opportunity for antiracist Whites to reduce racism by confronting bias when they see it. Put differently, White people who remain silent in the face of racism are squandering a precious opportunity to create social change. And by preventing a Black person from doing it, it has the dual advantage of saving a Black person from the negative consequences of being the confronter. Therefore, White people should resist the temptation of falling victim to White solidarity.[69] As mentioned during discussion of the PRESS model, even the most effective strategy is worthless if there is no willingness to incur the "sacrifice"—or the effort, cost, or inconvenience of acting. It boils down to how much you care, not whether something can be done. To paraphrase the words of the late congressman John Lewis once again: If you see something that is not right, say something. Do something.

ESTABLISHING CLEAR GOALS

At this point, your head may be spinning. I can't blame you. Given the pervasiveness of racism and bias, the actions you could choose to undertake in response can seem limitless. The best course of action is to start with just a handful of actions.

Research suggests that having fewer and more concrete goals can increase the likelihood of successful outcomes versus having very abstract or numerous goals.[70] For example, having the goal to lose weight is abstract. Having the goal to be a better person is very abstract. To have a better shot at reaching these goals, it helps to establish specific objectives. In the weight-loss example, a concrete goal might be consuming one thousand calories per day or spending forty-five minutes in the gym Monday through Friday. A concrete goal for being a "good person" might be saying hello and making eye contact with every stranger that you interact with or volunteering for a local charity five days a month. Having goals that are more specific and measurable increases the likelihood that you will achieve the end result.

It's also important to have goals that are realistic and attainable. As much as you care about the environment, having a goal of a negative carbon footprint or zero waste is simply not achievable for most people (you would never be able to buy anything online, due to the fact that it must be packaged). Remember, you can't boil the ocean by yourself. Carefully choose finite, reasonable goals that you can stick to. Although you can't reach zero waste, you can endeavor to recycle every piece of waste that enters your home. Although you can't function without electricity, you can use lower-wattage LED bulbs in all of your light fixtures. And although you might not live close enough to walk to work, you can purchase a hybrid or electric car, or ride your bike, carpool, or take public transportation instead of driving.

So let's apply this idea to the work of antiracism. My challenge to you is to choose three to five antiracist behaviors—whether it's being an advocate or an activist—and practice those religiously. Having actionable goals involves formulating a clear idea of what you can do to achieve the outcomes that are important to you. Here are five broad examples of actions that you can take to contribute to your own, or others', antiracism:

1. **Prosocial Civil Engagement.** Are you voting in every local, state, and national election? Do you volunteer time or resources to candidates whom you believe in? Are you writing letters to incumbent politicians? Are you helping to build the city's or neighborhood's sense of community and interconnectedness? Are you stepping outside your own comfort zone and getting

exposed to diverse people and cultures? Are there groups in your community that you can join, such as a book club dedicated to discussing works by authors of color?

2. **Selective Consumerism.** Pay attention to the practices of the retailers and service providers where you spend your money. What can you learn about the company's track record of diversity and racial justice? All companies are in business to make money, but some are in business *only* to make money. Go out of your way to support the "good" companies and/or boycott the "bad" ones. Educate yourself about local businesses that are owned by people of color, and actively support and promote these enterprises. If you are a business owner, seek non-White vendors and subcontractors.

3. **Mentorship and Sponsorship.** Dedicate time to the professional development of others at work who could benefit from your technical expertise or political support. Go out of your way to serve as a role model or mentor for youth who might be inspired by your work, especially those who may have fewer opportunities for relationship building.

4. **Civic Activism.** Engage in demonstrations and protests to draw attention to important issues and generate policy change.[71] Exercise your right to take to the street and make your voice heard when you see something that isn't right. Find opportunities to engage with diversity issues in real life, such as joining a committee dedicated to diversity and inclusion in your workplace.

5. **Financial Contribution.** There are many organizations whose mission is to bring about greater racial equity and social justice (e.g., NAACP, Southern Poverty Law Center, United Negro College Fund, Anti-Defamation League, Human Rights Campaign, National Association of Latino Elected and Appointed Officials, Partnership with Native Americans, etc.). What are local grassroots organizations that are dedicated to social justice

causes that are important to you? Ask yourself if you are in a position to financially support these organizations, and if so, consider contributing.

These are just a few general examples of actions that you can take to move the needle on racial equity. The goal of this chapter—and the book—is not to provide you with an exhaustive checklist of actions (though you may have noticed that this chapter is twice as long as some others in the book!), but rather to provide you with a new consciousness and perspective. My hope is that by opening your eyes, this book will help you move through your daily life armed with knowledge and inspired to seek everyday actions that help root out racism and bias amid the innumerable places it lurks in our society and within ourselves. It is up to you to figure out for yourself how best to apply this knowledge and perspective to the unique situations and challenges of your organization and community.

While the goal of "ending racism" seems so mystical, abstract, and unattainable, it doesn't have to be that way. First, make it concrete and finite in your own life. At the same time, we must acknowledge a limit to what individuals can accomplish on their own. Systemic racism calls for systemic interventions. In the next chapter, we'll turn our attention to the institutional side of ending racism. As a preview, I would argue that the vague and mysterious concept of systemic racism found within communities and organizations can be reduced to five big things. If we focused on these five interconnected foundations of oppression in a thoughtful and effective way, we could eliminate the lion's share—perhaps 90 percent or more—of systemic racism that exists in our country.

1. Voting rights
2. Economic inequality
3. Public education
4. Criminal justice
5. Healthcare disparities

Although all five of these factors represent institutional-level reforms, I mention them in this chapter on individual interventions because in a democratic system, every individual citizen can affect, and be affected by, institutions. This makes individual participation even more critical and impactful. However, leaders and organizations also play a role—perhaps an even bigger role—in creating and changing institutional structures. The final chapter dives deeper into the various steps that leaders and organizations can take to eradicate racism.

CHAPTER TWELVE

How Leaders and Organizations Can Create Greater Racial Equity

A t most organizations, little would get done without dedicated and effective leadership. This is especially true when it comes to promoting racial diversity, equity, and inclusion (DEI). The book's final chapter focuses on what leaders can do to combat racism in their organizations, as well as what their organizations can do to combat racism in society. Leaders often ask me to provide concrete examples of best practices in other organizations. I am often reluctant to do so. A cake recipe that works in New Orleans, at sea level, may not work in Denver, due to the higher altitude. Similarly, looking at one company's approach as an exact model for every other company is tricky. Every environment is different. Every industry is different. Every organization is different. Even different business units or geographical locations of the same corporation can have distinct needs, cultures, and challenges. With this caveat in mind, I will briefly describe the details of three organizations, across very distinct sectors—public, private, and higher education—that tackled their unique DEI goals in creative and effective ways.

MASSPORT: FLOUR IN THE BATTER, NOT ICING ON THE CAKE

The Massachusetts Port Authority, or Massport, operates several air transportation centers, including Boston Logan International Airport. It also operates ports and owns billions of dollars' worth of land in Boston's Seaport District and throughout Massachusetts. One source of revenue for Massport is rents received from commercial developments on its land (e.g., Boston Convention Center). Large organizations submit proposals to compete for lucrative development contracts, with the winners being selected by Massport.

When it came time to accept proposals for the half-billion-dollar hotel project on one of its parcels, the visionary leaders of the organization—including Massport board member L. Duane Jackson, a Black architect and developer, and Massport CEO Tom Glynn—put their heads together to decide what the organization could do to address the lack of racial diversity in the industry and the growing racial wealth disparity in the Boston area. (At the time, in 2017, the average household wealth of a White family in Boston was $247,500, but for a Black family that figure was just $8!)[1] Massport's leaders decided to change the criteria for how proposals were chosen for a $500 million hotel project that would be developed on a large parcel of land in the Seaport District. In addition to evaluating (1) track record of experience, (2) profitability from rents, and (3) architectural design, they added a fourth criterion called "comprehensive diversity and inclusion," which accounted for 25 percent of the proposal's overall score—making it just as important in the selection process as the other three criteria. This forced developers not only to think more deeply about diversity but also to take action—if they wanted a high enough score to land the contract.

Massport's approach was ingenious because it didn't impose quotas or constraints. It simply made clear that several facets of diversity would be evaluated as part of the 25 percent score, including:

- Extent of women/minority business participation in the areas of development, financing, design, construction, and ownership

- Quality of programs and initiatives for workforce development
- Contractor and supplier diversity programs
- Creative approaches to enhanced diversity and inclusion
- Local commitment and community outreach
- Level of specificity in proposal as to how the proposed women/minority goals would be achieved

Leaders of large development firms in Boston, who are almost exclusively White (and Irish American), acknowledged the racial homogeneity of the large-scale building industry and admitted that one tends to see the same people again and again, project after project. The oft-cited reasons for this were expertise and prior experience. That is, it's difficult to do a half-billion-dollar project if you have never done a half-billion-dollar project, making it a hard industry to break into. One developer, John Moriarty, who was completing a $900 million residential and retail complex in the Seaport District, said, "If you're going to spend $500 million, are you going to do it with someone who has done it before? Or are you going to do it with somebody who is just learning? Of course you're going to do it with someone who has a track record and your investors can feel comfortable with."[2]

Although Massport's new policy forced Moriarty out of his comfort zone, he was not one to pass up a big development opportunity. He reached out to local Black developer Greg Janey—who until that point had undertaken only smaller development projects. Moriarty and Janey soon began working together on a $25 million training-center project in Boston. Moriarty wanted to get experience working with Janey before bringing him into a $500 million project. Moriarty was quickly impressed with Janey's work on the training center, and the two became friends and business partners. Moriarty and Janey won the bid for the Massport hotel project, with Janey becoming a 30 percent partner in the $500 million venture. Together, they also reached out to one hundred minority subcontractors, as well as one of the few minority-owned architectural firms in the country, which also happened to be 40 percent women. All in all, about 30 percent of the businesses engaged in this massive project were women/minority, marking a tremendous increase in diversity for the development industry.

Based on this project's success, Massport has now made the policy an integral part of its business practices moving forward. All entities wanting to partner with Massport will have to now seriously consider how diversity will become part of their overall business plan. Diversity is not the icing on the cake—it's the flour in the batter. Before this policy, construction firms had little incentive to prioritize diversity. As one developer put it, "That's not to say that the development community is racist. What it is to say is that we're looking for the shortest distance between two points. [Massport had established these new] rules of engagement. But had Massport not set these rules of engagement, this is not the most cost-effective way to get the job done. It's because Massport took the very strong position that they did [that] people took it seriously."[3]

As stated in the previous chapter, sometimes people have to be compelled to eat brussels sprouts . . . and they later grow to like them. Massport's policy compelled people to behave differently from the way they would have if left to their own devices. However, the prior lack of engagement or commitment wasn't necessarily due to racism. People are busy. People are self-interested. Massport created an institutional-based incentive to embrace diversity, and in doing so, changed individual behavior and subsequently the culture of how business was done in Boston. This model is in the process of being adapted by other government agencies and municipalities and just might end up being a game changer. Later we will discuss ways in which some of the features of this model can be adapted to private corporations and other types of organizations.

HARVEY MUDD COLLEGE: FIX THE STRUCTURE, IMPROVE THE CULTURE

The second example comes from the higher education sector. Harvey Mudd College (HMC) is a prestigious liberal arts college in California focusing on science, technology, engineering, and math (STEM). For decades, Harvey Mudd's leaders and faculty have been trying to take steps to reduce the underrepresentation of women and racial minorities in STEM. One striking gap was the gender imbalance of students entering the college who intended to study computer science.

The leaders at HMC began by diagnosing the *root cause* of this disparity. Not surprisingly, they quickly discovered that many of the problems were inherited from society. Not only did men and women tend to have different reasons for studying computer science, but they tended to also have different levels of experience with computer science prior to entering college. To be clear, they did not have a different level of intelligence or potential but rather a different level of *experience*. This gap in experience is due to society treating boys and girls differently throughout secondary school—encouraging STEM subjects for boys and liberal arts subjects for girls—consistent with gender stereotypes.

To compensate for this gap, Harvey Mudd's leadership decided to create two different introductory computer science tracks—one for first-year students with no prior experience and one for first-year students with some prior experience in high school. The no-experience course tended to be around 50 percent women, whereas the some-experience course was predominantly male. By the end of the year, the students in both courses were on par with one another, and the groups were reintegrated the following semester. Through this structural change in how computer science was taught, the school began correcting the disparities that were produced by society.[4]

Maria Klawe, the president of Harvey Mudd, knew that creating the second track alone would not be enough. She also set out to change the school's culture more generally and create other incentives for underrepresented students to join. She understood that women and people of color were less likely to seek help once enrolled, despite the systemic factors that made their learning curve steeper. Klawe stated, "We've worked really hard on building a culture where asking for help is natural. . . . We must also create a culture in which our members feel empowered to take the necessary risks that lead to greater success as well as to the failures that lead to greater learning and personal growth."[5]

Klawe also changed the culture by encouraging students to see one another as partners, not competitors, and by creating a climate of mutual support. In addition, Klawe changed the on-campus imagery to reflect the diversity of the student body and the achievements of engineers and scientists from many different backgrounds. Recall the research cited in the last chapter showing that exposure to counterstereotypical images can have a huge impact on implicit bias.

To further increase exposure, she also began offering all-expense-paid trips to the Grace Hopper Celebration of Women in Computing, the nation's largest professional gathering of women in technology. This was done to give women an opportunity to meet role models in the tech industry. Finally, she worked with external partners—companies like Intel, Microsoft, Facebook, and Google—to establish early internship programs, believing that women and students of color would benefit from early internship experience in the program. Such efforts represented a major shift from the way higher education had typically operated, and Klawe demonstrated humility and a willingness to learn. "You'll never get it right immediately, and you have to be willing to be constantly reevaluating," as she put it.[6]

Klawe ran up against challenges from some faculty and members of the board of trustees who saw the college as a merit-based institution and did not believe the institution could become more diverse without lowering standards. As the speaker at the next trustee meeting, she decided to bring in Freeman Hrabowski, the president of the University of Maryland, Baltimore County, who transformed the predominantly White university into one of the top producers of minority scientists in the country. His stories from his own life and professional experience led to a total shift in attitudes. "People were crying," said Klawe. "[After his speech] the language just changed. Faculty, staff, trustees, students, parents were all saying, we've got to diversify the campus. Unsurpassed excellence and diversity at all levels became a core theme of Harvey Mudd College's strategic plan."[7]

Harvey Mudd's success in changing its culture is clearly reflected in the numbers. The percentage of women graduates in computer science increased from roughly 12 percent to 48 percent in the ten-year period from 2006 to 2016.[8]

JPMORGAN CHASE: BUILDING AN ECOSYSTEM OF SOCIAL IMPACT

The final example comes from the private sector. When JPMorgan Chase CEO Jamie Dimon decided he wanted to do something about racial inequality, he went big. The company built a program called "Advancing Black Pathways," which took on the broad goal of redressing racial economic disparities and making the economy work for everyone. This program, established in 2018, has three pillars: Wealth, Careers, and Education. The Wealth initiative focuses on helping to increase entrepreneurship, homeownership, financial wellness, and investment opportunities. For example, the firm provides access to capital through its Entrepreneurs of Color Fund, as well as online education through the Advancing Black Entrepreneurs program, which partners with *Black Enterprise* magazine, the National Minority Supplier Development Council, the National Urban League, and U.S. Black Chambers, Inc. The firm also offers down-payment assistance programs for people looking to buy a home, as well as home counseling and homeownership grants. Through Currency Conversations, launched in partnership with *Essence* in 2019, they're working to increase financial literacy in the Black community and put more people on a path to financial health.

The Careers initiative has the mission of increasing access to well-paying careers for Black people, as well as to provide support for Black executives. This effort builds on the company's existing Advancing Black Leaders strategy—which sought to increase the hiring, retention, and promotion of Black talent both within JPMorgan Chase and beyond. They have now expanded these efforts to the larger marketplace by offering a series of online classes and professional coaching in their Career Readiness Series and other online options.

Finally, the Education prong of the effort focuses on increasing access to educational and training opportunities for Black students. The firm has committed to creating apprenticeship, internship, and employment opportunities for four thousand Black students at JPMorgan

Chase by 2024. Although the initiative is less than two years old, they're already 40 percent of the way toward their hiring goal. In fact, JPMorgan Chase is the single biggest employer of students graduating from Howard University, Spelman College, and Morehouse College, three of the leading historically Black colleges and universities (HBCUs) in the United States, according to JPMorgan Chase executive Sekou Kaalund.

In addition to hiring opportunities, Advancing Black Pathways is providing financial support for students who attend historically Black colleges and universities through JPMorgan Chase's Student Financial Hardship Fund. Students are able to access these funds to cover a wide range of expenses, including outstanding tuition balances, apartment deposits, unanticipated car repairs, medical expenses, unpaid utility bills, and short-term food insecurity. Students can also use these funds to buy textbooks or travel home for family-related emergencies. Financial education for Black college students is another core focus for Advancing Black Pathways, and the program includes a financial e-learning curriculum that teaches basic personal finance. The series has already been delivered to thousands of HBCU students across the country.

What I find truly remarkable about the Advancing Black Pathways program is that it doesn't treat racial equity as just an aspiration, or a line on a mission statement, or even a policy—but an entire ecosystem of initiatives that work in concert with one another. Jamie Dimon has gone so far as to create a semiautonomous, well-funded business unit within JPMorgan Chase to address issues that are important to the corporation. It is run like a mini corporation with its own board—with prominent members such as Condoleezza Rice, Marc Morial, Kevin Hart, Soledad O'Brien, and Mellody Hobson, who is also a member of the board of JPMorgan Chase. The Advancing Black Pathways program is a prime example of what I call "corporate activism"—when corporations get involved to address problems in the broader society. Other recent examples are Nike and FedEx, companies that put pressure on the Washington Football Team to drop its offensive name and Native American mascot.

When I spoke to the head of Advancing Black Pathways, Sekou Kaalund, about how this institutionalization of antiracism came about at JPMorgan Chase, he recalled Jamie Dimon simply deciding in 2018 that he wanted to do more for the Black community. From there, Thasunda Brown Duckett, CEO of Chase Consumer Banking and executive sponsor of Advancing Black Pathways, went about putting smart people on the problem, including Kaalund, and gave them the support and resources that they needed. "When you're intentional and do the work and invest the resources, you can make a change," Kaalund says.

After less than two years, the program has been a roaring success by any measure, both internally and externally. Through the Advancing Black Leaders program JPMorgan Chase has increased the representation of Black executives by 60 percent. And at the top level, JPMorgan Chase employs more African American executives than the other three leading banks combined, according to Kaalund.

What does the bank get out of all this? "Clients want to do business with you when you do the right thing," says Kaalund. And he's right. The company is also seeing returns in employee engagement and well-being as a result of its efforts. And not just Black employees— Whites in Gen Z, who are more vocal on social justice issues than their parents' generation, don't want to work for or do business with companies that aren't diverse. The way I see it, JPMorgan Chase—by taking a strong stand on diversity—has well positioned itself for the decades ahead, in which the U.S. population and workforce will become increasingly diverse.

GENERAL LESSONS: THE CRITICAL IMPORTANCE OF LEADERSHIP

What all three examples above have in common is fearless and committed leadership. They also share the fact that at least one member of the institution's board was also strongly in favor of the initiative. That's an important detail because CEOs are not the demigods that people sometimes believe them to be. They report to a board of directors or, in the case of nonprofits and universities, to a board of trustees. In large for-profit companies, the chief executive's primary responsibility is to maximize shareholder value, which often does not prioritize diversity and inclusion efforts. The merits of the institutional logic that demands "maximizing shareholder value at any cost" is a debate for another book. But I would argue that efforts to end systemic racism are always in the long-term economic interest of a company. Change begins at the top—with the commitment and courage of the CEO to do things differently. The other lesson here is that it seems to help when CEOs also have at least one ally on the board. Interestingly, the board allies of the Massport and JPMorgan Chase CEOs were both Black, which also suggests that organizations need to put more Black people on their boards if they want profound and sustainable change around diversity.

I cannot think of a single case of radical change that has taken place at a large organization without the support of top leaders—whether it was a CEO, a board member, or both. In every case the change occurred because a leader stepped up and said, "This is what we should be doing," or carefully listened to and strongly supported employees' grassroots efforts to promote diversity. Nothing gets done at the organizational level without the blessing of the top brass. Without that, the chief diversity officer (if there is one) is simply playing a window-dressing game. Although CEO support is necessary, it is not sufficient. In addition, you need to address the "frozen middle," who often resist or oppose diversity initiatives because they do not understand them or because they see them as a threat to their own professional ascent. This starts with the leader building a compelling case for whatever change he or she is looking to make. Don't assume that the logic is obvious, as we covered in Chapter 1.

It also helps to know *why* this work is important to the organization. Is it window dressing/icing or part of the "batter" of the organization? Leaders sometimes say to me: "We know we should be doing something, but we don't know why." Examining the core values of the organization will help to clarify the utility of diversity and help the organization to establish priorities. Organizations should have no more than three to five core values, to ensure that they are truly central, deeply entrenched characteristics of the organization.[9]

WHAT CAN LEADERS DO TO PROMOTE RACIAL EQUITY?

Many of the strategies and tactics learned in the last chapter, such as greater intergroup contact, can be applied to the organizational context. There are creative ways to have icebreakers, scavenger hunts, and athletic activities that deliberately integrate people on teams and encourage them to work together. An inspiring real-world example is chronicled in the documentary *A Most Beautiful Thing,* based on the memoir of Arshay Cooper. It tells the story of Black high school teens in the 1990s on the west side of Chicago who took up rowing, and how being in the same boat—literally—brought rival gang members together in unity and solidarity. As adults, some of the teams have now extended offers to teach rowing to White police officers, and it has become a way to foster more positive relations between the police and community.

Another approach is decategorization, which focuses attention on the individual qualities of a person. One technique for increasing decategorization is an intervention that I call "speed dating." A person's social network at a company is instrumental to getting promotions, often through mentors, and particularly sponsors.[10] Leaders tend to be drawn to people who are more like themselves, and assume that people who look like them are more similar. However, people can often have more in common with others who do not look like them, despite assumptions to the contrary. Speed dating is a process in which leaders attend an event or gathering where they interact with a diverse set of people who meet the objective criteria for promotion (e.g., level of profit generation, educational credential, years of experience, etc.). Each leader must spend an allocated period of one-on-one time talking to and getting to know each of these employees. Doing so increases the likelihood that they will become impressed by the employees' expertise as well as discover similarities and common interests with diverse employees that they would not have expected to exist. This in turn makes it more likely that leaders will agree to sponsor diverse employees whom they never would have taken the initiative to meet due to the assumption that they had nothing in common.

In an ideal world, the level of emotional rapport, affinity, or similarity between a leader and an employee should be relatively unimportant. What should really matter is competence. However, research suggests that we do not live in that world.[11] Leaders should take care not to hold women and people of color to different standards of similarity or "homophily" than White males. An analysis of Fortune 500 boards from 1994 to 2006 showed that higher board diversity on race and gender characteristics was counterbalanced by lower diversity on more interpersonal-based characteristics.[12] In other words, women and racial-minority board members tended to have more in common with White male board members than the White board members had in common with one another. This suggests that women and people of color have to meet a higher bar of homophily, similarity, or affinity to be included. By finding people who look different from us but still think like us, we may undercut the advantages that diversity can provide.

Building on the research around counterstereotypical images, leaders should be mindful of the images and iconography in their physical spaces—and in the imagery associated with their business. Are the portraits of revered figures in the hallways and lobbies almost exclusively White males? Or is there a diversity of images? Hollywood executives could go a long way toward reducing implicit bias by simply making films that cast people of color in a more flattering light. Instead, they are disproportionately cast as criminals and villains, rather than as heroes. For example, one investigation examining roles in 26,000 U.S. films showed that Black people were cast as "thugs" or "gang members" in over 60 percent of these roles. In real life, only 13 percent of the population is Black and the majority (i.e., 65 percent) of actual gang members are *not* Black.[13] You can't be it if you can't see it. People of color need to see more positive role models.

Regarding the hypocrisy-induction approach discussed in the last chapter, organizations could be more mindful of internally acknowledging and highlighting inconsistencies between their values and their practices. Vivid examples of such inconsistencies are listed in the classic article "On the Folly of Rewarding A, While Hoping for B."[14] For example, organizations hope for long-term profit but reward quarterly earnings, or they hope for collaborative teamwork but reward individual effort. With the example of diversity, top leaders often want managers in the "frozen middle" to embrace and implement the company's diversity initiatives, but these managers are compensated and promoted based on efficiency and short-term profit. There is also little accountability for fulfilling the goals that the organization claims to value. Remember the Massport case—they held developers accountable for diversity in a clear, measurable, and unambiguous way.

THE POWER OF SOCIAL NORMS AND ORGANIZATIONAL CULTURE

We humans are a lot like sheep who are strongly inclined to follow the flock. For this reason, social norms—unspoken rules about what is socially common, appropriate, or acceptable—can have a powerful impact on our behaviors. Robert Cialdini and colleagues conducted a study to investigate what would be the most effective approach to getting citizens to change their behavior—in this case, to conserve more energy. Researchers surveyed each household to gauge their perceptions of why they thought it would be important to conserve energy: to save money, to protect the environment, or because other people are doing it. On average, people rated environmental protection as the most important reason, economic savings as the second most important reason, and other people doing it as the least important reason of all.

Next, they were interested in whether people would actually change their energy consumption, and if so, what would be the most effective way to get them to do it. To get an idea of how much energy each household was using already, the researchers took a baseline reading of the electrical meters of more than 350 households in the study a week before these households were randomly assigned to receive one of three types of flyers. Some households received a flyer urging them to reduce their energy consumption because it could save them $54 per month. Some households received a flyer urging them to reduce their energy consumption because it could prevent the release of up to 262 pounds of greenhouse gases per month. The third group of households received a flyer urging them to conserve energy because almost 80 percent of other residents in their city were doing it. A meter reading taken three weeks after the flyers were posted revealed that those in the social norms condition (i.e., 80 percent of your neighbors are doing it) showed, by far, the biggest drop in energy consumption of the three conditions.[15]

In short, norms are important because they affect behaviors. Organizations vary considerably in their norms around supporting a climate of racism or one of antiracism. A study by Arthur Brief and colleagues examined how norms created by leadership can exacerbate the expression of racism, particularly among those who already have racist attitudes. They investigated hiring decisions in the context of what they called the "business justification to discriminate." The study was inspired by the case of a large, national restaurant chain whose CEO believed that "Blacks should not be employed in any position where they would be seen by customers."[16] When no toxic culture of discrimination was present, neither White individuals high or low in prejudice discriminated against Black job candidates.[17] However, when a culture of discrimination was in place, high-prejudice Whites discriminated much more than low-prejudice Whites.[18]

Leaders have the ability to affect organizational culture through their words, actions, and policies, which in turn influence employees' decision and behaviors. Individual employees can have an impact too. Myriad studies have found that social norms around prejudice can have a huge impact on racial attitudes.[19] For example, one study found that hearing just one person denounce racism led to fewer expressions of racism from other people. On the flip side, hearing another person condone racism led to more expressions of racism from others.[20] Another study found that when people thought that their level of racism was higher than that of their peers, their racial attitudes improved. However, when they believed their peers were more racist, their racial attitudes got worse.[21] So why not recruit influencers and "cool kids" to help you model the behavior you want to see in the organization? With a concerted effort the climate can shift relatively quickly.

Leaders and employees alike have a lot of power to shape organizational culture, which creates downstream consequences for behaviors.[22] A climate is like fertilizer that allows certain types of seeds—or in this case traits or tendencies—to blossom and flourish. Although some organizational climates are more toxic than others, it would be too simplistic to simply classify them as "toxic" and "nontoxic." It's a bit more complicated than that. Let's dive more deeply into four types of organizational cultures around diversity.

THE FOUR TYPES OF CULTURES

Organizations vary considerably in their norms around supporting a climate of racism or one of antiracism. I put organizational cultures around diversity into four broad buckets: toxic, laissez-faire, prodiversity on paper, and prodiversity in practice.

Toxic organizations encourage overtly hostile, bullying, and anti-egalitarian behaviors toward women, LGBTQ+, people of color, and other groups, because they see such a culture as being indicative of masculinity, power, or status.[23] I estimate that about 15 percent of companies fall into this category, including some firms in the financial, tech, government, and mining sectors.

Laissez-faire organizations are apathetic toward diversity and tout themselves as being gender- or color-blind. However, as we learned in Chapter 2 (salmon in the stream) and Chapter 9 (people at the fence watching the soccer game), there is no such thing as color-blindness because there are currents and barriers everywhere. Therefore, doing nothing amounts to complicity in the perpetuation of racism. Nevertheless, many firms implicitly or explicitly espouse a hands-off approach. They figure it will happen organically, and if not, then so be it. I estimate that 35 percent of companies fall into this category.

Prodiversity on paper organizations hail diversity as being an integral part of their values and aspirations. However, there is little action beyond verbal commitments. At 40 percent, I estimate this is the largest of the four categories. Within it are two subcategories: (1) companies that want diversity but don't have it because they don't know what to do or simply haven't done it, and (2) companies that privately and candidly do *not* want diversity but nevertheless publicly extol the virtues of diversity.

Finally, *prodiversity in practice* organizations actively work toward building and enhancing diversity and achieve praiseworthy outcomes. I put about 10 percent of organizations into this category.

Organizations should try to decide which of these four categories they fall into, and whether they are satisfied being there. Two very simple ways that you can diagnose whether the culture is inclusive or not is to look at what happens when people make mistakes. How people are treated under normal circumstances will not tell you much about the level of racial bias—as illustrated by aversive racism theory. But how quickly or severely a woman and/or person of color is written off or punished for making a mistake may tell you a lot.[24] Being attuned to how easy it is for people of color to get into trouble for small things (what they are wearing, whether they go five minutes over on their lunch break, whether someone feels offended by something they said or how they said it) compared with how difficult it is for White males to get into trouble—no matter what they do—will also help you gauge the level of racial bias or inclusion.

Is your organization where you want it to be? If not, there are a number of steps that can be taken to change things. I will offer some suggestions in the next section.

INSTITUTIONAL POLICIES AND PRACTICES

There has been a trend in recent years to move away from an attempt to de-bias individuals (e.g., through unconscious bias training) to an effort to de-bias organizations by creating institutional policies and practices that disrupt both psychological and structural racism.

These include well-known strategies, many of them having to do with the hiring process, such as:

- Masking race or gender identifiers in hiring (e.g., removing names from résumés);
- Requiring diverse hiring slates (i.e., demanding that pools, short lists, and interview lineups contain diverse candidates);

- Broadening the scope of recruitment (e.g., going to historically Black colleges and universities);
- Requiring diverse panels during hiring (i.e., ensuring that the interviewers themselves are diverse *and* have equal power in decision making);
- Having structured interviews (e.g., asking everyone the same questions in the same order);
- Creating employee or business resource groups (e.g., for Black, Hispanic, LGBTQ+, women, or other affinity groups);
- Conducting simultaneous rather than sequential evaluations in hiring (i.e., evaluating candidates relative to one another rather than in isolation);[25]
- Increasing accountability (e.g., asking managers to provide justifications for their hiring decisions, and systematically evaluating the validity of these reasons);
- Creating a board of "truth tellers" (this is a group of individuals—one Fortune 500 CEO uses seven—whom a leader will meet with periodically to get candid feedback on how the organization's leadership is doing on diversity; it carries the benefit of a diversity of perspectives rather than one person speaking for the entire race, and the group setting reduces the vulnerability of any one individual);
- Increasing mentorship and sponsorship opportunities (e.g., the "speed dating" procedure described earlier, which increases access to leaders as well as individuation of candidates).

There are many other concrete steps that leaders can take to reduce systemic bias within their organization. However, one broad category of reform that can have a major impact on hiring, promotion, and retention is assessment. How is qualification or performance measured in an organization? Performance metrics—for selection, evaluation, merit raises, etc.—are all the rage. Although assessment and measurement are things that nearly all organizations do, very few organizations do them well. Gaining a deeper understanding of the theoretical and practical pitfalls of measurement—and how to avoid these traps—is something that will go a long way toward elim-

inating systemic racial bias in the design, administration, and interpretation of test results.

THE (IMPERFECT) ART AND SCIENCE
OF MEASUREMENT

Imagine that you are someone who has the long-term goal of staying
married forever once you walk down the aisle—divorce is not an option. Consequently, you wonder whether your current romantic partner truly loves you, because you believe that marital longevity is the
product of true love. So you set out to discover a fail-proof metric that
will indicate whether your partner's heart is true. The first metric
that crosses your mind is a simple survey question: "Do you really
love me?" with a response scale from zero to ten. Your true love cir-
cles "10," much to your delight. Case closed, right? Not so fast.

Self-report measures can be problematic for a number of reasons.
Maybe your partner circled "10" not because she loves you but because she didn't want to hurt your feelings. Bummer! So you move on
to a more sophisticated love meter—a physiological measure. You
connect your true love to a cardiogram that measures her beats per
minute when you're near. And whenever you come closer, lo and be-
hold, her heart rate increases. An indisputable sign of true love, right?
Well, not necessarily. Physiological instruments are more adept at de-
tecting arousal levels than discrete emotions. In other words, it can't
tell whether the increase in heart rate is caused by elation or irritation.

Next, it occurs to you that other people might be better at discern-
ing your true love's emotions than you are. We all know that it's difficult to see clearly when you're engulfed by the haze of infatuation.
You take her home to meet the family and later ask what they think.
After meeting her once, all four family members independently conclude that she adores you and urge you to propose. However, even in
this scenario, you can't be sure that this is evidence of true love. Maybe
she was putting on a show for the family. Or maybe the family just
wants you to get married already.

This seemingly straightforward example illustrates the challenges
and complications of measurement:

Challenge #1: Can the construct be accurately measured? The first challenge has to do with *construct validity,* or the extent to which a scale, device, or assessment actually measures what it intends to. Does the answer to the question "Do you really love me?" measure love or does it measure conflict avoidance? Maybe it even measures introspective ability—people themselves often don't quite know how they feel. Does the cardiogram measure love or merely increased heart rate? Is your family's consensus an indicator of her true love for you or a gauge of their gullibility—or motivated reasoning (perhaps they *want* to believe she loves you to speed the wedding along). The issue here is that many instruments and assessments do not actually measure what they purport to; they measure something else.

In physics, some instruments and measures have perfect construct validity, meaning what they are measuring (e.g., velocity) and how they measure it (i.e., calculating distance over time) are exactly the same. However, in the human realm, there are two problems. First, the concepts are fuzzy. What is love? What is intelligence? What is racism? People have vague ideas of what all of these concepts mean, but they lack the level of precision that a construct like velocity has. The second problem is that even if you can precisely define them, it's difficult to directly measure them the way you can measure speed. Simply put, there is no perfect measure for love, intelligence, potential, diligence, leadership ability, or any of the other factors that organizations are interested in. This complicates the assessment process.

The best way for leaders to get around this problem is to examine multiple different measures simultaneously. Returning to the love example, although all three measures have their flaws, if you look at all of them together, they can be extremely informative. *Convergent validity* is the term that scientists use to describe consistent results from many different measures. Although an answer of "10" on the love scale may have only a 15 percent level of confidence, truth, or certainty, if it's accompanied by elevated heart rate and the thumbs-up from your family members, then together they might increase your certainty level to 70 percent, for example. That is the power of convergent validity.

Now you understand why universities do not make decisions about applicants based on one factor (e.g., SAT scores). It's not that they are being politically correct. They are just being good scientists. You have to look at a bunch of indicators at the same time (e.g., GPA, letters of recommendation, community engagement, leadership potential, evidence of resilience, etc.) to be able to predict the outcome that you're interested in (e.g., success in life).

There are two lessons here for organizations—make sure your assessments actually measure what you intend them to, and never put all of your eggs in one assessment basket.

Challenge #2: Does the construct predict the outcome that I'm interested in? *Predictive validity* is the extent to which a measure correlates with the outcome of interest. For Harvard, it would be students who will make a positive impact on the world someday by finding a cure, ending world hunger, producing economic prosperity, inventing new technologies, creating world peace, being great leaders, or uplifting their communities in a significant way. Do SAT scores alone predict any of those outcomes? If not, why would you put excessive emphasis on them?

Does how much someone loves you—even if you could perfectly measure it—predict whether they will stay married to you for the rest of their life? Maybe not. When the honeymoon's over, passionate love may fade over time, even if it was genuine in the beginning. Even if the passion does endure, it may not be enough—as many folk songs attest. Indeed, one of the biggest predictors of divorce is financial strain—as social science research suggests.

Let's take another example. Although you can measure a wide receiver's running speed with perfect precision, speed may not strongly predict the outcome that you're interested in (e.g., the ability to score touchdowns). In addition to being fast, a successful wide receiver needs to be able to catch the football and adhere to the team's playbook to be in the right place to make the catch. Therefore, speed alone might be a fairly mediocre predictor of your outcome of interest, namely whether the player can score touchdowns.

The concept of predictive validity has profound implications for leaders. Even the best tests explain only 25 percent of the variance in outcomes.[26] That means that there is no crystal ball that will invariably predict who the "best candidate" will be. The best candidate is an *outcome,* not a trait—just as the Kentucky Derby winner is an outcome, not a trait. The horses actually have to run the race before you can determine, with any certainty, who the "best" horse is. Similarly, a best candidate does exist, but in order to be certain who it is, you would have to put all of the candidates in the position, leave them there for five years or so, then see who has performed the best. Who that highest performer will be is not something you can ever know at the time of hiring. It's a gamble, just like the Kentucky Derby. You can gather lots of information to help you wisely place a bet, but there is no test on earth that will invariably indicate who the best candidate will be. Even past performance is an imperfect indicator. Leaders who excelled at one organization may flop in a different organization. What you do have control over is how much you develop your employees. Focus on being a coach rather than a scout.

Challenge #3: How do I interpret test results? All tests are imperfectly reliable due to measurement error. Imagine there is a test of cognitive ability with scoring that ranges from zero to one hundred. The same person took the test three times and got three different scores—ninety-six the first time, ninety-one the second time, and ninety-four the third time. Does this fluctuation in test scores mean that the person's IQ is as variable as the weather? No, it just means that the test has imperfect reliability due to measurement "noise." This noise creates interpretation challenges.

If the same person can have different scores without it reflecting a difference in ability, then why can't two different people have different scores without it reflecting a difference in ability? The answer is that they can. One person can score ninety-six, another person can score ninety-one, and another person can score ninety-four without there being any difference whatsoever in ability, despite the fact that people might assume that the one who scored a ninety-six is the "best candidate."

The concept of *statistical banding,* proposed by Sheldon Zedeck, is the idea that there can exist a "band" or range of scores that do not significantly differ from one another. If five hundred people take a test and you rank them from one to five hundred, then persons ranked one through seventeen, for example, may not statistically differ from one another. This means that if you gave the test again, the person whose score ranked number one in the first round might rank number four in the second round, and the person who ranked number twelve in the first round might rank number one in the second round. Basically, the scores of people within a band are statistically interchangeable. Rather than having five hundred distinguishably different scores, you may have only thirty "bands" of scores, with fifteen to twenty people in each band.

For many people, this is a counterintuitive way of thinking about testing, because they assume that there is a difference between person 1 and person 2 and person 3 and so on. And there would be, if psychological measures, like digital timers, were super precise. But no psychological measure is. They all have a lot of noise.

What does all this mean for diversity? First, it means that leaders can seek diversity without sacrificing quality. Here's another anecdotal example. One of my colleagues jokes that he only got into Yale as an undergraduate because he is from Alaska. It would be easy for Yale to fill its roster admitting only students from California and New York, given the large populations of those states. However, one of the school's goals is to have geographical diversity, so that all fifty states (and many foreign countries) are represented. Why? Because a big part of learning and education is being exposed to people from many different walks of life. Someone who grew up in Manhattan can learn a lot from someone who lived off the grid in the Alaskan Yukon, and vice versa.

However, due to the vast numbers of people from New York and California and the very small number of people from Alaska, my colleague may have ended up number fifteen on the list of five hundred applicants based on SAT scores. And he may have been admitted over people who ranked one through fourteen. But that doesn't mean that he was less qualified.

Another problem with error is that it can come from sources that have nothing to do with the individual. For example, in her book *What Works: Gender Equality by Design* Harvard economist Iris Bohnet discusses how the SAT embeds gender bias. In the past, the test imposed a penalty for wrong answers, and because girls tend to be more risk averse than boys, they were less likely to guess if they were not sure of an answer. Nevertheless, if you can rule out one or two wrong answers, you are better off guessing, statistically speaking. Consequently, a portion of the gender difference in SAT math scores—with girls scoring lower than boys, on average—could be explained not by ability but by a willingness to guess. Once the College Board discovered this built-in error, they eliminated wrong-answer penalties and the gender gap significantly decreased.[27] This is similar to the concept of stereotype threat, discussed in Chapter 7, which affects scores for cultural reasons that have nothing to do with individual ability.

Another example of extrinsic error can be found with boys. What do you think is one of the biggest predictors of who ends up becoming a professional hockey player in the NHL? Surely it would be height? Or weight? Or aggression level, maybe? Actually, it's something as random as the month in which you are born. In fact, twice as many professional hockey players were born between January and March as between October and December (with a steady decline in numbers between March and October too).[28] This is because the cutoff birthday for youth hockey leagues is January 1. As a result, kids born earlier in the year tend to have a developmentally based physical advantage over those born later in the year, who are almost a year younger. It's a built-in systemic bias that has nothing to do with any inherent talent of the person, but rather reflects their age at the time of the commencement of hockey season.

To summarize this section:

1. All measures have flaws.
2. Multiple measures are better than one.
3. Measures do not perfectly predict outcomes of interest.
4. Strict rank ordering of scores capitalizes on noise. Use statistical bands.
5. Diversity is not incompatible with quality.
6. Outcomes are often determined by variables that are unrelated to talent (e.g., birth month).

I am not suggesting that organizations should never test. What I am suggesting is that they test more wisely. Most organizations do not, and it perpetuates racial and gender biases as a result. My advice would be to chuck the whole idea of the "best candidate." That kind of search amounts to chasing unicorns. Instead, focus on hiring well-qualified people who show good promise, and then invest time, effort, and resources into doing everything you can to help those people realize their full potential. Who knew in high school that Michael Jordan would become the basketball legend that he turned out to be? Who would have predicted Tom Brady's stellar future performance many years after his sixth-round pick in the 2000 NFL draft? As far as the NFL is concerned, predicting success with any amount of data, measurement, or assessment turns out to be a knotty affair. Despite large scouting departments, video of prior performance, and extensive tryouts, almost half of first-round picks in the NFL draft go on to be "busts."[29]

A FINAL NOTE ON "SACRIFICE"

Building diversity, equity, and inclusion requires the courage to do things differently. Leaders must have the guts and stamina—in addition to the understanding and desire—to work toward real and lasting change. Even the best strategy is useless if organizations lack the will or commitment to execute them.

Although nothing worth having is completely free, it won't cost as much as you think. Organizations often assume that diversity initiatives will require "sacrificing" at least two highly cherished values: fairness and quality. However, as we explored in Chapter 9, fairness often requires treating people differently in a way that makes sense. And as we just learned in the current chapter, quality is not as objective or static as people assume—there is no foolproof way to measure it and there are lots of ways to develop it.

In closing, keep in mind that it's not whether you have all of the answers—it's whether you're asking the right questions. Are you thinking about the problem in the most productive way? The leaders at Massport, Harvey Mudd College, and JPMorgan Chase were asking the right questions, made a commitment to taking bold action, and were able to move the needle. Positive results are achievable.

What outcomes would you like to see in your organization? What outcomes would you like to see in the world?

Ordinary individuals, business and community leaders, and large organizations all have a role to play. It's up to you to do the hard work of figuring out who you are as it relates to racism and equity, what is the change you want to see happen, and what are the concrete steps that you can take to achieve it. It's up to leaders to determine the core values and purpose of their organizations and whether and how diversity, equity, and inclusion efforts fit into the overall mission. They must also decide whether it's a priority, and whether they are willing to take on the necessary investment to see real results. That commitment is the real hurdle. The specifics of what to do are relatively straightforward—just like diets and exercise plans. Deciding that you are *willing* to give up the extra cookies is the hard part.

My hope is that this book has inspired you. I remain optimistic that racism is solvable—and I hope that you will join me in taking action to move us closer to a better world. By reading this book, you have invested energy in personal education and awareness. By connecting with friends, neighbors, coworkers, and strangers, you have taken on the critical task of Conversation. It's now time for action. How will you begin your journey upstream?

Taking Steps Toward Real Progress

CONVERSATION STARTERS

General Questions to Begin The Conversation:

What do you think?

1. Ask yourself: What are three techniques, studies, or examples that resonated with you from reading the chapters in this section? Was there anything in particular that you underlined, highlighted, or wrote down that you'd like to share? What made this information so intriguing, powerful, or noteworthy to you?

2. What were some examples that did *not* resonate with you— things that you took exception with? Which aspects of these techniques, approaches, or examples did you find inaccurate, objectionable, or impractical?

3. Which are strategies you think your family/friends would have a hard time adopting? Which ones might they be more amenable to?

How do you feel?

1. How did you feel before you began reading this section?

   How do you feel now, after finishing this section? What did you learn that you did not know before? How has this information affected the way you feel?

   How do you feel about your role in this process? Do you feel inspired and empowered by the information, or are you more hopeless and pessimistic?

2. Did this reading reveal any specific steps that you can take in your workplace or community to combat bias? If so, what are they?

MORE FOOD FOR THOUGHT: CONVERSATION IN CONTEXT

Breaking the Habit

Do you think that racism, and more specifically White supremacy, is in many ways analogous to addiction? It has great psychological and emotional appeal, making White people feel important, special, and powerful—like a drug. Despite its allure, it is also destructive. It disrupts relationships, careers, and communities. It produces negative psychological consequences such as guilt and shame. And many of its "users" are very much in denial. It also follows a cycle—of heavy usage, followed by a moment of clarity, abrupt renunciation of the habit, a period of rehabilitation, and ultimately a relapse.

Those who are caught up in the cycle want it to stop—they see the harm and damage that it does—but they don't know how.

Do you believe that the addiction metaphor is a helpful lens for understanding the nation's long-standing struggle with racism? If so, what should the rehabilitation process look like? How do we break the habit and stay clean, particularly when there are so many "pushers" who traffic in the substance?

Best Practices

Which of the three organizational examples discussed in Chapter 12 (i.e., Massport, Harvey Mudd College, JPMorgan Chase) resonated with you the most? Why? How might you import and adapt some of the lessons from any of these cases into your own organization?

Business Resource Groups

What role do you think business resource groups (BRGs) and employee resource groups (ERGs) play in creating a barrier against racism? Are they unnecessary in your opinion?

How can your organization build more functional partnerships between top leaders and employee/business resource groups? Are identity spaces an effort to separate Black people from White people or separate Black people from anti-Black racism? Do you think most White people in your organization see and understand the difference between these two things? Would an all-White BRG make sense? Why or why not?

Assessing Organizational Climate

Do you think your organization has an inclusive culture? What are things your organization can do to create psychological safety and reduce microaggressions or racial harassment?

Can people of color navigate their full range of emotions in the presence of White people without consequence? Are people of color able to be authentic? Based on what we covered in the measurement section, how might you go about assessing your organization's climate and culture around inclusivity?

Societal Change

Many lines of research suggest that a more honest approach to teaching history in schools would go a long way toward reducing racism. Parents don't want to discourage or disturb children, and as a result the public schools teach them not just a sugarcoated but a fictitious version of U.S. history. Should the honest but less flattering history of the United States be taught in public schools? Why do you think this hasn't been done? What are the advantages? What are the disadvantages?

Getting It Done

What are three things that you can do to combat racism personally, within yourself, or interpersonally, in other people? What are three things that you can do to change social norms around racism? What are three things you can do to create antiracist policies and practices at your organization? Finally, what are three things that you can do to promote greater racial equity in society?

What are things that leaders can do to combat racism internally, externally, and eternally? That is, how might they go about addressing it within their organization? In the broader society? And how might they go about making profound and sustainable change, both internally and externally?

Now ask these same questions in a group context. How can collectives work together to combat racism across all levels? How about internally, externally, and eternally? How can the combined wisdom, power, and resources of ordinary individuals, civic and corporate leaders, and large organizations be leveraged to increase the likelihood of successful eradication of racism?

Acknowledgments

This book was made possible by an army and a village. I salute the army of allies who have been in the trenches with me during my various stages of the book project. Thanks to Marilynn Brewer, Michael Norton, Stacey Sinclair, Tracy Dumas, Jonathan Haidt, Robin Ely, Jenny Fister Collins, Peter Glick, Theo Lorrain-Hale, Ian Simoy, Elorm Avorkame, Willis Bright, Leticia Haynes, Jonathan Pritchard, Naisha Bradley, Patricia Ledesma, Michaela Raymond, Rand Wentworth, Sofia Teixeira, Robert M. Livingston, George Liles, Paula Frank, Rebecca Raskin, Lisa Eby, Onjale Scott Price, Saaid Mendoza, Jackie Cureton, Laura Murphy, and Selin Kesebir for their insightful and invaluable comments and feedback on earlier drafts of the book. I am awed by the sheer genius and diversity of perspective contained within this group, and am fortunate to call so many of you my friends and family.

I offer special thanks to Harvard Kennedy School academic dean Iris Bohnet for providing the most precious commodity of all—time. Being on sabbatical made all the difference in enabling me to complete the book this decade. Your support and sponsorship, in so many ways, have been invaluable. Likewise, I appreciate the generosity of Ambassador Wendy Sherman and the Center for Public Leadership.

A huge round of applause and hearty praise for my very able and assiduous research assistants, Sa-Kiera Hudson, Daphne Penn, Dennis Sop, and Chu Wang, as well as my assistant, Louis Mitchell, who always keeps me focused, organized, and optimistic. I tip my hat to my extraordinary agent, Jim Levine, who has been so instrumental to the success of this book, as well as my very talented editor, Paul Whitlatch.

While the army is important, none of this would have been possible without my village—parents, stepparents, godparents, grandparents, aunts, "aunties," uncles, cousins, brothers, my "brother," neighbors, teachers, advisers, mentors, sponsors, and a loyal and loving crew of friends who have been with me for decades. You know who you are. I want to give a special thanks to two villagers, Patricia White and Toya Tichenor, who have been particularly helpful, supportive, and inspiring to me, not only through this long writing process but throughout my entire journey on this planet. My gratitude to "the village" knows no bounds.

Finally, I want to give a very, very special thanks to the village matriarch, Mattie "B." Summers, whose undying love, patience, encouragement, integrity, strength, pride, humor, guidance, protection, affection, grace, compassion, and unapologetic commitment to truth have shaped my entire being—my identity, my audacity, my alacrity, my soul, my purpose, my life. Thank you will never be enough.

I appreciate each reader's decision to allow my words to fill their minds and hearts. I am humbled by your decision to invest valuable time buried in the pages of this book. It is an honor and privilege that I do not take lightly. My ultimate hope is that your investment has been time well spent. Keep fighting the good fight!

Bibliography

Accapadi, M. M. 2007. "When White Women Cry: How White Women's Tears Oppress Women of Color." *College Student Affairs Journal* 26: 208–16.

Adorno, T. W., E. Frenkel-Brunswik, D. Levinson, and N. Sanford. 1950. *The Authoritarian Personality*. New York, New York: Harper & Brothers.

Akresh, I. R. 2011. "Wealth Accumulation Among U.S. Immigrants: A Study of Assimilation and Differentials." *Social Science Research* 40 (5): 1390–401. https://doi.org/10.1016/j.ssresearch.2009.08.004.

Alexander, M. G., M. B. Brewer, and R. W. Livingston. 2005. "Putting Stereotype Content in Context: Image Theory and Interethnic Stereotypes." *Personality and Social Psychology Bulletin* 31: 781–94.

Allport, G. W. 1954. *The Nature of Prejudice*. New York: Addison-Wesley.

Altemeyer, B. 1988. *Enemies of Freedom: Understanding Right-Wing Authoritarianism*. San Francisco: Jossey-Bass.

Altus, W. D. 1966. "Birth Order and Its Sequelae." *Science* 151 (3706): 44–49. http://doi.org/10.1126/science.151.3706.44.

Anderson, C., and G. J. Kilduff. 2009. "Why Do Dominant Personalities Attain Influence in Face-to-Face Groups? The Competence-Signaling Effects of Trait Dominance." *Journal of Personality and Social Psychology* 96 (2): 491–503. https://doi.org/10.1037/a0014201.

Anderson, K. O., C. R. Green, and R. Payne. 2009. "Racial and Ethnic Disparities in Pain: Causes and Consequences of Unequal Care." *Journal of Pain* 10 (12): 1187–204. https://doi.org/10.1016/j.jpain.2009.10.002.

Antonio, A. L., M. J. Chang, K. Hakuta, D. A. Kenny, S. Levin, and J. F. Milem. 2004. "Effects of Racial Diversity on Complex Thinking in College Students." *Psychological Science* 15 (8): 507–10.

Apfelbaum, E. P., S. R. Sommers, and M. I. Norton. 2008. "Seeing Race and Seeming Racist? Evaluating Strategic Colorblindness in Social Interaction." *Journal of Personality and Social Psychology* 95 (4): 918–32. https://doi.org/10.1037/a0011990.

Aronson, E., C. Fried, and J. Stone. 1991. "Overcoming Denial and Increasing the Intention to Use Condoms Through the Induction of Hypocrisy." *American Journal of Public Health* 81 (12): 1636–38. https://doi.org/10.2105/AJPH.81.12.1636.

Au, W. T., and J. Y. Y. Kwong. 2004. "Measurements and Effects of Social-Value Orientation in Social Dilemmas: A Review." In *Contemporary Psychological Research on Social Dilemmas*, edited by R. Suleiman, D. V. Budescu, I. Fischer, and D. M. Messick, 71–98. New York: Cambridge University Press.

Avenanti, A., A. Sirigu, and S. M. Aglioti. 2010. "Racial Bias Reduces Empathic Sensorimotor Resonance with Other-Race Pain." *Current Biology* 20 (11): 1018–22. https://doi.org/10.1016/j.cub.2010.03.071.

Baker, J., and A. J. Logan. 2007. "Developmental Contexts and Sporting Success: Birth Date and Birthplace Effects in National Hockey League Draftees 2000–2005." *British Journal of Sports Medicine* 41 (8): 515–17. https://doi.org/10.1136/bjsm.2006.033977.

Balaresque, P., G. R. Bowden, S. M. Adams, H. Leung, T. E. King, J. Goodwin, J. Moisan, C. Richard, A. Millward, A. G. Demaine, I. J. Wilson, C. Tyler-Smith, M. A. Jobling, G. Barbujani, and C. Previdere. 2010. "A Predominantly Neolithic Origin for European Paternal Lineages." *PLOS Biology* 8 (1): e1000285. https://doi.org/10.1371/journal.pbio.1000285.

Balaresque, P., N. Poulet, S. Cussat-Blanc, P. Gerard, L. Quintana-Murci, E. Heyer, and M. A. Jobling. 2015. "Y-Chromosome Descent Clusters and Male Differential Reproductive Success: Young Lineage Expansions Dominate Asian Pastoral Nomadic Populations." *European Journal of Human Genetics* 23 (January): 1413–22. https://doi.org/10.1038/ejhg.2014.285.

Baldiga, K. 2013. "Gender Differences in Willingness to Guess." *Management Science* 60: 434–48.

Bamshad, M., S. Wooding, B. A. Salisbury, and J. C. Stephens. 2004. "Deconstructing the Relationship Between Genetics and Race." *Nature Reviews Genetics* 5 (8): 598–609. https://doi.org/10.1038/nrg1401.

Banaji, M. R., and A. G. Greenwald. 2016. *Blindspot: Hidden Biases of Good People.* New York: Bantam.

Banakou, D., P. D. Hanumanthu, and M. Slater. 2016. "Virtual Embodiment of White People in a Black Virtual Body Leads to a Sustained Reduction in Their Implicit Racial Bias." *Frontiers in Human Neuroscience* 10 (November): 1–12. https://doi.org/10.3389/fnhum.2016.00601.

Banfield, J. C., and J. F. Dovidio. 2013. "Whites' Perceptions of Discrimination Against Blacks: The Influence of Common Identity." *Journal of Experimental Social Psychology* 49 (5): 833–41. https://doi.org/10.1016/j.jesp.2013.04.008.

Barbujani, G., S. Ghirotto, and F. Tassi. 2013. "Nine Things to Remember About Human Genome Diversity." *Tissue Antigens* 82 (3): 155–64. https://doi.org/10.1111/tan.12165.

Barclay, L. J., M. R. Bashshur, and M. Fortin. 2017. "Motivated Cognition and Fairness: Insights, Integration, and Creating a Path Forward." *Journal of Applied Psychology* 102 (6): 867–89.

Bardi, A., and S. H. Schwartz. 2003. "Values and Behavior: Strength and Structure of Relations." *Personality and Social Psychology Bulletin* 29 (10): 1207–20. https://doi.org/10.1177/0146167203254602.

Baron, A. S., and M. R. Banaji. 2006. "The Development of Implicit Attitudes." *Psychological Science* 17 (1): 53–58. https://doi.org/10.1111/j.1467-9280.2005.01664.x.

Barsh, G. S. 2003. "What Controls Variation in Human Skin Color?" *PLOS Biology* 1 (1): 19–23. https://doi.org/10.1371/journal.pbio.0000027.

Bastian, B., J. Jetten, and L. J. Ferris. 2014. "Pain as Social Glue: Shared Pain Increases Cooperation." *Psychological Science* 25 (11): 2079–85. https://doi.org/10.1177/0956797614545886.

Bazerman, M. H., G. F. Loewenstein, and S. B. White. 2018. "Reversals of Preference in Allocation Decisions: Judging an Alternative Versus Choosing Among Alternatives." *Administrative Science Quarterly* 37 (2): 220–40. https://doi.org/10.2307/2393222.

Benhabib, J., A. Bisin, and M. Luo. 2017. "Earnings Inequality and Other Determinants of Wealth Inequality." *American Economic Review* 107 (5): 593–97. https://doi.org/10.1257/aer.p20171005.

Berdahl, J. L., M. Cooper, P. Glick, R. W. Livingston, and J. C. Williams. 2018. "Work as a Masculinity Contest." *Journal of Social Issues* 74 (3): 422–48. https://doi.org/10.1111/josi.12289.

Bergh, R., N. Akrami, J. Sidanius, and C. G. Sibley. 2016. "Is Group Membership Necessary for Understanding Generalized Prejudice? A Reevaluation of Why Prejudices Are Interrelated." *Journal of Personality and Social Psychology* 111 (3): 367–95. https://doi.org/10.1037/pspi0000064.

Bergsieker, H. B., J. N. Shelton, and J. A. Richeson. 2010. "To Be Liked Versus Respected: Divergent Goals in Interracial Interactions." *Journal of*

Personality and Social Psychology 99 (2): 248–64. https://doi.org/10.1037/ a0018474.

Bernal, M. 1987. *Black Athena: The Afroasiatic Roots of Classical Civilization,* volumes 1–3. New Brunswick, N.J.: Rutgers University Press.

Bertrand, M., and S. Mullainathan. 2004. "Are Emily and Greg More Employable Than Lakisha and Jamal? A Field Experiment on Labor Market Discrimination." *American Economic Review* 94 (4): 991–1013. https://doi.org/10.1257/0002828042002561.

Best, R., and K. Rogers. 2020. "Do You Know How Divided White and Black Americans Are on Racism?" FiveThirtyEight, June 10, 2020. https://projects.fivethirtyeight.com/racism-polls/.

Bettencourt, B. A., M. B. Brewer, M. R. Croak, and N. Miller. 1992. "Cooperation and the Reduction of Intergroup Bias: The Role of Reward Structure and Social Orientation." *Journal of Experimental Social Psychology* 28 (4): 301–19. https://doi.org/10.1016/0022-1031(92)90048-O.

Blair, I. V., J. E. Ma, and A. P. Lenton. 2001. "Imagining Stereotypes Away: The Moderation of Implicit Stereotypes Through Mental Imagery." *Journal of Personality and Social Psychology* 81 (5): 828–41. https://doi .org/10.1037/0022-3514.81.5.828.

Blanchard, F. A., C. S. Crandall, J. C. Brigham, and L. A. Vaughn. 1994. "Condemning and Condoning Racism: A Social Context Approach to Interracial Settings." *Journal of Applied Psychology* 79 (6): 993–97. https:// doi.org/10.1037/0021-9010.79.6.993.

Blanchard, F. A., T. Lilly, and L. A. Vaughn. 1991. "Reducing the Expression of Racial Prejudice." *Psychological Science* 2 (2): 101–5. https://doi .org/10.1111/j.1467-9280.1991.tb00108.x.

Blanton, H., J. Jaccard, J. Klick, B. Mellers, G. Mitchell, and P. E. Tetlock. 2009. "Strong Claims and Weak Evidence: Reassessing the Predictive Validity of the IAT." *Journal of Applied Psychology* 94 (3): 567–82. https:// doi.org/10.1037/a0014665.

Bloom, P. 2016. *Against Empathy: The Case for Rational Compassion.* New York: Ecco.

Bloom, S. G. 2005. "Lesson of a Lifetime: Her Bold Experiment to Teach Iowa Third Graders About Racial Prejudice Divided Townspeople and Thrust Her onto the National Stage." *Smithsonian Magazine,* September 2005. https://www.smithsonianmag.com/science-nature/lesson-of-a -lifetime-72754306/.

Bohnet, I. 2016. *What Works: Gender Equality by Design.* Cambridge, Mass.: Belknap.

Bohnet, I., A. Van Geen, and M. Bazerman. 2016. "When Performance Trumps Gender Bias: Joint vs. Separate Evaluation." *Management Science* 62 (5): 1225–34. https://doi.org/10.1287/mnsc.2015.2186.

Bonilla-Silva. 2006. *Racism Without Racists: Color-Blind Racism and the Persistence of Racial Inequality in the United States*. 2nd ed. Lanham, Md.: Rowman & Littlefield.

Bonnet, C., and D. Valbelle. 2007. *The Nubian Pharaohs: Black Kings on the Nile*. Cairo and New York: American University in Cairo Press.

Brandt, M. J. 2013. "Do the Disadvantaged Legitimize the Social System? A Large-Scale Test of the Status-Legitimacy Hypothesis." *Journal of Personality and Social Psychology* 104 (5): 765–85. https://doi.org/10.1037/a0031751.

Brannon, T. N., and H. R. Markus. 2013. "Social Class and Race: Burdens but Also Some *Benefits* of Chronic Low Rank." *Psychological Inquiry* 24 (2): 97–101. https://doi.org/10.1080/1047840X.2013.794102.

Breech, J. 2018. "Terrell Owens Finally Explains Why He Had a Nearly 15-Year Beef with the Media." CBS Sports, August 5, 2018. https://www.cbssports.com/nfl/news/terrell-owens-finally-explains-why-he-had-a-nearly-15-year-beef-with-the-media/.

Brewer, M. B. 1979. "In-group Bias in the Minimal Intergroup Situation: A Cognitive-Motivational Analysis." *Psychological Bulletin* 86 (2): 307–24. https://doi.org/10.1037/0033-2909.86.2.307.

Brewer, M. B. 1991. "The Social Self: On Being the Same and Different at the Same Time." *Personality and Social Psychology Bulletin* 17 (5): 475–82. https://doi.org/10.1177/0146167291175001.

Brewer, M. B. 2016. "Intergroup Discrimination: Ingroup Love or Outgroup Hate?" In *The Cambridge Handbook of the Psychology of Prejudice,* edited by C. G. Sibley and F. K. Barlow, 90–110. Cambridge, UK: Cambridge University Press. https://doi.org/10.1017/9781316161579.005.

Brewer, M. B., and N. Miller. 1984. "Beyond the Contact Hypothesis: Theoretical Perspectives on Desegregation." In *Groups in Contact: The Psychology of Desegregation,* edited by N. Miller and M. B. Brewer, 281–302. Orlando: Academic Press.

Bridge, J. A., L. Asti, L. M. Horowitz, J. B. Greenhouse, C. A. Fontanella, A. H. Sheftall, K. J. Kelleher, and J. V. Campo. 2015. "Suicide Trends Among Elementary School–Aged Children in the United States from 1993 to 2012." *JAMA Pediatrics* 169 (7): 673–77. https://doi.org/10.1001/jamapediatrics.2015.0465.

Brief, A. P., J. Dietz, R. R. Cohen, S. D. Pugh, and J. B. Vaslow. 2000. "Just Doing Business: Modern Racism and Obedience to Authority as Explanations for Employment Discrimination." *Organizational Behavior and Human Decision Processes* 81 (1): 72–97. https://doi.org/10.1006/obhd.1999.2867.

Brown, K. T., T. N. Brown, J. S. Jackson, R. M. Sellers, and W. J. Manuel. 2003. "Teammates On and Off the Field? Contact with Black Teammates and the Racial Attitudes of White Student Athletes." *Journal of Applied Social Psychology* 33 (7): 1379–403. https://doi.org/10.1111/j .1559-1816.2003.tb01954.x.

Brown, T. N., J. S. Jackson, K. T. Brown, R. M. Sellers, S. Keiper, and W. J. Manuel. 2003. "'There's No Race on the Playing Field': Perceptions of Racial Discrimination Among White and Black Athletes." *Journal of Sport and Social Issues* 27 (2): 162–83. https://doi.org/10.1177/ 0193732502250715.

Brown-Iannuzzi, J. L., B. K. Payne, and S. Trawalter. 2013. "Narrow Imaginations: How Imagining Ideal Employees Can Increase Racial Bias." *Group Processes & Intergroup Relations* 16 (6): 661–70. https://doi.org/ 10.1177/1368430212467477.

Bryc, K., E. Y. Durand, J. M. Macpherson, D. Reich, and J. L. Mountain. 2015. "The Genetic Ancestry of African Americans, Latinos, and European Americans Across the United States." *American Journal of Human Genetics* 96 (1): 37–53. https://doi.org/10.1016/j.ajhg.2014.11.010.

Burger, J. M. 2009. "Replicating Milgram: Would People Still Obey Today?" *American Psychologist* 64 (1): 1–11. https://doi.org/10.1037/a0010932.

"Carmel's Own Data Supports I-Team 8 Investigation into Police Ticketing Black Drivers at Higher Rate." 2019. WishTV, December 4, 2019. https://www.wishtv.com/news/carmels-own-data-supports-i-team-8 -investigation/.

Caron, P. 2016. "Michelle Alexander Resigns from Ohio State Law Faculty for Seminary, Valuing 'Publicly Accessible Writing over Academic Careerism'; Law Without 'a Moral or Spiritual Awakening' Cannot Bring About Justice." TaxProf Blog, September 25, 2016. https://taxprof .typepad.com/taxprof_blog/2016/09/michelle-alexander-resigns-from -ohio-state-law-faculty-for-seminary-valuing-publicly-accessible-writ .html.

Castelli, L., L. De Amicis, and S. J. Sherman. 2007. "The Loyal Member Effect: On the Preference for Ingroup Members Who Engage in Exclusive Relations with the Ingroup." *Developmental Psychology* 43 (6): 1347–59. https://doi.org/10.1037/0012-1649.43.6.1347.

Castelli, L., K. Vanzetto, S. J. Sherman, and L. Arcuri. 2001. "The Explicit and Implicit Perception of In-group Members Who Use Stereotypes: Blatant Rejection but Subtle Conformity." *Journal of Experimental Social Psychology* 37 (5): 419–26. https://doi.org/10.1006/jesp.2000.1471.

Chaplin, G. 2004. "Geographic Distribution of Environmental Factors Influencing Human Skin Coloration." *American Journal of Physical Anthropology* 125 (3): 292–302. https://doi.org/10.1002/ajpa.10263.

Chapman, L. J., and J. P. Chapman. 1969. "Illusory Correlation as an Obstacle to the Use of Valid Psychodiagnostic Signs." *Journal of Abnormal Psychology* 74 (3): 271–80. https://doi.org/10.1037/h0027592.

Charles, K. K., and E. Hurst. 2003. "The Correlation of Wealth Across Generations." *Journal of Political Economy* 111 (6): 1155–82. https://doi.org/10.1086/378526.

Charlesworth, T. E. S., and M. R. Banaji. 2019. "Patterns of Implicit and Explicit Attitudes: I. Long-Term Change and Stability from 2007 to 2016." *Psychological Science* 30 (2): 174–92. https://doi.org/10.1177/0956797618813087.

Cheon, B. K., R. W. Livingston, J. Y. Chiao, and Y. Y. Hong. 2015. "Contribution of Serotonin Transporter Polymorphism (5-HTTLPR) to Automatic Racial Bias." *Personality and Individual Differences* 79: 35–38. https://doi.org/10.1016/j.paid.2015.01.019.

Cheon, B. K., R. W. Livingston, Y. Y. Hong, and J. Y. Chiao. 2013. "Gene × Environment Interaction on Intergroup Bias: The Role of 5-HTTLPR and Perceived Outgroup Threat." *Social Cognitive and Affective Neuroscience* 9 (9): 1268–75. https://doi.org/10.1093/scan/nst111.

Chetty, R., N. Hendren, M. R. Jones, and S. R. Porter. 2019. "Race and Economic Opportunity in the United States: An Intergenerational Perspective." *Quarterly Journal of Economics* 135 (2): 711–83. https://doi.org/10.1093/qje/qjz042.

Chirumbolo, A., L. Leone, and M. Desimoni. 2016. "The Interpersonal Roots of Politics: Social Value Orientation, Socio-political Attitudes and Prejudice." *Personality and Individual Differences* 91: 144–53. https://doi.org/10.1016/j.paid.2015.12.001.

Chow, R. M., B. S. Lowery, and C. M. Hogan. 2013. "Appeasement: Whites' Strategic Support for Affirmative Action." *Personality and Social Psychology Bulletin* 39 (3): 332–45. https://doi.org/10.1177/0146167212475224.

Christensen, K. D., T. E. Jayaratne, J. S. Roberts, S. L. R. Kardia, and E. M. Petty. 2010. "Understandings of Basic Genetics in the United States: Results from a National Survey of Black and White Men and Women." *Public Health Genomics* 13 (7–8): 467–76. https://doi.org/10.1159/000293287.

Chugh, D. 2018. *The Person You Mean to Be: How Good People Fight Bias.* New York: HarperCollins.

Clark, R., N. B. Anderson, V. R. Clark, and D. R. Williams. 1999. "Racism as a Stressor for African Americans: A Biopsychosocial Model." *American Psychologist* 54 (10): 805–16. https://pdfs.semanticscholar.org/bbe6/632bec7fd9cf8a741452db6ecb6bc3f0c391.pdf; http://hss.ucsf.edu/sites/hss.ucsf.edu/files/imported_pdf/clark_anderson_et_al_racism_as_stressor.pdf.

Coates, T.-N. 2010. "LeBron Treated Like 'a Runaway Slave.'" *Atlantic,* July 12, 2010. https://www.theatlantic.com/entertainment/archive/2010/07/lebron-treated-like-a-runaway-slave/59560/.

Cohen, D., F. Shin, X. Liu, P. Ondish, and M. W. Kraus. 2017. "Defining Social Class Across Time and Between Groups." *Personality and Social Psychology Bulletin* 43 (11): 1530–45. https://doi.org/10.1177/0146167217721174.

Collange, J., S. T. Fiske, and R. Sanitioso. 2009. "Maintaining a Positive Self-Image by Stereotyping Others: Self-Threat and the Stereotype Content Model." *Social Cognition* 27 (1): 138–49. https://doi.org/10.1521/soco.2009.27.1.138.

Collins, C. A., and D. R. Williams. 1999. "Segregation and Mortality: The Deadly Effects of Racism?" *Sociological Forum* 14 (3): 495–523. https://doi.org/10.1023/A:1021403820451.

Collins, J., and J. I. Porras. 1996. "Building Your Company's Vision." *Harvard Business Review,* September–October 1996.

Comer, R., and J. D. Laird. 1975. "Choosing to Suffer as a Consequence of Expecting to Suffer: Why Do People Do It?" *Journal of Personality and Social Psychology* 32 (1): 92–101. https://doi.org/10.1037/h0076785.

Cooley, E., H. Winslow, A. Vojt, J. Shein, and J. Ho. 2018. "Bias at the Intersection of Identity: Conflicting Social Stereotypes of Gender and Race Augment the Perceived Femininity and Interpersonal Warmth of Smiling Black Women." *Journal of Experimental Social Psychology* 74 (January): 43–49. https://doi.org/10.1016/j.jesp.2017.08.007.

Correll, J., B. Park, C. M. Judd, and B. Wittenbrink. 2002. "The Police Officer's Dilemma: Using Ethnicity to Disambiguate Potentially Threatening Individuals." *Journal of Personality and Social Psychology* 83 (6): 1314–29. https://doi.org/10.1037//0022-3514.83.6.1314.

Cox, W. T. L., and P. G. Devine. 2014. "Stereotyping to Infer Group Membership Creates Plausible Deniability for Prejudice-Based Aggression." *Psychological Science* 25 (2): 340–48. https://doi.org/10.1177/0956797613501171.

Craig, M. A., T. DeHart, J. A. Richeson, and L. Fiedorowicz. 2012. "Do unto Others as Others Have Done unto You?: Perceiving Sexism Influences Women's Evaluations of Stigmatized Racial Groups." *Personality and Social Psychology Bulletin* 38 (9): 1107–19. https://doi.org/10.1177/0146167212445210.

Craig, M. A., and J. A. Richeson. 2014a. "More Diverse Yet Less Tolerant? How the Increasingly Diverse Racial Landscape Affects White Americans' Racial Attitudes." *Personality and Social Psychology Bulletin* 40 (6): 750–61. https://doi.org/10.1177/0146167214524993.

Craig, M. A., and J. A. Richeson. 2014b. "On the Precipice of a 'Majority-

Minority' America: Perceived Status Threat from the Racial Demographic Shift Affects White Americans' Political Ideology." *Psychological Science* 25 (6): 1189–97. https://doi.org/10.1177/0956797614527113.

Crane, B., M. Thomas-Hunt, and S. Kesebir. 2019. "To Disclose or Not to Disclose: The Ironic Effects of the Disclosure of Personal Information About Ethnically Distinct Newcomers to a Team." *Journal of Business Ethics* 158 (4): 909–21. https://doi.org/10.1007/s10551-017-3714-0.

Crawford, N. G., D. E. Kelly, M. E. B. Hansen, M. H. Beltrame, S. Fan, S. L. Bowman, E. Jewett, A. Ranciaro, S. Thompson, Y. Lo, S. P. Pfeifer, J. D. Jensen, M. C. Campbell, W. Beggs, F. Hormozdiari, S. W. Mpoloka, G. G. Mokone, T. Nyambo, D. W. Meskel, G. Belay, J. Haut, H. Rothschild, L. Zon, Y. Zhou, M. A. Kovacs, M. Xu, T. Zhang, K. Bishop, J. Sinclair, C. Rivas, E. Elliot, J. Choi, S. A. Li, B. Hicks, S. Burgess, C. Abnet, D. E. Watkins-Chow, E. Oceana, Yun S. Song, E. Eskin, K. M. Brown, M. S. Marks, S. K. Loftus, W. J. Pavan, M. Yeager, S. Chanock, and S. A. Tishkoff. 2017. "Loci Associated with Skin Pigmentation Identified in African Populations." *Science* 358 (6365). https://doi.org/10.1126/science.aan8433.

Crisp, R. J., M. Hewstone, and M. Rubin. 2001. "Does Multiple Categorization Reduce Intergroup Bias?" *Personality and Social Psychology Bulletin* 27 (1): 76–89. https://doi.org/10.1177/0146167201271007.

Crockett, Z. 2016. "'Gang Member' and 'Thug' Roles in Film Are Disproportionately Played by Black Actors." *Vox,* September 13, 2016. https://www.vox.com/2016/9/13/12889478/black-actors-typecasting.

Cuddy, A. J. C., S. T. Fiske, and P. Glick. 2008. "Warmth and Competence as Universal Dimensions of Social Perception: The Stereotype Content Model and the BIAS Map." *Advances in Experimental Social Psychology* 40: 61–149. https://doi.org/10.1016/S0065-2601(07)00002-0.

Czopp, A. M., and M. J. Monteith. 2003. "Confronting Prejudice (Literally): Reactions to Confrontations of Racial and Gender Bias." *Personality and Social Psychology Bulletin* 29 (4): 532–44. https://doi.org/10.1177/0146167202250923.

Dagan, D., and S. Teles. 2016. *Prison Break: Why Conservatives Turned Against Mass Incarceration.* New York: Oxford University Press.

Darley, J. M., and P. H. Gross. 1983. "A Hypothesis-Confirming Bias in Labeling Effects." *Journal of Personality and Social Psychology* 44 (1): 20–33. http://doi.org/10.1037/0022-3514.44.1.20.

Darley, J. M., and B. Latane. 1968. "Bystander Intervention in Emergencies: Diffusion of Responsibility." *Journal of Personality and Social Psychology* 8 (4, part 1): 377–83. https://doi.org/10.1037/h0025589.

Dasgupta, N., and A. G. Greenwald. 2001. "On the Malleability of Automatic Attitudes: Combating Automatic Prejudice with Images of Admired and Disliked Individuals." *Journal of Personality and Social Psychology* 81 (5): 800–814. https://doi.org/10.1037/0022-3514.81.5.800.

Deegan, M. P., E. Hehman, S. L. Gaertner, and J. F. Dovidio. 2015. "Positive Expectations Encourage Generalization from a Positive Intergroup Interaction to Outgroup Attitudes." *Personality and Social Psychology Bulletin* 41 (1): 52–65. https://doi.org/10.1177/0146167214556240.

Desmond, M. 2019. "American Capitalism Is Brutal. You Can Trace That to the Plantation." *New York Times Magazine,* August 14, 2019.

DeSteno, D., N. Dasgupta, M. Y. Bartlett, and A. Cajdric. 2004. "Prejudice from Thin Air: The Effect of Emotion on Automatic Intergroup Attitudes." *Psychological Science* 15 (5): 319–24. https://doi.org/10.1111/j.0956-7976.2004.00676.x.

Devos, T., and M. R. Banaji. 2005. "American = White?" *Journal of Personality and Social Psychology* 88 (3): 447–66. https://doi.org/10.1037/0022-3514.88.3.447.

Di, Z. X., E. Belsky, and X. Liu. 2007. "Do Homeowners Achieve More Household Wealth in the Long Run?" *Journal of Housing Economics* 16 (3–4): 274–90. https://doi.org/10.1016/j.jhe.2007.08.001.

DiAngelo, R. 2011. "White Fragility." *International Journal of Critical Pedagogy* 3 (3): 54–70.

DiAngelo, R. 2018. *White Fragility: Why It's So Hard for White People to Talk About Racism*. Boston: Beacon Press.

Doerr, C., E. A. Plant, J. W. Kunstman, and D. Buck. 2011. "Interactions in Black and White: Racial Differences and Similarities in Response to Interracial Interactions." *Group Processes & Intergroup Relations* 14 (1): 31–43. https://doi.org/10.1177/1368430210375250.

Doran, G. T. 1981. "There's a S.M.A.R.T. Way to Write Management's Goals and Objectives." *Management Review* 70 (11): 35–36.

Dore, R. A., K. M. Hoffman, A. S. Lillard, and S. Trawalter. 2014. "Children's Racial Bias in Perceptions of Others' Pain." *British Journal of Developmental Psychology* 32 (2): 218–31. https://doi.org/10.1111/bjdp.12038.

Dovidio, J. F., and S. L. Gaertner. 2000. "Aversive Racism and Selection Decisions: 1989 and 1999." *Psychological Science* 11 (4): 315–19. https://doi.org/10.1111/1467-9280.00262.

Dovidio, J. F., and S. L. Gaertner. 2004. "Aversive Racism." In *Advances in Experimental Social Psychology,* edited by M. P. Zanna, 1–52. London: Elsevier Academic Press. https://doi.org/10.1016/S0065-2601(04)36001-6.

Dovidio, J. F., S. L. Gaertner, and K. Kawakami. 2003. "Intergroup Contact: The Past, Present, and the Future." *Group Processes & Intergroup Relations* 6 (1): 5–21. https://doi.org/10.1177/1368430203006001009.

Du Bois, W. E. B. 1968. *The Autobiography of W. E. B. Du Bois: A Soliloquy on Viewing My Life from the Last Decade of Its First Century*. New York: International Publishers.

Duckitt, J. 2001. "A Dual-Process Cognitive-Motivational Theory of Ideology and Prejudice." In *Advances in Experimental Social Psychology,* edited by M. P. Zanna, vol. 33, 41–113. New York: Academic Press.

Duckitt, J., and K. Fisher. 2003. "The Impact of Social Threat on Worldview and Ideological Attitudes." *Political Psychology* 24 (1): 199–222. https://doi.org/10.1111/0162-895X.00322.

Dunham, Y., and J. Emory. 2014. "Of Affect and Ambiguity: The Emergence of Preference for Arbitrary Ingroups." *Journal of Social Issues* 70 (1): 81–98. https://doi.org/10.1111/josi.12048.

Dupree, C. H., and S. T. Fiske. 2019. "Self-Presentation in Interracial Settings: The Competence Downshift by White Liberals." *Journal of Personality and Social Psychology* 117 (3): 579–604. https://doi.org/10.1037/pspi0000166.

Durante, F., S. T. Fiske, M. J. Gelfand, F. Crippa, C. Suttora, A. Stillwell, F. Asbrock, Z. Aycan, H. H. Bye, R. Carlsson, F. Björklund, M. Dagher, A. Geller, C. A. Larsen, A. H. A. Latif, T. A. Mähönen, I. Jasinskaja-Lahti, and A. Teymoori. 2017. "Ambivalent Stereotypes Link to Peace, Conflict, and Inequality Across 38 Nations." *Proceedings of the National Academy of Sciences of the United States of America* 114 (4): 669–74. https://doi.org/10.1073/pnas.1611874114.

Dweck, C. S. 2016. "What Having a 'Growth Mindset' Actually Means." *Harvard Business Review* 94 (1–2): 2–5.

Edmondson, A. 2012. *Teaming: How Organizations Learn, Innovate, and Compete in the Knowledge Economy.* San Francisco: Jossey-Bass.

Edwards, F., H. Lee, and M. Esposito. 2019. "Risk of Being Killed by Police Use of Force in the United States by Age, Race-Ethnicity, and Sex." *Proceedings of the National Academy of Sciences* 116 (34): 16793–98. https://doi.org/10.1073/pnas.1821204116.

Effron, D. A., J. S. Cameron, and B. Monin. 2009. "Endorsing Obama Licenses Favoring Whites." *Journal of Experimental Social Psychology* 45 (3): 590–93. https://doi.org/10.1016/j.jesp.2009.02.001.

Effron, D. A., D. T. Miller, and B. Monin. 2012. "Inventing Racist Roads Not Taken: The Licensing Effect of Immoral Counterfactual Behaviors." *Journal of Personality and Social Psychology* 103 (6): 916–32. https://doi.org/10.1037/a0030008.

Eibach, R. P., and J. Ehrlinger. 2006. "'Keep Your Eyes on the Prize': Reference Points and Racial Differences in Assessing Progress Toward Equality." *Personality and Social Psychology Bulletin* 32 (1): 66–77. https://doi.org/10.1177/0146167205279585.

Ely, R. J., and D. A. Thomas. 2001. "Cultural Diversity at Work: The Effects of Diversity Perspectives on Work Group Processes and Outcomes." *Administrative Science Quarterly* 46 (2): 229–73. https://doi .org/10.2307/2667087.

Ely, R. J., and D. A. Thomas. 2020. "Making Differences Matter Redux: A Guide to Managing in the 21st Century." *Harvard Business Review,* November–December 2020.

"Ending America's Opioid Crisis." n.d. The White House. Retrieved September 14, 2020. https://www.whitehouse.gov/opioids/.

Faber, D. R., and E. J. Krieg. 2002. "Unequal Exposure to Ecological Hazards: Environmental Injustices in the Commonwealth of Massachusetts." *Environmental Health Perspectives* 110 (supp. 2): 277–88. https:// doi.org/10.1289/ehp.02110s2277.

Federico, C. M., and J. Sidanius. 2002. "Racism, Ideology, and Affirmative Action Revisited: The Antecedents and Consequences of 'Principled Objections' to Affirmative Action." *Journal of Personality and Social Psychology* 82 (4): 488–501. https://doi.org/10.1037//0022-3514.82.4.488.

Fein, S., and S. J. Spencer. 1997. "Prejudice as Self-Image Maintenance: Affirming the Self Through Derogating Others." *Journal of Personality and Social Psychology* 73 (1): 31–44. https://doi.org/10.1037/0022-3514.73.1.31.

Fernando, J. W., N. Burden, A. Ferguson, L. V. O'Brien, M. Judge, and Y. Kashima. 2018. Functions of Utopia: How Utopian Thinking Motivates Societal Engagement." *Personality and Social Psychology Bulletin* 44 (5): 779–92. https://doi.org/10.1177/0146167217748604.

Finlay, K. A., and W. G. Stephan. 2000. "Improving Intergroup Relations: The Effects of Empathy on Racial Attitudes." *Journal of Applied Social Psychology* 30 (8): 1720–37. https://doi.org/10.1111/j.1559-1816.2000 .tb02464.x.

Fischer, A., V. Wiebe, S. Paabo, and M. Przeworski. 2004. "Evidence for a Complex Demographic History of Chimpanzees." *Molecular Biology and Evolution* 21 (5): 799–808. https://doi.org/10.1093/molbev/msh083.

Fisher, D. M., S. T. Bell, E. C. Dierdorff, and J. A. Belohlav. 2012. "Facet Personality and Surface-Level Diversity as Team Mental Model Antecedents: Implications for Implicit Coordination." *Journal of Applied Psychology* 97 (4): 825–41. https://doi.org/10.1037/a0027851.

Fiske, S. T., A. J. C. Cuddy, P. Glick, and J. Xu. 2002. "A Model of (Often Mixed) Stereotype Content: Competence and Warmth Respectively Follow from Perceived Status and Competition." *Journal of Personality and Social Psychology* 82 (6): 878–902. https://doi.org/10.1037//0022-3514.82 .6.878.

Freeman, H. P., and R. Payne. 2000. "Racial Injustice in Health Care." *New England Journal of Medicine* 342 (14): 1045–47. https://doi.org/10.1056/ NEJM200004063421411.

Freeman, R. B., and W. Huang. 2014. "Collaboration: Strength in Diversity." *Nature* 513 (7518): 305. https://doi.org/10.1038/513305a.

Furnham, A. 2003. "Belief in a Just World: Research Progress over the Past Decade." *Personality and Individual Differences* 34 (5): 795–817. https://doi.org/10.1016/S0191-8869(02)00072-7.

Furnham, A., and H. C. Boo. 2011. "A Literature Review of the Anchoring Effect." *Journal of Socio-Economics* 40 (1): 35–42. https://doi.org/10.1016/j.socec.2010.10.008.

Fyock, J., and C. Stangor. 1994. "The Role of Memory Biases in Stereotype Maintenance." *British Journal of Social Psychology* 33 (3): 331–43. https://doi.org/10.1111/j.2044-8309.1994.tb01029.x.

Gaertner, S. L. 1973. "Helping Behavior and Racial Discrimination Among Liberals and Conservatives." *Journal of Personality and Social Psychology* 25 (3): 335–41. https://doi.org/10.1037/h0034221.

Gaertner, S. L., and J. F. Dovidio. 1977. "The Subtlety of White Racism, Arousal, and Helping Behavior." *Journal of Personality and Social Psychology* 35 (10): 691–707. https://doi.org/10.1037/0022-3514.35.10.691.

Gaertner, S. L., J. F. Dovidio, and B. A. Bachman. 1996. "Revisiting the Contact Hypothesis: The Induction of a Common Ingroup Identity." *International Journal of Intercultural Relations* 20 (3–4): 271–90. https://doi.org/10.1016/0147-1767(96)00019-3.

Gan, M., D. Heller, and S. Chen. 2018. "The Power in Being Yourself: Feeling Authentic Enhances the Sense of Power." *Personality and Social Psychology Bulletin* 44 (10): 1460–72. https://doi.org/10.1177/0146167218771000.

Gates, B. 2015. "The Next Outbreak? We're Not Ready." TED Talk, March 2015. www.ted.com/talks/bill_gates_the_next_outbreak_we_re_not_ready?language=en.

GBAO Strategies. 2019. "Survey of the South." https://static1.squarespace.comstatic/5b743ca3b27e39474fcbead6/t/5db2848b3668b23b4196420a/1571980427669/E+Pluribus+Unum+Fund+Southern+States+Topline+Results+-+Embargoeduntil102519.pdf.

Gee, G. C., A. Hing, S. Mohammed, D. C. Tabor, and D. R. Williams. 2019. "Racism and the Life Course: Taking Time Seriously." *American Journal of Public Health* 109 (S1): S43–S47. https://doi.org/10.2105/AJPH.2018.304766.

Georgeac, O., and A. Rattan. 2019. "Does the 'Business Case for Diversity' Help or Hurt Minorities and Women?" Paper presented at the 79th Annual Meeting of the Academy of Management, Boston.

Ghavami, N., and L. A. Peplau. 2013. "An Intersectional Analysis of Gender and Ethnic Stereotypes: Testing Three Hypotheses." *Psychology of Women Quarterly* 37 (1): 113–27. https://doi.org/10.1177/0361684312464203.

Gilbert, D. T., and J. G. Hixon. 1991. "The Trouble of Thinking: Activation and Application of Stereotypic Beliefs." *Journal of Personality and Social Psychology* 60 (4): 509–17. https://doi.org/10.1037//0022-3514.60.4.509.

Gladwell, M. 2005. *Blink: The Power of Thinking Without Thinking.* New York: Little, Brown.

Gladwell, M. 2008. *Outliers: The Story of Success.* New York: Little, Brown.

Goff, P. A., J. L. Eberhardt, M. J. Williams, and M. C. Jackson. 2008. "Not Yet Human: Implicit Knowledge, Historical Dehumanization, and Contemporary Consequences." *Journal of Personality and Social Psychology* 94 (2): 292–306. https://doi.org/10.1037/0022-3514.94.2.292.

Goff, P. A., M. A. Thomas, and M. C. Jackson. 2008. "'Ain't I a Woman?': Towards an Intersectional Approach to Person Perception and Group-Based Harms." *Sex Roles* 59 (5–6): 392–403. https://doi.org/10.1007/s11199-008-9505-4.

Gollwitzer, P. M., and B. Schaal. 1998. "Metacognition in Action: The Importance of Implementation Intentions." *Personality and Social Psychology Review* 2 (2): 124–36. https://doi.org/10.1207/s15327957pspr0202_5.

Goodman, A. H., Y. T. Moses, and J. L. Jones, eds. 2012. *Race: Are We So Different?* Chichester, UK: John Wiley & Sons. https://doi.org/10.1002/9781118233023.

Goyal, M. K., N. Kuppermann, S. D. Cleary, S. J. Teach, and J. M. Chamberlain. 2015. "Racial Disparities in Pain Management of Children with Appendicitis in Emergency Departments." *JAMA Pediatrics* 169 (11): 996–1002. https://doi.org/10.1001/jamapediatrics.2015.1915.

Grant, A. 2013. *Give and Take: Why Helping Others Drives Our Success.* New York: Penguin.

Green, C. R., K. O. Anderson, T. A. Baker, L. C. Campbell, S. Decker, R. B. Fillingim, D. A. Kaloukalani, K. E. Lasch, C. Myers, R. C. Tait, K. H. Todd, and A. H. Vallerand. 2003. "The Unequal Burden of Pain: Confronting Racial and Ethnic Disparities in Pain." *Pain Medicine* 4 (3): 277–94. https://doi.org/10.1046/j.1526-4637.2003.03034.x.

Greenberg, J., and T. Pyszczynski. 1985. "Compensatory Self-Inflation: A Response to the Threat to Self-Regard of Public Failure." *Journal of Personality and Social Psychology* 49 (1): 273–80. https://doi.org/10.1037/0022-3514.49.1.273.

Greenwald, A. G., D. E. McGhee, and J. L. K. Schwartz. 1998. "Measuring Individual Differences in Implicit Cognition: The Implicit Association Test." *Journal of Personality and Social Psychology* 74 (6): 1464–80. https://doi.org/10.1037/0022-3514.74.6.1464.

Greenwald, A. G., T. A. Poehlman, E. L. Uhlmann, and M. R. Banaji. 2009. "Understanding and Using the Implicit Association Test: III. Meta-analysis of Predictive Validity." *Journal of Personality and Social Psychology* 97 (1): 17–41. https://doi.org/10.1037/a0015575.

Gulker, J. E., A. Y. Mark, and M. J. Monteith. 2013. "Confronting Prejudice: The *Who, What, and Why* of Confrontation Effectiveness." *Social Influence* 8 (4): 280–93. https://doi.org/10.1080/15534510.2012.736879.

Gutiérrez, A. S., and M. M. Unzueta. 2013. "Are Admissions Decisions Based on Family Ties Fairer Than Those That Consider Race? Social Dominance Orientation and Attitudes Toward Legacy vs. Affirmative Action Policies." *Journal of Experimental Social Psychology* 49 (3): 554–58. https://doi.org/10.1016/j.jesp.2012.10.011.

Hacker, A. 1992. *Two Nations: Black and White, Separate, Hostile, Unequal.* New York: Scribner.

Hafer, C. L., and B. L. Correy. 1999. "Mediators of the Relation Between Beliefs in a Just World and Emotional Responses to Negative Outcomes." *Social Justice Research* 12 (3): 189–204. https://doi.org/10.1023/A:1022144317302.

Haidt, J., and J. Graham. 2007. "When Morality Opposes Justice: Conservatives Have Moral Intuitions That Liberals May Not Recognize." *Social Justice Research* 20 (1): 98–116. https://doi.org/10.1007/s11211-007-0034-z.

Halevy, N., E. Y. Chou, T. R. Cohen, and R. W. Livingston. 2012. "Status Conferral in Intergroup Social Dilemmas: Behavioral Antecedents and Consequences of Prestige and Dominance." *Journal of Personality and Social Psychology* 102 (2): 351–66. https://doi.org/10.1037/a0025515.

Hall, E. V., and R. W. Livingston. 2012. "The Hubris Penalty: Biased Responses to 'Celebration' Displays of Black Football Players." *Journal of Experimental Social Psychology* 48 (4): 899–904. https://doi.org/10.1016/j.jesp.2012.02.004.

Hamad, R. 2018. "How White Women Use Strategic Tears to Silence Women of Colour." *Guardian,* May 7, 2018. https://www.theguardian.com/commentisfree/2018/may/08/how-white-women-use-strategic-tears-to-avoid-accountability.

Hamilton, D. L., and R. K. Gifford. 1976. "Illusory Correlation in Interpersonal Perception: A Cognitive Basis of Stereotypic Judgments." *Journal of Experimental Social Psychology* 12 (4): 392–407. https://doi.org/10.1016/S0022-1031(76)80006-6.

Han, S. 2018. "Neurocognitive Basis of Racial Ingroup Bias in Empathy." *Trends in Cognitive Sciences* 22 (5): 400–421. https://doi.org/10.1016/j.tics.2018.02.013.

Hanel, P. H. P., G. R. Maio, and A. S. R. Manstead. 2019. "A New Way to Look at the Data: Similarities Between Groups of People Are Large and Important." *Journal of Personality and Social Psychology* 116 (4): 541–62. http://dx.doi.org/10.1037/pspi0000154.

Hannah-Jones, N. 2019. "Our Democracy's Founding Ideals Were False When They Were Written. Black Americans Have Fought to Make Them True." *New York Times Magazine*. December 20, 2019. https://www.nytimes.com/interactive/2019/08/14/magazine/black-history-american-democracy.html.

Harpending, H., and A. Rogers. 2000. "Genetic Perspectives on Human Origins and Differentiation." *Annual Review of Genomics and Human Genetics* 1 (6): 361–85. https://doi.org/10.1146/annurev.genom.1.1.361.

Hartley, E. 1946. *Problems in Prejudice*. New York: Kings Crown Press.

Hehman, E., E. W. Mania, and S. L. Gaertner. 2010. "Where the Division Lies: Common Ingroup Identity Moderates the Cross-Race Racial-Recognition Effect." *Journal of Experimental Social Psychology* 46 (2): 445–48. https://doi.org/10.1016/j.jesp.2009.11.008.

Henry, P. J., and D. O. Sears. 2002. "The Symbolic Racism 2000 Scale." *Political Psychology* 23 (2): 253–83. https://doi.org/10.1111/0162-895X.00281.

Herrnstein, R., and C. Murray. 1994. *The Bell Curve: Intelligence and Class Structure in American Life*. New York: Free Press.

Hertwig, R., and C. Engel. 2016. "Homo Ignorans: Deliberately Choosing Not to Know." *Perspectives on Psychological Science* 11: 359–72.

Herzberg, F. 2003. "One More Time: How Do You Motivate Employees?" *Harvard Business Review,* January 2003.

Hester, N., and K. Gray. 2018. "For Black Men, Being Tall Increases Threat Stereotyping and Police Stops." *Proceedings of the National Academy of Sciences* 115 (11): 2711–15. https://doi.org/10.1073/pnas.1714454115.

Hewstone, M. 1994. "Revision and Change of Stereotypic Beliefs: In Search of the Elusive Subtyping Model." *European Review of Social Psychology* 5 (1): 69–109. https://doi.org/10.1080/14792779543000020.

Hewstone, M., and R. Brown. 1986. "Contact Is Not Enough: An Intergroup Perspective on the 'Contact Hypothesis.'" In *Contact and Conflict in Intergroup Encounters,* edited by M. Hewstone and R. Brown, 1–44. Oxford and New York: Blackwell.

Hicken, M. T., H. Lee, J. Ailshire, S. A. Burgard, and D. R. Williams. 2013. "'Every Shut Eye, Ain't Sleep': The Role of Racism-Related Vigilance in Racial/Ethnic Disparities in Sleep Difficulty." *Race and Social Problems* 5 (2): 100–112. https://doi.org/10.1007/s12552-013-9095-9.

Hjelmgaard, K. 2020. "Reparations Bill Gets New Attention Amid BLM. Could Other Nations Provide a Blueprint?" *USA Today,* July 10, 2020.

Ho, A. K., J. Sidanius, F. Pratto, S. Levin, L. Thomsen, N. Kteily, and J. Sheehy-Skeffington. 2012. "Social Dominance Orientation: Revisiting the Structure and Function of a Variable Predicting Social and Political Attitudes." *Personality and Social Psychology Bulletin* 38 (5): 583–606. https://doi.org/10.1177/0146167211432765.

Hochschild, A. R. 2016. *Strangers in Their Own Land: Anger and Mourning on the American Right*. New York: New Press.

Hoever, I. J., D. van Knippenberg, W. P. van Ginkel, and H. G. Barkema. 2012. "Fostering Team Creativity: Perspective Taking as Key to Unlocking Diversity's Potential." *Journal of Applied Psychology* 97 (5): 982–96. https://doi.org/10.1037/a0029159.

Holoien, D. S., and J. N. Shelton. 2012. "You Deplete Me: The Cognitive Costs of Colorblindness on Ethnic Minorities." *Journal of Experimental Social Psychology* 48 (2): 562–65. https://doi.org/10.1016/j.jesp.2011.09.010.

Holzer, H. J., S. Raphael, and M. A. Stoll. 2002. "Will Employers Hire Ex-Offenders? Employer Preferences, Background Checks, and Their Determinants." Institute for Research on Poverty Discussion Paper No. 1243–02.

Horowitz, J. M., A. Brown, and K. Cox. 2019. *Race in America 2019.* Pew Research Center, April 2019. https://www.pewsocialtrends.org/wp-content/uploads/sites/3/2019/04/Race-report_updated-4.29.19.pdf.

Hsee, C. K., S. Blount, G. F. Loewenstein, and M. H. Bazerman. 1999. "Preference Reversals Between Joint and Separate Evaluations of Options: A Review and Theoretical Analysis." *Psychological Bulletin* 125 (5): 576–90. https://doi.org/10.1037/0033-2909.125.5.576.

Hunsinger, M., R. Livingston, and L. Isbell. 2013. "The Impact of Loving-Kindness Meditation on Affective Learning and Cognitive Control." *Mindfulness* 4 (3): 275–80. https://doi.org/10.1007/s12671-012-0125-2.

Ibarra, H. 1992. "Homophily and Differential Returns: Sex Differences in Network Structure and Access in an Advertising Firm." *Administrative Science Quarterly* 37 (3): 422–47. https://doi.org/10.2307/2393451.

Ibarra, H. 2019. "A Lack of Sponsorship Is Keeping Women from Advancing into Leadership." *Harvard Business Review,* August 2019.

Institute for Policy Studies. n.d. "Wealth Inequality: Our World's Deepest Pockets—'Ultra High Net Worth Individuals'—Hold an Astoundingly Disproportionate Share of Global Wealth." Inequality.org. https://inequality.org/facts/global-inequality/.

Isenberg, N. 2016. *White Trash: The 400-Year Untold History of Class in America*. New York: Viking.

Jablonski, N. G., and G. Chaplin. 2000. "The Evolution of Human Skin Coloration." *Journal of Human Evolution* 39 (1): 57–106. https://doi.org/10.1006/jhev.2000.0403.

Jablonski, N. G., and G. Chaplin. 2010. "Human Skin Pigmentation as an Adaptation to UV Radiation." *Proceedings of the National Academy of Sciences of the United States of America* 107 (S2): 8962–68. https://doi.org/10.1073/pnas.0914628107.

Jackman, M. R., and M. Crane. 1986. " 'Some of My Best Friends Are

Black . . .': Interracial Friendship and Whites' Racial Attitudes." *Public Opinion Quarterly* 50 (4): 459. https://doi.org/10.1086/268998.

Jackson, P. B., and D. R. Williams. 2006. "The Intersection of Race, Gender, and SES: Health Paradoxes." In *Gender, Race, Class, & Health: Intersectional Approaches,* edited by A. J. Schulz & L. Mullings, 131–62. San Francisco: Jossey-Bass.

Jacoby-Senghor, D. S., S. Sinclair, C. T. Smith, and J. L. M. Skorinko. 2019. "Implicit Bias Predicts Liking of Ingroup Members Who Are Comfortable with Intergroup Interaction." *Personality and Social Psychology Bulletin* 45 (4): 603–15. https://doi.org/10.1177/0146167218793136.

Jehn, K. A., G. B. Northcraft, and M. A. Neale. 1999. "Why Differences Make a Difference: A Field Study of Diversity, Conflict, and Performance in Workgroups." *Administrative Science Quarterly* 44 (4): 741–63. https://doi.org/10.2307/2667054.

Johansson, F. 2017. *The Medici Effect: What Elephants and Epidemics Can Teach Us About Innovation.* 2nd ed. Cambridge, Mass.: Harvard Business School Press.

Johnson, A. 2017. "That Was No Typo: The Median Net Worth of Black Bostonians Really Is $8." *Boston Globe,* December 11, 2017. https://www.bostonglobe.com/metro/2017/12/11/that-was-typo-the-median-net-worth-black-bostonians-really/ze5kxC1jJelx24M3pugFFN/story.html.

Jones, E. E., and V. A. Harris. 1967. "The Attribution of Attitudes." *Journal of Experimental Social Psychology* 3 (1): 1–24. https://doi.org/10.1016/0022-1031(67)90034-0.

Jorde, L. B., and S. P. Wooding. 2004. "Genetic Variation, Classification and 'Race.'" *Nature Genetics* 36 (11): 1–6. https://doi.org/10.1038/ng1435.

Jost, J. T., J. Glaser, A. W. Kruglanski, and F. J. Sulloway. 2003. "Political Conservatism as Motivated Social Cognition." *Psychological Bulletin* 129 (3): 339–75. https://doi.org/10.1037/0033-2909.129.3.339.

Jost, J. T., and O. Hunyady. 2003. "The Psychology of System Justification and the Palliative Function of Ideology." *European Review of Social Psychology* 13 (1): 111–53. https://doi.org/10.1080/10463280240000046.

Judge, T. A., and D. M. Cable. 2004. "The Effect of Physical Height on Workplace Success and Income: Preliminary Test of a Theoretical Model." *Journal of Applied Psychology* 89 (3): 428–41. https://doi.org/10.1037/0021-9010.89.3.428.

Kahneman, D. 2011. *Thinking, Fast and Slow.* New York: Farrar, Straus and Giroux.

Kaiser, C. R., B. Major, I. Jurcevic, T. L. Dover, L. M. Brady, and J. R. Shapiro. 2013. "Presumed Fair: Ironic Effects of Organizational Diversity Structures." *Journal of Personality and Social Psychology* 104 (3): 504–19. https://doi.org/10.1037/a0030838.

Kaiser, C. R., and C. T. Miller. 2001. "Stop Complaining! The Social Costs of Making Attributions to Discrimination." *Personality and Social Psychology Bulletin* 27 (2): 254–63. https://doi.org/10.1177/0146167201272010.

Kaiser, C. R., and J. S. Pratt-Hyatt. 2009. "Distributing Prejudice Unequally: Do Whites Direct Their Prejudice Toward Strongly Identified Minorities?" *Journal of Personality and Social Psychology* 96 (2): 432–45. https://doi.org/10.1037/a0012877.

Kang, S. K., K. A. DeCelles, A. Tilcsik, and S. Jun. 2016. "Whitened Résumés: Race and Self-Presentation in the Labor Market." *Administrative Science Quarterly* 61 (3): 469–502. https://doi.org/10.1177/0001839216639577.

Karmali, F., K. Kawakami, and E. Page-Gould. 2017. "He Said What? Physiological and Cognitive Responses to Imagining and Witnessing Outgroup Racism." *Journal of Experimental Psychology: General* 146 (8): 1073–85. https://doi.org/10.1037/xge0000304.

Kawakami, K., E. Dunn, F. Karmali, and J. F. Dovidio. 2009. "Mispredicting Affective and Behavioral Responses to Racism. *Science* 323: 276–78.

Keister, L. A. 2008. "Conservative Protestants and Wealth: How Religion Perpetuates Asset Poverty." *American Journal of Sociology* 113 (5): 1237–71. https://doi.org/10.1086/525506.

Kelly, K. 2020. "The Short Tenure and Abrupt Ouster of Banking's Sole Black C.E.O." *New York Times,* October 3, 2020. https://www.nytimes.com/2020/10/03/business/tidjane-thiam-credit-suisse.html.

Kendi, I. X. 2017. *Stamped from the Beginning: The Definitive History of Racist Ideas in America.* New York: Bold Type.

Kendi, I. X. 2019. *How to Be an Antiracist.* New York: One World.

Kerr, S. 1975. "On the Folly of Rewarding A, While Hoping for B." *Academy of Management Journal* 18 (4): 769–83. https://doi.org/10.2307/255378.

Killewald, A. 2013. "Return to *Being Black, Living in the Red:* A Race Gap in Wealth That Goes Beyond Social Origins." *Demography* 50 (4): 1177–95. https://doi.org/10.1007/s13524-012-0190-0.

Killewald, A., F. T. Pfeffer, and J. N. Schachner. 2017. "Wealth Inequality and Accumulation." *Annual Review of Sociology* 43 (1): 379–404. https://doi.org/10.1146/annurev-soc-060116-053331.

Kirkland, S. L., J. Greenberg, and T. Pyszczynski. 1987. "Further Evidence of the Deleterious Effects of Overheard Derogatory Ethnic Labels." *Personality and Social Psychology Bulletin* 13 (2): 216–27. https://doi.org/10.1177/0146167287132007.

Kittles, R. A., and K. M. Weiss. 2003. "Race, Ancestry, and Genes: Implications for Defining Disease Risk." *Annual Review of Genomics and Human*

Genetics 4 (1): 33–67. https://doi.org/10.1146/annurev.genom.4.070802 .110356.

Knowles, E. D., B. S. Lowery, R. M. Chow, and M. M. Unzueta. 2014. "Deny, Distance, or Dismantle? How White Americans Manage a Privileged Identity." *Perspectives on Psychological Science* 9 (6): 594–609. https://doi.org/10.1177/1745691614554658.

Koch, L. M., A. M. Gross, and R. Kolts. 2001. "Attitudes Toward Black English and Code Switching." *Journal of Black Psychology* 27 (1): 29–42. https://doi.org/10.1177/0095798401027001002.

Kraus, M. W., I. N. Onyeador, N. M. Daumeyer, J. M. Rucker, and J. A. Richeson. 2019. "The Misperception of Racial Economic Inequality." *Perspectives on Psychological Science* 14 (6): 899–921. https://doi.org/10 .1177/1745691619863049.

Kraus, M. W., J. M. Rucker, and J. A. Richeson. 2017. "Americans Misperceive Racial Economic Equality." *Proceedings of the National Academy of Sciences of the United States of America* 114 (39): 10324–31. https://doi.org/ 10.1073/pnas.1707719114.

Kteily, N., T. Saguy, J. Sidanius, and D. M. Taylor. 2013. "Negotiating Power: Agenda Ordering and the Willingness to Negotiate in Asymmetric Intergroup Conflicts." *Journal of Personality and Social Psychology* 105 (6): 978–95. https://doi.org/10.1037/a0034095.

Kuhlman, D. M., C. R. Camac, and D. A. Cunha. 1986. "Individual Differences in Social Orientation." In *Experimental Social Dilemmas,* edited by H. A. M. Wilke, D. Messick, and C. Rutte, 234. Frankfurt, Bern, and New York: Peter Lang.

Kuhlman, D. M., and A. F. Marshello. 1975. "Individual Differences in Game Motivation as Moderators of Preprogrammed Strategy Effects in Prisoner's Dilemma." *Journal of Personality and Social Psychology* 32 (5): 922–31. https://doi.org/10.1037/0022-3514.32.5.922.

Kunda, Z. 1990. "The Case for Motivated Reasoning." *Psychological Bulletin* 108 (3): 480–98. https://doi.org/10.1037/0033-2909.108.3.480.

Kurzban, R., J. Tooby, and L. Cosmides. 2001. "Can Race Be Erased? Coalitional Computation and Social Categorization." *Proceedings of the National Academy of Sciences of the United States of America* 98 (26): 15387–92. https://doi.org/10.1073/pnas.251541498.

Lai, C. K., A. L. Skinner, E. Cooley, S. Murrar, M. Brauer, T. Devos, J. Calanchini, Y. J. Xiao, C. Pedram, C. K. Marshburn, S. Simon, J. C. Blanchar, J. A. Joy-Gaba, J. Conway, L. Redford, R. A. Klein, G. Roussos, F. M. H. Schellhaas, M. Burns, . . . B. A. Nosek. 2016. "Reducing Implicit Racial Preferences: II. Intervention Effectiveness Across Time." *Journal of Experimental Psychology: General* 145 (8): 1001–16. https://doi .org/10.1037/xge0000179.

Lamont, M., L. Adler, B. Y. Park, and X. Xiang. 2017. "Bridging Cultural
    Sociology and Cognitive Psychology in Three Contemporary Research
    Programmes." *Nature Human Behaviour* 1 (12): 866–72. https://doi.org/
    10.1038/s41562-017-0242-y.

Landmann, H., and U. Hess. 2018. "Testing Moral Foundation Theory: Are
    Specific Moral Emotions Elicited by Specific Moral Transgressions?"
    Journal of Moral Education 47 (1): 34–47. https://doi.org/10.1080/03057240
    .2017.1350569.

Latane, B., and J. M. Darley. 1970. *The Unresponsive Bystander: Why Doesn't
    He Help?* New York: Appleton-Century Crofts.

Lavine, H., M. Lodge, J. Polichak, and C. Taber. 2002. "Explicating the
    Black Box Through Experimentation: Studies of Authoritarianism and
    Threat." *Political Analysis* 10 (4): 343–61. https://doi.org/10.1093/pan/
    10.4.343.

Lawrence, V. W. 1991. "Effect of Socially Ambiguous Information on White
    and Black Children's Behavioral and Trait Perceptions." *Merrill-Palmer
    Quarterly* 37 (4): 619–30.

Layous, K., E. M. Davis, J. Garcia, V. Purdie-Vaughns, J. E. Cook, and
    G. L. Cohen. 2017. "Feeling Left Out, but Affirmed: Protecting Against
    the Negative Effects of Low Belonging in College." *Journal of Experi-
    mental Social Psychology* 69: 227–31. https://doi.org/10.1016/j.jesp.2016
    .09.008.

Lee, T. 2019. "How America's Vast Racial Wealth Grew: By Plunder." *New
    York Times Magazine,* August 14, 2019.

Leffler, E. M., K. Bullaughey, D. R. Matute, W. K. Meyer, L. Se, A. Venkat,
    P. Andolfatto, and M. Przeworski. 2012. "Revisiting an Old Riddle:
    What Determines Genetic Diversity Levels Within Species?" *PLOS Bi-
    ology* 10 (9): 1–9. https://doi.org/10.1371/journal.pbio.1001388.

Lepper, M. R., D. Greene, and R. E. Nisbett. 1973. "Undermining Children's
    Intrinsic Interest with Extrinsic Reward: A Test of the 'Overjustifica-
    tion' Hypothesis." *Journal of Personality and Social Psychology* 28 (1):
    129–37. https://doi.org/10.1037/h0035519.

Lerner, M. J. 1980. "The Belief in a Just World." In *The Belief in a Just
    World. Perspectives in Social Psychology,* 9–30. Boston: Springer US.
    https://doi.org/10.1007/978-1-4899-0448-5_2.

Leung, A. K.-y., W. W. Maddux, A. D. Galinsky, and C.-y. Chiu. 2008.
    "Multicultural Experience Enhances Creativity: The When and How."
    American Psychologist 63 (3), 169–181.

Levendusky, M. S. 2017. "Americans, Not Partisans: Can Priming American
    National Identity Reduce Affective Polarization?" *Journal of Politics* 80
    (1): 59–70. https://doi.org/10.1086/693987.

Lewin, K. 1952. "Group Decision and Social Change." In *Readings in Social

Psychology, edited by G. E. Swanson, T. M. Newcomb, and E. L. Hartley, 197–211. New York: Henry Holt & Company.

Lewis, G. J., and T. C. Bates. 2017. "The Temporal Stability of In-group Favoritism Is Mostly Attributable to Genetic Factors." *Social Psychological and Personality Science* 8 (8): 897–903. https://doi.org/10.1177/1948550617699250.

Liebrand, W. B. G., R. W. T. L. Jansen, V. M. Rijken, and C. J. M. Suhre. 1986. "Might Over Morality: Social Values and the Perception of Other Players in Experimental Games." *Journal of Experimental Social Psychology* 22 (3): 203–15. https://doi.org/10.1016/0022-1031(86)90024-7.

Livingston, R. W. 2002. "The Role of Perceived Negativity in the Moderation of African Americans' Implicit and Explicit Racial Attitudes." *Journal of Experimental Social Psychology* 38 (4): 405–13. https://doi.org/10.1016/S0022-1031(02)00002-1.

Livingston, R. W. 2020. "How to Promote Racial Equity in the Workplace." *Harvard Business Review,* September–October, 64–72.

Livingston, R. W. 2013. "Gender, Race, and Leadership: An Examination of the Challenges Facing Non-prototypical Leaders." Paper presented at the Gender & Work Research Symposium: Challenging Conventional Wisdom, Boston.

Livingston, R. W., T. R. Cohen, and N. Halevy. 2012. "Empowering the Wolf in Sheep's Clothing." Unpublished manuscript.

Livingston, R. W., and B. B. Drwecki. 2007. "Why Are Some Individuals Not Racially Biased? Susceptibility to Affective Conditioning Predicts Nonprejudice Toward Blacks." *Psychological Science* 18 (9): 816–23. https://doi.org/10.1111/j.1467-9280.2007.01985.x.

Livingston, R. W., and N. A. Pearce. 2009. "The Teddy-Bear Effect: Does Having a Baby Face Benefit Black Chief Executive Officers?" *Psychological Science* 20 (10): 1229–36. https://doi.org/10.1111/j.1467-9280.2009.02431.x.

Livingston, R. W., A. S. Rosette, and E. F. Washington. 2012. "Can an Agentic Black Woman Get Ahead? The Impact of Race and Interpersonal Dominance on Perceptions of Female Leaders." *Psychological Science* 23 (4): 354–58. https://doi.org/10.1177/0956797611428079.

Locke, E. A., and G. P. Latham. 2015. "New Directions in Goal-Setting Theory." *Psychological Science* 15 (5) (October): 265–68. https://doi.org/10.1111/j.1467-8721.2006.00449.x.

Locke, E. A., K. N. Shaw, L. M. Saari, and G. P. Latham. 1981. "Goal Setting and Task Performance: 1969–1980." *Psychological Bulletin* 90 (1): 125–52. https://doi.org/10.1037/0033-2909.90.1.125.

Lowery, B. S., C. D. Hardin, and S. Sinclair. 2001. "Social Influence Effects on Automatic Racial Prejudice." *Journal of Personality and Social Psychology* 81 (5): 842–55. https://doi.org/10.1037/0022-3514.81.5.842.

Lowery, B. S., E. D. Knowles, and M. M. Unzueta. 2007. "Framing Inequity Safely: Whites' Motivated Perceptions of Racial Privilege." *Personality and Social Psychology Bulletin* 33 (9): 1237–50. https://doi.org/10.1177/0146167207303016.

Lucas, B. J., and N. S. Kteily. 2018. "(Anti-)egalitarianism Differentially Predicts Empathy for Members of Advantaged Versus Disadvantaged Groups." *Journal of Personality and Social Psychology* 114 (5): 665–92. https://doi.org/10.1037/pspa0000112.

Lueke, A., and B. Gibson. 2015. "Mindfulness Meditation Reduces Implicit Age and Race Bias: The Role of Reduced Automaticity of Responding." *Social Psychological and Personality Science* 6 (3): 284–91. https://doi.org/10.1177/1948550614559651.

Luo, M. 2009. "'Whitening' the Résumé." *New York Times,* December 5, 2009. https://www.nytimes.com/2009/12/06/weekinreview/06Luo.html.

Lyons-Padilla, S., H. R. Markus, A. Monk, S. Radhakrishna, R. Shah, N. A. "Daryn" Dodson, and J. L. Eberhardt. 2019. "Race Influences Professional Investors' Financial Judgments." *Proceedings of the National Academy of Sciences of the United States of America* 116 (35): 17225–30. https://doi.org/10.1073/pnas.1822052116.

Macrae, C. N., and G. V. Bodenhausen. 2000. "Social Cognition: Thinking Categorically About Others." *Annual Review of Psychology* 51 (1): 93–120. https://doi.org/10.1146/annurev.psych.51.1.93.

Maddox, K. B., and S. A. Gray. 2002. "Cognitive Representations of Black Americans: Reexploring the Role of Skin Tone." *Personality and Social Psychology Bulletin* 28 (2): 250–59. https://doi.org/10.1177/0146167202282010.

Maddux, W. W., and A. D. Galinsky. (2009). "Cultural Borders and Mental Barriers: The Relationship Between Living Abroad and Creativity." *Journal of Personality and Social Psychology* 96 (5), 1047–1061.

Mahalingam, R. 2003. "Essentialism, Culture, and Power: Representations of Social Class." *Journal of Social Issues* 59 (4): 733–49. https://doi.org/10.1046/j.0022-4537.2003.00087.x.

Mannix, E., and M. A. Neale. 2005. "What Differences Make a Difference?: The Promise and Reality of Diverse Teams in Organizations." *Psychological Science in the Public Interest* 6 (2): 31–55. https://doi.org/10.1111/j.1529-1006.2005.00022.x.

Maroto, M. 2016. "Growing Farther Apart: Racial and Ethnic Inequality in Household Wealth Across the Distribution." *Sociological Science* 3: 801–24. https://doi.org/10.15195/v3.a34.

Martin, A. R., M. Lin, J. M. Granka, J. W. Myrick, X. Liu, A. Sockell, E. G. Atkinson, C. J. Werely, M. Möller, M. S. Sandhu, D. M. Kingsley, E. G. Hoal, X. Liu, M. J. Daly, M. W. Feldman, C. R. Gignoux, C. D. Bustamante, and B. M. Henn. 2017. "An Unexpectedly Complex Architecture for Skin Pigmentation in Africans." *Cell* 171 (6): 1340–53. https://doi.org/10.1016/j.cell.2017.11.015.

Mattan, B. D., J. T. Kubota, T. Li, S. A. Venezia, and J. Cloutier. 2019. "Implicit Evaluative Biases Toward Targets Varying in Race and Socioeconomic Status." *Personality and Social Psychology Bulletin* 45 (10): 1512–27. https://doi.org/10.1177/0146167219835230.

McChesney, K. Y. 2015. "Teaching Diversity: The Science You Need to Know to Explain Why Race Is Not Biological." *SAGE Open* 5 (4). https://doi.org/10.1177/2158244015611712.

McClintock, C. G., and W. B. Liebrand. 1988. "Role of Interdependence Structure, Individual Value Orientation, and Another's Strategy in Social Decision Making: A Transformational Analysis." *Journal of Personality and Social Psychology* 55 (3): 396–409. https://doi.org/10.1037/0022-3514.55.3.396.

McConahay, J. B. 1986. "Modern Racism, Ambivalence, and the Modern Racism Scale." In *Prejudice, Discrimination, and Racism,* edited by J. F. Dovidio and S. L. Gaertner, 91–125. Orlando: Academic Press.

McDonald, M. L., G. D. Keeves, and J. D. Westphal. 2018. "One Step Forward, One Step Back: White Male Top Manager Organizational Identification and Helping Behavior Toward Other Executives Following the Appointment of a Female or Racial Minority CEO." *Academy of Management Journal* 61 (2): 405–439. https://doi.org/10.5465/amj.2016.0358.

McGinnies, E. 1949. "Emotionality and Perceptual Defense." *Psychological Review* 56 (5): 244–51. https://doi.org/10.1037/h0056508.

McGlothlin, H., and M. Killen. 2006. "Intergroup Attitudes of European American Children Attending Ethnically Homogeneous Schools." *Child Development* 77 (5): 1375–86. https://doi.org/10.1111/j.1467-8624.2006.00941.x.

McGlothlin, H., and M. Killen. 2010. "How Social Experience Is Related to Children's Intergroup Attitudes." *European Journal of Social Psychology* 40 (4): 625–34. https://doi.org/10.1002/ejsp.733.

McNeil, D. G., Jr. 1997. "In Africa, Making Offices Out of an Anthill." *New York Times,* February 13, 1997.

Meleady, R., T. Hopthrow, and R. J. Crisp. 2013. "Simulating Social Dilemmas: Promoting Cooperative Behavior Through Imagined Group Discussion." *Journal of Personality and Social Psychology* 104 (5): 839–53. https://doi.org/10.1037/a0031233.

Mendoza, S. A., P. M. Gollwitzer, and D. M. Amodio. 2010. "Reducing the Expression of Implicit Stereotypes: Reflexive Control Through Implementation Intentions." *Personality and Social Psychology Bulletin* 36 (4): 512–23. https://doi.org/10.1177/0146167210362789.

Merton, R. K. 1948. "The Self-Fulfilling Prophecy." *The Antioch Review* 8 (2): 193–210. http://doi.org/10.2307/4609267.

Metzl, J. M. 2019. *Dying of Whiteness: How the Politics of Racial Resentment Is Killing America's Heartland*. New York: Basic Books.

Mijs, J. J. B. 2018. "Visualizing Belief in Meritocracy, 1930–2010." *Socius: Sociological Research for a Dynamic World* 4 (1). https://doi.org/10.1177/2378023118811805.

Milano, B. 2020. "Why 'Truth' Beats Facts." *Harvard Gazette,* February 21, 2020. https://news.harvard.edu/gazette/story/2020/02/talk-explores-what-truth-actually-means/.

Milgram, S. 1963. "Behavioral Study of Obedience." *Journal of Abnormal and Social Psychology* 67 (4): 371–78. https://doi.org/10.1037/h0040525.

Milkman, K. L., M. Akinola, and D. Chugh. 2015. "What Happens Before? A Field Experiment Exploring How Pay and Representation Differentially Shape Bias on the Pathway into Organizations." *Journal of Applied Psychology* 100 (6): 1678–712. https://doi.org/10.1037/apl0000022.

Ministero, L. M., M. J. Poulin, A. E. K. Buffone, and S. DeLury. 2018. "Empathic Concern and the Desire to Help as Separable Components of Compassionate Responding." *Personality and Social Psychology Bulletin* 44 (4): 475–91. https://doi.org/10.1177/0146167217741345.

Misra, S., P. T. D. Le, E. Goldmann, and L. H. Yang. 2020. "Psychological Impact of Anti-Asian Stigma Due to the COVID-19 Pandemic: A Call for Research, Practice, and Policy Responses." *Psychological Trauma: Theory, Research, Practice, and Policy* 12 (5): 461–64. https://doi.org/10.1037/tra0000821.

Monin, B., and D. T. Miller. 2001. "Moral Credentials and the Expression of Prejudice." *Journal of Personality and Social Psychology* 81 (1): 33–43. https://doi.org/10.1037/0022-3514.81.1.33.

Moore-Berg, S. L., and A. Karpinski. 2019. "An Intersectional Approach to Understanding How Race and Social Class Affect Intergroup Processes." *Social and Personality Psychology Compass* 13 (1): 1–14. https://doi.org/10.1111/spc3.12426.

Mueller, K., K. Hattrup, S.-O. Spiess, and N. Lin-Hi. 2012. "The Effects of Corporate Social Responsibility on Employees' Affective Commitment: A Cross-Cultural Investigation." *Journal of Applied Psychology* 97 (6): 1186–200. https://doi.org/10.1037/a0030204.

Muhammad, K. G. 2019. *The Condemnation of Blackness: Race, Crime, and the Making of Modern Urban America*. Cambridge, Mass.: Harvard University Press.

Mullen, B., and J. M. Smyth. 2004. "Immigrant Suicide Rates as a Function of Ethnophaulisms: Hate Speech." *Psychosomatic Medicine* 66 (3): 343–48.

Murray, P. 2020. "Protestors' Anger Justified Even if Actions May Not Be." Monmouth Polling Institute, June 2, 2020. https://www.monmouth.edu/polling-institute/reports/monmouthpoll_US_060220/.

Myrdal, G. 1944. *An American Dilemma: The Negro Problem and Modern Democracy*. 2 volumes. New York: Harper & Brothers.

Nai, J., J. Narayanan, I. Hernandez, and K. Savani. 2018. "People in More Racially Diverse Neighborhoods Are More Prosocial." *Journal of Personality and Social Psychology* 114 (4): 497–515. https://doi.org/10.1037/pspa0000103.

National Safety Council. 2017. "Odds of Dying." Injury Facts. https://injuryfacts.nsc.org/all-injuries/preventable-death-overview/odds-of-dying/.

Nelson, J. C., G. Adams, and P. S. Salter. 2013. "The Marley Hypothesis: Denial of Racism Reflects Ignorance of History." *Psychological Science* 24 (2): 213–18. https://doi.org/10.1177/0956797612451466.

Newman, B. J., C. D. Johnston, and P. L. Lown. 2015. "False Consciousness or Class Awareness? Local Income Inequality, Personal Economic Position, and Belief in American Meritocracy." *American Journal of Political Science* 59 (2): 326–40. https://doi.org/10.1111/ajps.12153.

Nir, S. M. 2020. "The Bird Watcher, That Incident and His Feelings on the Woman's Fate." *New York Times,* May 27, 2020. https://www.nytimes.com/2020/05/27/nyregion/amy-cooper-christian-central-park-video.html.

Nolan, J. M., P. W. Schultz, R. B. Cialdini, N. J. Goldstein, and V. Griskevicius. 2008. "Normative Social Influence Is Underdetected." *Personality and Social Psychology Bulletin* 34, 913–23.

Norton, M. I., and D. Ariely. 2011. "Building a Better America—One Wealth Quintile at a Time." *Perspectives on Psychological Science* 6 (1): 9–12. https://doi.org/10.1177/1745691610393524.

Norton, M. I., and S. R. Sommers. 2011. "Whites See Racism as a Zero-Sum Game That They Are Now Losing." *Perspectives on Psychological Science* 6 (3): 215–18. https://doi.org/10.1177/1745691611406922.

Norton, M. I., J. A. Vandello, and J. M. Darley. 2004. "Casuistry and Social Category Bias." *Journal of Personality and Social Psychology* 87 (6): 817–31. https://doi.org/10.1037/0022-3514.87.6.817.

Nosek, B. A., M. R. Banaji, and A. G. Greenwald. 2002. "Harvesting Implicit Group Attitudes and Beliefs from a Demonstration Web Site." *Group Dynamics* 6 (1): 101–15. https://doi.org/10.1037/1089-2699.6.1.101.

Nunley, J. M., A. Pugh, N. Romero, and R. A. Seals. 2015. "Racial Discrimination in the Labor Market for Recent College Graduates: Evidence from a Field Experiment." *B.E. Journal of Economic Analysis and Policy* 15 (3): 1093–125. https://doi.org/10.1515/bejeap-2014-0082.

Obama, B. 2006. *The Audacity of Hope: Thoughts on Reclaiming the American Dream*. New York: Crown.

Obeid, N., N. Argo, and J. Ginges. 2017. "How Moral Perceptions Influence Intergroup Tolerance: Evidence from Lebanon, Morocco, and the United States." *Personality and Social Psychology Bulletin* 43 (3): 381–91. https://doi.org/10.1177/0146167216686560.

Ogbu, J. U. 1978. *Minority Education and Caste: The American System in Cross-Cultural Perspective*. New York: Academic Press.

Page, S. 2007. *The Difference: How the Power of Diversity Creates Better Groups, Firms, Schools, and Societies*. Princeton, N.J.: Princeton University Press.

Pager, D. 2003. "The Mark of a Criminal Record." *American Journal of Sociology* 108 (5): 937–75. https://doi.org/10.1086/374403.

Palamar, J. J., S. Davies, D. C. Ompad, C. M. Cleland, and M. Weitzman. 2015. "Powder Cocaine and Crack Use in the United States: An Examination of Risk for Arrest and Socioeconomic Disparities in Use." *Drug and Alcohol Dependence* 149: 108–16. https://doi.org/10.1016/j.drugalcdep.2015.01.029.

Paluck, E. L. 2009. "Reducing Intergroup Prejudice and Conflict Using the Media: A Field Experiment in Rwanda." *Journal of Personality and Social Psychology* 96 (3): 574–87. https://doi.org/10.1037/a0011989.

Paluck, E. L., and D. P. Green. 2009. "Deference, Dissent, and Dispute Resolution: An Experimental Intervention Using Mass Media to Change Norms and Behavior in Rwanda." *American Political Science Review* 103 (4): 622–44. https://doi.org/10.1017/S0003055409990128.

Paradies, Y., J. Ben, N. Denson, A. Elias, N. Priest, A. Pieterse, A. Gupta, M. Kelaher, and G. Gee. 2015. "Racism as a Determinant of Health: A Systematic Review and Meta-analysis." *PLOS ONE* 10 (9): 1–48. https://doi.org/10.1371/journal.pone.0138511.

Park, S. H., and J. D. Westphal. 2013. "Social Discrimination in the Corporate Elite: How Status Affects the Propensity for Minority CEOs to Receive Blame for Low Firm Performance." *Administrative Science Quarterly* 58 (4): 542–86. https://doi.org/10.1177/0001839213509364.

Payne, B. K., H. A. Vuletich, and J. L. Brown-Iannuzzi. 2019. "Historical Roots of Implicit Bias in Slavery." *Proceedings of the National Academy of Sciences of the United States of America* 116 (24): 11693–98. https://doi.org/10.1073/pnas.1818816116.

Payne, B. K., H. A. Vuletich, and K. B. Lundberg. 2017. "The Bias of

Crowds: How Implicit Bias Bridges Personal and Systemic Prejudice." *Psychological Inquiry* 28 (4): 1–64. https://doi.org/10.1080/1047840X .2017.1335568.

Peck, T. C., S. Seinfeld, S. M. Aglioti, and M. Slater. 2013. "Putting Yourself in the Skin of a Black Avatar Reduces Implicit Racial Bias." *Consciousness and Cognition* 22 (3): 779–87. https://doi.org/10.1016/j.concog.2013 .04.016.

Petersen, M. B., D. Sznycer, A. Sell, L. Cosmides, and J. Tooby. 2013. "The Ancestral Logic of Politics: Upper-Body Strength Regulates Men's Assertion of Self-Interest over Economic Redistribution." *Psychological Science* 24 (7): 1098–103. https://doi.org/10.1177/0956797612466415.

Petrow, G. A., J. E. Transue, and T. Vercellotti. 2018. "Do White In-group Processes Matter, Too? White Racial Identity and Support for Black Political Candidates." *Political Behavior* 40 (1): 197–222. https://doi.org/ 10.1007/s11109-017-9422-8.

Pettigrew, T. F. 1958. "Personality and Sociocultural Factors in Intergroup Attitudes: A Cross-National Comparison." *Journal of Conflict Resolution* 2 (1): 29–42. https://doi.org/10.1177/002200275800200104.

Pettigrew, T. F. 1997. "Generalized Intergroup Contact Effects on Prejudice." *Personality and Social Psychology Bulletin* 23 (2): 173–85. https:// doi.org/10.1177/0146167297232006.

Pettigrew, T. F., and L. R. Tropp. 2006. "A Meta-analytic Test of Intergroup Contact Theory." *Journal of Personality and Social Psychology* 90 (5): 751–83. https://doi.org/10.1037/0022-3514.90.5.751.

Pfeffer, J. 2015. *Leadership BS: Fixing Workplaces and Careers One Truth at a Time*. New York: HarperCollins.

Phelan, J. E., and L. A. Rudman. 2010. "Reactions to Ethnic Deviance: The Role of Backlash in Racial Stereotype Maintenance." *Journal of Personality and Social Psychology* 99 (2): 265–81. https://doi.org/10.1037/a0018304.

Phillips, K. W., and D. L. Loyd. 2006. "When Surface and Deep-Level Diversity Collide: The Effects on Dissenting Group Members." *Organizational Behavior and Human Decision Processes* 99 (2): 143–60. https://doi .org/10.1016/j.obhdp.2005.12.001.

Pieterse, A. L., N. R. Todd, H. A. Neville, and R. T. Carter. 2012. "Perceived Racism and Mental Health Among Black American Adults: A Meta-analytic Review." *Journal of Counseling Psychology* 59 (1): 1–9. https://doi.org/10.1037/a0026208.

Pietraszewski, D., L. Cosmides, and J. Tooby. 2014. "The Content of Our Cooperation, Not the Color of Our Skin: An Alliance Detection System Regulates Categorization by Coalition and Race, but Not Sex." *PLOS ONE* 9 (2): e88534. https://doi.org/10.1371/journal.pone.0088534.

Pinsker, J. 2015. "The Financial Perks of Being Tall." *The Atlantic,* May 18, 2015.

Plant, E. A., and D. A. Butz. 2006. "The Causes and Consequences of an Avoidance-Focus for Interracial Interactions." *Personality and Social Psychology Bulletin* 32 (6): 833–46. https://doi.org/10.1177/0146167206287182.

Plant, E. A., and P. G. Devine. 1998. "Internal and External Motivation to Respond Without Prejudice." *Journal of Personality and Social Psychology* 75 (3): 811–32. https://doi.org/10.1037/0022-3514.75.3.811.

Pliner, P. 1982. "The Effects of Mere Exposure on Liking for Edible Substances." *Appetite* 3 (3): 283–90. https://doi.org/10.1016/S0195-6663(82)80026-3.

Plous, S., ed. 2003. *Understanding Prejudice and Discrimination.* New York: McGraw-Hill Humanities/Social Sciences/Languages.

Prati, F., R. J. Crisp, R. Meleady, and M. Rubini. 2016. "Humanizing Outgroups Through Multiple Categorization." *Personality and Social Psychology Bulletin* 42 (4): 526–39. https://doi.org/10.1177/0146167216636624.

Pratto, F., J. Sidanius, L. M. Stallworth, and B. F. Malle. 1994. "Social Dominance Orientation: A Personality Variable Predicting Social and Political Attitudes." *Journal of Personality and Social Psychology* 67 (4): 741–63. https://doi.org/10.1037/0022-3514.67.4.741.

Prentice, D. A., and D. T. Miller. 2007. "Psychological Essentialism of Human Categories." *Current Directions in Psychological Science* 16 (4): 202–6. https://doi.org/10.1111/j.1467-8721.2007.00504.x.

Purdie-Vaughns, V., and R. Eibach. 2008. "Intersectional Invisibility: The Distinctive Advantages and Disadvantages of Multiple Subordinate-Group Identities." *Sex Roles* 59: 377–91. http://link.springer.com/article/10.1007/s11199-008-9424-4.

Putnam, R. D., and S. R. Garrett. 2020. *The Upswing: How America Came Together a Century Ago and How We Can Do It Again.* New York: Simon & Schuster.

Pyszczynski, T., and J. Greenberg. 1987. "Toward an Integration of Cognitive and Motivational Perspectives on Social Inference: A Biased Hypothesis-Testing Model." In *Advances in Experimental Social Psychology* 20: 297–340. https://doi.org/10.1016/S0065-2601(08)60417-7.

Quillian, L., D. Pager, O. Hexel, and A. H. Midtbøen. 2017. "Meta-analysis of Field Experiments Shows No Change in Racial Discrimination in Hiring over Time." *Proceedings of the National Academy of Sciences* 114 (41): 10870–75. https://doi.org/10.1073/pnas.1706255114.

Ramos, M. R., M. R. Bennett, D. S. Massey, and M. Hewstone. 2019. "Humans Adapt to Social Diversity over Time." *Proceedings of the National Academy of Sciences* 116 (25): 12244–49. https://doi.org/10.1073/pnas .1818884116.

Rattan, A., and N. Ambady. 2014. "How 'It Gets Better': Effectively Communicating Support to Targets of Prejudice." *Personality and Social Psychology Bulletin* 40 (5): 555–66. https://doi.org/10.1177/ 0146167213519480.

Rattan, A., and C. S. Dweck. 2018. "What Happens After Prejudice Is Confronted in the Workplace? How Mindsets Affect Minorities' and Women's Outlook on Future Social Relations." *Journal of Applied Psychology* 103 (6): 676–87. https://doi.org/10.1037/apl0000287.

Rattan, A., K. Savani, N. V. R. Naidu, and C. S. Dweck. 2012. "Can Everyone Become Highly Intelligent? Cultural Differences in and Societal Consequences of Beliefs About the Universal Potential for Intelligence." *Journal of Personality and Social Psychology* 103 (5): 787–803. https://doi .org/10.1037/a0029263.

Rees, H. R., A. M. Rivers, and J. W. Sherman. 2019. "Implementation Intentions Reduce Implicit Stereotype Activation and Application." *Personality and Social Psychology Bulletin* 45 (1): 37–53. https://doi.org/10.1177/ 0146167218775695.

Reicher, S. D., A. Templeton, F. Neville, L. Ferrari, and J. Drury. 2016. "Core Disgust Is Attenuated by Ingroup Relations." *Proceedings of the National Academy of Sciences of the United States of America* 113 (10): 2631–35. https://doi.org/10.1073/pnas.1517027113.

Reynolds, G. A., A. Thernstrom, T. Gaziano, G. Heriot, P. N. Kirsanow, A. D. Melendez, A. L. Taylor, and M. Yaki. 2010. *The Multiethnic Placement Act: Minorities in Foster Care and Adoption.* U.S. Commission of Civil Rights, July 2010.

Richardson, V. 2018. "First Round Picks Only Have a 53% Success Rate and Other Troubling Draft Thoughts." Riot Report, March 27, 2018. https:// theriotreport.com/scout-camp-2018-about-the-author/.

Richeson, J. A., and R. J. Nussbaum. 2004. "The Impact of Multiculturalism Versus Color-Blindness on Racial Bias." *Journal of Experimental Social Psychology* 40 (3): 417–23. https://doi.org/10.1016/j.jesp.2003 .09.002.

Richeson, J. A., and J. N. Shelton. 2007. "Negotiating Interracial Interactions: Costs, Consequences, and Possibilities." *Current Directions in Psychological Science* 16 (6): 316–20. https://doi.org/10.1111/j.1467-8721 .2007.00528.x.

Rivera, L. 2012. "Hiring as Cultural Matching: The Case of Elite Professional Service Firms." *American Sociological Review* 77: 999–1022.

Rohrer, J. M., B. Egloff, and S. C. Schmukle. 2015. "Examining the Effects of Birth Order on Personality." *Proceedings of the National Academy of Sciences* 112 (46): 14224–29. https://doi.org/10.1073/pnas.1506451112.

Rosalsky, G. 2019. "Is the American Tax System Regressive?" NPR, October 29, 2019. www.npr.org/sections/money/2019/10/29/774091313/is-the -american-tax-system-regressive?t=1597330595693.

Rosenberg, N. A., J. K. Pritchard, J. L. Weber, H. M. Cann, K. K. Kidd, L. A. Zhivotovsky, and M. W. Feldman. 2002. "Genetic Structure of Human Populations." *Science* 298 (5602): 2381–85. https://doi.org/ 10.1126/science.1078311.

Rosenthal, R., and L. F. Jacobson. 1968. "Teacher Expectations for the Disadvantaged." *Scientific American* 218 (4): 19–23. http://doi.org/10.1038/ scientificamerican0468-19.

Rosette, A. S., G. J. Leonardelli, and K. W. Phillips. 2008. "The White Standard: Racial Bias in Leader Categorization." *Journal of Applied Psychology* 93 (4): 758–77. https://doi.org/10.1037/0021-9010.93.4.758.

Rosette, A. S., and R. W. Livingston. 2012. "Failure Is Not an Option for Black Women: Effects of Organizational Performance on Leaders with Single Versus Dual-Subordinate Identities." *Journal of Experimental Social Psychology* 48 (5): 1162–67. https://doi.org/10.1016/j.jesp.2012.05.002.

Ross, L. 1977. "The Intuitive Psychologist and His Shortcomings: Distortions in the Attribution Process." *Advances in Experimental Social Psychology* 10: 173–220. https://doi.org/10.1016/S0065-2601(08)60357-3.

Rothstein, R. 2016. "School Policy Is Housing Policy: Deconcentrating Disadvantage to Address the Achievement Gap." In *Race, Equity, and Education,* edited by P. A. Noguera, J. C. Pierce, and R. Ahram, 27–43. Cham, Switz.: Springer International. https://doi.org/10.1007/978-3-319 -23772-5_2.

Rucker, J. M., A. Duker, and J. A. Richeson. 2019. "Structurally Unjust: How Lay Beliefs About Racism Relate to Perceptions of and Responses to Racial Inequality in Criminal Justice." Preprint, January 7, 2019. https://doi.org/10.31234/osf.io/sjkeq.

Rudman, L. A., R. D. Ashmore, and M. L. Gary. 2001. "'Unlearning' Automatic Biases: The Malleability of Implicit Prejudice and Stereotypes." *Journal of Personality and Social Psychology* 81 (5): 856–68. https://doi .org/10.1037//0022-3514.81.5.856.

Ruiz, N. G., J. M. Horowitz, and C. Tamir. 2020. "Many Black and Asian Americans Say They Have Experienced Discrimination Amid the COVID-19 Outbreak." Pew Research Center, July 1, 2020. https://www .pewsocialtrends.org/2020/07/01/many-black-and-asian-americans-say -they-have-experienced-discrimination-amid-the-covid-19-outbreak/.

Rutherford, A. 2020. *How to Argue with a Racist: What Our Genes Do (and Don't) Say About Human Difference*. New York: The Experiment.

Sagar, H. A., and J. W. Schofield. 1980. "Racial and Behavioral Cues in Black and White Children's Perceptions of Ambiguously Aggressive Acts." *Journal of Personality and Social Psychology* 39 (4): 590–98. https://doi.org/10.1037/0022-3514.39.4.590.

Sandel, M. J. 2009. *Justice: What's the Right Thing to Do?* New York: Farrar, Straus and Giroux.

Saslow, E. 2018. *Rising Out of Hatred: The Awakening of a Former White Nationalist.* New York: Anchor.

Sattler, D. N., and N. L. Kerr. 1991. "Might Versus Morality Explored: Motivational and Cognitive Bases for Social Motives." *Journal of Personality and Social Psychology* 60 (5): 756–65. https://doi.org/10.1037//0022-3514.60.5.756.

Schildkraut, D. J. 2017. "White Attitudes About Descriptive Representation in the US: The Roles of Identity, Discrimination, and Linked Fate." *Politics, Groups, and Identities* 5 (1): 84–106. https://doi.org/10.1080/21565503.2015.1089296.

Schilke, O., and L. Huang. 2018. "Worthy of Swift Trust? How Brief Interpersonal Contact Affects Trust Accuracy." *Journal of Applied Psychology* 103 (11): 1181–97. https://doi.org/10.1037/apl0000321.

Schwartz, S. H. 2012. "An Overview of the Schwartz Theory of Basic Values." *Online Readings in Psychology and Culture* 2 (1): 1–20. https://doi.org/10.9707/2307-0919.1116.

Sechrist, G. B., and C. Stangor. 2005. "Prejudice as Social Norms." In *Social Psychology of Prejudice: Historical and Contemporary Issues,* edited by C. S. Crandall and M. Schaller, 167-87. Lawrence, Kans.: Lewinian Press.

Sesko, A. K., and M. Biernat. 2010. "Prototypes of Race and Gender: The Invisibility of Black Women." *Journal of Experimental Social Psychology* 46 (2): 356–60. https://doi.org/10.1016/j.jesp.2009.10.016.

Seuss, Dr. 1961. *The Sneetches and Other Stories.* New York: Random House.

Shalby, C. 2017. "What's the Difference Between 'Looting' and 'Finding'? 12 Years After Katrina, Harvey Sparks a New Debate." *Los Angeles Times,* August 29, 2017.

Shariff, A. F., D. Wiwad, and L. B. Aknin. 2016. "Income Mobility Breeds Tolerance for Income Inequality: Cross-National and Experimental Evidence." *Perspectives on Psychological Science* 11 (3): 373–80. https://doi.org/10.1177/1745691616635596.

Sheftall, A. H., L. Asti, L. M. Horowitz, A. Felts, C. A. Fontanella, J. V. Campo, and J. A. Bridge. 2016. "Suicide in Elementary School–Aged Children and Early Adolescents." *Pediatrics* 138 (4): e20160436. https://doi.org/10.1542/peds.2016-0436.

Shelton, J. N., and J. A. Richeson. 2006. "Interracial Interactions: A Relational Approach." *Advances in Experimental Social Psychology* 38: 121–81. http://www.sciencedirect.com/science/article/pii/S0065260106380033.

Shelton, J. N., J. A. Richeson, and J. Salvatore. 2005. "Expecting to Be the Target of Prejudice: Implications for Interethnic Interactions." *Personality & Social Psychology Bulletin* 31 (9): 1189–202. https://doi.org/10.1177/0146167205274894.

Sherif, C. W., and M. Sherif. 1953. *Groups in Harmony and Tension: An Integration of Studies of Intergroup Relations*. New York: Harper & Brothers.

Shih, M., T. L. Pittinsky, and N. Ambady. 1999. "Stereotype Susceptibility: Identity Salience and Shifts in Quantitative Performance." *Psychological Science* 10 (1): 80–83. https://doi.org/10.1111/1467-9280.00111.

Shim, S.-H., R. Livingston, K. W. Phillips, and S. S. K. Lam. 2020. "The Impact of Leader Eye Gaze on Disparity in Member Influence: Implications for Process and Performance in Diverse Groups." *Academy of Management Journal* (published online August 24, 2020). https://doi.org/10.5465/amj.2017.1507.

Sibley, C. G., M. S. Wilson, and J. Duckitt. 2007. "Antecedents of Men's Hostile and Benevolent Sexism: The Dual Roles of Social Dominance Orientation and Right-Wing Authoritarianism." *Personality and Social Psychology Bulletin* 33 (2): 160–72. https://doi.org/10.1177/0146167206294745.

Sidanius, J., S. Levin, and F. Pratto. 1996. "Consensual Social Dominance Orientation and Its Correlates Within the Hierarchical Structure of American Society." *International Journal of Intercultural Relations* 20 (3–4): 385–408. https://doi.org/10.1016/0147-1767(96)00025-9.

Sidanius, J., and F. Pratto. 1999. *Social Dominance: An Intergroup Theory of Social Hierarchy and Oppression*. Cambridge, UK: Cambridge University Press.

Sidanius, J., F. Pratto, and L. Bobo. 1996. "Racism, Conservatism, Affirmative Action, and Intellectual Sophistication: A Matter of Principled Conservatism or Group Dominance?" *Journal of Personality and Social Psychology* 70 (3): 476–90. https://doi.org/10.1037/0022-3514.70.3.476.

Sierminska, E. M., J. R. Frick, and M. M. Grabka. 2010. "Examining the Gender Wealth Gap." *Oxford Economic Papers* 62 (4): 669–90. https://doi.org/10.1093/oep/gpq007.

Sinclair, L., and Z. Kunda, Z. 1999. "Reactions to a Black Professional: Motivated Inhibition and Action of Conflicting Stereotypes." *Journal of Personality and Social Psychology* 77: 885–904.

Sinclair, S., E. Dunn, and B. Lowery. 2005. "The Relationship Between Parental Racial Attitudes and Children's Implicit Prejudice." *Journal of Experimental Social Psychology* 41 (3): 283–89. https://doi.org/10.1016/j.jesp.2004.06.003.

Smith, B. 2008. "Are the NFL's Celebration Rules Racist?" Bleacher Report,

October 23, 2008. https://bleacherreport.com/articles/72851-are-the-nfls
-celebration-rules-racist.

Smith, I. H., K. Aquino, S. Koleva, and J. Graham. 2014. "The Moral Ties
That Bind . . . Even to Out-groups: The Interactive Effect of Moral
Identity and the Binding Moral Foundations." *Psychological Science* 25
(8): 1554–62. https://doi.org/10.1177/0956797614534450.

Sommers, S. R. 2006. "On Racial Diversity and Group Decision Making:
Identifying Multiple Effects of Racial Composition on Jury Delibera-
tions." *Journal of Personality and Social Psychology* 90 (4): 597–612. https://
doi.org/10.1037/0022-3514.90.4.597.

Sommers, S. R., and M. I. Norton. 2006. "Lay Theories About White Racists: What Constitutes Racism (and What Doesn't)." *Group Processes &
Intergroup Relations* 9 (1): 117–38. https://doi.org/10.1177/
1368430206059881.

Son Hing, L. S., W. Li, and M. P. Zanna. 2002. "Inducing Hypocrisy to Reduce Prejudicial Responses Among Aversive Racists." *Journal of Experimental Social Psychology* 78 (1): 71–78. https://doi.org/10.1006/jesp.2001
.1484.

Sowell, T. 2019. *Discrimination and Disparities*. New York: Basic Books.

Stangor, C., G. B. Sechrist, and J. T. Jost. 2001. "Changing Racial Beliefs by
Providing Consensus Information." *Personality and Social Psychology
Bulletin* 27 (4): 486–96. https://doi.org/10.1177/0146167201274009.

Steele, C. M. 1992. "Race and the Schooling of Black Americans." *Atlantic,*
April 1992.

Steele, C. M. 2010. *Whistling Vivaldi: How Stereotypes Affect Us and What We
Can Do*. New York: W. W. Norton.

Stell, A. J., and T. Farsides. 2016. "Brief Loving-Kindness Meditation Reduces Racial Bias, Mediated by Positive Other-Regarding Emotions."
Motivation and Emotion 40 (1): 140–47. https://doi.org/10.1007/s11031
-015-9514-x.

Stephens, G. J., L. J. Silbert, and U. Hasson. 2010. "Speaker-Listener Neural
Coupling Underlies Successful Communication." *Proceedings of the National Academy of Sciences* 107 (32): 14425–30. https://doi.org/10.1073/
pnas.1008662107.

Stevenson, B. 2019. "Why American Prisons Owe Their Cruelty to Slavery."
New York Times Magazine, August 14, 2019.

Stewart, B. D., and B. K. Payne. 2008. "Bringing Automatic Stereotyping
Under Control: Implementation Intentions as Efficient Means of
Thought Control." *Personality and Social Psychology Bulletin* 34 (10):
1332–45. https://doi.org/10.1177/0146167208321269.

Stone, J., E. Aronson, A. L. Crain, M. P. Winslow, and C. B. Fried. 1994.
"Inducing Hypocrisy as a Means of Encouraging Young Adults to Use

Condoms." *Personality and Social Psychology Bulletin* 20 (1): 116–28. https://doi.org/10.1177/0146167294201012.

Stone, D., B. Patton, and S. Heen. 2010. *Difficult Conversations: How to Discuss What Matters Most*. New York: Penguin.

Stroessner, S. J. 1996. "Social Categorization by Race or Sex: Effects of Perceived Non-normalcy on Response Times." *Social Cognition* 14 (3): 247–76. https://doi.org/10.1521/soco.1996.14.3.247.

Sue, D. W., C. M. Capodilupo, and A. M. B. Holder. 2008. "Racial Microaggressions in the Life Experience of Black Americans." *Professional Psychology: Research and Practice* 39 (3): 329–36. https://doi.org/10.1037/0735-7028.39.3.329.

Sue, D. W., C. M. Capodilupo, G. C. Torino, J. M. Bucceri, A. M. B. Holder, K. L. Nadal, and M. Esquilin. 2007. "Racial Microaggressions in Everyday Life: Implications for Clinical Practice." *American Psychologist* 62 (4): 271–86. https://doi.org/10.1037/0003-066X.62.4.271.

Sue, D. W., and M. G. Constantine. 2007. "Racial Microaggressions as Instigators of Difficult Dialogues on Race: Implications for Student Affairs Educators and Students." *College Student Affairs Journal* 26 (2): 136–43.

Sykes, B. 2001. *The Seven Daughters of Eve*. New York: W. W. Norton.

Tajfel, H., M. G. Billig, R. P. Bundy, and C. Flament. 1971. "Social Categorization and Intergroup Behavior." *European Journal of Social Psychology* 1: 149–78.

Tannenbaum, D. 2012. "Do Gender Differences in Risk Aversion Explain the Gender Gap in SAT Scores?" Working paper, University of Chicago.

Tatum, B. D. 2017. *Why Are All the Black Kids Sitting Together in the Cafeteria?* 2nd ed. New York: Basic Books.

Thomas, E. L., J. F. Dovidio, and T. V. West. 2014. "Lost in the Categorical Shuffle: Evidence for the Social Non-prototypicality of Black Women." *Cultural Diversity and Ethnic Minority Psychology* 20 (3): 370–76. https://doi.org/10.1037/a0035096.

Thomsen, L., E. G. T. Green, and J. Sidanius. 2008. "We Will Hunt Them Down: How Social Dominance Orientation and Right-Wing Authoritarianism Fuel Ethnic Persecution of Immigrants in Fundamentally Different Ways." *Journal of Experimental Social Psychology* 44 (6): 1455–64. https://doi.org/10.1016/j.jesp.2008.06.011.

Todd, K. H., C. Deaton, A. P. D'Adamo, and L. Goe. 2000. "Ethnicity and Analgesic Practice." *Annals of Emergency Medicine* 35 (1): 11–16. https://doi.org/10.1016/S0196-0644(00)70099-0.

Tomaka, J., J. Blascovich, R. M. Kelsey, and C. L. Leitten. 1993. "Subjective, Physiological, and Behavioral Effects of Threat and Challenge Appraisal." *Journal of Personality and Social Psychology* 65 (2): 248–60. https://doi.org/10.1037/0022-3514.65.2.248.

Touryalai, H. 2013. "Ready, Set, Clean! Secrets to Cleaning a Marriott Hotel Room." *Forbes,* June 26, 2013. https://www.forbes.com/sites/halahtouryalai/2013/06/26/ready-set-clean-secrets-to-cleaning-a-marriott-hotel-room/#794c588f7276.

Trail, T. E., J. N. Shelton, and T. V. West. 2009. "Interracial Roommate Relationships: Negotiating Daily Interactions." *Personality & Social Psychology Bulletin* 35 (6): 671–84. https://doi.org/10.1177/0146167209332741.

Trawalter, S., K. M. Hoffman, and A. Waytz. 2012. "Racial Bias in Perceptions of Others' Pain." *PLOS ONE* 7 (11): 1–8. https://doi.org/10.1371/journal.pone.0048546.

Trawalter, S., J. A. Richeson, and J. N. Shelton. 2009. "Predicting Behavior During Interracial Interactions: A Stress and Coping Approach." *Personality and Social Psychology Review* 13 (4): 243–68. https://doi.org/10.1177/1088868309345850.

Tröster, C., A. Mehra, and D. van Knippenberg. 2014. "Structuring for Team Success: The Interactive Effects of Network Structure and Cultural Diversity on Team Potency and Performance." *Organizational Behavior and Human Decision Processes* 124 (2): 245–55. https://doi.org/10.1016/j.obhdp.2014.04.003.

Tversky, A., and D. Kahneman. 1973. "Availability: A Heuristic for Judging Frequency and Probability." *Cognitive Psychology* 5 (2): 207–32. https://doi.org/10.1016/0010-0285(73)90033-9.

Tyler, T. R., R. J. Boeckmann, H. J. Smith, and Y. J. Huo. 2019. *Social Justice in a Diverse Society*. New York: Routledge.

Tyson, T. 2017. *The Blood of Emmett Till*. New York: Simon & Schuster.

Ufkes, E. G., S. Otten, K. I. Van Der Zee, E. Giebels, and J. F. Dovidio. 2012. "Urban District Identity as a Common Ingroup Identity: The Different Role of Ingroup Prototypicality for Minority and Majority Groups." *European Journal of Social Psychology* 42 (6): 706–16. https://doi.org/10.1002/ejsp.1888.

United States Sentencing Commission. 1995. "1995 Report to the Congress: Cocaine and Federal Sentencing Policy." https://www.ussc.gov/research/congressional-reports/1995-report-congress-cocaine-and-federal-sentencing-policy.

United States Sentencing Commission. 2003. "2003 Datafile. Table 34: Race of Drug Offenders for Each Drug Type." https://www.ussc.gov/sites/default/files/pdf/research-and-publications/annual-reports-and-sourcebooks/2003/table34_0.pdf.

Unzueta, M. M., and B. S. Lowery. 2008. "Defining Racism Safely: The Role of Self-Image Maintenance on White Americans' Conceptions of Racism." *Journal of Experimental Social Psychology* 44 (6): 1491–97. https://doi.org/10.1016/j.jesp.2008.07.011.

Vagins, D. J., and J. McCurdy. 2006. "Cracks in the System: Twenty Years of the Unjust Federal Crack Cocaine Law." ACLU, October 2006. https://www.aclu.org/files/pdfs/drugpolicy/cracksinsystem_20061025.pdf.

van Dijk, E., D. De Cremer, and M. J. J. Handgraaf. 2004. "Social Value Orientations and the Strategic Use of Fairness in Ultimatum Bargaining." *Journal of Experimental Social Psychology* 40 (6): 697–707. https://doi.org/10.1016/j.jesp.2004.03.002.

Vandivere, S., K. Malm, and L. Radel. 2009. *Adoption USA: A Chartbook Based on the 2007 National Survey of Adoptive Parents*. U.S. Department of Health and Human Services, Office of the Assistant Secretary for Planning and Evaluation.

Van Hiel, A., and I. Mervielde. 2005. "Authoritarianism and Social Dominance Orientation: Relationships with Various Forms of Racism." *Journal of Applied Social Psychology* 35 (11): 2323–44. https://doi.org/10.1111/j.1559-1816.2005.tb02105.x.

Van Lange, P. A. M. 1999. "The Pursuit of Joint Outcomes and Equality of Outcomes." *Journal of Personality and Social Psychology* 77 (2): 337–49.

Van Lange, P. A. M., R. Bekkers, A. Chirumbolo, and L. Leone. 2012. "Are Conservatives Less Likely to Be Prosocial Than Liberals? From Games to Ideology, Political Preferences and Voting." *European Journal of Personality* 26 (5): 461–73. https://doi.org/10.1002/per.845.

Van Lange, P. A. M., E. M. N. De Bruin, W. Otten, and J. A. Joireman. 1997. "Development of Prosocial, Individualistic, and Competitive Orientations: Theory and Preliminary Evidence." *Journal of Personality and Social Psychology* 73 (4): 733–46. https://doi.org/10.1037/0022-3514.73.4.733.

Van Lange, P. A. M., and D. M. Kuhlman. 1994. "Social Value Orientations and Impressions of Partner's Honesty and Intelligence: A Test of the Might Versus Morality Effect." *Journal of Personality and Social Psychology* 67 (1): 126–41. https://doi.org/10.1037//0022-3514.67.1.126.

Vezzali, L., A. Cadamuro, A. Versari, D. Giovannini, and E. Trifiletti. 2015. "Feeling Like a Group After a Natural Disaster: Common Ingroup Identity and Relations with Outgroup Victims Among Majority and Minority Young Children." *British Journal of Social Psychology* 54 (3). https://doi.org/10.1111/bjso.12091.

Vijaya, R. M. 2019. "Dangerous Skin Bleaching Has Become a Public Health Crisis. Corporate Marketing Lies Behind It." *Washington Post,* June 15, 2019. https://www.washingtonpost.com/politics/2019/06/15/dangerous-skin-bleaching-has-become-public-health-crisis-corporate-marketing-lies-behind-it/.

Villarosa, L. 2019. "How False Beliefs in Physical Racial Difference Still Live in Medicine Today." *The New York Times,* August 14, 2019.

Vohs, K. D., N. L. Mead, and M. R. Goode. 2006. "The Psychological Consequences of Money." *Science* 314 (5802): 1154–56. https://doi.org/10 .1126/science.1132491.

Voigt, R., N. P. Camp, V. Prabhakaran, W. L. Hamilton, R. C. Hetey, C. M. Griffiths, D. Jurgens, D. Jurafsky, and J. L. Eberhardt. 2017. "Language from Police Body Camera Footage Shows Racial Disparities in Officer Respect." *Proceedings of the National Academy of Sciences* 114 (25): 6521–26. https://doi.org/10.1073/pnas.1702413114.

Voorspoels, W., A. Bartlema, and W. Vanpaemel. 2014. "Can Race Really Be Erased? A Pre-registered Replication Study." *Frontiers in Psychology* 5 (September): 1–7. https://doi.org/10.3389/fpsyg.2014.01035.

Walravens, S., and H. Cabot. 2016. "Tech CEO Shares Difficulties of Raising Venture Capital in a Down Market." *Forbes,* May 13, 2016. https:// www.forbes.com/sites/geekgirlrising/2016/05/13/how-this-startup -founder-is-braving-the-slowdown-in-venture-capital-funding/ #1c3dfa284241.

Watson, W. E., K. Kumar, and L. K. Michaelsen. 1993. "Cultural Diversity's Impact on Interaction Process and Performance: Comparing Homogeneous and Diverse Task Groups." *Academy of Management Journal* 36 (3): 590–602. https://doi.org/10.5465/256593.

Waytz, A., J. Dungan, and L. Young. 2013. "The Whistleblower's Dilemma and the Fairness-Loyalty Tradeoff." *Journal of Experimental Social Psychology* 49 (6): 1027–33. https://doi.org/10.1016/j.jesp.2013.07.002.

Waytz, A., K. M. Hoffman, and S. Trawalter. 2015. "A Superhumanization Bias in Whites' Perceptions of Blacks." *Social Psychological and Personality Science* 6 (3): 352–59. https://doi.org/10.1177/1948550614553642.

Webber, D., M. Babush, N. Schori-Eyal, A. Vazeou-Nieuwenhuis, M. Hettiarachchi, J. J. Bélanger, M. Moyano, H. M. Trujillo, R. Gunaratna, A. W. Kruglanski, and M. J. Gelfand. 2018. "The Road to Extremism: Field and Experimental Evidence That Significance Loss-Induced Need for Closure Fosters Radicalization." *Journal of Personality and Social Psychology* 114 (2): 270–85. https://doi.org/10.1037/pspi0000111.

Weber, R., and J. Crocker. 1983. "Cognitive Processes in the Revision of Stereotypic Beliefs." *Journal of Personality and Social Psychology* 45 (5): 961–77. https://doi.org/10.1037/0022-3514.45.5.961.

Weisbuch, M., M. L. Slepian, C. P. Eccleston, and N. Ambady. 2013. "Nonverbal Expressions of Status and System Legitimacy: An Interactive Influence on Race Bias." *Psychological Science* 24 (11): 2315–21. https://doi .org/10.1177/0956797613490745.

Whitley, B. E. 1999. "Right-Wing Authoritarianism, Social Dominance Orientation, and Prejudice." *Journal of Personality and Social Psychology* 77 (1): 126–34. https://doi.org/10.1037/0022-3514.77.1.126.

Wilkerson, I. 2020. *Caste: The Origins of Our Discontents*. New York: Random House.

Wilkinson, R., and K. Pickett. 2019. *The Inner Level: How More Equal Societies Reduce Stress, Restore Sanity and Improve Everyone's Well-Being*. New York: Penguin Press.

Willard, G., K. Isaac, and D. R. Carney. 2015. "Some Evidence for the Nonverbal Contagion of Racial Bias." *Organizational Behavior and Human Decision Processes* 128: 96–107. https://doi.org/10.1016/j.obhdp.2015 .04.002.

Williams, J. C. 2017. *White Working Class*. Boston: Harvard Business Review Press.

Williams, M. J., and J. L. Eberhardt. 2008. "Biological Conceptions of Race and the Motivation to Cross Racial Boundaries." *Journal of Personality and Social Psychology* 94 (6): 1033–47. https://doi.org/10.1037/0022-3514 .94.6.1033.

Winig, L., and R. W. Livingston. 2019. "The Massport Model: Integrating Diversity and Inclusion into Public-Private Partnerships." Case study, Harvard University, John F. Kennedy School of Government, March 13, 2019.

Winig, L., and R. W. Livingston. 2020. "Harvey Mudd College: Organizational Strategy and Commitment Lead to Sizeable Gains of Diversity in STEM." Case study, Harvard Kennedy School.

Woodcock, A., P. R. Hernandez, M. Estrada, and P. W. Schultz. 2012. "The Consequences of Chronic Stereotype Threat: Domain Disidentification and Abandonment." *Journal of Personality and Social Psychology* 103 (4): 635–46. https://doi.org/10.1037/a0029120.

Woolley, A. W., C. F. Chabris, A. Pentland, N. Hashmi, and T. W. Malone. 2010. "Evidence for a Collective Intelligence Factor in the Performance of Human Groups." *Science* 330 (6004): 686–88. https://doi.org/10.1126/ science.1193147.

Word, C. O., M. P. Zanna, and J. Cooper. 1974. "The Nonverbal Mediation of Self-Fulfilling Prophecies in Interracial Interaction." *Journal of Experimental Social Psychology* 10 (2): 109–20. https://doi.org/10.1016/0022 -1031(74)90059-6.

Wyatt, S. B., D. R. Williams, R. Calvin, F. C. Henderson, E. R. Walker, and K. Winters. 2003. "Racism and Cardiovascular Disease in African Americans." *American Journal of the Medical Sciences* 325 (6): 315–31. https://doi.org/10.1097/00000441-200306000-00003.

Yengde, S. 2019. *Caste Matters*. New York: Penguin Books.

Yoshino, K. 2006. *Covering: The Hidden Assault on Our Civil Rights*. New York: Random House.

Zakrisson, I. 2005. "Construction of a Short Version of the Right-Wing Authoritarianism (RWA) Scale." *Personality and Individual Differences* 39 (5): 863–72. https://doi.org/10.1016/j.paid.2005.02.026.

Zarate, M. A., and E. R. Smith. 1990. "Person Categorization and Stereotyping. *Social Cognition* 8 (2): 161–85. https://doi.org/10.1521/soco.1990.8.2.161.

Zedeck, S., and W. F. Cascio. 1984. Psychological Issues in Personnel Decisions." *Annual Review of Psychology* 35 (1): 461–518. https://doi.org/10.1146/annurev.ps.35.020184.002333.

Zhang, L. 2017. "A Fair Game? Racial Bias and Repeated Interaction Between NBA Coaches and Players." *Administrative Science Quarterly* 62 (4): 603–25. https://doi.org/10.1177/0001839217705375.

Zhu, D. H., W. Shen, and A. J. Hillman. 2014. "Recategorization into the In-group: The Appointment of Demographically Different New Directors and Their Subsequent Positions on Corporate Boards." *Administrative Science Quarterly* 59 (2): 240–70. https://doi.org/10.1177/0001839214530951.

Ziegert, J. C., and P. J. Hanges. 2005. "Employment Discrimination: The Role of Implicit Attitudes, Motivation, and a Climate for Racial Bias." *Journal of Applied Psychology* 90 (3): 553–62. https://doi.org/10.1037/0021-9010.90.3.553.

Zimmerman, J. L., and C. Reyna. 2013. "The Meaning and Role of Ideology in System Justification and Resistance for High- and Low-Status People." *Journal of Personality and Social Psychology* 105 (1): 1–23. https://doi.org/10.1037/a0032967.

Notes

Introduction

1. GBAO Strategies 2019.
2. Lepper et al. 1973.
3. Herzberg 2003.
4. Stephens, Silbert, and Hasson 2010.
5. Meleady, Hopthrow, and Crisp 2013.
6. Lewin 1952; see also Sechrist and Stangor 2005.
7. Dovidio and Gaertner 2004.

PART I: CONDITION

Chapter One: Do We All Believe That Racism Exists?

1. Norton and Sommers 2011.
2. Horowitz, Brown, and Cox 2019.
3. Murray 2020.
4. Best and Rogers 2020.
5. National Safety Council 2017.
6. Tversky and Kahneman 1973.
7. Furnham and Boo 2011.
8. Eibach and Ehrlinger 2006.
9. Nelson, Adams, and Salter 2013.
10. Du Bois 1968.
11. Milano 2020; Sandel 2009.

12. McGinnies 1949.

13. Kunda 1990.

14. Pyszczynski and Greenberg 1987.

15. Lowery, Knowles, and Unzueta 2007.

16. Knowles et al. 2014.

17. Jones and Harris 1967; Ross 1977.

18. Lerner 1980.

19. Norton, Vandello, and Darley 2004; Furnham 2003; Lerner 1980.

20. Comer and Laird 1975; Hafer and Correy 1999.

21. Kraus, Rucker, and Richeson 2017.

22. Norton, Vandello, and Darley 2004.

23. DiAngelo 2011.

24. Unzueta and Lowery 2008.

25. Steele 1992.

26. Tomaka et al. 1993.

Chapter Two: What Is "Racism," Anyway?

1. Sommers and Norton 2006.

2. Rucker, Duker, and Richeson 2019.

3. Sommers and Norton 2006.

4. Ibid.

5. I will use the terms *implicit bias, modern racism, aversive racism* (a type of modern racism), and *unconscious bias* interchangeably throughout the book.

6. McGlothlin and Killen 2006.

7. Baron and Banaji 2006; Lawrence 1991; Sagar and Schofield 1980.

8. Sinclair, Dunn, and Lowery (2005) examined implicit racial attitudes of fourth- and fifth-grade children as well as parental identification, or how much they liked, admired, and wanted to be like their parents. They also measured parents' racial attitudes toward Blacks. They found a correlation between children's and parents' racial biases only for children who identified with their parents. This suggests that the children's racial attitudes are not just passively learned from parents, but function as a way for children to emulate their parents. These findings are hopeful in a way, because they suggest that parents who have a good relationship with their children can have a strong positive influence on their attitudes and values.

9. Shalby 2017.

10. Tyson 2017.

11. Darley and Latane 1968; Latane and Darley 1970.

12. Gaertner and Dovidio 1977.

13. Cox and Devine 2014.

14. Dovidio and Gaertner 2000.

15. Effron, Miller, and Monin 2012; Monin and Miller 2001.

16. Effron, Cameron, and Monin 2009.

17. Apparently, sometimes nations strategically employ moral credentials as well. A former student, Pavel Kanygin, granted me permission to discuss what he experienced while working as a journalist for the free-press Russian newspaper *Novaya Gazeta*. Pavel had been kidnapped several times for reporting truthful but damning evidence about the Kremlin. When I asked him why Vladimir Putin wouldn't just shut down a newspaper that he perceived to be a nuisance, the response was that having at least one paper that wasn't controlled by the government gives the Kremlin leverage to argue against other nations' claims that Russia suppresses free speech. In short, *Novaya Gazeta* is a moral credential for the Kremlin. Ironically, permitting a little free speech gives the Kremlin more latitude to create structures that broadly suppress free speech.

18. Kaiser et al. 2013.

19. Kang et al. 2016.

20. Kaiser and Miller 2001.

21. Quillian et al. 2017.

22. Nunley et al. 2015.

23. Brown-Iannuzzi, Payne, and Trawalter 2013.

24. Greenwald, McGee, and Schwartz 1998.

25. Charlesworth and Banaji 2019; Lai et al. 2016; Livingston 2002; Nosek, Banaji, and Greenwald 2002.

26. Blanton et al. 2009; but see Greenwald et al. 2009.

27. Kendi 2019.

28. Lamont et al. 2017; Payne et al. 2017; Payne et al. 2019.

29. Blair, Ma, and Lenton 2001; Charlesworth and Banaji 2019; Lai et al. 2016; Lowery, Hardin, and Sinclair 2001; Rudman, Ashmore, and Gary 2001.

30. Rucker, Duker, and Richeson 2019; Unzueta and Lowery 2008.

31. Brewer 1979; Brewer 2016.

32. E.g., Banaji and Greenwald 2016 and Chugh 2018.

Chapter Three: How Does Social Disadvantage Differ for Blacks and Whites?

1. Hochschild 2016; Williams 2017; but see also Layous, Davis, Garcia, Purdie-Vaughns, Cook, and Cohen 2017.

2. DiAngelo 2018; Kendi 2016; Muhammad 2019; Myrdal 1944.

3. Maddox and Gray 2002.

4. Vijaya 2019.

5. Wilkerson 2020.

6. Mahalingam 2003; Yengde 2019.

7. For the sake of simplicity, I have defined *privilege* as financial wealth, although privilege or class can be defined by education, occupational prestige, family background, or social behavior as well. (Cohen et al. 2017.)

8. See Sidanius and Pratto 1999.

9. Hannah-Jones 2019.

10. Devos and Banaji 2005.

11. Hannah-Jones 2019.

12. Sidanius and Pratto 1999.

13. Cohen et al. 2017.

14. Mattan et al. 2019.

15. Moore-Berg and Karpinski 2019.

16. Bertrand and Mullainathan 2004.

17. Pager 2003; see also Holzer, Raphael, and Stoll 2002.

18. This study differs from Bertrand and Mullainathan's study in a couple of important ways. First, it used in-person testers rather than paper résumés. This means that White and Black actors went to job sites in person rather than sending in written résumés. The second major difference is that individual privilege was directly manipulated—some applicants declared having been convicted of a felony. Specifically, the crime consisted of a nonviolent felony drug conviction of possession with intent to distribute, and the applicant had served eighteen months of prison time.

19. For example, see the documentary *13th* (2016), directed by Ava DuVernay.

20. Hertwig and Engel 2016.

21. Yoshino 2006.

22. Kang et al. 2016; Luo 2009.

23. To be clear, these data are descriptive, not prescriptive. In other words, they indicate that Whitening one's response does increase the likelihood of getting a callback. They do not speak to the question of whether one "should" Whiten one's résumé. The issue of whether one should conform to the system for personal gain, or challenge the system for collective gain, is a personal choice and one that is not the focus of this chapter. The dilemma of personal versus collective benefit will resurface in many different ways in subsequent chapters and is a worthwhile topic of conversation.

24. There are two similar questions posed by this 2019 Pew Survey, one assessing perceptions of their own ability to get ahead and a second that assesses their perceptions of their group's ability to get ahead "in our country these days." The data contained in this paragraph reflect responses to the first question.

25. The fact that this individual even knows about the existence of the Bos-

ton Brahmins is an indicator of some level of privilege, as one friend astutely pointed out. Indeed, the average Bostonian, or American, has never heard of this group. By the same logic, if you can name the secret societies at Yale, then you are likely a Yalie.

26. "Carmel's Own Data" 2019.
27. Voigt et al. 2017.
28. Edwards, Lee, and Esposito 2019.
29. Hacker 1992.
30. Hochschild 2016; Isenberg 2016; Williams 2017; Metzl 2019.
31. Brannon and Markus 2013; Moore-Berg and Karpinski 2019.

Chapter Four: What Are the Structural Origins of Racism?

1. Norton and Ariely 2011.
2. Kraus, Rucker, and Richeson 2017; Kraus et al. 2019.
3. Sidanius and Pratto 1999.
4. Ibid.
5. A multitude of theories in social psychology, political science, and sociology, including the classic Marxist notion of *false consciousness,* make the argument that, on some level, a stable group-based social hierarchy requires not just oppression from the top (i.e., institutional terror) but also tacit cooperation and complicity from a sizable proportion of the population at the bottom (facilitated by legitimizing myths), since they usually far outnumber those at the top. But clearly, not everyone is "falsely conscious" or complicit. There are many individuals and organizations that resist the status quo.
6. Institute for Policy Studies n.d.
7. Livingston and Pearce 2009; Lyons-Padilla et al. 2019; Rosette, Leonardelli, and Phillips 2008; Pinsker 2015.
8. Akresh 2011; Benhabib, Bisin, and Luo 2017; Charles and Hurst 2003; Di, Belsky, and Liu 2007; Judge and Cable 2004; Keister 2008; Killewald 2013; Killewald, Pfeffer, and Schachner 2017; Maroto 2016; Newman, Johnston, and Lown 2015; Sierminska, Frick, and Grabka 2010.
9. Walravens and Cabot 2016.
10. Bill Gates predicted the 2020 pandemic years before it happened. (Gates 2015.)
11. Mijs 2018.
12. Shariff, Wiwad, and Aknin 2016.
13. Brandt 2013; Zimmerman and Reyna 2013.
14. After considering whether slaves would be counted as people who contribute to the population of a given state, for the purpose of determining the number of seats in Congress, it was decided that only three out of five Black people would be counted as part of the population.

15. This work can be studied in much greater detail by reading *Slavery by Another Name* by Douglas A. Blackmon, *The New Jim Crow* by Michelle Alexander, and *Stamped from the Beginning* by Ibram X. Kendi, and/or by watching the two-hour documentary *13th,* directed by Ava DuVernay.

16. Sidanius, Levin, and Pratto 1996.

17. United States Sentencing Commission 1995.

18. United States Sentencing Commission 2003; Vagins and McCurdy 2006.

19. Payne, Vuletich, and Brown-Iannuzzi 2019.

20. Rothstein 2016.

21. Ho et al. 2012; Pratto et al. 1994.

22. Bergh et al. 2016; Hiel and Mervielde 2005; Ho et al. 2012. Moreover, high-SDO individuals may actually favor out-groups that are deemed as high status and worthy of admiration. If we put this into the context of immigration, an American high in social dominance orientation might welcome a poor immigrant from Sweden but show contempt toward a poor immigrant from Somalia. Similarly, they might welcome a wealthy immigrant from India but not a poor immigrant from India.

23. To be clear, my goal and intent is to create a vivid and comprehensible metaphor about protection and danger, *not* to imply that police officers are dogs. Police officers are humans—many with a very high potential for compassion and sacrifice.

24. Nir 2020.

Chapter Five: How Does "Threat" Perpetuate Racial Inequality?

1. Craig and Richeson 2014a; Craig and Richeson 2014b.

2. Lee 2019.

3. Stevenson 2019.

4. For just a few examples, see *We Were Eight Years in Power* by Ta-Nehisi Coates; *The Obamas and a (Post) Racial America?* by Gregory S. Parks and Matthew W. Hughey; and *Change They Can't Believe In: The Tea Party and Reactionary Politics in America* by Christopher S. Parker and Matt A. Barreto.

5. Rosette, Leonardelli, and Phillips 2008.

6. McDonald et al. 2018.

7. Park and Westphal 2013.

8. Rosette and Livingston 2012.

9. The tendency for Whites to lash out against Black achievement is not universal. Some research has shown that White people who endorse the status quo prefer racial group members who exhibit "status-appropriate" (e.g., submissive) nonverbal behaviors, whereas White people who do not support the status quo show the opposite effect, preferring high-status cues among Blacks. (Weisbuch, Slepian, Eccleston, and Ambady 2013.)

Despite this variability, research reveals that the aggregated response to people of color who defy hierarchical prescriptions is negative.

10. Lyons-Padilla et al. 2019.

11. Kelly 2020.

12. Phelan and Rudman 2010.

13. One interesting question here is whether the "backlash" is expected from Whites or from other Blacks. The answer is that it is often both. But as discussed in Chapter 4, both can originate from consensually shared stereotypes and internalization of hierarchical prescriptions.

14. There is considerable theoretical and empirical evidence supporting the idea that success is often what triggers aggression toward out-groups. Susan Fiske and colleagues' Stereotype Content Model describes what they call "envious prejudice," where groups are reviled *because* they are seen as too competent. (Fiske et al. 2002.) This characterizes prejudice against Jewish people, who are perceived as competent but not warm. (Cuddy, Fiske, and Glick 2008.)

15. Coates 2010.

16. Breech 2018.

17. Smith 2008.

18. The NFL's celebration policy underwent a major overhaul in 2017 to permit certain types of performances after touchdowns.

19. Hall and Livingston 2012.

20. In the past, there were debates about whether Black players were even capable of being quarterbacks. It was assumed that they were suited for brute-force positions but not more tactical or strategic positions, presumably because they lacked the necessary intelligence. To this day, journalists have observed that White quarterbacks are described as intelligent and irreplaceable, whereas Black quarterbacks are described as athletic and nonessential.

21. Livingston and Pearce 2009.

22. Cooley et al. 2018.

23. Koch, Gross, and Kolts 2001.

24. Hester and Gray 2018.

25. Kaiser and Pratt-Hyatt 2009.

26. Steele 2010.

27. I want to be clear that my exposition of this work is purely descriptive, not prescriptive. It is worth mentioning that although these disarming mechanisms may facilitate the progress of an individual, they do not facilitate social progress as a whole, and, if anything, do the opposite.

28. Livingston and Pearce 2009.

29. Livingston, Rosette, and Washington 2012.

30. Livingston 2013.

31. Rosette and Livingston 2012.

32. Ghavami and Peplau 2013; Goff, Thomas, and Jackson 2008; Purdie-Vaughns and Eibach 2008; Sesko and Biernat 2010; Thomas, Dovidio, and West 2014.

33. Altemeyer 1988; Zakrisson 2005.

34. Adorno et al. 1950.

35. Altemeyer 1988; Duckitt 2001; Jost and Hunyady 2003.

36. Lavine et al. 2002.

37. Van Hiel and Mervielde 2005; Sibley, Wilson, and Duckett 2007; Thomsen, Green, and Sidanius 2008; Whitley 1999.

38. Altemeyer 1988.

39. Federico and Sidanius 2002; Henry and Sears 2002; Sidanius, Pratto, and Bobo 1996.

40. Livingston and Drwecki 2007.

41. Gaertner 1973.

42. Dupree and Fiske 2019.

43. Milkman, Akinola, and Chugh 2015.

44. Craig et al. 2012.

45. Fein and Spencer 1997.

46. Collange, Fiske, and Sanitioso 2009; Fein and Spencer 1997.

47. Sinclair and Kunda 1999.

Chapter Six: What Are the Psychological and Evolutionary Origins of All Intergroup Biases?

1. Seuss 1961.

2. Brewer 1979; Taifel et al. 1971.

3. Brewer 1991.

4. Dunham and Emory 2014.

5. Lewis and Bates 2017.

6. Reicher et al. 2016.

7. Taifel et al. 1971.

8. Petersen et al. 2013.

9. Gladwell 2005; Judge and Cable 2004.

10. Many scientists argue that what "used to be" was actually egalitarianism, not dominance. That is, hunter-gatherer groups were more communal and egalitarian than societies today because (1) they often killed larger game than one person could possibly consume before decay set in and (2) the advent of weapons made physical strength less important in deciding who could be killed. (See Wilkinson and Pickett 2019 for a deeper discussion.)

11. Sidanius and Pratto 1999.

12. Rutherford 2020.

13. Bernal 1987; Bonnet and Valbelle 2007.
14. Gilbert and Hixon 1991; Macrae and Bodenhausen 2000.
15. Chapman and Chapman 1969.
16. Hamilton and Gifford 1976.
17. Ibid.
18. Specifically, eighteen members of group A and nine members of group B did good stuff, whereas eight members of group A and four members of group B did bad stuff.
19. Kahneman 2011.
20. Fyock and Stangor 1994.
21. Stroessner 1996; Zarate and Smith 1990.

Chapter Seven: Is Inequality Due to Racism or Race?

1. Christensen et al. 2010.
2. Herrnstein and Murray 1994.
3. More details about Derek's story can be found in the book *Rising Out of Hatred* by Eli Saslow, which was published about one year after my interview with Derek.
4. Prentice and Miller 2007; Williams and Eberhardt 2008.
5. Goff, Eberhardt, Williams, and Jackson 2008.
6. Anderson, Green, and Payne 2009; Freeman and Payne 2000; Goyal et al. 2015; Green et al. 2003; Todd et al. 2000.
7. Villarosa 2019.
8. Waytz, Hoffman, and Trawalter 2015.
9. Dore et al. 2014; Trawalter, Hoffman, and Waytz 2012.
10. People who have essentialist beliefs are more likely to endorse stereotypes and other racist beliefs. They are also less likely to endorse policies to reduce social inequality. (Rattan et al. 2012.)
11. Sykes 2001.
12. Leffler et al. 2012.
13. Harpending and Rogers 2000.
14. Bamshad et al. 2004; Fischer et al. 2004; Jorde and Wooding 2004.
15. Rosenberg et al. 2002.
16. Bamshad et al. 2004; Barbujani, Ghirotto, and Tassi 2013.
17. This example is for illustration purposes only, and the one-in-one-hundred likelihood should not be taken literally. In reality, the likelihood is likely to be much lower than one in one hundred, perhaps even one in one million, and would depend on a number of factors that are not specified in the current example. The reason that I did not state the probability as being closer to zero is because Mom and Dad in this example are not genetically related to each other. Thus, there is a slim chance that on a random round the mom and dad of both families could

be chosen and the parent from one family might be more genetically related to the parent from the other family.

18. Bamshad et al. 2004.

19. This finding is particularly ironic given Watson's racist commentaries
    over the decades regarding the prevalence of inherent racial differences.

20. Barbujani, Ghirotto, and Tassi 2013.

21. The likelihood of greater between-race similarity in the Bamshad et al.
    study was 33 percent for Native Americans, 36 percent for Africans, and
    38 percent for Asians. These exact percentages should be interpreted
    with caution because there is some "sampling error" due to the fact that
    only a relatively small subset of all the tribes or ethnicities from each
    race was included in the study. What can be concluded is that the like-
    lihood of greater between-race similarity is much closer to 50 percent
    than to 1 percent, and this high likelihood is approximately the same
    across all races.

22. Bryc et al. 2015.

23. Many White nationalists cite Neanderthal ancestry among Europeans,
    and the larger brains of Neanderthals, as evidence of White genetic su-
    periority. There are at least four problems with this argument. First,
    many Europeans have no Neanderthal ancestry at all, and many other
    groups, including Melanesians and Aboriginals, do have Neanderthal
    ancestry. Second, the proportion of Neanderthal ancestry, among Euro-
    peans who do have it, is extremely small. Third, brain size does not ex-
    clusively determine intelligence. If it did, sperm whales would be five
    times smarter than humans. Finally, anthropologists concur that the Ne-
    anderthals of central Europe were *not* intellectually superior to *Homo sa-
    piens* from Africa. If anything, the exact opposite was true.

24. Balaresque et al. 2010; Balaresque et al. 2015.

25. Residents of Charlotte, North Carolina, might be shocked to find out
    that their city, and Mecklenburg County, in which it sits, were named in
    honor of a Black queen.

26. Bloom 2005.

27. Kittles and Weiss 2003; McChesney 2015.

28. Jablonski and Chaplin 2010.

29. Ibid.

30. Chaplin 2004.

31. Crawford et al. 2017.

32. Barsh 2003.

33. Martin et al. 2017.

34. Ogbu 1978.

35. Merton 1948; Rosenthal and Jacobson 1968; Darley and Gross 1983.

36. Steele 2010.

37. Shih, Pitinsky, and Ambady 1999.
38. Gladwell 2008; Altus 1966; see also Rohrer, Egloff, and Schmukle 2015.
39. Sowell 2019.
40. Hanel, Maio, and Manstead 2018.
41. Goodman, Moses, and Jones 2012; McChesney 2015.

Forum One: How to Talk About the Problem

1. Livingston 2020.
2. Kahneman 2011.
3. Stone, Patton, and Heen 2010.
4. Bergsieker, Shelton, and Richeson 2010.
5. See Edmonson 2012; Johansson 2017; Page 2007.
6. Jehn, Northcraft, and Neale 1999.
7. Hjelmgaard 2020.
8. Voigt et al. 2017.

PART II: CONCERN

Chapter Eight: How Much Do White People Care About Racism?

1. Chow, Lowery, and Hogan 2013.
2. Kawakami et al. 2009.
3. Karmali, Kawakami, and Page-Gould 2017.
4. Sue et al. 2007.
5. Kaiser and Miller 2001.
6. Castelli, Amicis, and Sherman 2007.
7. Castelli et al. 2001.
8. Jacoby-Senghor et al. 2019.
9. Petrow, Transue, and Vercellotti 2018; Schildkraut 2017.
10. DiAngelo 2018.
11. Greenberg and Pyszczynski 1985.
12. Kirkland, Greenberg, and Pyszczynski 1987.
13. Willard, Isaac, and Carney 2015.
14. Avenanti, Sirigu, and Aglioti 2010; Han 2018.
15. For example, in October 2017, President Trump declared the opioid crisis a public health emergency. ("Ending America's Opioid Crisis" n.d.)
16. E.g., Accapadi 2007; DiAngelo 2018; Hamad 2018.
17. Bloom 2016.
18. Ministero et al. 2018.
19. Kuhlman and Marshello 1975; Sattler and Kerr 1991; Van Lange et al. 1997.
20. Van Lange 1999.
21. Chirumbolo, Leone, and Desimoni 2016.

22. Van Lange et al. 2012.

23. van Dijk, De Cremer, and Handgraaf 2004.

24. Liebrand et al. 1986; Sattler and Kerr 1991; Van Lange and Kuhlman 1994.

25. Duckitt and Fisher 2003; Kuhlman, Camac, and Cunha 1986.

26. Chirumbolo, Leone, and Desimoni 2016.

27. Grant 2013.

28. Au and Kwong 2004.

29. Van Lange et al. 2012, Study 3.

30. McClintock and Liebrand 1988; Van Lange 1999.

31. Pfeffer 2015.

32. Anderson and Kilduff 2009.

33. Halevy et al. 2012; Livingston, Cohen, and Halevy 2012.

34. Schwartz 2012.

35. Interestingly, research by Vohs, Mead, and Goode (2006) shows that priming people with the concept of money can cause them to be less likely to help other people, to sit farther away from other people, and to prefer solo over group activities.

36. Bardi and Schwartz 2003.

37. Caron 2016.

Chapter Nine: The Moral Cost of Condoning Racism

1. Haidt and Graham 2007.

2. Some would argue that the U.S. tax system is progressive only in theory, whereas in practice it's a flax tax, at best, or a regressive tax system, at worst, where wealthier households end up paying a much lower tax rate than middle- and working-class households. (Rosalsky 2019.)

3. Tyler et al. 2019.

4. Gutiérrez and Unzueta 2013.

5. Barclay, Bashshur, and Fortin 2017.

6. Bridge et al. 2015; Sheftall et al. 2016.

7. Mullen and Smyth 2004.

8. Reynolds et al. 2010; Vandivere, Malm, and Radel 2009.

9. Paradies et al. 2015; Pieterse et al. 2012.

10. Clark et al. 1999; Collins and Williams 1999; Gee et al. 2019; Hicken et al. 2013; Jackson and Williams 2006; Wyatt et al. 2003.

11. Steele 2010.

12. Woodcock et al. 2012.

13. Chetty et al. 2019.

14. Payne, Vuletich, and Brown-Iannuzzi 2019.

15. Burger 2009; Milgram 1963.

16. Haidt and Graham 2007.

17. Waytz, Dungan, and Young 2013.
18. Landmann and Hess 2018; Smith et al. 2014.
19. Dagan and Teles 2016, 129.

Chapter Ten: The Practical Importance of Redressing Racism
1. Page 2007.
2. To be clear, diversity and quality are not mutually exclusive. You could have a homogeneous set of rusty hammers or a pristine set of diverse titanium tools. I pitted the two extremes against each other to more clearly illustrate the point that diversity can trump quality.
3. Johansson 2017.
4. McNeil 1997.
5. Touryalai 2013.
6. Jehn, Northcraft, and Neale 1999.
7. Crane, Thomas-Hunt, and Kesebir 2019.
8. Putnam and Garrett 2020.
9. Woolley et al. 2010.
10. Hoever et al. 2012.
11. Antonio et al. 2004; Fisher et al. 2012; Freeman and Huang 2014; Sommers 2006; Tröster, Mehra, and van Knippenberg 2014; Watson, Kumar, and Michaelsen 1993; but see Mannix and Neale 2005 for a review.
12. Phillips and Loyd 2006.
13. Sommers 2006.
14. Ely and Thomas 2020.
15. Mueller et al. 2012.
16. Georgeac and Rattan 2019.
17. Ely and Thomas 2001.
18. Ramos et al. 2019.
19. Nai et al. 2018.
20. Allport 1954.
21. Hartley 1946.
22. Bergh et al. 2016.
23. Misra et al. 2020; Ruiz, Horowitz, and Tamir 2020.
24. Ruiz, Horowitz, and Tamir 2020.
25. Horowitz, Brown, and Cox 2019.
26. Bonilla-Silva 2006.
27. Desmond 2019.
28. Metzl 2019.
29. Faber and Krieg 2002.
30. Hannah-Jones 2019.
31. Wilkinson and Pickett 2019.
32. Leung et al. 2008; Maddux and Galinsky 2009.

PART III: CORRECTION

Chapter Eleven: What Everyone Can Do to Promote Racial Equity

1. Nelson, Adams, and Salter 2013; Rudman, Ashmore, and Gary 2001.
2. Schilke and Huang 2018.
3. Norton and Sommers 2011.
4. Nelson, Adams, and Salter 2013; Sommers and Norton 2006; Unzueta and Lowery 2008.
5. Kaiser et al. 2013.
6. Plant and Devine 1998.
7. Fernando et al. 2018.
8. Obama 2006.
9. Deegan et al. 2015.
10. Dweck 2016.
11. Rattan and Dweck 2018.
12. Plous 2003.
13. Pliner 1982.
14. Allport 1954.
15. Dovidio, Gaertner, and Kawakami 2003; Pettigrew and Tropp 2006.
16. Jackman and Crane 1986.
17. K. T. Brown et al. 2003; T. N. Brown et al. 2003.
18. Pettigrew 1997.
19. McGlothlin and Killen 2010.
20. Charlesworth and Banaji 2019.
21. Saslow 2018.
22. Zhang 2017.
23. Brewer and Miller 1984; Hewstone and Brown 1986; Pettigrew and Tropp 2006.
24. Hewstone 1994; Weber and Crocker 1983.
25. Livingston 2002.
26. Bergsieker, Shelton, and Richeson 2010; Kteily et al. 2013; Rattan and Ambady 2014; Richeson and Shelton 2007; Trail, Shelton, and West 2009.
27. Bergsieker, Shelton, and Richeson 2010.
28. Holoien and Shelton 2012; Shelton, Richeson, and Salvatore 2005.
29. Tatum 2017.
30. Yoshino 2006.
31. Gan, Heller, and Chen 2018.
32. Sue et al. 2007; Sue, Capodilupo, and Holder 2008; Sue and Constantine 2007.
33. Richeson and Shelton 2007; Shelton and Richeson 2006; Trawalter, Richeson, and Shelton 2009.
34. Shim et al. 2020; Word, Zanna, and Cooper 1974.

35. Bastian, Jetten, and Ferris 2014.
36. Kurzban, Tooby, and Cosmides 2001; but see also Alexander, Brewer, and Livingston 2005; Durante et al. 2017; and Fiske et al. 2002 for more complex models of friend/foe coalitional affiliation.
37. Kurzban, Tooby, and Cosmides 2001; Pietraszewski, Cosmides, and Tooby 2014; Voorspoels, Bartlema, and Vanpaemel 2014.
38. Banfield and Dovidio 2013; Bettencourt et al. 1992; Crisp, Hewstone, and Rubin 2001.
39. Banfield and Dovidio 2013; Gaertner, Dovidio, and Bachman 1996; Levendusky 2017; McConahay 1986; Vezzali et al. 2015.
40. Brewer and Miller 1984.
41. Ufkes et al. 2012.
42. Obeid, Argo, and Ginges 2017.
43. Hehman, Mania, and Gaertner 2010.
44. Lai et al. 2016.
45. Crisp, Hewstone, and Rubin 2001; Prati et al. 2016.
46. Crisp, Hewstone, and Rubin 2001.
47. Gollwitzer and Schaal 1998; Rees, Rivers, and Sherman 2019.
48. Lai et al. 2016; Mendoza et al. 2010; Rees, Rivers, and Sherman 2019; Stewart and Payne 2008.
49. Correll et al. 2002.
50. Mendoza, Gollwitzer, and Amodio 2010.
51. Lai et al. 2016.
52. Dasgupta and Greenwald 2001.
53. Banakou, Hanumanthu, and Slater 2016; see also Peck et al. 2013.
54. Finlay and Stephan 2000.
55. Aronson, Fried, and Stone 1991; Stone et al. 1994.
56. Song Hing, Li, and Zanna 2002.
57. Webber et al. 2018.
58. Collange, Fiske, and Sanitioso 2009; Fein and Spencer 1997.
59. Craig et al. 2012.
60. DeSteno et al. 2004.
61. Livingston and Drwecki 2007.
62. Jost et al. 2003.
63. Cheon et al. 2013; Cheon et al. 2015.
64. Hunsinger, Livingston, and Isbell 2013; Lueke and Gibson 2015; Stell and Farsides 2016.
65. Czopp and Monteith 2003; Gulker, Mark, and Monteith 2013.
66. Gulker, Mark, and Monteith 2013.
67. Kaiser and Miller 2001.
68. Czopp and Monteith 2003.
69. DiAngelo 2011.

70. Locke et al. 1981; Locke and Latham 2015; Doran 1981.
71. Kendi 2019.

**Chapter Twelve: How Leaders and Organizations
Can Create Greater Racial Equity**

1. Winig and Livingston 2019; Johnson 2017.
2. Winig and Livingston 2019, p. 15.
3. Ibid., p. 19.
4. Winig and Livingston 2020.
5. Ibid, p. 11.
6. Ibid.
7. Ibid., p. 10.
8. Ibid.
9. Collins and Porras 1996.
10. Ibarra 1992.
11. Rivera 2012.
12. Zhu, Shen, and Hillman 2014.
13. Crockett 2016.
14. Kerr 1975.
15. Nolan et al. 2008.
16. Steve Watkins, "Racism du Jour at Shoney's," *Nation,* 1993, 424–27, as cited in Brief et al. 2000.
17. This finding may seem to contradict earlier studies showing discrimination across the board. Keep in mind that hiring for fast-food and restaurant positions may operate differently from hiring for more white-collar jobs.
18. Brief et al. 2000; see also Ziegert and Hanges 2005.
19. Allport 1954; Blanchard, Lilly, and Vaughn 1991; Blanchard et al. 1994; Pettigrew 1958; Sherif and Sherif 1953; Stangor, Sechrist, and Jost 2001.
20. Blanchard et al. 1994.
21. Stangor, Sechrist, and Jost 2001.
22. Paluck 2009; Paluck and Green 2009.
23. Berdahl et al. 2018.
24. Rosette and Livingston 2012.
25. Bohnet, Van Geen, and Bazerman 2016; Hsee et al. 1999; Loewenstein and White 2018.
26. Zedeck and Cascio 1984.
27. Bohnet 2016; Baldiga 2013; Tannenbaum 2012.
28. Baker and Logan 2007.
29. Richardson 2018.

Index

About the Author

ROBERT LIVINGSTON is a social psychologist whose research has appeared in *The New York Times, The Wall Street Journal,* and *Harvard Business Review.* For two decades, he has served as a diversity consultant to scores of Fortune 500 companies, public-sector agencies, and nonprofit organizations. He has held professorships at the University of Wisconsin–Madison, Northwestern University's Kellogg School of Management, and the University of Sussex, where he was the founding director of the Centre for Leadership, Ethics, and Diversity (LEAD). He currently serves on the faculty of Harvard University's John F. Kennedy School of Government.